LAW BOOKS IN ACTION

Law Books in Action: Essays on the Anglo-American Legal Treatise explores the history of the legal treatise in the common law world. Rather than looking at treatises as shortcuts from 'law in books' to 'law in action,' the essays in this collection ask what treatises can tell us about what troubled legal professionals at a given time, what motivated them to write what they did, and what they hoped to achieve. This book, then, is the first study of the legal treatise as a 'law book in action', an active text produced by individuals with ideas about what they wanted the law to be, not a mere stepping-stone to codes and other forms of legal writing, but a multifaceted genre of legal literature in its own right, practical and fanciful, dogmatic and ornamental in turn. This book will be of interest to legal scholars, lawyers, and judges, as well as to anyone else with a scholarly interest in law in general, and legal history in particular.

Law Books in Action

Essays on the Anglo-American Legal Treatise

Edited by

Angela Fernandez

and

Markus D Dubber

•HART•
PUBLISHING

OXFORD AND PORTLAND, OREGON

2012

Published in the United Kingdom by Hart Publishing Ltd
16C Worcester Place, Oxford, OX1 2JW
Telephone: +44 (0)1865 517530
Fax: +44 (0)1865 510710
E-mail: mail@hartpub.co.uk
Website: http://www.hartpub.co.uk

Published in North America (US and Canada) by
Hart Publishing
c/o International Specialized Book Services
920 NE 58th Avenue, Suite 300
Portland, OR 97213-3786
USA
Tel: +1 503 287 3093 or toll-free: (1) 800 944 6190
Fax: +1 503 280 8832
E-mail: orders@isbs.com
Website: http://www.isbs.com

British Library Cataloguing in Publication Data
Data Available

ISBN: 978-1-84946-141-2

Typeset by Hope Services, Abingdon
Printed and bound in Great Britain by
Lightning Source UK Ltd

Dedicated to the memory of AWB Simpson (1931–2011)

CONTENTS

CONTRIBUTORS

G Blaine Baker is Professor Emeritus, Faculty of Law and Institute of Private and Comparative Law, McGill University, Montreal.

Lyndsay Campbell is Assistant Professor, Law & Society Program, Faculty of Arts and Faculty of Law, University of Calgary.

Markus D Dubber is Professor of Law, Faculty of Law, University of Toronto.

Lindsay Farmer is Professor of Law, University of Glasgow, Scotland.

Angela Fernandez is Associate Professor of Law, Faculty of Law, University of Toronto.

Philip Girard is University Research Professor and Professor of Law, History and Canadian Studies, Dalhousie University, Halifax, Nova Scotia.

Roman J Hoyos is Associate Professor, Southwestern Law School, Los Angeles, California.

Kunal M Parker is Professor of Law and Dean's Distinguished Scholar, University of Miami School of Law.

Jim Phillips is Professor of Law, Faculty of Law, University of Toronto and is editor in chief of the Osgoode Society for Canadian Legal History.

Christopher Tomlins is Chancellor's Professor of Law, School of Law, University of California, Irvine.

Stephen Waddams is University Professor and the holder of the Goodman/Schipper chair, Faculty of Law, University of Toronto.

Barry Wright is Professor of Law, History and Criminology, Carleton University, Ottawa.

Introduction: Putting the Legal Treatise in Its Place

ANGELA FERNANDEZ AND MARKUS D DUBBER*

IN 1976, WHILE working on the first volume of *The Transformation of American Law*, Morton Horwitz noted that treatises were 'the most neglected and really important sources of American legal history'.[1] Little has changed since then: treatises are still neglected, they are still really important, and not only in American legal history, but in common law history as a whole. This book aims to give legal treatises their due by undertaking an international and comparative analysis of the significance of the common law treatise in modern legal history and historiography.

The hypothesis here is that, provided one does not treat them as statements of *lex lata* (the law as it is) no matter what their authors might claim, but as a more or less stable mixture of elements of *lex lata* and *lex ferenda* (the law as it should be), treatises can provide insight into conceptions of law in general and of a particular area of law, into ideas about the project of legal scholarship, legal education (and learning), legal commentary, about the very notion of the ideal in law, and the relationship between the real and the ideal, into the role of law in broader projects, including projects of nation-building, of (scientific) systematisation, of rationalisation, and of civilisation, modernisation, and therefore also codification, and, ultimately, into the relationship between the individual, the community (however defined), and the law (and perhaps even the state, depending on one's view of the law's, and the lawyer's, role within the state apparatus).

I. WHAT IS A (LEGAL) TREATISE?

The attempt to settle on 'the' definition of 'the' treatise is as futile and uninteresting as most definitional quests – and perhaps more so, given the variety of books making an appearance in the pages of this collection that are called 'treatise',

* Angela Fernandez and Markus D Dubber are both professors of Law at the University of Toronto, Faculty of Law. They gratefully acknowledge the generous support of the Social Sciences and Humanities Research Council of Canada (SSHRCC), Aid to Research Workshops and Conferences, funds from which were used to support this project and the workshop 'The Treatise in Legal History' held at the Faculty of Law, University of Toronto in October 2010.

[1] MJ Horwitz, 'Part III – Treatise Literature' (1976) 69 *Law Library Journal* 460.

either by their author or others. Still, a project on the legal treatise would do well, at the outset, to arrive at a working definition of its subject matter, however preliminary and non-exhaustive. For starters, to get a sense of what a *legal* treatise is, it might make sense to get clear(er) on what a treatise is. The *Oxford English Dictionary* ventures a definition of treatise that is as good as any other:

> A book or writing which treats of some particular subject; commonly (in mod. use always), one containing a formal or methodological discussion or exposition of the principles of the subject; formerly more widely used for a literary work in general.[2]

Three points must be emphasised. First, there is the general and capacious sense of *treatment*, a feature shared by any book or writing on a particular subject. Anything between two covers 'treats' its topic. Second, we must notice the more narrow focus on *principles*, so important to the legal treatise in particular. And third, there is the point about the presentation of principles in a methodological *discussion* or *exposition*. We take it that what makes a treatise *legal* is its focus on legal sources – cases, statutes, codes, constitutional text or legal doctrine – along with its implied claim of offering authoritative interpretation of those sources.

The essays in this collection take to heart a broad approach to the legal treatise in the sense that they include discussion of a number of kinds of legal literature that one might not ordinarily think of as a treatise, eg the institute-structured commentaries of William Blackstone and James Kent. These works 'treat' their legal topics in the required discursive way, even if some would question their status as treatises based on the way that they range across many topics (usually those included in some variation on the persons-things-actions triad Justinian's *Institutes* borrowed from Gaius) rather than focusing on a single legal topic like English treatises such as William Jones' book on bailments or John Joseph Powell on contracts.[3] In addition to essays focusing on commentaries, readers will find included here a chapter on a justice of the peace manual and another on criminal law codification. Each of these forms of legal literature certainly presents legal principles, alphabetised in the former case and conceptually arranged in the latter case of a code. What seems to be lacking is the third feature mentioned above, namely, a discursive presentation, probably connected to the second *Oxford English Dictionary* definition of a treatise as '[a] story, a tale, a narrative (spoken or written)' and its third meaning as a 'descriptive treatment,

[2] 'Treatise, n. 1a' (2nd edn, 1989); online version November 2010. www.oed.com.myaccess.library.utoronto.ca/Entry/205390; accessed 14 March 2011. Earlier version first published in *New English Dictionary*, 1914.

[3] AWB Simpson, 'The Rise and Fall of the Legal Treatise: Legal Principles and the Forms of Legal Literature' (1981) 48 *University of Chicago Law Review* 632, 633 (stating that 'the treatise is a monograph, purporting to deal only with a single branch of the law that is conceived of as possessing some quality of unity; treatises, like institutional works, are not comprehensive, though they are similar in other respects'); J Langbein, 'Chancellor Kent and the History of Legal Literature' (1993) 93 *Columbia Law Review* 547, 586 (stating that '[t]he distinguishing trait of institutionalist writing is the effort to be comprehensive, to describe the private law of an entire legal system in a single work. This breadth of field contrasts sharply with the treatise writer's effort to delimit a single topic in exhaustive depth').

description, account (of something)'.[4] Codes and manuals (as well as other forms of legal literature that use alphabetisation to present legal information like a law dictionary, a commonplace book, an abridgement or a digest) are too staccato in the way in which they speak. There is not enough narrative or descriptive fill to count as a treatise. However, there is no doubt that these works perform a similar rationalising and systematising function to the traditional legal treatise, and we operate on the premise that thinking about them alongside and in relationship to the legal treatise is a useful exercise.

We have divided the essays into type of law book under discussion, rough geography and to some extent chronology. The first division consists of the two essays on institute-structured commentaries, Kunal Parker on Blackstone's *Commentaries* (Chapter one) and Philip Girard comparing Blackstone and Kent's *Commentaries* with an institute-writer from Nova Scotia, Beamish Murdoch (Chapter two). The second division contains the three essays in the book on American legal treatises – one of us, Angela Fernandez on Tapping Reeve's treatise on domestic relations, *Baron and Femme* (1816) (Chapter three), Blaine Baker on Joseph Story's *Commentaries on the Conflicts of Laws* (1834) (Chapter four) and Roman Hoyos writing about a book that emerged after the United States Civil War on the legal principles involved in state constitutional conventions, John A Jameson's *The Constitutional Convention* (1867) (Chapter five). The third section contains the United Kingdom pieces, Stephen Waddams on English contract law treatises (Chapter six), Lindsay Farmer on English and Scots criminal law treatise writers (Chapter seven) and Lyndsay Campbell on English libel law treatises in North America (Chapter eight). The fourth and final section of the book contains Barry Wright's essay on colonial criminal law codification (Chapter nine) and Jim Phillips' piece on a Nova Scotia justice of the peace manual (Chapter 10). This is followed by a commentary by Chris Tomlins discussing the ways in which he sees the essays inter-relating (Chapter 11). We highlight here a number of themes that we believe emerge from the collection.

II. LAW BOOKS IN ACTION

Legal historians know well how unreliable a legal treatise is in terms of operating as a source for understanding what the law on the ground was at a particular time and place. One need only think of Roscoe Pound's famous distinction between 'law in books' and 'law in action'.[5] Much of the thrust of law and society studies of the last 40 years has been premised on the idea that 'law in books' tells us very little about 'law in action'.[6] Treatises may be (ab)used as shortcuts to the detailed

[4] *Oxford English Dictionary* (n 2), 'Treatise n 1b & c'.

[5] R Pound, 'Law in Books and Law in Action' (1910) 44 *American Law Review* 12.

[6] But see RW Gordon, 'Critical Legal Histories' (1984) 36 *Stanford Law Review* 57, 120–23 (on the usefulness of 'mandarin' legal materials, ie case law and treatise literature).

study of legal developments, in doctrine and in the streets. One need not be a proponent of social history over the history of ideas to dismiss the use of treatises as the legal historian's Cliffs Notes.[7] As rationalising and systematising works, legal treatises seem to be unlikely places to find out how the law was actually operating. Indeed, they would be much more likely to set out some kind of synthesising aspiration, a kind of plea to judges, legal practitioners and students to think of things in the way that the treatise-writer recommends, drawing on hints to that effect in whatever cases can be found.

Stephen Waddams, the only contributor to this volume who has written a treatise, has used the term 'forensic convention' to describe the way in which the treatise-writer speaks as if he or she is arguing at the bar itself, offering in effect a plea or pleading.[8] Since doctrinal writing is not a formal source of law in a common law system, the voice in which the treatise-writer speaks will likely be quiet and deferential.[9] Ideally, from the treatise-writer's perspective, once the judges are convinced to adopt the recommended view, that makes it 'law' and the treatise-writer can quietly reflect that success in a subsequent edition, of which there always seem to be many. Joel Prentiss Bishop, an extremely prolific American treatise-writer of the late nineteenth century, was particularly vocal about highlighting the importance of the treatise-writer over the judge. And he was not very deferential.[10] Yes, the judges get to decide the case, but the treatise-writer gets to say what the case really decides.[11] Legal treatises are supposed to describe the law and report it in something like a neutral or objective way; but they do an awful lot of advocacy with respect to shaping what that law is. Why treatise-writers took up the topics they did and argued in the ways they did can make for a fascinating back story, often more interesting as a matter of legal history than the actual words on the pages of the books.

[7] See, eg Paul Halliday's brilliant critical history of habeas corpus, which seeks to offer a history of the 'Great Writ' 'that is better grounded empirically and broader conceptually than the one still routinely invoked in courtrooms and public debates', and thereby also to illustrate the pitfalls of historical analysis of law that limits itself to a reading of treatises and printed case reports, while ignoring 'countless parchment court records and case reports surviving only in manuscript'. P Halliday, *Habeas Corpus: From England to Empire* (Cambridge, MA, Harvard University Press, 2010) 3–4.

[8] S Waddams, *Principle and Policy in Contract Law: Competing or Complementary Concepts?* (Cambridge, Cambridge University Press, 2011) 56 (describing 'the forensic convention' as 'the convention that the writers were indirectly addressing an English judge, as a barrister might do, and seeking to persuade him of the actual state of contemporary English law').

[9] Simpson (n 3) 638 ('the text writer, unless he himself is a judge, possesses as an individual no authority derived from office').

[10] See, eg JP Bishop, *First Book of the Law: Explaining the Nature, Sources, Books, and Practical Applications of Legal Science, and Methods of Study and Practice* (Boston, MA, Little, Brown, 1868) 130 ('oftentimes, the judges do not apprehend the true reasons of their decisions'), 250 ('[I]f the author of a legal treatise is as able a lawyer as the judge, his disquisitions upon the law are, as a general rule, more nicely accurate than those of the judge can be,' given the judge's 'duty . . . to decide no more than the simple question in controversy'). See SA Siegel, 'Joel Bishop's Orthodoxy' (1995) 13 *Law and History Review* 215; see also Hoyos, in this volume.

[11] See, eg AWB Simpson, 'The Beauty of Obscurity: *Raffles v Wichelhaus and Busch* (1864)' in AWB Simpson (ed), *Leading Cases in the Common Law* (Oxford University Press, 1995) 135–62 (on how the treatise-writers and casebook editors turned a one-line judgment into a leading contracts case).

At least two of the essays in this collection are explicit examples of that kind of back story. So, for instance, Roman Hoyos (Chapter five) describes how John A Jameson's book emerged from the uncertainty surrounding constitutional conventions, particularly the state constitutional conventions authorising Southern secession in the American Civil War, and a concern about disorder. It was particularly important as a 'first' book, since it established a field of law that would not have been recognised as such until the book made it so.[12] The authority brought by the form of the legal treatise was key to the writer's point that 'yes constitutional conventions were a concern', while sending out the reassuring message 'don't worry, this can be dealt with as a matter of law' – any irrational, arbitrary, disorderly, political uncertainty can be made to be orderly, rational, certain and predictable according to formal, systematic and scientific rule.

The essay by Angela Fernandez (Chapter three) on Tapping Reeve's book on the law of domestic relations is another example of the back story of a treatise, also a 'first' treatise. However, rather than claiming to bring order to the essentially disorderly mass of cases, a common claim of many late nineteenth-century treatise-writers (see Hoyos), Reeve's book is unusual for its failure to refer to the positive law and its insistence on pure principle. Fernandez explains how Reeve rejected the common law maxim that husband and wife were one person in law, advocated for a married woman's right to make a will and convinced his students at the Litchfield Law School to pass a statute to that effect. He did all this in the face of strong counter-authority (eg Coke, Blackstone and Connecticut case law). Reeve's claim to be describing English law for an American audience was really an attempt to reflect the norms of *his* Connecticut, just at the moment at which as a 'fading Federalist' he was losing the larger political and religious project in which he was invested.

Both of these back story essays demonstrate that legal treatises as a topic of historical investigation can go beyond the words the authors wrote on the page in order to enquire about what the authors of these books thought they were doing in writing them or, at least, what the books in effect did in their wider social and political worlds. The accounts given here make it impossible to view legal treatises as simply carriers of purportedly neutral, objective, rationalising and systematising principles. Their substance was deeply normative, while much of their authority was predicated precisely on their appearing not to be. This approach requires at the very least looking with a sceptical eye on what the treatise-writer says in the preface to the work about what the work is for and trying to ask instead about what the work in fact did. To scramble Pound's distinction between 'law in books' and 'law in action', we might think of this as 'law books in action'.[13]

[12] See T Agape and V Lim, 'John Cobb Cooper: At the Frontiers of International Law' available at www.ccil-ccdi.ca/ccil-the-essays/student-essays-from-the-university-of-toronto-project/ (on the creation of the subfield of air and space law).

[13] Companion literatures here would include work on the history of the book (see, eg DD Hall, *Cultures of Print: Essays in the History of the Book* (Amherst, MA, University of Massachusetts Press, 1996)), law book publishing (see, eg M Hoeflich, *Legal Publishing in Antebellum America* (New York, NY, Cambridge University Press, 2010)) and literature on lawyers' libraries (see, eg A Fernandez,

The third example, less of a back story than Hoyos or Fernandez since it does not focus on the author of the treatise and the original context for its creation but is certainly an example of 'law books in action', is the essay by Lyndsay Campbell (Chapter eight) on Thomas Starkie's *A Treatise on the Law of Slander* (1813) and its reception in North America. The 1830 London edition of Starkie elaborated on a defence of 'qualified privilege' that Joseph Howe, a newspaperman prosecuted for publishing criticisms of Nova Scotia's magistracy, was able to use to convince a Halifax jury to acquit him in 1835. However, that approach went nowhere in neighbouring Massachusetts, where debate about libel and slander focused on a defence based on truth. We cannot know, of course, if the treatise was the thing that convinced the jury in Howe's case. However, Campbell's explanation of the role it played in this trial shows a law book figuring in very real on-the-ground events that were unlikely to have turned out this way in the United States.

III. STEPPING STONES

Philip Girard (Chapter two) makes the argument in his essay that we should not think of institute-literature like Blackstone or Kent's *Commentaries* as a stepping-stone on the way to the treatise (as John Langbein has claimed).[14] Treatises and commentaries co-existed and indeed interacted. The many editions of Blackstone's *Commentaries* (also featured in Chapter one by Kunal Parker) show a continued use for and interest in that text, as do the subsequent editions of Kent's *Commentaries*. Girard points out the back-and-forth exchange, for example, between Kent's *Commentaries* and one of Joseph Story's treatises.

Barry Wright (Chapter nine) makes a similar argument about our understanding of a code, which cannot always be understood as the place that the treatise was a stepping-stone *to* (as Brian Simpson has claimed).[15] While this was true in the case of the Canadian criminal code, modelled largely on the failed 1878–80 draft code prepared for England by James Fitzjames Stephen (who wrote both a treatise and a digest before his code), it was not so in the earlier case of Thomas Macaulay's Indian Penal Code (drafted by 1837 and enacted in the wake of the

'Albert Mayrand's Private Law Library: An Investigation of the Person, the Law of Persons, and 'Legal Personality' in a Collection of Law Books' (2003) 53 *University of Toronto Law Journal* 37; DJ Hulsebosch, 'An Empire of Law: Chancellor Kent and the Revolution in Books in the Early Republic' (2009) 60 *Alabama Law Review* 377).

[14] Langbein (n 3) 593 ('within the realm of doctrinal writing . . . the institutionalist genre could not withstand the competition from later forms of legal literature. Doctrinal writing can be done better when it is separated from the need for schoolbook simplicity that characterizes the institutionalist tradition. Breadth is the enemy of depth, and when breadth is no longer needed, depth will prevail. As a result, everywhere in the Western legal systems, the institutes gave way to the treatise, and that is what happened in the United States').

[15] Simpson (n 3) 666 ('[a] number of treatises were written in the form of codes, the code being the next logical step in the process of systematization beyond the discursive treatise').

Mutiny or the First War of Independence in India in 1860). While there were 'hints of the treatise' in things Macaulay had written as he was preparing his code that took a synthetic and discursive approach (the *Examples* and to a greater extent his explanatory *Notes*), Wright argues that Macaulay's code must really be understood as inspired by Jeremy Bentham's critique of Blackstone's attempt to rationalise the common law. Unlike Stephen, who used the conservative approach of trying to accommodate the common law, there was no stepping-stone treatise for Macaulay. His experiment for colonial India was meant to make a radical break with the past and the common law authority that more traditional forms of legal literature like a treatise or a digest would be at pains to catalogue. However, Stephen's 'cautious' approach, beginning with a treatise, moving to a digest 'and then on to a narrow code that retained common law' was perfect for late-nineteenth-century Canada, where common law traditions were weaker than they were in England and codification of the criminal law came to be seen as key to establishing and keeping order and stability in the new Dominion.

In the United States, over a century after Macaulay's codification efforts and a good half century after the passage of Canada's Criminal Code of 1892, Herbert Wechsler conceived of the American Law Institute's Model Penal Code (1952–62) as following what he regarded as Stephen's path to codification. In fact, it is useful to think of the Model Penal Code project as a treatise project first, and a code second. Wechsler, as Chief Reporter of the Model Code, consciously followed the example of Stephen, who regarded, or at least presented, his 1878 draft of an English criminal code as merely the codified form of his *A General View of the Criminal Law* (1863) and *A Digest of the Criminal Law* (1877). To this day, the Model Penal Code itself is the best textbook of 'American criminal law', and, along with the Commentaries, the best treatise on the subject. In Wechsler's view, the Model Penal Code, in other words, was but a treatise codified.

Note here that the Model Penal Code was not a code derived from a treatise, but a treatise in code form. Unlike in the case of contracts and torts, say, there were no great criminal law treatises in the making, or for that matter on the shelves (the early efforts by such enterprising nineteenth-century publishing pioneers like Bishop and Wharton notwithstanding).[16] The absence of a respectable criminal law treatise, in fact, was taken as evidence of the poor, and relatively backward, state of American criminal law, which accounted for the Institute's decision to draft a model criminal code, rather than producing a restatement, as it did, for instance, in contracts and torts; there was no criminal law worth restating. Given that there was no treatise, nor was there time to produce one en route to a code, Wechsler and his collaborators produced a treatise-cum-code, later supplemented by six volumes of commentary, which produced a text on American criminal law unmatched in breadth and depth to this day.

[16] On the poverty of American criminal law treatise-writing, and American criminal law scholarship in general, see GOW Mueller, *Crime, Law, and the Scholars: A History of Scholarship in American Criminal Law* (Seattle, WA, University of Washington Press, 1969).

Given the enormity of the task of reforming American criminal law – and his Legal Process view of the legal world – Wechsler realised that merely capturing criminal law norms in codified forms would not be enough. Judges and other system participants would always have to exercise discretion in interpreting the provisions of the code, and that discretion required guidance. This guidance came in the form of interpretive instructions (for instance, on the proper interpretation of ambiguous offence definitions, most notably the requisite *mens rea*) but, more important, shaped the code as a whole. The code is far more comprehensive and detailed than, say, the German criminal code precisely because it was also a treatise – it taught criminal justice system participants criminal law in a systematic way (note here the parallel to Wright's discussion of Macaulay's *Examples* as teaching devices, designed to illustrate the operation of code provisions).

So codes could be treatises; but treatises could be codes as well. As Farmer points out (Chapter seven), in the absence of comprehensive, or reliable, case reports, treatises in late eighteenth-century Britain added up to 'a form of de facto codification of the criminal law, as a means of solving co-ordination problems'. A treatise, written by (often young) practitioners for practitioners, thus functioned as a 'codification . . . of practical knowledge'. These practical works, unlike the ambitious English codification movements of the early nineteenth century, Farmer reports, were less concerned with conceptual innovation than with educating the practising bar.

India, and colonialism more generally, occupy an odd, and fascinating, place in the history of treatise- and code-writing, not only in the common law world, but in civil law countries as well. As the contributions to this volume reveal, several of our treatise- and code-writers either spent a great deal of time in India or concerned themselves with matters Indian, from the more obvious (Macaulay and Stephen, see Wright) to the less obvious (Henry Colebrook, William Jones, even Pollock, who cited not only Savigny, but also 'with full approval' provisions from the Indian Contract Act, see Waddams).[17] Wright calls India a 'colonial laboratory for utilitarian reform' and chalks up Stephen's failure in the Mother Country to the widely-shared sense, among Englishmen, that the Indian code, while perhaps useful 'to keep things simple for the native population and magistrates of limited ability', was ill-suited to a country as sophisticated as England, and a bar

[17] Pollock worked on six editions of a book on the Indian Contract Act from 1905 to the 1930s. See N Duxbury, *Frederick Pollock and the English Juristic Tradition* (Oxford, Oxford University Press, 2004) 77. Pollock also drafted a Code of Civil Wrongs for the government of India, included as an appendix to the second edition of his Law of Torts (1890). He travelled to lecture at the University of Calcutta in the fall of 1893 on fraud, misrepresentation and mistake, lectures that were published in 1894. See Pollock to Holmes, 9 August, 1893, in M De Wolfe Howe (ed), *Holmes-Pollock Letters: The Correspondence of Mr Justice Holmes and Sir Frederick Pollock, 1874–1932* vol 1 (Cambridge, MA, Harvard University Press, 1941) 45. Pollock's father-in-law was an official in British India; See J Gorham Palfrey, 'Introduction' to the *Holmes-Pollock Letters* xv (in 1873 'Pollock married Miss Georgina Harriet Deffell, daughter of John Deffell of Calcutta'). British India Era Papers indicate that Deffell was a sheriff in Calcutta (then Bengal) in the 1850s. See also Pollock to Holmes, 18 August 1913, 209 (noting that William Jones 'tackled Sanskrit at Calcutta, and was the first Englishman who really knew much of it').

as well-trained and common-sensical as the English.[18] While Stephen might have been right to regard, and praise, Macaulay's *Notes* as a 'succinct critical treatise on English criminal law in the 1830s', as Wright puts it, clearly English judges and lawyers thought there was no need for a code-cum-treatise to show them the way around their very own law. There is an interesting parallel here to the – woefully understudied – German colonial legal experience. As Wolfgang Naucke has pointed out, German criminal law scholars and early criminologists at the turn of the twentieth century regarded German colonial criminal law, and German colonial criminal codes in particular, as an opportunity to implement their treatmentist (rehabilitative/incapacitationist) projects in a form, and to an extent, unimaginable in Germany itself, where the German Criminal Code of 1871 (itself based on the Prussian Criminal Code of 1851) remained firmly committed to the idea of a retributive, guilt-based criminal law.[19]

Outside of the criminal law context, the idea that treatises acted as stepping stones to codes is often claimed in the case of the French Civil Code of 1802, where commentators have long identified the treatises of Robert Joseph Pothier as having made that codification possible.[20] However, it is also common to hear the claim that works like Kent's *Commentaries* and Story's treatises helped *stave off* codification in the United States.[21]

Kent was called the 'doctor of the laws', and part of the reason was that his *Commentaries* had saved those laws from codification.[22] Story was a more

[18] Pollock thought the codified route preferable. He wrote to Holmes '[c]ompare the Indian Penal Code with the amazing muddle English criminal law has drifted into through (among other causes) the combined meddling & timidity of the Legislature'. And he invited Holmes to 'get up a sort of moot in print' on codification generally, him for and Holmes against. See Pollock to Holmes, 26 July 1877 in Holmes-Pollock Letters ibid 7–8. Holmes seems to have declined the invitation and wrote five years later, 'I don't attach much importance to the codifying furore – except for India'. Pollock to Holmes, 8 April 1882 in Holmes-Pollock Letters ibid 21.

[19] See W Naucke, 'Deutsches Kolonialstrafrecht 1886–1918' (1988) 7 *Rechtshistorisches Journal* 297.

[20] Simpson (n 3) 667, 675.

[21] See, eg R Pound, *The Formative Era of American Law* (Boston, MA, Little, Brown, 1938) 152–53. The lectures the book was based on were delivered at Tulane University in honour of the Louisiana jurist and codifier, Edward Livingston, and so must have been a sharp theme for this audience. Pound called the Kent/Story approach 'taught law' or 'tough law' (evoking a phrase of Frederick Maitland) and emphasised how this tradition helped stave off codification in all states but Louisiana. As he put it, 'the great text writers of the formative era were able to bring it about that the English common law should be the basis of the law in all but one of the United States' Ibid 148 (emphasis added). This was typical of Pound, who as John Witt has put it, was always able to 'situate himself right at the boundaries of his audience's tolerance – to provoke, but never to disturb, to be iconoclastic and forceful but never radical or revolutionary, to startle while confirming his audience's deepest convictions'. *John Fabian Witt, Patriots and Cosmopolitans: Hidden Histories of American Law* (Boston, MA, Harvard University Press, 2007) 230.

[22] JT Horton, *James Kent: A Study in Conservatism, 1763–1847* (New York, NY, D Appleton-Century Company, 1939) 306 (calling Kent 'doctor of laws to the whole republic'). See also DJ Hulsebosch, *Constituting Empire: New York and the Transformation of Constitutionalism in the Atlantic World, 1664–1830* (Chapel Hill, NC, University of North Carolina Press, 2005) 299 ('in practice the codification controversy was a conflict between two groups of lawyers: those who wanted to unify American law through treatises and legal education, and those who wanted to do so as delegates of state legislatures'), 280 ('Kent and other Federalist heirs resisted most codification efforts because they arose at the state rather than the national level. The federal government lacked the power to enact a private-law code').

complicated case, as Kent Newmyer has explained, as his treatises were meant to pave the way toward codification for settled areas of commercial law. However, his larger goal as a 'moderate' in the codification debates of the 1830s was to scuttle radical, novel, extensive, experimental, total codification.[23] Didactic legal works like commentaries and treatises, in other words, could support the argument that codification was either not required at all or at best was appropriate at the margins (eg David Dudley Field's code of procedure for New York State). The message was 'do not worry about the common law; there is no need for a code; it's not a mess, it's not chaos; it's not just a jumble of cases; we have got it under control' (see Hoyos on the need to fabricate disorder in the antidote to that disorder, the treatise). Such claims were premised on the point that the more discursive didactic literature simplified the legal universe in the way that a code would (or at least was often expected to) (see Blaine Baker in this volume on Story's codifying).

Indeed, the view of legal treatises operating as the stepping-stone to a code and the idea that the legal treatise would act as a defence against codification made the same assumption: legal treatises provide a unifying and simplifying function. This is, however, a problematic assumption.

In the United States at least, many of the treatises that were produced in the nineteenth century arguably made things more complex rather than less by loading new editions of English and native works with layers upon layers of citations. As Dirk Hartog has pointed out, these books might have been originally written as 'repositories of legal truth', filled with principle for which the precedents cited were mere illustrations. However, lawyers bought these books as compendia, as repositories of all the possible positions that could be raised with regard to a particular legal problem. They bought them for the footnotes and the indexes, as shortcuts to precedents and arguments they would use as well as those they would have to counter. And the treatise writers responded to the market demand with larger and larger editions that incorporated and distinguished every possible variation and alternative. Instead of countering complexity with coherence, in the end the treatises recreated complexity.[24]

Lawyers wanted cases. They wanted the ability to generate complexity, which, after all, is the water they swim in. So, for instance, Stephen Waddams (Chapter six) discusses the interesting example of Henry Colebrooke who offered a contract law treatise in 1818 that tried to be all principle without cases and it fell flat. Regardless of what a text-writer might say in his preface about the principles that

Hence when Pollock asks Holmes whether Holmes thinks codification 'a humbug' in the sense that codification is itself undesirable 'or only that there is no advantage in doing it by legislative authority', Pollock fails to grasp this important federal-state distinction. See Pollock to Holmes, 26 July 1877 *Holmes- Pollock Letters* (n 17) 7.

[23] See RK Newmyer, *Supreme Court Justice Joseph Story: Statesman of the Old Republic* (Chapel Hill, NC, University of North Carolina Press, 1985) 278. The thought was that 'moderate' codification would 'clear up areas of confusion, enhance uniformity, and rescue working lawyers from drudgery and impending chaos' (279).

[24] H Hartog, *Man and Wife in America: A History* (Cambridge, MA, Harvard University Press, 2000) 16.

would drive the inquiry (or symmetry, order, science, etc), a discussion of the law would be expected to include references to cases or other primary sources of positive law, including codes. That is what Colebrooke seems not to have understood. Waddams tells us that Colebrooke was never able to write a preface to his work. Perhaps he did not understand (as someone like CG Addison did) that a preface might say one thing (very high-sounding) and the book do another (give cases that could be used as authorities slotted onto a more or less developed theoretical framework).

This says something important about legal treatises, which might well be different from other kinds of treatises and might well be true of law books more generally: they exist in the shadow of legal practice. A good, successful legal treatise must take precedent and practice into account. It cannot be all principle. That is what makes Tapping Reeve's *Baron and Femme* come dangerously close to looking like a bad treatise, as much as one might like his rejection of Blackstone on one-person-in-law. Hence, in the same way that we cannot see commentaries-treatises-codes as stepping stones towards a *telos* like the transparent and perhaps ultimately self-interpreting simplicity that the Shangri-La code was imagined to inaugurate, we must take seriously the fact that these books were not meant to be read from cover to cover for their overarching conceptual argument. Indeed, the framework in many cases was little more than a way of creating categories in which to put things (eg the Gaian triad, persons-things-actions).[25] Many, if not most, of these books were meant to be dipped into for this or that point and its corresponding authorities. The Scottish institute-writer George Joseph Bell said his own work was useful 'for the sudden occasions of practice'.[26] In other words, these works were intended to allow the practitioner to *step in and out* of the text, a text the form of which was not necessarily moving backwards or forwards in any particular direction, eg towards codification or the institute-structure, or away from it.

Lindsay Farmer (Chapter seven) takes up the point about use and the legal treatise in his essay explicitly, asking specifically about how principled English and Scottish criminal law was. Not very, Farmer argues. 'Criminal law was conceived of primarily as a practical subject, and that utility to the practitioner was the organising principle both in terms of structure and substance'. Rather than drawing distinctions between institutional works and handbooks and other texts, Farmer asks us to think about what they had in common, namely, operating as actual sources of law for criminal lawyers. As he puts it, 'in the absence of detailed case reports and other sources, they *are* the law for the developing profession'. So, for example, for the Scottish criminal law writer David Hume, nephew of the famous philosopher, principle and practice were inseparable – 'the principle *is*

[25] The Gaian triad has been called 'one of the most distinctive and enduring systems of thought in Western history'. See DR Kelley, 'Gaius Noster: Substructures of Western Thought' (1979) 84 *The American Historical Review* 619, 620.

[26] KGC Reid, 'From Text-Book to Book of Authority: The *Principles* of George Joseph Bell' (2011) 15 *Edinburgh Law Review* 6, 12.

the practice'. It would be misguided therefore to assume that principle was more appropriately expressed in 'higher' forms of legal literature and practice in some 'lower' form like a justice of the peace manual. Farmer argues that treatise-writers were achieving a kind of de facto codification with these works, rather than acting as a stepping-stone to codification or operating as a defence against it.

Jim Phillips (Chapter 10) examines one justice of the peace manual in depth, prepared in the 1830s by an imperious judge and assemblyman, John George Marshall, for the use of magistrates in Nova Scotia. Calling this book a 'counter treatise', Phillips argues that it embodied 'low law', highly positivistic and statute-based, to be used on the ground by justices of the peace, ordinary men who were not trained in the law and, indeed, for whom Marshall seems to have held not a little contempt. Marshall's book was meant to instruct, Phillips claims, not persuade as a treatise would. The work was 'an instructional guide, pure and simple, written for a class of people desperately in need, in his [Marshall's] view, of instruction'.

We should note that the form of 'low law' Phillips describes is not confined to the alphabetised manual form. So, for instance, Zephaniah Swift's *A System of the Laws of the State of Connecticut: In Six Books* (1795–96) was actually written in part for justices of the peace and used by them in states like Ohio that looked to Connecticut when they were settled.[27] That was despite the fact that Swift used the institute form, strongly associated with high principle. However, Swift was very positivistic (see Fernandez contrasting him with Tapping Reeve). As Philip Girard explains in his essay (Chapter two), comparing the institute-structure in Blackstone and Kent to the Nova Scotia institute-structured book, Beamish Murdoch's *Epitome of the Laws of Nova Scotia*, Murdoch's work was very practical and statutory. It contained 'a wealth of detail about local statutes, civil and criminal procedure, and actual practice and usage'. In other words, work that was positivistic, statute-oriented and practice-oriented could exist in high forms, as well as low ones.

Conversely, the 'highest' kind of legal treatise could be directed at 'lower' audiences. Take Savigny's famous treatise on possession. It was translated from the German into English by Sir Erskine Perry, Chief Justice of the Bombay Supreme Court. Perry dedicated the work to 'the members of the Honourable Company's Service engaged in the administration of justice in India'.[28] Such individuals cannot be expected to have 'the same scientific knowledge of the law which follows only upon deep study and exclusive attention to the subject'.[29] However, these officials of the East India Company, Perry supposed, would rush to consume this book by 'the greatest master of Roman law in Europe'.[30] Why? '[A]n accurate

[27] See EC Goodwin, *The Magistracy Rediscovered: Connecticut, 1636–1818* (Ann Arbor, MI, UMI Research Press, 1981) 95–96.

[28] E Perry, 'Preface' to Von Savigny's *Treatise on Possession or the Jus Possessionis of the Civil Law* 6th edn (London, S Sweet, 1848) iii.

[29] Ibid iv.

[30] Ibid.

knowledge of the distinction between Possession and Property, and of the legal protection afforded to the former in order to repress violence and breaches of the public peace' was especially valuable to colonial administrators, Perry implied.[31] This book, in other words, was high law for the unscientifically-oriented lowly.[32]

IV. THE ORNAMENTAL

Blaine Baker's essay (Chapter four) deals with an American figure essential to any collection on the legal treatise: Joseph Story. Story wrote so many treatises and there were so many editions of the books, many of them on very boring topics, one can easily see why not much has been written about them. Baker argues that Story's treatises should be understood in relationship to his other systematising writing – an alphabetised digest, a consolidation of state statutes, his codification initiatives and even his encyclopaedia entries. The treatise was just one of the forms Story used, even if it was the one he managed to make work most successfully. However, no simple stepping-stone story emerges. Baker focuses on Story's *Commentaries on the Conflicts of Laws* (1832), explaining how that book is dominated by Story's concerns about individuals engaged in exchange transactions across state lines rather than conflicts between the laws of independent sovereign nations. 'Although Story had limited interest in genuinely transnational private-law discord', Baker writes

> [s]ituating a domestic, private law problem in the context of international practice and the law of nations was in some measure a rhetorical flourish on Story's part, intended to add appealing classical cachet to choice-of-law rules at risk of being ignored or rejected by parochial state courts.

Story was a cosmopolitan. As Baker notes, 'a single page of *Commentaries on Conflicts*, for example, has . . . quotations from Louis Boullenois, Achille Rodemburg, Paul Voet, John Voet, Charles D'Argentré and Ulricus Huberus'. However, this was, at least in part 'rhetorical flourish', 'intended to add appealing classical cachet' to a set of much more mundane domestic problems relating to the lack of coordination among state courts on rules directly affecting property, trade and commerce. Like one of Story's most important judicial decisions, *Swift v Tyson* and its creation of a federal common law,[33] establishing a set of fixed and determined choice of law rules was about augmenting national power in order to create strong national markets. These concerns were resolutely domestic, not international.

[31] Ibid.
[32] Apparently, when he retired, just four years after the translation, Perry 'occupied himself, with strange ingratitude, in advocating for the abolition of the Honourable Company'. CHS Fifoot, *Judge and Jurist in the Reign of Victoria* (London, Stevens and Sons, 1959) 87 n 3. See also J Keay, *The Honourable Company: History of the English East India Company* (London, HarperCollins, 1991).
[33] *Swift v Tyson*, 41 U.S. 1 (1842).

Stephen Waddams (Chapter six) also describes the way in which cosmopolitan sources operated in an ornamental way for English contract law writers. This was most apparent in the little failed book prepared by Colebrook. Waddams writes that '[t]he book is replete with references to Roman law, to the French Civil Code, to Hindu law and to civilian writers, including Barbeyrac, Pufendorf, Godefroy, Grotius, Domat, Pothier and Erskine'. However, more commercially and intellectually successful writers like Frederick Pollock also referred to the civil law, the writings of Savigny and Pothier, who was praised by many for his 'manly' style. The continental promise of order, elegance and science created a powerful drug, and Pothier's treatise on the law of obligations was available in English (unlike Savigny whom Waddams notes Pollock insisted on quoting in German for an English audience who were unlikely to have been able to appreciate the nuance Pollock sought to preserve). However, Waddams explains how the principles taken from the civil law, and specifically from Pothier, turned out to be too wide for common law lawyers in many cases and how even Pollock retreated from Savigny's emphasis on intention as Pollock moved closer towards Holmes and the American emphasis on reasonable expectations. The extent of actual deep influence of the civil law on the English contract law writers might have been minimal; however, Waddams notes an attachment to 'an *idea* or ideal of civil law, closely associated as it was with order, science, elegance, logic and principle'. Ironically, Pollock's admiration for Pothier's 'elaborate and elegant works' in general did not keep him from rejecting specific positions taken by Pothier as 'cumbrous and inelegant', suggesting that Pollock was not content to imitate Pothier's elegance but to exceed it.

Elegance, at the same time, was treated with considerable suspicion in the common law world – perhaps partly because of its association with civil law in general, and French law in particular. Farmer notes, for instance, that Hume's late eighteenth-century treatise on Scots criminal law sought to 'avoid . . . strained and artificial rules of law', while Waddams quotes Pollock's approval, over a hundred years later, of 'the modern tendency to look to 'the realization of reasonable expectations' as the ground of just claims rather than an artificial equation of wills or intentions', thus throwing Savigny, and presumably his own enthusiastic previous endorsement of Savigny, under the shiny new wheels of American Legal Realism.[34] Blackstone, of course, was frequently both lauded and chided for his elegance, not only by Bentham (quoted by Wright as snarkily dismissing the *Commentaries* as an 'elegant palliative to the inherently chronic confusion of the common law') but also by the likes of Thomas Jefferson, who bemoaned the waning influence of Coke on Littleton, that 'black-letter text' filled with 'uncouth but cunning learning' as the fashionable 'honeyed Mansfieldism of Blackstone became the students' hornbook'.

[34] The Legal Realists had no use for elegance for elegance's sake. For a typical dismissal of the 'intellectual passion for *elegantia juris*, for symmetry of form and substance', see BN Cardozo, *The Nature of the Judicial Process* (New Haven, CT, Yale University Press, 1921) 34.

Unlike 'the deep and rich mines of Coke, Littleton', fact- and case-based, well-grounded, proudly inelegant in its reportorial restraint, Blackstone's suspiciously elegant *Commentaries* had been 'perverted . . . to the degeneracy of legal science'. Their attempt to systematise and scientise the material, with an apparently aloof 'elegance', ill concealed the celebration of central authority hidden behind an apparently abstract, and objective, system of legal principles. Here the treatise, or rather the elegant treatise, carries the whiff of despotism ordinarily associated with codes, which as Wright points out, Macaulay considered 'almost the only blessing, perhaps the only blessing, which absolute governments are better fitted to confer on a nation than popular governments'. (This is not to say, incidentally, that Jefferson was opposed to codification, provided he drafted the code and in drafting the code he relied heavily on Coke, to the point of imitating Coke's marginal style and medieval spelling habits.)[35]

The interrelation between treatise and code, however, once again turns out to be less straightforward than one might think. Not only are there codes-as-treatises and treatises-as-codes, but treatises, even elegant ones, do not necessarily serve the centralising and controlling functions often ascribed to codes (at least in the common law world, while codification elsewhere has the exact opposite connotation of subjecting state power to comprehensive, systematic, visible, and therefore monitorable and enforceable legal constraint). In Germany, for instance, treatises have been said to serve the end of subjecting state power to principled (and, yes, scientific or, if you prefer, 'scientific') control by the law professoriate, which one commentator went so far as to elevate and institutionalise as a fourth – externally critiquing – branch of government.[36]

This critical, or normative, function of the treatise is often associated with its scientific ambition. Certainly the German law professor who writes a legal treatise traditionally has seen herself as doing legal science, and her claim to influence derives from her status as a legal scientist who occupies a position of objectivity, from which she critically assesses positive law (*lex lata*) and from which she proposes corrections to any errors she might discover (*lex ferenda*). This is not to say, however, that the treatise (or the *Lehrbuch*) is unique in its legal scientific ambition. In Germany, law has been considered a science since (at least) the early nineteenth century and all legal scholars have been regarded, and have regarded themselves, as scientists by definition (and occupation), whether they write a treatise, a code commentary, a case comment, an article or a monograph (even an op-ed piece in a general newspaper, though they may need to simplify their scientific analysis for a lay audience).[37]

[35] See MD Dubber, '"An Extraordinarily Beautiful Document": Jefferson's Bill for Proportioning Crimes and Punishments and the Challenge of Republican Punishment' in MD Dubber and L Farmer (eds), *Modern Histories of Crime and Punishment* (Stanford, CA, Stanford University Press, 2007) 115.

[36] B Schünemann, 'Strafrechtsdogmatik als Wissenschaft' in B Schünemann *et al* (eds), *Festschrift für Claus Roxin* (Berlin, de Gruyter, 2001) 1, 8.

[37] On German legal science, see M Reimann, 'Nineteenth Century German Legal Science' (1990) 31 *Boston College Law Review* 837; MD Dubber, 'The Promise of German Criminal Law: A Science of Crime and Punishment' (2005) 6 *German Law Journal* 1049.

The association between the idea of law as science (or, the common non-committal, 'science') and the idea of the treatise in particular is characteristic of the common law world, where the very project of legal science (and within that project, of different conceptions of legal science) has been contested for decades, if not centuries.[38] The appeal of the treatise as a marker for the scientific ambitions of the common law thus reflects both a yearning, however conflicted, to move beyond a non-scientific, or insufficiently scientific, conception of law and a recognition of the possibility of that conception. At the same time, and for the same reason, anxiety about the idea of a treatise reflects anxiety about the idea of a scientific conception of law.

The connection between the ideas, and ideals, elegance and science also deserves more critical attention than it occasionally receives. The artificiality of elegance, the veneer of sophistication, the pretence of learning, the putting on of airs, can be distinguished from the pursuit of, and the attempt to claim, the objectivity, systematicity, comprehensiveness and complexity of science. Elegance is not rigour. Whatever might have been said about Savigny and his fellow nineteenth-century Romanists, German legal science – as opposed to German Roman law scholarship – since then could hardly be described as motivated by a concern for elegance and, in fact, might be just as well, if not better, regarded as driven by a disdain for elegance that rivals Jefferson's, if for entirely different reasons.

While citations to, and even quotations from, civil law legal scientists may have signalled a common law treatise-writer's attempt to associate his project with a foreign idea of law as science, often more sensed than fully grasped or endorsed, the ornamental significance of these cross-systemic references should not be discounted. Why would the author of a legal treatise orient (or at least pepper) the work in this way? Why pretend to be cosmopolitan when the concern was actually domestic (Story)? Why quote in German text that most readers will not be able to understand, or agonise over whether or not Pothier was right about a fine point relating to offer and acceptance (Pollock)?[39]

Part of the answer has to do with stature and reputation and what these legal scholars would have thought necessary to achieve greatness. Kent wanted to be recognised as the American Blackstone. Story sought after and attained an international reputation with his books, quite a feat since England would have viewed the United States of the 1830s and early 1840s as a backwater. Each of these jurists wanted to be the Pothier of their time and jurisdiction, to be known as a great legal scientist.[40] Greatness included learnedness, filtering it in a way that also demonstrated it. Repackaging pretend Roman and civil law was one way to do this. In

[38] See H Schweber, 'The Science of Legal Science: The Model of the Natural Sciences in Nineteenth-Century American Legal Education' (1999) 17 *Law and History Review* 421.

[39] See Waddams (n 8) 307–10.

[40] See D Hulsebosch, 'Debating the Transformation of American Law: James Kent, Joseph Story, and the Legacy of the Revolution' in DW Hamilton and AL Brophy (eds), *Transformations in American Legal History: Essays in Honor of Professor Morton J Horwitz* (Cambridge, MA, Harvard University Press, 2009) 1 (emphasising differences between Kent and Story).

fact, Pothier did this himself when he reworked Justinian's *Digest*.[41] Pollock seems to have been genuinely interested in Pothier and Savigny. However, Waddams shows us that Pollock also wished to appear, at least to Holmes, to have been ahead of the curve on reasonable expectations in contract law.[42] If Pollock had any hope of being recognised as a legal scientist with international stature, presumably Holmes would have to concur in that judgment. Individuals in these small rarefied circles were very dependent on each other for their promotion and recognition, which could be a fickle process.[43] Waddams describes what Jones' book on bailments and Evans' English translation of the *Law of Obligations* did for Pothier among English lawyers who might otherwise have never known who he was. A cosmopolitan orientation, even if it was largely ornamental, meant that a treatise-writer got to play in a larger and more learned circle of scholars, thereby increasing the chances of notoriety, name-recognition and a shot at greatness.

When the author of a didactic work made a conscious choice to keep the focus local – Zephaniah Swift and his *System of the Laws of the State of Connecticut* or Beamish Murdoch's *Epitomes* – this would take them and their work out of these circles. Not only did Swift refer to the state in the title of his book, he also referred to 'laws' in the plural. Nothing could more clearly communicate that he was positivistic. No claim was made about 'the law' in the singular. It was this sense of 'our lady the common law' that later academic jurists like Pollock and Holmes took themselves to be investigating and explaining and writing to each other about.[44] Murdoch, Girard tells us (Chapter two), was also focused on the local and the legislative. He was not interested in commercial law, a tremendous

[41] See JE de Montmorency, 'Robert-Joseph Pothier and French Law' (1914) 13 *Journal of the Society of Comparative Legislation* 265, 278–79.

[42] Holmes had filtered 'learned law' in his editing of the 12th edition of *Kent's Commentaries*. Langbein (n 3) 566–70 (on 'learned law'), 565 (noting the Holmes edition).

[43] Holmes was very free in making such judgments in his correspondence with Pollock. See, eg Holmes to Pollock, 17 June 1880, in *Holmes-Pollock, Letters* (n 17) 15 (speaking about Melville M Bigelow who wrote a history of procedure in England from the Norman Conquest that '[h]e is a man whom I greatly respect for his sincere love of learning which he has proved in spite of poverty etc., but there is nothing incisive or masterly about him – so that whatever he does will have to be done over again. He is, however, *getting to be a really learned man*') (emphasis added); Holmes to Pollock, 23 March 1883, 21 (speaking about James Fitzjames Stephen, 'I am reading Stephen's *Criminal Law*. My opinion of him as a law writer does not grow higher, as I read this or his former books. He knows nothing, it seems to me, of the scientific aspects of the history of law, and is to my mind rather a model of a fine old 18th century controversialist than a philosopher. He would knock the stuffing out of an antagonist upon a point of dogma I don't doubt, in the handsomest way. He is an adult male animal, but he hasn't the intuition of [Henry Sumner] Maine or the higher class of writers'); Holmes to Pollock, 4 March 1888, 31 (speaking about Maine at the time of his death and noting that while *Ancient Law* 'brilliantly caught and popularized' the science of law, '[h]e seems to have been impatient of investigation himself and I do not think will leave much mark on the actual structure of jurisprudence, although he helped many others do so'). Bigelow was a young scholar in Boston also using a historical approach to understand English law whom Holmes likely saw as a rival. Holmes' issues with intellectual generosity were manifold. So, for instance, he denied that Maine's influence extended to himself despite the fact that his lectures on the common law corresponded to the chapters in Maine's *Ancient Law*. See M De Wolfe Howe, *Justice Oliver Wendell Holmes*, vol 2 *The Proving Years 1870–1882* (Cambridge, MA, Belknap Press, 1963) 139 (on Bigelow), 148–49 (on Maine).

[44] See *Holmes-Pollock Letters*, ibid; Richard Cosgrove, *Our Lady the Common Law: An Anglo-American Legal Community, 1870–1930* (New York, NY, New York University Press, 1987).

contrast with Kent and Story. And Murdoch, who unlike Blackstone and Kent enjoyed legal practice, was not very interested in the elaborate or scholarly. Girard quotes Murdoch warning the 'young collegian' to avoid taking excessive 'pride of classic lore'. 'While his learning may be an ornament, and perhaps give grace and intensity to his eloquence, yet it is rather a holiday garb'. Murdoch's text was not, like Kent and Blackstone's, 'ready-made for export and empire'. Probably, for that reason, it did not need a story about the importance of commercial law as a civilising function.[45]

If Swift and Murdoch had problems with name-recognition, there was no such issue for William Blackstone. As Kunal Parker explains in his essay on *Blackstone*'s *Commentaries* (Chapter one), Blackstone's text shifted from being an object of use to an object in a museum admired for its style. What that style was is very difficult to say. There is certainly dogma and oversimplification, but many much less influential didactic works have had this. Is the style merely ornamental? Or is it somehow essential to the central role this set of books has played? Parker explains the way in which editors of Blackstone's work eventually gave up trying to update the text to a particular time and jurisdiction and simply accepted that what was important about the text was just that it was Blackstone. In his description of the text's journey from use to style and the text taking up its place as a museumised object, Parker asks us to think about what has stayed the same in relation to this text over time. Rather than focusing on difference or change over time, we can see something important about Blackstone's text as a kind of museum exhibit of how one (particularly influential) eighteenth-century English gentleman thought he could renovate a Gothic castle and live comfortably in it.

V. CONCLUSIONS

We could write for a very long time about all the different things that the essays in this collection are doing: describing how individual law books operated in a political event (Campbell), invented – or at least cordoned off – a field of law (Hoyos, Farmer), offered a local iteration in the institute form (Girard), presented the local as if it were English common law that could operate for the American nation (Fernandez) and adopted national concerns and embedded them into a cosmopolitan and international context (Baker). There is a sub-theme in the chapters relating to the end user of the text – justices of the peace, who were being lectured to and instructed so as to harness them in (Phillips), criminal lawyers, who

[45] Hulsebosch, 'Debating the Transformation of American Law' (n 40) 6 (noting that both Kent and Story embraced commerce, which '[i]n the sociology of the Scottish Enlightenment, which both learned from British books . . . was the primary index of civilization'). See also Baker in this volume, quoting from Story who dramatically stated that a nation that ignored the disorderliness created by inter-state conflicts of law 'would soon find its whole commercial intercourse reduced to a state, like that, in which it now exists with savage tribes, with the barbarous nations of Sumatra, and with the other portions of Asia, washed by the Pacific'.

needed a way to access and cite the law (Farmer), students, who received the dogmatic principles of contract from Anson, as opposed to the more thoughtful and nuanced Pollock (Waddams) and magistrates in India, who could use Macaulay's code to impose a straightforward version of British justice on the native population (Wright).

We are cognisant that the longer we write, the longer it will take readers to get to the essays themselves, which contain so much more than we have been able to highlight here. We must, however, say a word about what the essays in the collection do not treat. As the title of the collection indicates, these essays are focused on the Anglo-American legal treatise. The books our authors have chosen to write about are all common law works from the United States, the United Kingdom and Canada (with the exception of Barry Wright on the Indian Penal Code). The civil law arguably triggered common law interest in the form but there are no essays on civil law legal treatises per se, not to mention treatises in other legal traditions such as Islamic law or on fields of law like international law.[46] Even within the Anglo-American tradition, no one here has written about earlier works like *Littleton on Tenures* or 'the ultimate treatises'[47] or 'mega treatises'[48] of the late nineteenth century in the United States – Williston, Wigmore, Powell, Scott or Corbin. Rather than striving for an ever-elusive coverage, we have opted for a collection of essays that highlight important features of the treatise as a form of legal literature, as a law book in action, as a work that complicates simple stepping-stone stories about the relationships among the treatise and codes or institutes and other forms of legal literature, and as a talky text that can and often does contain important ornamental aspects.

One question that we do not address in great detail is what happened to the treatise as a form of literature in the twentieth century. Roscoe Pound recounted this evolution in *The Formative Era in American Law*, where he gave a stepping-stone story, casebooks were the 'necessary forerunner[s] . . . of the great treatises',[49] the 'ultimate' or 'mega' treatises. And those 'great treatises' paved the way for the American Law Institute Restatement projects.[50] How did the United States get from this 'Age of the Treatise' to the study of doctrine being seen as *passé* by the

[46] Holmes interestingly used the fact that international law was 'a subject which lawyers do practically study' and that there were 'rules of conduct *so definite as to be written in textbooks*, and sanctioned in many cases by the certainty that a breach will be followed by war' as his reasons for recognising it as part of the law. De Wolfe Howe, *The Proving Years* 71 n 22 (emphasis added).

[47] Simpson (n 3) 674.

[48] Langbein (n 3) 593.

[49] Pound, (n 21) 165. So, for instance, Williston produced his collection of cases before his treatise. See S Williston, *The Law of Contracts* (New York, NY, Baker, Voorhis, 1920); S Williston, *A Selection of Cases on the Law of Contracts* (Boston, MA, Little, Brown, 1903–04). Wigmore's treatise was published shortly after his casebook. See JH Wigmore, *A Treatise on the System of Evidence in Trials at Common Law: Including the Statutes and Judicial Decisions of Jurisdictions of the United States* (Boston, MA, Little, Brown, 1904); JH Wigmore, *A Selection of Cases on Evidence: For the Use of Students of Law* (Boston, MA, Little, Brown, 1906).

[50] For instance, Williston produced his *A Selection of Cases on the Law of Contracts* in 1903–04, the treatise on *The Law of Contracts* in 1920, and his work for the American Law Institute's Restatement of the law of contracts in the late 1920s and early 1930s.

late 1970s and early 1980s? Simpson identified the lack of enthusiasm for doctrine in the United States with the rise and effects of legal realism.[51] There is clearly some truth to this observation, although there are many jurisdictions that had significant 'realist' or 'sociological' movements in which treatises continued to be produced.[52] Treatise-writing was not just an outmoded vestige of 'Langdellian formalism', or 'Classical Legal Thought', if you prefer.[53] Corbin, for instance, saw his treatise as a Legal Realist alternative to Williston's formalism, one that drew on inductive case analysis rather than deductive reasoning from higher principles to lower doctrines. Corbin's treatise, after all, appeared only in 1950, long after Legal Realism had replaced formalism as the orthodoxy in American legal thought.[54] (Even the first edition of Williston was published in 1920, at the very end of the 'heyday' of legal formalism.) Karl Llewellyn, who regarded Corbin as his 'father in the law', complained bitterly about his fellow Legal Realists' dismissal of doctrinal analysis, and of treatise and Restatement writing in particular. Although no treatise-writer himself, Llewellyn, like Corbin, played a central part in the American Law Institute's work. His Uniform Commercial Code, more explicitly than Corbin's Restatement of Contracts, implemented the core Legal Realist claim that it was impossible to deduce the resolution of every issue from a set of principles by leaving space for local legal communities (in this case communities of merchants) to frame and resolve issues based on their experience and expertise.[55] Farnsworth's contracts treatise, first published in 1982, can be seen as a more explicitly normative, if not to say neo-formalist, alternative to Corbin's Realist project.[56] Prosser's torts treatise, first published in 1941, too was more intellectually ambitious – and in particular animated by then-dominant Legal Realist thought – than it would appear in hindsight, after a series of editions that, as in all such works, tend to dilute the conceptual clarity of the original vision.[57]

That said, few if any legal scholars in the United States today wake up filled with a burning desire to devote their professional lives to the production of a treatise, great or not so great. While short treatlets survive on the margins of the American legal textbook market, neither students nor teachers, not to mention courts or practising lawyers or, for that matter, legislators or their aides, feel the need to bury their noses in heavy tomes of treatise learning. The Great Treatise very much

[51] Simpson (n 3) 677 (stating that the realist movement 'involved a scepticism and even a cynicism about the significance of legal doctrine in the determination of cases'), 678 ('a movement that minimizes the importance of legal doctrine is hardly likely to generate enthusiasm for the work of analyzing doctrine and expounding it as the principled science of law').

[52] See A Hunt, *Sociological Movement in Law* (London, Macmillan, 1978). Thanks to Blaine Baker for this point and this reference.

[53] See TC Grey, 'Langdell's Orthodoxy' (1983–84) 45 *University of Pittsburgh Law Review* 1, 2 (using the term 'classical orthodoxy'); D Kennedy, 'Two Globalizations of Law and Legal Thought: 1850–1968' (2003) 36 *Suffolk University Law Review* 631, 633 (using the term 'Classical Legal Thought', which he made famous).

[54] See F Kessler, 'Arthur Linton Corbin' (1969) 78 *Yale Law Journal* 517.

[55] See JQ Whitman, 'Commercial Law and the American *Volk*: A Note on Llewellyn's German Sources for the Uniform Commercial Code' (1987) 97 *Yale Law Journal* 156.

[56] EA Farnsworth, *Contracts* (Boston, MA, Little Brown, 1982).

[57] L William, *Prosser, Handbook of the Law of Torts* (St Paul, MN, West, 1941).

has gone the way of the Great Men of the Law; just as the American Law Institute is not what it once was, and ALI giants like Herbert Wechsler no longer roam the halls of American law schools, so Model Codes or even Restatements no longer demand the attention of the producers or the consumers of legal literature in the United States.[58]

Other common law countries, such as Canada, however, continue to generate treatises on the standard range of topics, including – even – in criminal law, a subject long neglected in its Neighbour to the South. In the Mother Country, too, scholars and practitioners continue to churn out treatises, though the name may have fallen out of favour, perhaps so as not to scare off students and lawyers eager for a quick hit of doctrine. In civil law countries, say Germany, the production of comprehensive – and heavy – tomes of doctrinal analysis continues, both in the form of *Lehrbücher* and (often multi-volume) treatises-cum-code-commentaries, though here too shorter forms of legal educational literature have found a willing market.

Given the treatise's shape-shifting resilience over the past few centuries and its intimate connection with ideas of legal scholarship, legal education, and even of law itself, it would be foolish to count it out, now or in the future, in civil law countries or in the common law world. Perhaps even in an apparently hostile environment such as American legal scholarship, where 'doctrine' has for some time been a four-letter word, a fundamental and widespread reassessment of the very project of so-called interdisciplinary ('law and') legal scholarship may usher in a renaissance, or at least a reassessment, of the treatise in one form or another, as the disciplinary pendulum swings back from the 'and' to the 'law' and the analysis of law reasserts itself, both chastened and complicated in the wake of insights gleaned from decades of peering into law from the outside.[59]

[58] MD Dubber, 'The Model Penal Code and European Criminal Law' in A Klip (ed), *Substantive Criminal Law of the European Union* (Antwerp, Maklu, 2011) 209.

[59] See, eg S Lavi, 'Turning the Tables on "Law and . . .": A Jurisprudential Inquiry into Contemporary Legal Theory' (2011) 96 *Cornell Law Review* 811.

1

Historicising Blackstone's *Commentaries on The Laws of England*

KUNAL M PARKER*

I. INTRODUCTION: DIFFERENCE, SAMENESS AND THE COMMENTARIES

IN THE FIRST edition of *The Mysterious Science of the Law* (1941), Daniel Boorstin described Blackstone's *Commentaries on the Laws of England* as 'perhaps the most important single book . . . in the history of the common law'. This was especially true, according to Boorstin, if one focused on the *Commentaries*' impact in the United States: 'Justinian's role in the reception of the civil law in western Europe', Boorstin claimed, 'was Blackstone's in the reception of the common law in America'.[1] In his preface to the 1958 edition of *The Mysterious Science of the Law*, Boorstin went even further: 'In the history of American institutions, no other book – except the Bible – has played so great a role. . . .'[2]

While they might not have praised the *Commentaries* in quite such grandiloquent terms, eighteenth-century Americans, like eighteenth-century Britons generally, were quick to recognise the *Commentaries*' importance. On the eve of the Declaration of Independence, Edmund Burke observed in Parliament that nearly as many copies of the *Commentaries* had been sold in the American colonies as in England.[3] The text was intimately familiar to American legal elites. America's most prominent Chief Justice, John Marshall, had read the *Commentaries* four times before he turned 30.[4] Later in life, the eminent New York jurist James Kent would declare that the *Commentaries* had 'inspired [him], at the age of 15, with awe'

* Professor of Law and Dean's Distinguished Scholar, University of Miami School of Law. I would like to thank Angela Fernandez, Mary Anne Franks, Christopher Tomlins, and the participants at the conference on 'The Treatise in Legal History' held at the Faculty of Law, University of Toronto in October 2010, for their comments on earlier drafts of this paper.

[1] DJ Boorstin, *The Mysterious Science of the Law* (Cambridge, MA, Harvard University Press, 1941) vii, 4.

[2] Ibid, (1958 edn) Preface).

[3] E Burke, 'Speech on Moving His Resolutions for Conciliation with the Colonies, March 22, 1775' in *The Works of the Right Honorable Edmund Burke* (Boston, MA, Little, Brown, 1865).

[4] See DR Nolan, 'Sir William Blackstone and the New American Republic: A Study of Intellectual Impact' (1976) 51 *New York University Law Review* 731–57.

and convinced him to become a lawyer.[5] In 1795, Connecticut's Zephaniah Swift praised Blackstone for having 'reduced order out of chaos'.[6] In 1803, Virginia's leading legal authority, Henry St George Tucker, remarked that, until the appearance of the *Commentaries*, 'the students of law in England, and its dependencies, were almost destitute of any scientific guide to conduct their studies'.[7] Indeed, Robert Ferguson has concluded that '[a]ll of our formative documents – the Declaration of Independence, the Constitution, the Federalist Papers, and the seminal decisions of the Supreme Court under John Marshall – were steeped in [the *Commentaries*]'.[8]

The *Commentaries* cast a long shadow over the nineteenth century as well. Blackstone's text served as the model not only for the pioneering treatises of the early nineteenth century such as James Kent's *Commentaries on American Law* (1826–30), but also for lesser known treatises such as Henry St George Tucker's *Commentaries on the Laws of Virginia* (1831). More than 65 years after the *Commentaries* first appeared, a set was acquired by the young Abraham Lincoln, who later in life recommended the text to aspiring lawyers as an important source of instruction. The *Commentaries* continued to be used in law school instruction until the very end of the nineteenth century. The US Supreme Court and other courts cited them repeatedly.

And yet, what is curious is that, despite their extraordinary longevity, the *Commentaries* were viewed, very soon after their appearance, in both England and America, as being out of date, even as out of step with the movement of history. In his famous 1803 'republican' edition of the *Commentaries*, St George Tucker was at pains to assure his readers that, in the aftermath of the American Revolution, the *Commentaries* 'could only safely be relied on as a methodical guide . . . or at most, in apprising the student of what the *law had been*; to know *what it now is*, he must resort to very different sources of information'.[9] This was a result of profound changes not only in obvious areas such as the constitutional system described in the *Commentaries*, but also in areas such as the law of real and personal property, where Tucker discerned an 'almost total change'.[10]

This sense that the *Commentaries* were out of step with the times, both in England and America, is reflected in the plethora of 'updated' editions that poured forth from the moment of the text's first appearance. The first English editions of the four volumes of the *Commentaries* appeared in quarto between 1765 and 1769. Four editions of the first three volumes had appeared by 1770, as

[5] W Kent, *Memoirs and Letters of James Kent* (Boston, MA, Little, Brown, 1989) 18.

[6] A Zephaniah Swift, '*System of the Laws of the State of Connecticut* (Windham, John Byrne, 1795–96)' 1, 41.

[7] H St George Tucker (ed), *Blackstone's Commentaries with Notes of Reference to the Constitution and Laws of the Federal Government of the United States and of the Commonwealth of Virginia* (5 vols) (Philadelphia, PA, William Young Birch & Abraham Small, 1803) (hereinafter 'Tucker Edition') vol 1, Preface, iii.

[8] AF Robert, *Law and Letters in American Culture* (Cambridge, MA, Harvard University Press, 1984) 11.

[9] T Edition (n 7) Preface, v (emphasis in the original).

[10] Ibid x.

Blackstone hastened to correct errors and make stylistic changes. The first edition in octavo appeared in Dublin. The first English octavo edition – and the fifth edition of the overall work – appeared in 1773. Eight editions were published during Blackstone's lifetime, the last appearing in 1778. Thereafter, English editions appeared in 1783 (9th edition by Richard Burn), 1787 (10th edition; a reprint), 1791 (11th edition; a reprint), 1793–95 (12th edition by Andrew Christian), 1800 (13th edition by Andrew Christian), 1803 (14th edition by Edward Christian), 1809 (15th edition by Edward Christian), 1811 (16th edition by JF Archbold), 1825 (17th edition by JT Coleridge), 1826 (18th edition by J Chitty; often reproduced in the United States), 1836 (19th edition by Hovenden and Ryland), 1841–44 (20th edition by James Stewart), and 1844 (21st edition by Hargrave, Sweet, Couch and Welsby). Serjeant Stephen's 1841 *New Commentaries on the Laws of England*, based on the *Commentaries*, largely supplanted subsequent English editions of the *Commentaries* for the remainder of the nineteenth century.

The first American edition of the *Commentaries* appeared in 1771–72, when an enterprising publisher claimed to offer a cheaper version of the *Commentaries* at the price of $8 a set (the English edition was sold at $26 a set).[11] Thereafter, there was a Boston edition of 1799 based on the ninth English edition and St George Tucker's 'republican' edition of 1803 (also based on the ninth edition English edition). Many American editions published during the nineteenth century were reprints of English ones. During the second half of the nineteenth century, however, there were major American editions by George Sharswood (1860), Thomas Cooley (1870) and William G Hammond (1890). American editions continued to be produced in the early twentieth century. William Carey Jones' 1915 edition was followed by William Draper Lewis' 1922 edition.

This incessant re-issuing of the *Commentaries* is testimony to a paradox: their continuing vitality, on the one hand, and a mounting sense of their obsolescence, on the other. How do we conjoin these? In a collection devoted to examining the history of the treatise, I suggest, the paradoxical history of Blackstone's *Commentaries* might be useful in opening up the question of what it means, in the first place, to historicise.

I will first offer a conventional history, a story of change over time, a story of how the fate of Blackstone's *Commentaries* tracks the fate of many objects that start out as objects of active manipulation (what I shall call objects of 'use') and end up as museum objects of distanced aesthetic contemplation (what I shall call objects of 'style'). In offering this 'use' to 'style' historical narrative, I do not, of course, suggest that objects of style thereby cease to have uses. Far from it. The Greek vessels that once served as objects of use in an ancient kitchen do not cease to have uses – including, or even especially, political uses – when they become objects of style, objects of aesthetic interest trapped behind panes of glass in a

[11] W Blackstone, *Commentaries on the Laws of England* (Philadelphia, PA, Printed for Subscribers, 1771).

museum. If ancient Greek vessels no longer carry oil or wine, for example, they serve to confirm the integrity of a narrative of Western history that is inculcated in the hundreds of museum-goers that file past them silently every day.

In the context of the history of Blackstone's *Commentaries*, as I shall show, the 'use' to 'style' narrative tracks how the *Commentaries* were treated by a succession of editors as we move across the nineteenth century. Over the course of the nineteenth century, the *Commentaries* ceased to be actively manipulated by editors (objects of use) and were increasingly recognised for their textual integrity (objects of style). This 'use' to 'style' narrative confirms something that we historians *already* 'know' to be the truth of objects, namely, that objects belong in contexts that themselves change over time. There is something comforting – and historically true – about this narrative.

But the fate of Blackstone's *Commentaries*, while it sanctions the 'use' to 'style' historical narrative, also reveals something more uncanny: sameness over time. This is not sameness in the sense that historians might appreciate: the ubiquity of historical context itself as something that is always available to make sense of objects. Rather, it is a sameness that reaches beyond historical context even as it does not defy it, a sameness that unsettles our deepest historical faiths. The sameness over time that Blackstone's *Commentaries* reveal might be worth tarrying over, if only because it reveals the blank spot in our efforts as historians.

II. FROM 'USE' TO 'STYLE': ONE HISTORY OF BLACKSTONE'S COMMENTARIES

Blackstone fully recognised the importance of understanding law in historical context. At the very opening of the *Commentaries*, he observes that the law student of the mid-eighteenth century has to be taught the various 'originals' of English law. Of these, by far the most important is the feudal:

> These originals should be traced to their fountains, as well as our distance will permit; to the customs of the Britons and Germans, as recorded by Caesar and Tacitus; to the codes of the northern nations on the continent, and more especially to those of our own Saxon princes; to the rules of the Roman law, either left here in the days of Papinian, or imported by Vacarius and his followers; but, above all, to that inexhaustible reservoir of legal antiquities and learning, the feodal law, or, as Spelman has entitled it, the law of nations in our western orb (emphasis added).[12]

Indeed, Blackstone insists, it is impossible to understand 'either the civil constitution of this kingdom . . . or the laws which regulate it's [sic] landed property' without an understanding of feudal law.[13]

[12] W Blackstone, *Commentaries on the Laws of England: A Facsimile of the First Edition of 1765–1769* (Chicago, IL, University of Chicago Press, 1979) (hereinafter 'University of Chicago Edition') (4 vols) vol 1, 35–36.

[13] Ibid vol 2, 44.

Blackstone's sense that feudalism had left its mark on the common law went along with his sense that England was now in a commercial age. His understanding of history as a move from feudal to commercial, and of law as something to be seen in historical context, had been articulated authoritatively by Blackstone's Scottish contemporaries (Kames, Smith and others), who were anxious to rid law of its feudal trappings and to fit it to the needs of the commercial present. Occasionally, Blackstone strikes a Kamesian note when he says that feudal restrictions on the transferability of property are inconsistent with the needs of a commercial economy. Applauding the erosion of 'feodal severity' in regard to the alienability of land, Blackstone concludes: '[P]roperty best answers the purposes of civil life, especially in commercial countries, when its transfer and circulation are totally free and unrestrained'.[14] Indeed, Blackstone tells us that the new commercial economy has witnessed the rise into prominence of personal property, a species of property more or less entirely disregarded by older writers on the common law.[15] To be sure, scholars have correctly cited Blackstone as evidence of the 'continued awkwardness of common lawyers in treating commercial topics'.[16] The *Commentaries* are much sounder in discussing real property than personal property. And Blackstone was no jurist like Lord Mansfield, who sought to reshape the common law to fit the needs of merchants through massive importations of continental principles and the consultation of special merchant juries. Nevertheless, it seems difficult to argue that Blackstone was not acutely conscious of living through a momentous historical shift and that he was unaware that the common law should be judged in terms of this historical shift and fitted to its context.

However, despite a strong historical sensibility that allows him to make sense of the common law in terms of its feudal origins and its commercial present, Blackstone remains wedded to the continuity of the common law, to its ability to collapse difference over time into sameness. In sharp contrast with his great critic Jeremy Bentham, Blackstone would celebrate the figure of the common law judge precisely for the judge's ability to mould the old common law to modern uses through a skilful use of legal fictions. Blackstone's celebrated metaphor is that of the common law as an 'old Gothic castle' that the common law judge fits out for modern, ie eighteenth century – living:

> When, therefore, by the gradual influence of foreign trade and domestic tranquility, the spirit of our military tenures began to decay, and at length the whole structure was removed, the judges quickly perceived that the forms and delays of the old feudal actions, (guarded with their several outworks of essoins, vouchers, aid-prayers, and a hundred other formidable entrenchments) were ill suited to that more simple and com-

[14] Ibid 288.

[15] 'But of later years, since the introduction and extension of trade and commerce, which are entirely occupied in this species of property, and have greatly augmented it's [sic] quantity and of course it's [sic] value, we have learned to conceive different ideas of it'. Ibid 385.

[16] D Lieberman, *The Province of Legislation Determined: Legal Theory in Eighteenth-Century Britain* (Cambridge; New York, NY, Cambridge University Press, 1985) 103.

mercial mode of property which succeeded the former, and required a more speedy decision of right, to facilitate exchange and alienation. Yet they wisely avoided soliciting any great legislative revolution in the old established forms, which might have been productive of consequences more numerous and extensive than the most penetrating genius could foresee; but left them as they were, to languish in obscurity and oblivion, and endeavoured by a series of minute contrivances to accommodate such personal actions, as were then in use, to all the most useful purposes of remedial justice. . . . And, since the new expedients have been refined by the practice of more than a century, and are sufficiently known and understood, they in general answer the purpose of doing speedy and substantial justice, much better than could now be effected by any great fundamental alterations. The only difficulty that attends them arises from their fictions and circuities: but, when once we have discovered the proper clew, that labyrinth is easily pervaded. *[We] inherit an old Gothic castle, erected in the days of chivalry, but fitted up for a modern inhabitant. The moated ramparts, the embattled towers, and the trophied halls, are magnificent and venerable, but useless, and therefore neglected. The inferior apartments, now accommodated to daily use, are cheerful and commodious, though their approaches may be winding and difficult.*[17]

Some might call for the English to move out of the old Gothic castle of the common law; but the common law judge, ie Blackstone – would rather make the eighteenth century Englishman at home in it. In this metaphor, we recognise that the common law inherited from the centuries following the Conquest is an object of active use. As in the case of a family living in a building erected centuries earlier, some parts of the old common law might be neglected, some maintained, some rearranged, some put to new uses. But throughout, the family continues to inhabit the same building. It is not abandoned.[18]

Blackstone's description of how the common law method allowed eighteenth-century Englishmen to inhabit the old Gothic castle of the common law adumbrates the fate of his own text. Over the course of the nineteenth century, Blackstone's own text *became* the old Gothic castle he so evocatively described.

[17] University of Chicago Edition (n 12) vol 3, 268–69 (emphasis added).

[18] In a brilliant recent essay, Carol Matthews has drawn attention to Blackstone's lifelong interest in architecture and specifically to his distaste for the Gothic architectural style and his preference for classical architectural order. See C Matthews, 'A "Model of the Old House": Architecture in Blackstone's Life and the *Commentaries*' in W Prest (ed), *Blackstone and His Commentaries: Biography, Law, History* (Oxford, Hart Publishing, 2009). On Blackstone and architecture, see also W Prest, 'Blackstone as Architect: Constructing the *Commentaries*' (2003) 15 *Yale Journal of Law and Humanities* 103–33.

Blackstone described the Gothic architectural style as having 'something oddly artificial in it. Huge ponderous Roofs being raised on slender pillars, or rather Groups of Staves; great masses of Stone, like Rocks, hanging in the Air without any visibly sufficient Support, and threatening every instant to fall. Every thing is crammed with Roses, Lace, Crosses, Monkeys, and other Quaintnesses, which glut the eye instead of filling it, by means of such a profusion of silly Ornaments. Whereas in the Greek Architecture there is not a single Member or Ornament but has its Priority as well as Beauty'. Quoted in Matthews, 'A "Model of the Old House"' 31–32. Matthews draws attention to the similarity between Blackstone's distaste for the Gothic style and his distaste for the feudal law as a way of underscoring Blackstone's historicist critique of the common law. Ibid 31. As should be clear from my own discussion of Blackstone's historicism, with its sense of the movement of history from the feudal to the commercial, I agree entirely with Matthews' sense of Blackstone's historicism. I find it *even more* noteworthy, then, that Blackstone uses the metaphor of the old Gothic castle not to argue that the common law should be abandoned, but that it should be lived in comfortably.

Like that old Gothic castle, the *Commentaries* had to be fitted out for modern use. In what follows, I describe how a succession of legal writers created new knowledge not only upon, but literally inside, the body of Blackstone's text.[19]

What is striking about the earliest English and American editions of the *Commentaries* is their level of aggressiveness vis-à-vis the text itself. In an age of slow communications, poor reporting of statutes and court decisions, and rudimentary legal instruction, the *Commentaries* were one of the few places Anglo-American judges, lawyers and law students could turn in order to obtain an understanding of the state of the law. Precisely *because* the *Commentaries* were an object of such active use and manipulation, their shortcomings were acutely apparent and needed urgently to be fixed. Editors, commentators and annotators thus treated Blackstone's *Commentaries* exactly as Blackstone himself had treated the common law. The old Gothic castle of the *Commentaries* could not be abandoned. Therefore, it had to be fitted out for modern living.

This sense of having to inhabit and update the *Commentaries* is discernible in the prefaces that accompanied the *Commentaries*' various editions, as editors both attempted to explain their intrusive editorial practices and to affirm the importance of the text they intruded upon. Nineteenth-century English editors were every bit as conscious of historical change as American ones. Joseph Chitty's famous and widely circulated 1826 edition of the *Commentaries* recognised openly that the *Commentaries* were the product of another age, another context. There were some, Chitty argued, who might call for the *Commentaries* to be placed in the hands of readers as they had been originally published, 'without annotations or additions.' This would make sense were new editions of the *Commentaries* intended 'merely as a history of English jurisprudence, having no other object than to inform the reader upon the facts and data of a past age'. But such was not the case. The very importance and centrality and uniqueness of the *Commentaries* in early-nineteenth-century English life were what made them impossible to abandon. As 'the first book of instruction to which the attention of the student is directed', the *Commentaries* should not convey anything incorrect or superseded, 'nor be silent upon any of those relations in social, political, and commercial life, which have sprung up since the time of the learned author'.[20] To cabin the *Commentaries* in the moment of their first writing 'would be to consign these volumes to a place in the library beneath their rank and importance; and to circumscribe their utility and value within limits very much narrower than they were designed, and are calculated to fill'. The *Commentaries* had to be recognised

[19] Readers of this essay should also read Michael Hoeflich's wonderful essay, 'American Blackstones.' See M Hoeflich, 'American Blackstones' in W Prest (ed), *Blackstone and His Commentaries: Biography, Law, History* (Oxford, Hart Publishing, 2009) 172–84. Hoeflich emphasises, as I do, the multiplicity of the American Blackstones that proliferated in different editions of the Commentaries over the course of the nineteenth century. However, Hoeflich does not advance the 'use' to 'style' narrative—or its unscrambling—that I offer and that allows me to make sense of these different American Blackstones as part of, and as a challenge to, historical knowledge.

[20] W Blackstone, *Commentaries on the Laws of England* (London, W Walker, 1826) (hereinafter 'Chitty Edition') Preface, iii.

as belonging to the past, but also, because of their importance, to be carried 'forward with the stream of time . . .'[21]

Similarly, in 1831, the Virginia lawyer Henry St George Tucker confessed his utter dependence on the *Commentaries* when he described his initial attempts to produce a course of lectures on the laws of Virginia to be delivered at a new law school in Winchester, VA. As he put it:

> With these views [ie, the idea that he should produce a series of lectures on the laws of Virginia] he immediately commenced the prosecution of his plan; but his diffidence of his own ability, and the want of sufficient time for the digesting of an original course of lectures, conspired to induce him to adopt Mr. Blackstone's Commentaries as a text book, and to connect with it such additional matter as seemed advantageous, in the form of annotations.[22]

These annotations were initially delivered orally in the form of lectures, but lectures on such an abstruse subject proved ineffective. Tucker then decided to print the annotations and deliver the sheets to his students. When Tucker determined to compile these sheets into what he called 'the shape of an original work', he determined to 'retain whatever was most essential in the admirable work of Mr Blackstone'.[23]

By the 1840s, editors of the *Commentaries* frequently bemoaned the obsolescence of the *Commentaries* even as they continued to put forth new editions. James Stewart's 1844 London edition began by setting forth the difficulties of working on a text that was eight decades old:

> Could a work, which was fast passing away as a whole, be advantageously adopted as an elementary book, or referred to with safety in practice? Was it possible to restore it in some degree to its original value in both these particulars? Could those portions which were becoming dead and obsolete be revived? Time had already seized a large portion of its contents.[24]

But the 'great principles of the common law' laid forth in the *Commentaries* – as distinguished from, say, Blackstone's discussion of the eighteenth-century electoral system – remained 'untouched, and as useful as ever'.[25] For this reason, Stewart maintained, the present generation 'still turns to Blackstone as its first and best guide; and we may almost despair of the appearance of another author uniting all [Blackstone's] qualifications'.[26]

The impossibility of abandoning the old Gothic castle of the *Commentaries*, combined with the corresponding imperative to fit them out for modern living, took the aggressive forms of manipulation that usually attend the active use of an object. Chitty described his edition as 'loading these volumes with the legal

[21] Ibid iv.

[22] H St George Tucker, *Commentaries on the Law of Virginia: Comprising a Course of Lectures Delivered to the Winchester Law School* (Winchester, Officer of the Winchester Virginian, 1831) 1.

[23] Ibid i.

[24] W Blackstone, Commentaries on the Laws of England, J Stewart (ed), 2nd edn (London, E Spettigue, 1844) (hereinafter 'Stewart Edition') vol 1, xiii.

[25] Ibid xiv.

[26] Ibid xv.

accumulations of the last half century'.[27] Henry St George Tucker offered a text in which Blackstone's language and Tucker's own annotations were combined, but also carefully distinguished from one another: 'The passages of Blackstone are indicated by inverted commas . . . and as his analysis has been rigidly pursued, and his work is the groundwork of the present, it has been deemed unnecessary to quote him particularly'.[28] This work of intersplicing, Tucker suggested, was very hard: 'The interweaving of the original work of one author with the commentary of another is not a matter of easy accomplishment. In such a patch work the *piecing* must be obvious . . .'[29]

But Tucker did more than simply indicate the difference between Blackstone's language and his own. In basing his lectures on the *Commentaries*, he also decided to discard large entire chunks of Blackstone's text. Various outmoded and cumbersome portions of the inherited old Gothic castle of the *Commentaries* were thus pulled down and carted off. Tucker described his omission of portions of Blackstone's text as dictated by the imperatives of use:

> [T]he discarding of such portions of the Commentaries as were either obsolete or matters of curiosity merely, was absolutely necessary in order to bring the contemplated course of lectures within the compass allotted to them; yet it was a source of deep regret to be compelled to break the continuity of Mr. Blackstone's work. . . .

Yet all these objections were surmounted by a single consideration. The object of the lecturer was not display: It was, *to be useful* . . .[30]

Robert Malcolm Kerr's 1857 London edition did not discard portions of the text Kerr considered obsolete, as Tucker had done, but simply shifted them from the body of the text to the footnotes.[31] James Stewart's 1844 London edition also reworked the text, but through the novel method of changing tenses. Stewart described this peculiar method of updating Blackstone as follows:

> Under these circumstances, it appeared to me, that if the changes in the law since his time were added continuously; if the portions altered were thrown into the past tense, and the whole were considered with the view of stating the law as it now stands; an acceptable service might be rendered to the profession and the public at large.

Stewart proudly claimed that the changing of tenses allowed him to preserve the integrity of Blackstone's text: 'I have given, thus altered, the whole of the text of Blackstone'.[32]

[27] Chitty Edition (n 20) iv.

[28] Tucker, *Commentaries on the Law of Virginia* (n 22) i–ii.

[29] Ibid ii.

[30] Ibid ii.

[31] Kerr described his method thus: 'Those portions of the Commentaries which have become entirely obsolete, but are still curious or interesting either in a historical point of view or with reference to the altered state of the law, have been converted into *notes*, reference being made at the same time to the page of the original work'. W Blackstone, *Commentaries on the Laws of England*, RM Kerr (ed) (London, J Murray, 1857) (hereinafter 'Kerr Edition') viii.

[32] Stewart Edition (n 24) xv. Kerr's edition also engaged in the changing of tenses. Kerr referred to instances in his edition of 'those words which in the original text of Sir William Blackstone were in the present, but in the present edition are in the past tense; many pages, and indeed chapters of the Commentaries having become purely historical'. Kerr Edition (n 31) vol 1, viii.

Perhaps the most aggressive active use of the *Commentaries* was that of Serjeant Stephen, who in 1841 came out with *New Commentaries on the Laws of England (Partly Founded on Blackstone)*.[33] The title reveals much. Stephen admitted that Blackstone's *Commentaries* remained 'without a rival', but found that endless footnoting obliged the reader 'to transfer his attention incessantly, from the text to the commentary . . .'[34] Stephen's solution was to introduce 'the necessary alterations into the text itself', and he determined to '[discard] all solicitude about the measure of my adherence to the original work, [and] to interweave my own composition with it, as freely as the purpose of general improvement might seem to require'.[35] Stephen determined to depart from Blackstone's language whenever he felt 'dissatisfied with [Blackstone's] performance, as well as where any change in the law had made a departure indispensable'.[36] He warned the reader: 'Large portions . . . of original composition [ie, Stephen's own] will be found frequently to occur in a continuous form . . .'[37] So large, indeed, were the chunks of Stephen's own prose relative to Blackstone's that the latter's were placed in brackets, rather than the former's. The *New Commentaries* were more Stephen's text larded with bits of text from Blackstone.

Notwithstanding these novel forms of fitting out the *Commentaries* for nineteenth-century use (discarding text, relegating text to footnote, intersplicing it with original text, changing tenses), footnoting as a way of alerting the reader to changes in the law remained the privileged way of inhabiting the *Commentaries*. This was, in itself, not new. But footnoting in the context of successive editions of the *Commentaries* became not just a matter of adding to Blackstone's text, but of building upon the footnotes of others who had added to Blackstone's text, layering footnotes on footnotes. The *Commentaries* thus became a kind of multi-authored composite, crowded with the comments of a range of writers, an old building with many layers, the work not of one architect and many masons, but, it would appear, of multiple architects, masons and bricklayers all crowded under a single name. The saleability of an edition of the *Commentaries* was linked precisely to its ability to gather as many different footnotes, by as many different updaters, as possible. The New York 1832 edition offered its readers 'the late alterations of the law in England, as furnished by the notes of Lee, Hovenden, and Ryland'.[38] George Sharswood's 1860 Philadelphia edition advertised itself thus:

> Besides the editions of Archbold, Christian, and Chitty, which have been republished in this country, the editor has drawn largely upon the valuable notes of Mr Justice Coleridge. The late English editions by James Stewart and Robert Malcolm Kerr – in which all the recent alterations by statutes have been referred to and incorporated –

[33] HJ Stephen, *New Commentaries on the Laws of England (Partly Founded on Blackstone)* 4 vols (London, Henry, Butterworths, 1841)) (hereinafter 'New Commentaries').

[34] Ibid, 'Preface, iv'.

[35] Ibid v.

[36] Ibid vi.

[37] Ibid.

[38] W Blackstone, *Commentaries on the Laws of England* (New York, NY, Collins & Hannay, 1832) [Preface].

> have been freely used, and an occasional note will be found from the late abridgement of Blackstone by Samuel Warren; and the attention of the student is especially called to the notes added to the last chapter of the work, on the rise, progress, and gradual improvement of the laws of England, for valuable sketches by Coleridge, John William Smith, Stewart, Warren, and Kerr, of the latest enactments, to which the American editor has ventured to add some remarks upon American jurisprudence. Barron Field's Analysis – a most important aid to the student in the work of self-examination – has been added at the end.[39]

The *Commentaries* remained vital during the second half of the nineteenth century, but the stance of editors changed. Increasingly, editors were beginning to pay attention to the integrity of Blackstone's text, to recover his language in its fullness. The *Commentaries* were becoming less an object of active use, the place to which the law student and lawyer turned, and were coming to be recognised explicitly for their style. To be sure, this was a complex process with many twists and turns.

A full century after the *Commentaries* had first appeared, Thomas Cooley's 1871 Chicago edition emphasised that '[l]apse of time does not seem to diminish their attractions, or to lessen materially their practical value'.[40] The *Commentaries* were still 'the best book in which to take a comprehensive view of English and American law . . .'[41] Indeed, the *Commentaries* were even more useful in America than in England, Cooley maintained, because they represented 'the law in something near the condition in which our ancestors brought it to America, leaving us to trace in our statutes and decisions its subsequent changes here, unembarrassed by irrelevant information about parliamentary legislation which in no way concerns us'.[42] Kent's *Commentaries on American Law*, themselves almost a half century old, had not superseded Blackstone's text: 'The admirable lectures of Chancellor Kent every student is expected to master *after* he has made himself familiar with the Commentaries of Mr Justice Blackstone'.[43]

Unlike previous editors, however, Cooley was determined *not* to leave out that which was obsolete from Blackstone's text: 'Things which are abolished or obsolete may, nevertheless, have furnished the reasons for the things which remain . . .'[44] Nevertheless, Cooley was clear about the object of his edition, which remained the conventional one of updating: 'The main purpose in giving to the public a new edition of the Commentaries of Blackstone, was to present the changes in the law which had taken place since the last preceding edition appeared . . .'[45]

But even as Cooley wrote, new political, social and intellectual currents had begun to swirl around him. In the post-Civil War United States, the common law,

[39] W Blackstone, 'Commentaries on the Laws of England' in G Sharswood (ed) (Philadelphia, PA, Childs & Peterson, 1860) (2 vols) vol 1, iii.
[40] W Blackstone, 'Commentaries on the Laws of England' in TM Cooley (ed) (Chicago, IL, Callaghan & Cockcroft, 1871) 1 v.
[41] Ibid v.
[42] Ibid vi.
[43] Ibid xv.
[44] Ibid v.
[45] Ibid xxxi.

especially as it was joined to the US Constitution by a conservative federal judiciary, was under attack. In Great Britain, a century of Utilitarian-inspired statutory reform, combined with the positivist and historicist understanding of law pioneered by figures such as Sir Henry Maine, made the common law method of establishing continuity through the weaving of fictions increasingly anachronistic. There were changes in the method of legal instruction that turned students away from treatises and towards cases. There was also an explosion of treatises upon a range of specialised subjects. The world was changing too quickly, it was frequently alleged, for legal disputes to be resolved through common law doctrine. It was time, finally, to move out of the old Gothic castle of Blackstone's *Commentaries*.

By the 1890s, accordingly, legal thinkers characterised Blackstone's *Commentaries* not as a text that had to be filled in with references to the latest law, a means of conveying changes in law, but as something valuable in and of itself, as evidence of Blackstone's own thinking. After having been an object of active use, the *Commentaries* were becoming an object of aesthetic contemplation, an object valued for their style. This does not mean, of course, the *Commentaries*' use value was thereby diminished. In being recuperated for their style, the *Commentaries* were elevated to the status of a classic and rendered a certain origin point of the modern Anglo-American legal tradition, their Olympian integrity a microcosm of late-nineteenth-century law's claim to be a self-contained whole, removed from – and therefore to be defended against – the encroachments of politics.[46]

William G Hammond's monumental 1890 edition is exemplary in this regard. From the early nineteenth century, it had been the practice in American editions of the *Commentaries* to select such American cases as showed a divergence of American authority from Blackstone. But Hammond rejected such approaches. Updating Blackstone, he argued, was no longer necessary:

> [W]hile they serve the purpose of making the Commentaries a handy reference book upon questions as to what the law is when the edition is prepared, they do little to fix the student's attention upon Blackstone's reasoning, which to the student is altogether the most valuable part of his work. . . . *It is now altogether too late to convert the Commentaries into a digest of the newest law, and the student who uses them for that purpose only . . . will miss the chief benefit of studying this authority.*[47]

Hammond emphasised the importance of not interfering with the work's perfection, its internal proportions and intrinsic harmonies:

> The more attentively I have read the Commentaries with the view of selecting passages for annotation, the stronger has been my sense of the caution with which such notes should be added, and of the mischief that might be done in distracting the student's attention from a continuous reading of the text. The symmetry of the whole is so perfect, the proportion of the respective parts is so well preserved, that additions here and

[46] I am grateful to Christopher Tomlins for this suggestion.

[47] W Blackstone, *Commentaries on the Laws of England*, W Hammond (ed) (San Francisco, Bancroft-Whitney, 1890) Preface, xii (emphasis added).

> there can hardly be made without marring it. The student will gain little by being told that this rule or that is now modified in New York, or Missouri, or California, if the stress laid on the rule spoils the harmony of the whole.[48]

Indeed, Hammond explicitly referred back to Blackstone's own metaphor of a building, but a building not to be lived in but to be appreciated as a whole, ie from a distance – as an exemplar of its time. It was more important to give the student 'a clear and just conception of the edifice of law with which our fathers began their national history . . . than to learn the modern shape of this or that chamber at the expense of the entire plan'.[49]

Hammond's emphasis on recovering the *Commentaries*' style rather than on putting them to active use translated into an obsessive detailing of the changes Blackstone himself had made in the different editions published during his lifetime. Hammond recognised that

> [t]o the intensely practical lawyer, this careful and minute examination of the text may seem almost unprofessional, but it certainly is justified in the case of a writer who gave himself, so much attention to literary form and finish, and to accuracy of expression. Blackstone's style has been admired by every one capable of appreciating good English or exactness in the expression of thought. And the more carefully it is studied, the higher will that appreciation be.[50]

Indeed, the reader who chose to compare the stylistic changes Blackstone made between one edition and another would see 'to what constant labor the easy grace of his style is due'.[51] To this end, Hammond added numbers from 1 to 9 to various words in the text to indicate to the reader when specific words had been added or replaced in the first nine editions of the *Commentaries.*

As part of this endeavour to recover the 'original' Blackstone, Hammond went through various editions of the *Commentaries* before deciding upon the eighth edition of 1778, the last published during Blackstone's own lifetime. Most editions in the late nineteenth century were reprints of the ninth edition of 1783, which had been published after Blackstone's death and edited by Richard Burn. Even though Burn had claimed to be working from Blackstone's manuscripts, Hammond observed – somewhat snobbishly, but as befitting someone acutely conscious of style – that anyone familiar with Blackstone's style and with Burn's may be pardoned 'for sometimes doubting the self-restraint of the latter'.[52] But ironically, the emphasis on Blackstone's style – and a downplaying of the old enterprise of updating the *Commentaries* – led Hammond to downplay Blackstone's *own* updating efforts. Hammond said that he had considered saving space by omitting 'Blackstone's own additions [that had served to update the text], which have no permanent interest and mar the general harmony and

[48] Ibid.
[49] Ibid.
[50] Ibid xiv.
[51] Ibid.
[52] Ibid xvi.

proportion of his treatment; but it seemed best to retain them, that the work might be given exactly as Blackstone left it'.[53] Style – rather than content – was what imbued the *Commentaries* with 'permanent interest'.

Hammond's alternative to what he considered a crass updating of the *Commentaries* was unique. He would not dispense with footnotes. But how, exactly, was one to footnote what had become an object to be admired from afar for its style, an object rendered a monument or museum piece? Hammond's strategy is revealing of the fate of the *Commentaries* in the twentieth century. In his footnotes, rather than pointing to the latest law, Hammond would show how '[t]he courts themselves have annotated the text by their reference to it in their published opinions, all of which are collected in the references to it given at the foot of each page'.[54] To this end, with the help of a team of researchers, Hammond pored over 2500 volumes of the American law reports, scouring them for every reference to Blackstone contained in the judges' opinions. He distinguished those in which Blackstone's language was quoted, especially where the doctrine was approved or criticised, from mere citations, 'but not omitting even these'. The goal was nothing less than a demonstration of the overall influence of the monument that the *Commentaries* had become, an attempt to mark where the *Commentaries* had extruded themselves into American jurisprudence.

As befitting a strategy that transformed the *Commentaries* into an object of contemplation for its style, Hammond was also clear that Blackstone's immediate relevance to American jurisprudence was on the wane. He put it thus:

> No coming century can furnish such notes of the same relative importance with this first one, alike in the life of the text and of its development in American jurisprudence; nor will the work need to be done again, provided only that its execution has corresponded to the requirements of the plan.[55]

The idea, of course, was that the twentieth century would not regard the *Commentaries* as important in the same way the nineteenth had.

To be sure, in the context of the arduous task of editing the *Commentaries*, the 'stylisation' of Blackstone inaugurated by Hammond was not universally followed. William Carey Jones' 1915 edition rejected Hammond's turning away from mere updating. At the same time, however, Jones largely accepted Hammond's conviction that the *Commentaries* were now a classic, and, as such, beyond simple reproach or criticism for their rightness or wrongness on this or that issue. Jones found that 'the Commentaries have long since so thoroughly vindicated themselves and now rest so solidly upon their own merits, that it is useless to perpetuate in notes the controversies aroused by the attacks of Bentham, Austin, and others of the utilitarian school'.[56] Other early-twentieth-century editors

[53] Ibid.
[54] Ibid xiii.
[55] Ibid.
[56] W Blackstone, 'Commentaries on the Laws of England' in WC Jones (ed) (San Francisco, Bancroft-Whitney, 1915) x.

followed Hammond more explicitly. William Draper Lewis' 1922 Philadelphia edition claimed-like every past edition of the *Commentaries* – to break new ground and to accomplish 'certain things not heretofore attempted', but nevertheless also revealed the imprint of Hammond's editorial approach. The materials used in his edition would be fourfold:

> First, the published results of modern research into the history of our law, such as the works of Maine, of Pollock and Maitland, of Vinogradoff. Second, the statutes in England and the United States which modify the statements made in the text. Third, the notes of my predecessors. Fourth, the cases decided and the textbooks published since Blackstone's day which have referred to him as authority.

The fourth set of materials – inspired, as should be clear, by Hammond – was, in Lewis' view, 'by far the most important'.[57] Nevertheless, faithful to an older tradition of annotating Blackstone, Lewis also claimed to have selected notes from the editions of Archbold, Christian, Coleridge, Chitty, Stewart, Kerr and others.

The monumentalisation or museumisation of Blackstone in the twentieth century continued apace. At a Special Session of the American Bar Association in London, July 20–25, 1924, a statue of Sir William Blackstone, initially 'veiled in Old Glory and the Union Jack', was presented 'to the lawyers of England by the lawyers of America'.[58] But even as the chairman of the American Blackstone Committee emphasised Blackstone's importance in American law, he acknowledged that 'in the last quarter of a century Blackstone has ceased to be the guide, philosopher and friend of every student of the law, and, indeed, is known to many of the later generations as a dim, shadowy figure of the past, rather than as the vital force he was to their fathers'.[59]

This sense of Blackstone as a 'dim shadowy figure of the past' might not be entirely accurate when describing the way twentieth-century legal thinkers have seen Blackstone. We know a great deal about Blackstone. From Daniel Boorstin to Duncan Kennedy, scholars in the second half of the twentieth century have studied Blackstone as exemplifying a certain mindset, often that of the conservative eighteenth-century common law thinker. There is no shortage of conferences, monographs, edited collections and articles on Blackstone. Courts continue to mention him here and there. He shows up with some regularity in the casebooks used in American law Schools, Blackstone is far from 'dim' or 'shadowy'.

For all that, it is absolutely correct that Blackstone has ceased to be the object of active use and manipulation that he was for so much of the nineteenth century. We might turn occasionally to Blackstone for a canonical statement of the old common law position, but we no longer learn our law through him. He is often invoked, but rarely read cover to cover. He has become a classic, a monument, an origin point of a certain kind. Perhaps nothing exemplifies this more than the

[57] W Blackstone,'Commentaries on the Laws of England' in W Draper Lewis (ed) (Philadelphia, PA, Geo T Bisel, 1922) iii.

[58] 'Presentation of Blackstone Memorial' (1924) 10 *American Bar Association Journal* 571.

[59] Ibid 579.

University of Chicago Press' decision to reissue in 1979 the first edition (1765–69) of the *Commentaries*. In Blackstone's own lifetime, to say nothing of the rest of the nineteenth century, the first edition of the *Commentaries* was out of date. The fact that the University of Chicago turned to this edition tells us something about our fetishisation of the purity – and the style – of Blackstone's text. We are tourists content to take a few photographs of the edifice of Blackstone's work, now appreciated for its integrity and seen as an exemplar of its period, before walking away.

III. FROM 'STYLE' TO 'STYLE': ANOTHER HISTORY OF BLACKSTONE'S COMMENTARIES

It will be readily discerned that I have provided a certain history of Blackstone's *Commentaries* as they moved from being objects of active use to objects of style. Once the *Commentaries* had ceased to serve a vital function as the vehicle for conveying the state of the law, they became objects of scholarly solicitude, their integrity reinstated, their style recuperated, the awkward glosses and manipulations of a century expunged. The efforts to recover the 'original' Blackstone for his style are of a piece, I have suggested, with the American Bar Association's gift of Blackstone's bust to the English bar. Such a gesture would have made no sense for much of the nineteenth century when English and American lawyers struggled with – and complained loudly about – the anachronisms of Blackstone's text, fully aware of the outdatedness of the old Gothic castle of the text, but unable to move out of it.

To historians, this story of the career of the *Commentaries* will be a readily comprehensible one. Historians will understand the shift from active use to a recuperation of style as confirming the (already known) truth that objects are different over time, that they are the products of contexts that themselves shift over time. This is true of everything from Greek vases to the Bible to Shakespeare's plays to the doctrine of *assumpsit*. Why should Blackstone's *Commentaries* be any different? They were actively manipulated and their integrity ignored so long as they were immediately relevant; they became the object of scholarly solicitude, their integrity recovered, once they ceased to be immediately relevant.

And yet it might not be quite so easy to tell the history of Blackstone's *Commentaries* as one from use to style, from being relevant to living legal practice to being a museum object. The problem, it turns out, is style itself.

Hammond was hardly the first editor of the *Commentaries* to have emphasised their style. Far from being the end point, as it has been in my narrative, style has been associated with the *Commentaries* throughout their long life. Indeed, style lies at the heart of the *Commentaries*' origins.

Blackstone's style was recognised and highlighted from the very first appearance of the *Commentaries*. Trained as a classical scholar, the author of critical notes on Shakespeare, the winner of a prize for a poem on Milton, Blackstone wrote with a style acknowledged by friends and enemies alike. Lord Mansfield approved of the *Commentaries* for students, because students would find there analytic reasoning 'diffused in a pleasing style and that he knew no other work to recommend to them'.[60] Blackstone's inveterate enemy, Jeremy Bentham, praised the *Commentaries* for their style, even as he recognised that the seductions of Blackstone's style made the *Commentaries* all the more dangerous:

> Correct, elegant, unembarrassed, ornamented, the *style* is such, as could scarce fail to recommend a work still more vicious in the point of *matter* to the multitude of readers. He it is, in short, who first of all institutional writers has taught Jurisprudence to speak the language of the Scholar and the Gentleman: put a polish upon that rugged science: cleansed her from the dust and cobwebs of the office: and if he has not enriched her with that precision that is drawn only from the sterling treasury of the sciences, has decked her out, however, to advantage, from the toilette of classic erudition: enlivened her with metaphors and allusions; and sent her abroad in some measure to instruct and in still greater measure to entertain, the most miscellaneous and even the most fastidious societies.[61]

Praising Blackstone's style was, in fact, *de rigueur* among all the various English and American editors who tortured the text throughout the nineteenth century to suit their various purposes. We might have to confront the troubling fact that it was precisely the *Commentaries*' style that compelled their use, even as the late-nineteenth-century recovery of their style marked a turning *away* from their use and a turning *towards* their monumentalisation or museumisation. The paradox is that an entire generation of editors of the *Commentaries* continued to inhabit the old Gothic castle of the *Commentaries* precisely because of the *Commentaries*' style, even as they tortured Blackstone's text in ways that subsequent appreciations of its style would find violent and barbaric.

St George Tucker stuck with the *Commentaries* despite their apparent outdatedness in post-revolutionary America because of 'the exalted opinion he entertained of the Commentaries as a model of methodical elegance and legal perspicuity: a work in which the author has united the various talents of the philosopher, the antiquarian, the historian, the jurist, the logician and the classic . . .' In annotating the *Commentaries*, Tucker maintained, he had chosen to 'avail himself not only of the Commentator's incomparable method, but of his . . . classical purity and precision as a scholar . . .'[62]

Various editors, American and English, who massacred Blackstone's text over the course of the nineteenth century in the name of use were equally – and acutely – conscious of the text's style. Indeed, it might not have been the comprehensiveness of Blackstone's text that made them turn to him, but his style. Style rendered Blackstone's text enduring and above mere changes in the law. John Archbold's popular 1811 edition of the *Commentaries* extolled

[60] Cited in JS Waterman, 'Mansfield and Blackstone's Commentaries' (1934) 1 *University of Chicago Law Review* 549–51.

[61] J Bentham, *A Fragment on Government* in FC Montague (ed) (Oxford, Clarendon Press, 1891) 116.

[62] Tucker Edition (n 7) vi.

> [t]he great correctness of the work, the admirable arrangement of its parts, and the beauty and simplicity of the style, [which] render it more than probable that we shall never see another work, upon the same subject and in so small a compass, to equal it.[63]

The anonymous editor of the 1832 New York edition referred to the *Commentaries*' style as 'so simple and clear . . . that, however much the details of the law may be changed, they will always be read with interest'.[64]

'Style' is, at least in part, what might have kept editors from producing entirely new texts and hanging on to fragments of Blackstone when so much in the text appeared anachronistic. Serjeant Stephen, whose *New Commentaries on the Laws of England (Partly Founded on Blackstone)* was perhaps the most thorough or aggressive edition of the nineteenth century in putting Blackstone's text to active use, claimed that he had refrained from producing an entirely new text in part because of Blackstone's style. He put it thus:

> The unimpaired portion of Blackstone's Commentaries comprise many passages, which (free in other respects from objection) are so far valuable at least, that they bear the stamp of his authority, and many others whose merit is of the highest order, being distinguished by all the grace and spirit of diction, the justness of thought and the affluence of various learning, to which he owes his fame. These relics, which are in considerable danger of perishing by their incorporation in a work now falling into decay, may be lawfully converted, by any new Commentator on the Laws, to his own purpose . . .[65]

Early-nineteenth-century editors were, indeed, aware that their aggressive editing involved a marring of the style that had drawn them to Blackstone in the first place. Henry St George Tucker regretted that his butchering of the *Commentaries* had destroyed 'the beautiful symmetry for which [the work] is remarkable'. He compared Blackstone's style with his own less felicitous one as follows:

> And, lastly, the editor was not insensible that his hasty composition, and his awkward and involved style, would, in contrast with the style of his author, awaken the recollection of the *purpureus assuitur pannus* of the latin poet: except, indeed, that here Mr Blackstone's cloth of Tyrean purple is the principal fabric, while the patches that are sewed upon it are my homely linsey-woolsey.[66]

Searjeant Stephen was highly conscious of having detracted – as a result of his method of inserting text – from what he called 'the beauty of the page'.[67]

Praise of Blackstone's style, then, did not pick up when the *Commentaries* ceased to be 'useful'. Blackstone's style is something that had been with the *Commentaries* all along, at some points sanctioning their fragmentation and use at the hands of aggressive editors, at other points sanctioning the recovery of their 'original' integrity. If I have told one story of how the *Commentaries* travelled

[63] W Blackstone, *Commentaries on the Laws of England* in JF Archbold (ed) (London, M&S Brooke for W Reed, 1811) vii.

[64] W Blackstone, *Commentaries on the Laws of England* (n 38).

[65] Stephen, *New Commentaries* (n 33) v.

[66] Tucker, *Commentaries on the Law of Virginia* (n 22) ii.

[67] Stephen, *New Commentaries* (n 33) xvi.

through the nineteenth century, first as an object of use and then as an object of style, it seems important to scramble that story and to tell another one of the *Commentaries*' career as a journey from style to style. For the *Commentaries*' style is the sameness over time out of which difference has been enabled, sanctioning initial active use and subsequent museumisation. The text's difference over time, in other words, is the product of qualities that were recognised over the centuries as being the same.

IV. CONCLUSION: HISTORY AND CLICHÉ

It remains, then, to come to terms with the *Commentaries*' style, which – I have suggested – remained the same over time. Most historians, myself included, might be loath to recognise in Blackstone's style something truly transhistorical, universal, conforming to aesthetic norms that are divorced from historical context. There are ready historian's responses to such claims. Style can itself be historicised, rendered the artifact of a concrete historical period: Renaissance, Baroque, Neoclassical, and so on. Hammond's recovery of the style of the *Commentaries* was, after all, an attempt to fit the text (back) into its mid-eighteenth-century context. Alternatively, historians might historicise the appreciation of style as itself the subject of historical contextualisation. Seventeenth-century audiences responded differently to Molière and Shakespeare, as we know, from the way we now do. We are used to reciting how eighteenth- and nineteenth-century audiences supplied Shakespeare's plays with endings that suited their taste, whereas we would now consider it sacrilegious to tamper with his texts. It should not be surprising that early-nineteenth-century commentators responded to Blackstone's style one way, while late-nineteenth-century commentators responded to it in another.

But there seems to be something a bit more troubling about Blackstone's style. Even if one rejects the idea that Blackstone's style can be entirely divorced from historical context, as I do, Blackstone's style cannot be readily domesticated through conventional historical norms of contextualisation.

In a brilliant 1909 article entitled 'Blackstone's Commentaries' devoted in large part to exploring nothing other than Blackstone's style, AV Dicey identified Blackstone as the product of an age of eloquence:

> Blackstone . . . lived at a time when the learned world was still a reality, when there was an established standard of style and when men of letters could address themselves, even when writing on such a subject as law, neither to experts, nor to practitioners, nor to that unsatisfactory class now known as gentle readers. The audience of whom Johnson, Goldsmith, Hume, Adam Smith, Gibbon, Burke, and Blackstone courted and received the approbation, was made of the educated gentlemen of England.[68]

[68] AV Dicey, 'Blackstone's Commentaries' (1930–31) 4 *Cambridge Law Journal* 286 (reprint from 1909) 296, 298.

But pinning down Blackstone's style to a concrete and identifiable mid-eighteenth-century moment of literary efflorescence does not seem adequate to capture the many ways in which successive editors of the *Commentaries* repeatedly spoke about the text's style. Dicey's famous line—'The Commentaries *live* by their style' – itself seems to recognise that there is more at stake.[69]

Even as Dicey located Blackstone as the product of the world of mid-eighteenth-century letters, he emphasised that Blackstone's style could not be pinned down. It consisted, Dicey argued, of 'power of expression, clearness of aim, literary judgment or tact'.[70] It allowed its owner to weave through the various perils of legal exposition. Thus, on the basis of style, Dicey argued, Blackstone had avoided the excesses of 'logical formalism', on the one hand, and 'pedantic antiquarianism', on the other. There was, Dicey cautioned, '[n]o formula [that could] tell any man what is the method by which to avoid both of these opposite errors'. But, Dicey argued, Blackstone had unerringly negotiated a path through them.

I am not suggesting that Dicey's explanation of the success of Blackstone's style – Blackstone's ability to weave through the dilemmas of legal writing, to steer clear of the lures of extremes – accounts for why commentators over the past two centuries turned to Blackstone, whether to use him or to museumise him for his style. Indeed, none of the various editors of Blackstone's *Commentaries* cited Dicey's exact reasoning – style as the means of calibrating the antinomy between 'legal formalism' and 'pedantic antiquarianism' (an antinomy that is itself the product of late-nineteenth-century jurisprudential debate) as the reason for turning to Blackstone. Instead, I invoke Dicey's discussion of Blackstone's style for the former's sense that there is 'no formula' adequate for thinking about Blackstone's style, no way to break it down, no way to disaggregate it, no way to contain it by rendering it replicable, no way – in short – to historicise it perfectly.

In the endless invocations of Blackstone's style that one encounters in every discussion of the *Commentaries*, the historian – or at least this historian – must confront the obdurate fact of simply having 'no formula' for discussing the endless recurrence to Blackstone's style by the various editors who invoked it for all kinds of purposes, from torturing Blackstone's text to recovering its integrity, from inserting their own text into Blackstone's text to detailing obsessively the changes Blackstone himself made, from updating the *Commentaries* to refusing to update them. Blackstone's style, as an object of inquiry, defies historical inquiry by remaining the same across time, by sanctioning a range of mutually opposed uses. But it does not remain the 'same' across time as an artifact of the world of mid-eighteenth-century letters or as something entirely divorced from historical context. Instead, it simply defies our 'formulas', whether historicist or otherwise. Invoked over and over and over again, in its ubiquity and sameness across time, but sanctioning the most opposed practices over time, Blackstone's style gradually loses its meaning. It becomes something akin to *cliché*. In one sense, perhaps what

[69] Ibid 294 (emphasis added).

[70] Ibid 295.

I am interested in is how *cliché* might – or, more accurately, might not – become the object of historical analysis. The *cliché* might be given temporal origins, but in its constant exceeding of any given context, in its inability to fit any one context adequately even as it straddles different contexts effortlessly, in its loss of *meaning*, in its colourlessness and flatness, it seems to resist our efforts, defies our 'formulas'. So it is, I submit, with Blackstone's style, widely invoked and *de rigueur* in all the different uses to which we have put the *Commentaries* for the past two and a half centuries.

2

'Of Institutes and Treatises': Blackstone's *Commentaries*, Kent's *Commentaries* and Murdoch's *Epitome of the Laws of Nova-Scotia*

PHILIP GIRARD*

THE INSTITUTIONAL WORK has a long and venerable history in Western law, beginning with the Institutes of Gaius in ad 160 and of Justinian in ad 533, and followed, after a millennial hiatus, by a flowering of such works in France, Holland, Scotland and Germany in the seventeenth century, and Spain, Italy, Scandinavia and England in the eighteenth. In the New World, authors in the state of Connecticut (1795–96), Hispanic America (1818–20), the United States as a whole (1826–30) and the British North American colony of Nova Scotia (1832–33) turned to the institutional form in order to fashion accounts of the entirety of the law in their own jurisdictions. The characteristics of the institutional form have been summarised by JW Cairns:

> They are often (though by no means always) in the vernacular; they are frequently linked to the introduction of university education in the national law; they are influenced in organization by Justinian's Institutes; they attempt to be comprehensive; they deal with a national law; and they are often fairly elementary in nature.[1]

To this list might be added another feature of institutional writing, at least in the case of the English-language institutists: their situating of the law in its historical, political and cultural context. While the rational ordering of legal categories and doctrines was a paramount concern of the institutists, so was the desire to show that the national law served the public good; and this could only be done by referring to the actual state of society in the nation in question. The institutists were social scientists and men of letters, in addition to being learned in the law.

* Philip Girard is University Research Professor and Professor of Law, History and Canadian Studies at Dalhousie University, Halifax, Nova Scotia. He would like to thank the Social Sciences and Humanities Research Council of Canada for funding assistance in the preparation of this chapter.

[1] JW Cairns, 'Blackstone, an English Institutist: Legal Literature and the Rise of the Nation-State' (1984) 4 *Oxford Journal of Legal Studies* 318–27.

Thus, law was both subject and object for them, not just an object as it became for the treatise-writers.

The relationship between the institutional work and the treatise has generally been portrayed as antagonistic. The distinguishing feature of an institutional work is, according to John Langbein, breadth, that of the legal treatise, depth. Eventually, he argues, the legal treatise completely superseded the institutional work: 'Doctrinal writing can be done better when it is separated from the need for schoolbook simplicity that characterises the institutionalist tradition. Breadth is the enemy of depth, and when breadth is no longer needed, depth will prevail'.[2]

Such lapidary formulations have their appeal. Two elements of this story may be challenged, however. The first is the characterisation of the relationship between institute and treatise as a competitive Darwinian struggle leading to the former's demise. Arguably, what is impressive about institutional writing is not so much its ultimate decline but its continuing vigour until the very end of the nineteenth century. Thomas Cooley, the giant of US constitutional jurisprudence, produced an edition of Blackstone's *Commentaries* in 1872–73, well over a century after the work's initial publication, and revised it twice, in 1879 and 1884 (discussed in the chapter by Kunal Parker); James DeWitt Andrews produced a fourth edition in 1899 after Cooley's death. There were continuing editions of Kent down to the 14th and last edition by John Gould in 1896; and even if, as we shall see, there were no subsequent editions of the *Epitome of the Laws of Nova-Scotia* (published 1832–33), provenance information indicates that it was still circulating among lawyers in eastern Canada in the 1860s and 70s.

I begin with the proposition that the institute and the treatise were not inherently in conflict, but could and did co-exist for a long time. They did so because lawyers continued to have a need for both breadth and depth in their understanding of the legal order, both as students and novice lawyers and throughout their careers. Cooley and his contemporaries

> viewed the 'institutional' arrangement of Blackstone's work as the best way to give the beginning law student a view of the whole of the Anglo-American common law, unburdened by technical details. [After Blackstone] the student . . . could then move on to . . . Kent's Commentaries on American Law. Only after having mastered these two overviews should one commence to study the specialised treatises on American law which had begun to appear in quantity during the antebellum period.[3]

Not only did institute and treatise co-exist, but they also interacted in diverse ways. Langbein himself admits that some of Kent's chapters had a 'treatise-like' quality, such that they were stripped out of the *Commentaries* and sold as separate treatises both in the US and abroad. A Canadian lawyer did the same with Blackstone's treatment of real property in 1864, but then partially 're-institutionalised' it by adding a long introduction on the reception of English law

[2] J Langbein, 'Chancellor Kent and the History of Legal Literature' (1993) 93 *Columbia Law Review* 547, 586, 593.

[3] M Hoeflich, 'American Blackstones' in W Prest (ed), *Blackstone and His Commentaries: Biography, Law, History* (Oxford, Hart Publishing, 2009) 181.

in Upper Canada and the early history of the province.[4] At the turn of the century another Canadian lawyer rewrote Blackstone's first volume as a treatise on the law of persons in Ontario, declaring that the 'Revised Statutes of the Dominion and of this Province must be always beside any person who wishes to learn the law of this country'.[5] In other words, the author had localised Blackstone as a treatise on this body of provincial law. To take a final example of the institute-treatise boundary: Kent criticised a decision of Joseph Story on jurisdiction over maritime insurance in the first edition of his *Commentaries*, which Story defended in his own *Commentaries on the Constitution*, only to have Kent critique it more extensively in his third edition, thus creating a dialogue between institute and treatise.[6]

There are certainly some differences between the scope and function of institutional works and treatises, but they also shared enough features that the boundary between them was more fluid than the conflictual dynamic proposed by the Langbein interpretation. Brian Simpson, who also subscribes to the basic dichotomy between institute and treatise, unwittingly provides an example of the blurry boundary between them by characterising Zephaniah Swift's *A System of the Laws of the State of Connecticut* (1795–96) – in form, certainly an institutional work – as the first American 'law treatise'.[7]

My second caveat concerning the Langbein account is whether labelling institutional works as works of 'schoolboy simplicity' is accurate or fair. In trying to sharpen the contrast between institute and treatise, Langbein contradicts his own copious evidence of the extravagant learning that Kent poured into his *Commentaries*. All of the works examined here comprise some 2000 pages of clear but highly erudite prose, and demonstrate an astonishing breadth and depth of reading in the legal sources of local and foreign jurisdictions and in a wide variety of non-legal literature. They are elementary works only in the sense that they concentrate on the elements, or fundamentals, of the legal tradition in question, not in the sense that they discuss only the obvious, or unduly simplify complex matters.[8] While criticism of the existing law is not their principal goal, all three writers

[4] A Leith, *Commentaries on the Laws of England Applicable to Real Property by William Blackstone, Adapted to the Present State of the Law in Upper Canada* (Toronto, ON, WC Chewett, 1864, 1880). It was reworked by ED Armour as *A Treatise on the Law of Real Property founded on Leith & Smith's edition of Blackstone's Commentaries* (Toronto, Canada Law Book, 1901, 2nd edn 1916).

[5] RE Kingsford, *Commentaries on the Laws of Ontario: Being Blackstone's Commentaries on the Laws of England, Adapted to the Province of Ontario* (Toronto, ON, Carswell, 1896) v.

[6] D Hulsebosch, 'Debating the Transformation of American Law: James Kent, Joseph Story, and the Legacy of the Revolution' in DW Hamilton and AL Brophy (eds), *Transformations in American Legal History: Essays in Honor of Professor Morton J Horwitz* (Cambridge, MA, Harvard University Press, 2009).

[7] AWB Simpson, 'The Rise and Fall of the Legal Treatise: Legal Principles and the Forms of Legal Literature' (1981) 48 *University of Chicago Law Review* 632, 669. I thank Angela Fernandez for pointing this out.

[8] I have the sense that the somewhat pejorative use of the word 'elementary' – as in Sherlock Holmes's famous riposte, 'elementary, my dear Watson' – is of relatively recent origin, but have not been able to verify this. Hulsebosch, 'Debating the Transformation' (n 6), 16 provides an example of Joseph Story using the word in a more robust sense. Speaking of a reputed lawyer whom Story thought lacked insight and creativity, he observed: 'He would apply settled principles with great precision, but it may be doubtful if he could create elementary ones'.

provide some critique of particular doctrines and suggestions for reform.[9] And like most books, readers may appreciate them differently at different stages of life; thus British North American students were advised to read Blackstone several times during their apprenticeship, both to deepen their understanding of the text on its own terms and to 'localise' the *Commentaries*' transatlantic knowledge.[10]

Ironically, institutional writing in the Anglo-American world was only finally superseded by the spread of the university legal education that had initially spurred its production. University education in law meant that learning the law was no longer restricted to the auto-didact reading Blackstone's or Kent's 'lectures' by candlelight. Institutional writing was also eclipsed by the rise of legal formalism, which was hostile to the propensity of the institutists to include references to the cultural, political and social context of the law. As Canadian author RE Kingsford noted in his 1896 adaptation of Blackstone's first volume for local use, he had 'expunged any historical references which I considered unnecessary . . . omitted all illustrations by analogy from the civil law, and all classical allusions'. By the end of the nineteenth century, law was safely 'in the box', a box which, for the institutists, had been porous enough to let society flow in and out.

Having established that treatises and institutional works should be considered in dialogue with one another, this chapter will now discuss the contribution of institutional works to legal literature, while keeping their relationship to the legal treatise in view. Comparison of these three works reveals insights which cannot be gained by examining each in isolation. Part I will introduce briefly the authors, their works and their historical contexts. Part II will compare the works' format, organisation and audience. Part III will look at the role of the institutional work in nation-building. Part IV, by way of conclusion, will look at how the 'scale' of law, in Christopher Tomlins's words, plays out in different ways in these three works.

I. INTRODUCING THE INSTITUTISTS

Blackstone's *Commentaries*,[11] Kent's *Commentaries*[12] and Murdoch's *Epitome*[13] were written in three quite different societies, with somewhat divergent goals in mind. William Blackstone (1723–80) wrote as Britain was about to defeat France in the Seven Years' War and become the pre-eminent global power. With a population of nearly six million in 1750, England was already a wealthy society, albeit one in which wealth was grossly unevenly distributed. It had a complex, hierarchical class system reflected in the legal profession itself, where high-status

[9] Cairns, 'Blackstone, an English Institutist' (n 1) 326.

[10] B Murdoch, *Epitome of the Laws of Nova-Scotia* (Halifax, NS, Joseph Howe, 1832–33) vol 1, 14.

[11] Blackstone's *Commentaries on the Laws of England* will be cited to the first edition (University of Chicago reprint edition, 1979) by volume and page number.

[12] Kent's *Commentaries on American Law* will be cited to the first edition (1826–30) by volume and page number.

[13] Murdoch's *Epitome of the Laws of Nova-Scotia* will be cited by volume and page number.

barristers (about 350 active in 1750) were sharply distinguished from far less respectable attorneys and solicitors, who numbered some 3 or 4000 as Blackstone wrote. Blackstone was admitted as a barrister but did not achieve great success in practice. He based his *Commentaries* on lectures he gave at Oxford, where he had obtained a doctorate in civil law. There is some debate, discussed below, about what audience Blackstone had in mind; but whatever his motivation, he provided a new intellectual basis for English law, hitherto so dominated by the medieval writ system, by pointing toward – if he did not quite articulate – a common law oriented around substantive rights rather than remedies, procedural law, and jurisdictional rules.[14] Innovative in the canon of English legal literature, the *Commentaries* achieved immediate success not only in England but also in its colonies and elsewhere over the next century and more.[15]

James Kent (1763–1847) wrote his *Commentaries* in retirement after a long judicial career in New York.[16] At the time he wrote in the 1820s the United States was a rising power with some twelve million inhabitants and a rapidly growing economy, though it was still much less wealthy than England. It had some 22 000 lawyers by 1850, of whom some 4400 lived in the state of New York. Kent received a BA from Yale and was admitted to the bar in 1785 after an apprenticeship with the Attorney-General of New York; he practised law for some years but hated it. Fortunately he was appointed a professor of law at Columbia in 1793 with a stipend of £200 which enabled him to withdraw from law practice; Federalist political connections smoothed his appointment to the New York Supreme Court in 1798 at the age of 35. Forcibly retired in 1823, Kent returned to Columbia where his lectures became the basis of the *Commentaries on American Law*. This work was directed at 'students, and . . . the junior members of the profession',[17] but it is clear from its best-seller status and multiple editions that it was used avidly by practising lawyers beyond their novice years.

Beamish Murdoch (1800–76) was born on the edge of empire, in Halifax, Nova Scotia, and was called to the bar there in 1822. Founded in 1749 as a bastion from which to attack Louisbourg, the importance of Halifax as a naval base only increased during the American Revolution, the Napoleonic wars, and the War of 1812; after peace descended in 1815, the colony struggled to re-invent itself as British defence spending diminished sharply. By 1830, when Murdoch was writing his *Epitome*, the population of Nova Scotia was about 125 000, some 15 000

[14] SFC Milsom, 'The Nature of Blackstone's Achievement' (1981) 1 *Oxford Journal of Legal Studies* 1.

[15] The most convenient approach to Blackstone and his oeuvre is through two recent works: W Prest, *William Blackstone: Law and Letters in the Eighteenth Century* (Oxford, Oxford University Press, 2008); and W Prest (ed), *Blackstone and His Commentaries: Biography, Law, History* (Oxford, Hart Publishing, 2009).

[16] On Kent, see generally Langbein, 'Chancellor Kent' (n 2); Hulsebosch, 'Debating the Transformation' (n 6) and his 'An Empire of Law: Chancellor Kent and the Revolution in Books in the Early Republic' (2008–09) 60 *Alabama Law Review* 377; T Horton, J Kent: *A Study in Conservatism, 1763–1847* (New York, NY, Appleton-Century, 1939); A Fernandez, '*Pierson v. Post*: A Great Debate, James Kent, and the Project of Building a Learned Law for New York State' (2009) 34 *Law and Social Inquiry* 301.

[17] Kent's *Commentaries* Preface to vol 1, iv.

of whom called Halifax home. It was by far the smallest and poorest of the three 'institutional' jurisdictions considered here, although a small elite and nascent middle class could exist in comfort. A number of local newspapers and literary magazines, along with Murdoch's *Epitome* and JG Marshall's justice of the peace manual (1837, 1846) (considered in Jim Phillips's contribution to this volume), also spoke to a certain cultural efflorescence under the *Pax Britannica*.

Murdoch's heritage was 'Planter' rather than Loyalist, his protestant Irish ancestors having arrived in Nova Scotia in the 1760s. His five-year apprenticeship with Attorney-General of Nova Scotia Richard Uniacke and his sons afforded him access to a large law library and encouraged his intellectual bent. It also served as an education in the enlightened humanism of the Anglo-Irish elite of the 1760s and 70s, the atmosphere in which Uniacke himself had come of age before emigrating from Ireland to the New World. There was a university in Nova Scotia, King's College at Windsor, founded by the Loyalists in 1789, but Murdoch's family could not afford to send him there. Of all our three institutists, Murdoch was the only one who supported himself throughout his life by the practice of law, who actually seemed to enjoy it, and who achieved a reputation as a leading lawyer.[18] But he was also alone in not achieving the high academic and judicial posts of a Blackstone or a Kent. Partly this reflected the limited opportunities available in a small colony, but it also resulted from Murdoch being out of sympathy with the rising tide of reform politics leading to responsible government, effectively launched by the Joseph Howe trial (discussed in Lyndsay Campbell's chapter in this volume). His decision to compose a full-blown four-volume work aimed at a jurisdiction with a total of 73 lawyers in 1830 speaks to the appeal of the institutional tradition and to a certain hubris – as well as a lack of commercial judgement – on Murdoch's part.[19]

II. MISSIONS

Within its broad parameters, the institutional form was a flexible one, and each of our authors used it for somewhat different purposes though they also shared some. All declared their intentions in prefaces and elsewhere, but all had undeclared motives as well. In advertising the lectures which formed the basis of the *Commentaries*, Blackstone claimed that they were aimed at young gentlemen rather than budding barristers, an assertion often taken at face value.[20] But given his forceful critique of contemporary modes of preparation for the bar, it seems likely that

[18] P Girard, *Lawyers and Legal Culture in British North America: Beamish Murdoch of Halifax* (Toronto, ON, University of Toronto Press, 2011).

[19] See generally P Girard, 'Themes and Variations in Early Canadian Law: Beamish Murdoch and his *Epitome of the Laws of Nova-Scotia*' (1993) 11 *Law and History Review* 101.

[20] eg Prest, *William Blackstone* (n 15) 115.

he had both groups in mind.[21] Kent and Murdoch aimed their works first at aspiring lawyers but also claimed they would be 'useful and ornamental to gentlemen in every pursuit, and especially to those who are to assume places of public trust',[22] or in Murdoch's case, 'useful and acceptable to magistrates, persons of property, and business, &c'.[23] All thus claimed to present an overview of the law that would assist young lawyers but could also be appreciated by laypersons.

Undeclared intentions are better understood by situating the authors at their respective moments of composition. Blackstone and Murdoch were both relatively young, about 30, when they composed their works. Academic glory in Blackstone's case, and the desire for recognition by the legal and political establishment in Murdoch's, motivated them in addition to their public spiritedness. The institutional form with its broad legal-historical sweep, more so than the narrower and more formalistic legal treatise, was the vehicle best suited for these purposes. Kent was in his 60s when he wrote his *Commentaries*, and had already completed an illustrious judicial career. The desire for fame is not so evident in his case, but he was in a sense the most ambitious of the three: he wished to shape how American lawyers and judges understood and applied their law, to reconcile them to the continued validity and utility of English precedent, to preach the benefits of judge-made law above those of codification, to create a national law out of the mass of state and federal statutes and jurisprudence, and thereby firmly to establish the US as a civilised actor in the international community (see Blaine Baker's chapter in this volume on Joseph Story).

What 'law' the authors chose to deal with also influenced the shape of their works. For Blackstone the common law was at the heart of the *Commentaries*. Equity plays almost no role in the work, with only a dozen index references scattered over 2000 pages, and a chapter in volume III that John Langbein calls 'baffling' in its deliberate minimisation of equity's historic role in modernising the common law.[24] Blackstone referred frequently to statutes, but usually via footnote references rather than overt discussion and often as part of a historical discussion rather than a statement of contemporary law; whole fields of statutory law, such as the poor law, he simply ignored. Kent too was concerned mainly with the common law, synthesised from state and federal judicial decisions and English precedents. In a well-known passage, he confided that he did

> not much care what the law is in Vermont or Delaware or Rhode Island, or many other states. Cannot we assume American common law to be what is declared in the federal courts and in the courts of the states I have mentioned [New York, Pennsylvania, Massachusetts, Maryland and South Carolina] . . . without troubling ourselves with every local peculiarity? I shall assume what I have to say, to be the law of every state,

[21] Blackstone's *Commentaries* vol 1, 26–34. D Lemmings, 'Blackstone and Law Reform by Education: Preparation for the Bar and Lawyerly Culture in Eighteenth-Century England' (1998) 16 *Law and History Review* 211.

[22] Kent's *Commentaries* Preface to vol 1, vii.

[23] Murdoch's *Epitome* vol 1, 3.

[24] Langbein, Introduction to Blackstone's *Commentaries*, vol 3 (n 11) viii.

where an exception is not shown, because I mean to deal in general Principles and those positive regulations, legislative and judicial, which constitute the basis of all American jurisprudence.[25]

Although Kent cited mostly New York and English decisions, he purported to declare a national law. Lawyers across the country accepted, indeed welcomed that approach, and presumably took note of their own 'local peculiarities' where relevant.

Murdoch was the odd man out here: for him provincial statutes were the primary source of law, and the absence of their systematisation the main goal of the work as declared in its preface. He did not have to deal with the problem of federalism, as Kent did, because he dealt with a sole jurisdiction. Nor did he have to deal with the whole sweep of English legal history, as Blackstone did. A staunch adherent of the traditional British doctrine of the mixed and balanced constitution, Murdoch was content to adopt without elaboration the content of British constitutional law as applying to the colony.[26] He nonetheless wished to carve out a space for a distinctive Nova Scotian tradition in the private law which, like Zephaniah Swift, he conceived as much simpler and more 'free' than its English parent.[27] This larger cultural mission puts Murdoch squarely in the institutist tradition. His focus on statutes in one sense made him the most forward-looking of our three institutists, given the rise of legislation as a tool of the state in the nineteenth century. But in his attempt to illustrate a distinctive Nova Scotian legal culture, he resembled Blackstone more than Kent.

III. FORMAT, ORGANISATION AND AUDIENCE

It is now generally agreed that in writing the *Commentaries*, Blackstone used the institutional format in order to provide some structure to English law, but that in doing so he failed to provide a convincing account of how the English common law actually worked.[28] As Michael Lobban has stated, '[b]ecause Blackstone had sought to fit the common law into an institutional structure which stressed the importance of rules and natural law as an organising concept, and had sought to portray the common law as static and unchanging in its principles, he failed adequately to explore the customary base of law or its remedial nature in a systematic way'.[29] In spite of the commercial success of the *Commentaries*, English lawyers

[25] Kent to P DuPonceau, 29 December 1826, cited in Hulsebosch, 'An Empire of Law' (n 16) 387.

[26] P Girard, '"I will not pin my faith to his sleeve": Beamish Murdoch, Joseph Howe, and Responsible Government Revisited' (2001) 4 *Journal of the Royal Nova Scotia Historical Society* 1.

[27] Girard, 'Themes and Variations' (n 19) 105.

[28] HJ Berman and CJ Reid, Jr, 'The Transformation of English Legal Science: From Hale to Blackstone' (1996) 45 *Emory Law Journal* 437 deny that Blackstone was influenced by the Roman institutists but are unpersuasive on this point.

[29] M Lobban, *The Common Law and English Jurisprudence* (Oxford, Oxford University Press, 1991) 41.

remained suspicious of it. Blackstone had misconstrued the law: it was not, they believed, a system of principles and rules which only needed the occasional use of history to explain the odd idiosyncrasy, but it was rather a complex and detailed system of forms which could only be simplified and distorted by reducing it to the rules that Blackstone had.[30]

Whatever his failures as a theorist, Blackstone was thought to have succeeded in showing how English law was interwoven with English society, how it reflected its values (or at least those of its dominant classes) and how it helped to shape England's political structures and institutions. As a reviewer of the first edition declared, 'Our masterly Commentator takes a wider range, and unites the qualities of the historian and politician, with those of the lawyer . . . Mr Blackstone is perhaps the first who has treated the body of the law in a liberal, elegant, and constitutional manner'.[31]

What might seem fundamental flaws in the English context seemed virtues in North America, where the *Commentaries* proved an attractive model for apprentices, lawyers and law-writers anxious to render the law accessible to all. Although the *Commentaries* were institutional in form, they were used more like treatises, as with the Canadian authors cited above. North American lawyers were conscious of the importance of history for the common law, but they wanted a usable past, preferably served up in a portable and relatively succinct fashion.[32]

At the organisational level, the three works made quite different choices, reflecting their understandings of law and their particular missions. Blackstone's organisation has been most discussed because it seems most puzzling to the modern reader. He made no clear distinction between public and private law, and discussed most of what we could call constitutional law (a term Blackstone himself did not use) as part of the law of persons, with the monarch and members of the two houses of parliament understood simply as persons with particular rights, privileges and immunities. This choice in turn reflected contemporary understandings of law and society as essentially intermingled, without a clear division between state and citizenry. Blackstone's conception of private law centres on property law (land law in particular) almost to the exclusion of contract and tort, and he has very little to say about commercial law.

Kent's organisation is more familiar to the modern reader. He has left the traditional triad of persons, things and actions behind, and replaced it with a major division between public law and private law. The emphasis is very much on substantive law principles as derived from a learned discussion of case law both American and English, and it would not be wrong to see the *Commentaries* as a series of mini-treatises on such things as the law of domestic relations, insurance, partnership and so on. Unlike Blackstone, personal property (and thus, in effect, commercial law) has been promoted ahead of real property. Little is said about procedure and statutes are mostly relegated to footnotes. It is Kent's omissions

30 Ibid 47.

31 Cited by Prest, *William Blackstone* (n 15) 220.

32 M Hoeflich, 'American Blackstones' in *Blackstone and His Commentaries* (n 3).

that distinguish him from Blackstone and Murdoch, three in particular: he provides no introduction to the *Commentaries*; he says virtually nothing about the legal profession; and he does not address criminal law.

Kent's *Commentaries* do not begin, as most institutional works do, with a section on the nature of law in general, or advice about how to study law. For his part, Blackstone starts with four introductory chapters prior to Book I, entitled 'Of the Study of Law', 'On Laws in General', 'The Laws of England' and 'Countries Subject to the Laws of England'. Murdoch follows Blackstone on the first three (the first on legal study being entirely his own composition, the second and third more or less summaries of Blackstone's chapters), and then adds several chapters on the early history of the colony and the doctrine of reception to replace Blackstone's chapter on law throughout the empire. Kent, by contrast, launches directly into the law of nations in Part I of volume I, follows that with Part II on the constitutional law of the United States, and only in Part III of volume I does he discuss the sources of law at the state and federal level. By the time we reach the law of persons in Part IV, it is clear that we are dealing with persons only in their private relations, although the section begins with an account of the constitutional rights of individuals.

The absence of any introductory section in Kent's *Commentaries* seems odd in what was supposedly meant to be an 'elementary' work. Kent may have avoided a section on the nature of law in general because he never claimed to be a legal theorist and always described his interest in law as of a practical nature. The closest Kent got to a definition of law in the *Commentaries* was a purely empirical and positivist one: 'Municipal law is a rule of civil conduct prescribed by the supreme power in a state. It is composed of written and unwritten, or statute and common law'.[33] This is the opening sentence of Part III, on the sources of law, a section which is admittedly somewhat introductory but placed 400 pages into the text. The absence of a 'proper' introduction is even stranger in light of Kent's prior publication of two such efforts.[34]

Kent chose to say almost nothing about the legal profession itself.[35] In a work supposedly addressed to lawyers, this is more puzzling than the omission of legal philosophy, and is in stark contrast to both Blackstone and Murdoch. Combined with the absence of introductory material, one cannot avoid the impression that Kent was trying to intimidate rather than assist the budding jurist. It is almost as if his *Commentaries* were meant to be an anti-institutional work, to make the law less accessible rather than more so. He warned that

> [t]o attain a competent knowledge of the common law in all its branches has now become a very serious undertaking, and it requires steady and lasting perseverance, in

[33] Kent's *Commentaries* vol 1, 419.

[34] Kent, *An Introductory Lecture to a Course of Law Lectures Delivered Nov. 17, 1794* (New York, NY, Francis Childs, 1794), Repr in (1903) 3 *Columbia Law Review* 330. 'A Lecture, introductory to a course of law lectures in Columbia College. Delivered February 2, 1824', reproduced in Perry Miller; *The Legal Mind in America from Independence to the Civil War* (New York, NY, Doubleday Publishing, 1962).

[35] His entire discussion is at Kent's *Commentaries* vol 1, 286–87.

> consequence of the number of books which now beset and encumber the path of the student.[36]

Kent noted that there were some 648 volumes of English texts, digests and case law (aside from statutes) and some 200 volumes of such American materials. To read all these, he admitted, 'would be a melancholy waste or misapplication of strength and time' but, astonishingly, he provided no suggestions or reading list to assist the young lawyer in overcoming this problem.[37] Kent undoubtedly deplored the contemporary trend to reducing barriers to entry to the legal profession – though the phenomenon goes unmentioned in the *Commentaries*. Here he seems to be actively discouraging those candidates who might quail at having to deal with an 850-book library. The message is clear: 'only the scholarly need apply'.

Finally, where both Blackstone and Murdoch devoted large sections of their works to the criminal law, Kent wrote nothing on it. He never justified this decision in the *Commentaries* itself, and devoted only a few pages to the protection of personal security by the criminal law and the legitimacy of the death penalty. This omission is probably the best indicator of Kent's elitism, and reveals again the anti-institutional character of his work. Kent may have believed he was addressing himself to students as well as members of the profession, but if so, he was mentally addressing a highly elite group of students who had no need to know where the criminal law fit into the scheme of American law, probably because their clientele was expected to be wealthy and respectable.

Murdoch managed to blend Blackstone and Kent in his organisational scheme by fusing the public and private law division made by Kent with the Roman trilogy of persons, things and actions. He did not need to begin with international law, as Kent did, because Nova Scotia was a colony. After his introductory chapters Murdoch began with Part I of Book I 'On Government', which included not only an overview of the provincial constitution but a long section on regulatory law as contained in the provincial statutes; thus we have chapters on laws connected with agriculture; trade; religion, morals (including the licensing laws), charity (including the poor law) and education; health and amusement; and the militia and billeting. All of these manifestations of the police power were beneath Kent's notice, and largely beneath Blackstone's, who, when he considered them, usually did so as part of the penal law; he had virtually nothing to say about the poor law, for instance, a highly important part of English law at the local level. Murdoch had relatively little to say about commercial law as a domain of private law, but quite a bit to say about its public law aspects (ie the regulation of trade), and in this respect was virtually the inverse of Kent.

Part II of Murdoch's Book I is entitled 'Of the Government of Families'. It follows Blackstone and Kent with regard to the sub-categorisation of the law of persons (husband and wife, master and servant, etc) but is unique with respect to the strong link to the public sphere. JW Cairns observes that:

[36] Ibid vol 1, 441.

[37] Ibid 442. Nor had he done so in his 1824 introductory lecture.

> [Blackstone's] society was still one in which the system of rule – king, nobility, church, commoners – was intimately part of the general societal system affecting not only government but family and other relations between persons. In a sense, the family was an institution of government: and many institutional writers linked the institution of the family directly to that of government.[38]

Interestingly, this is a link that Blackstone himself does not make explicit. Considering as he does the rights of the governors of England as part of the law of persons, when he has finished with what we would call constitutional law, he states:

> Having thus commented on the rights and duties of persons, as standing in the public relations of magistrates and people; the method I have marked out now leads me to consider their rights and duties in *private* oeconomical relations [ie husband and wife, master and servant, etc][39]

Murdoch's transition was quite different: 'The public government and general regulation of society having been considered, I will now advert to the government of families'.[40] Kent, like Blackstone, considered the law of domestic relations as essentially a matter of private rights, but for Murdoch they still possessed something of a public, governmental character. In this he reflected wider currents of thought in British North America, as Canadian law proved remarkably resistant to most liberalising trends in family law emanating from the nineteenth-century US in matters such as divorce, illegitimacy, adoption and custody.[41]

Murdoch's treatment of the law of property followed Blackstone's rather than Kent's: he privileged real property, devoting some 225 pages to it, while personal property merited only 50 pages, 15 of which dealt with wills of personal property. This disparity seems at odds with Murdoch's observations that in Nova Scotia 'immovable and movable property are subjected with few exceptions to the same rules of acquisition and transfer', such that 'our landed property has in all cases the general character . . . of allodial land'.[42] Murdoch justified his treatment of the complex law of future interests with the observation that 'the increasing value of real estate in the Province, and the tendency arising now to make settlements by devise, will eventually bring it more into use than heretofore'.[43] But Murdoch must have known that Nova Scotia's economy was based mainly on providing shipping services and on trade and commerce in movable goods, especially fish and lumber; he owned a share in a valuable Halifax wharf at which such trade was carried on. He even declared that colonial lawyers 'may emphatically be called' men of business.[44] But neither in his treatment of personal property nor of con-

[38] Cairns, 'Blackstone, an English Institutist' (n 1) 346.
[39] Blackstone's *Commentaries* vol 1, 410.
[40] Murdoch's *Epitome* vol 2, 1.
[41] P Girard with J Phillips, 'Re-thinking the 'Nation' in National Legal History: A Canadian Perspective' (2011) 29 *Law and History Review* 607, 615.
[42] Murdoch's *Epitome* vol 2, 80.
[43] Ibid vol 2, 128.
[44] Ibid vol 1, 8.

tracts did he pay much attention to commercial law. Even partnerships, the basic business vehicle of the day, rated only four pages (compared to Kent's 40). With the example of Kent available, this must have been a deliberate choice rather than a rote imitation of Blackstone, but one that is somewhat difficult to explain.[45] It is not that Murdoch was anti-commercial, but rather that he privileged other kinds of rights over those associated with commerce; we will return to this point below.

If Murdoch's treatment of commercial law was unsatisfactory, his volumes three and four in some respects improved, in different ways, upon Kent and Blackstone. In volume III he devoted nearly 200 pages to the 'Civil Courts of Common Law', considering in turn the jurisdiction of various courts, actions, limitation of actions, procedure, pleadings, juries, evidence, the execution of judgments and costs. Kent ignored virtually all of these as too practical, part of the daily grind of lawyers' work which he 'always extremely hated'.[46] Murdoch's volume IV covered criminal law, which Kent ignored as we have seen, and equity, which Blackstone and to some extent even Kent (ironically, for a former chancellor of New York) underplayed.[47]

The question of audience is the key to all three works. Blackstone aimed his work at England's governing class and at budding barristers, not at the attorneys and solicitors who did the grunt work of the law. Detail was not that important to him; rather he wished to portray the common law comprehensively as part of English society and governance, and as the cultural birthright of the English people. Kent also aimed his work at a high mandarinate of the legal, judicial and political establishments, not at everyday lawyers – the fact that he authorised a sort of *Kent for Dummies* is the best evidence of this.[48] But the context in which he wrote gave his work a different cast. While he did not wish to undo the Revolution, he greatly feared its tendencies to democracy and individualism, which he believed would undermine the rule of the educated and the propertied. Kent was uneasy about the fundamental values of the American people as revealed in the Jacksonian innovations of expanded suffrage, elected judges and an open legal profession.[49] Thus he wished to erect a formidable scholarly wall around the law, to depict it as the rightful preserve of a select group of initiates who could maintain the security of property and good governance against democratic excess. And what better way to do that than to focus on the common law, declared by judges, rather than statutes, the creatures of unpredictable legislatures? And better

[45] Murdoch initially planned to write a fifth volume devoted to 'mercantile contracts, not strictly belonging to the title of personal property' (vol 1, 48), but it never appeared. Thus, while aware of commercial law, Murdoch did not regard it with the same urgency as the other topics he chose to address in print.

[46] Cited in Hulsebosch, 'An Empire of Law' (n 16) 389, n 41.

[47] Z Swift, *A System of the Laws of the State of Connecticut* (Windham, CT, Printed by John Byrne, 1795–96) also devotes distinct books in vol 4 to criminal law and equity; it is not clear if Murdoch was aware of his work; see Girard, 'Themes and Variations' (n 19) 105.

[48] A Kinne, *The Most Important Parts of Kent's Commentaries Reduced to Questions and Answers* 2nd edn (New York, NY, W E Dean, 1840); Langbein, 'Chancellor Kent' (n 2) 566, n 95.

[49] Hulsebosch, 'Debating the Transformation' (n 6) 21, concludes that Kent 'took Jacksonian democracy in stride' but that is not the way I read him.

yet, to focus on the notion that 'the rule of law was not the property of any one state, [but rather] floated above them, [such that] all states were held to it'.[50] In Kent's mind locality was tied to the threat of democracy, while the judiciary acted as a higher power untethered by geography.

Where Kent feared locality, Murdoch celebrated it. Local statutes were the best evidence of the true values of Nova Scotia's people, which included a commitment to British ordered liberty but went two better than the mother country by enshrining those values in the private law, thus embracing a spirit of equality and cultural pluralism unknown in Britain itself.[51] When the movement for colonial autonomy embroiled provincial politics a few years later, Murdoch would have reason to question whether his optimistic portrayal of consensus values was accurate, but in the early 1830s political parties had yet to appear on the local scene. Along with this high cultural mission, the *Epitome* was aimed at novice lawyers in a much more direct and utilitarian way than either Kent or Blackstone. It contained a wealth of detail about local statutes, civil and criminal procedure, and actual practice and usage, set out in an easy and readable style, that could only have been obtained by a combination of extensive research and practical experience.

Where Kent equated the lawyer with the scholar, Murdoch took a much more balanced and realistic approach to the lawyers in his audience, whom he knew combined the roles of barrister and solicitor. He treasured the law as a learned profession but at the same time recognised that serving one's clients in North America required a good deal of business savvy. Thus he issued twin warnings to those aspiring lawyers who possessed a university education, and to those who did not:

> The young collegian is not to expect, that any precocity of genius evinced in scholastic pursuits, will in the world be accepted in lieu of the habits and acquirements of a man of business, such as a colonial lawyer may emphatically be called. . . . Let him not in pride of classic lore, undervalue the most minute or humble departments of his profession. While his learning may be an ornament, and perhaps give grace and intensity to his eloquence, yet it is rather a holiday garb; while method and accuracy in things which appear trivial are essential and indispensable, to success in any profession.[52]

But, he continued,

> Those who enter upon the study of law without the benefit of a college education, should be cautioned against the indulgence of an opposite error. They should guard against any impressions, that would lessen in their estimation the value of learning. . . . [They should] allow no occasion when they may add to their limited stock of learning, to pass by unimproved. . . . An early acquaintance with legal proceedings and principles is of the highest value to the future lawyer. . . . But if the human mind, at so early a period, be confined to one science, and kept until manhood forcibly bent into this one solitary channel of study, we must calculate on its becoming narrow, and full of the

[50] Hulsebosch, 'An Empire of Law' (n 16) 401.

[51] Swift, *A System of the Laws of Connecticut* (n 47), also praised local statutes and saw them as the best evidence of republican liberty, as opposed to British liberty.

[52] Murdoch's *Epitome* vol 1, 8.

> peculiar prejudices of its *caste*. . . . The student, whose information is limited to law reading alone must have his notions, even on law principles, obscure. . . .[53]

Murdoch's *Epitome* fulfils this joint mission well, displaying the scholarly heft and broad socio-historical context requisite for a learned work on the law, while also providing the practical knowledge that the lawyer will need to navigate the local legal order. This localisation of transatlantic law was a considerable intellectual achievement in its own terms, but there is no doubt that it prevented Murdoch from becoming a British North American Kent, just as it had prevented Zephaniah Swift from being recognised as a 'national' jurist (see Angela Fernandez's contribution to this collection on this point).

III. INSTITUTISTS AND THE NATION

As noted earlier, the institutional work has been linked to the rise of the nation-state. Considering our three institutists in this light reveals differing conceptions of how law is linked to the nation-state, from positivist, instrumentalist understandings to those having to do more with soft law and legal culture. In the European context the link between institutional works and the nation-state came about when centralising monarchies wished to weld various regional or provincial customs into a single national law. In England the common law had already played this role, but in the 1760s various courts still used civil law, canon law or manorial law instead of the common law. JW Cairns once suggested that Blackstone wished to ensure that the common law was seen as 'the' national law by elevating it over its rivals, while David Lemmings maintained more recently that the common law had already won this battle by the 1760s.[54] Even if Lemmings is correct on this particular point, it cannot be denied that the *Commentaries* exude what AWB Simpson has called 'a spirit of nationalistic self-satisfaction'.[55] Frequent references to the common law as 'our law' and attempts to distinguish the Anglo-Saxon law from later Norman interpretations (dimly viewed by Blackstone) abound. The reason for them is not so much related to the technical legal position of the common law in English judicature as to its place in the hearts and minds of the English people. Blackstone was concerned as much with the legal culture of the nation as its law. But the nation in which he wished to instill a sense of the history and values of the common law comprised not the entire English population but the much smaller political nation: principally male Protestants (preferably Anglicans) of the gentry and land-owning classes.

Kent was faced with discussing the law of a federal nation. While he could not ignore the states, as much as possible he tried to state the law as if it had already

[53] Ibid 9–10.

[54] Cairns, 'Blackstone, an English Institutist' (n 1) 328–39; Lemmings, 'Blackstone and Law Reform by Education' (n 21) 249, n 146.

[55] Simpson, 'Rise and Fall' (n 7) 658.

been harmonised among them, footnoting instances where that was not possible. Unlike Blackstone, Kent was not so much concerned with the relationship of law and society through legal culture, because he did not find himself in sympathy with the main social and political trends of Jacksonian America. Rather he was concerned with an important but narrow fragment of lawyers' legal thought: how to rehabilitate English law as the intellectual ballast for a unified American common law. This lends to Kent's *Commentaries* a more hard-edged, more analytic, more purely legal tone than one finds in either Blackstone or Murdoch.

The one area in which Kent found himself in accord with his society was in its devotion to commerce and the accumulation of property. Here the role of the state was clear: to stand aside and let the wondrous laws of economics work their magic. With the exception of setting limits to the accumulation of property by corporations, 'the legislature have no right to limit the extent of the acquisition of property'.[56] Furthermore, '[c]ivil government is not entitled . . . as a general rule, to regulate the use of property in the hands of the owners, by sumptuary laws, or by any other visionary schemes of frugality and equality'.[57] Kent pointed to Britain to prove that there was no conflict between liberty and the accumulation of wealth; there, he asserted, 'the abundant returns of industry, the fruits of genius, the boundless extent of commerce, the exuberance of wealth and the cultivation of the liberal arts, with the unfettered use of all those blessings', proved this point.[58]

In fact there were any number of laws at both the state and municipal level that 'regulate[d] property in the hands of the owners',[59] but Kent, unlike Murdoch, chose to ignore them. For him, property was an absolute right to be protected at all costs from the depredations of the misguided and envious lower classes. Kent could not prevent such people from getting the vote, but he could weave a web of erudite law to entangle them should they try to implement any 'visionary schemes of frugality [or] equality'. His legal nation-building was thus at odds with the political trends of Jacksonian America. Where in the US, unlike Blackstone's England, the political nation was rapidly coming to comprise all adult white males, Kent addressed himself to a smaller subset of the citizenry: what we might call the white commercial nation. Afro-Americans ('a degraded caste', in his view) were beyond the pale but Kent had considerable sympathy for native Americans, whom he thought had been treated by all levels of government with 'rapacity, violence & perfidy'. Their 'fast approaching Destruction' meant that he could avoid considering their claims to legal protection, but he failed to perceive that it was the very unleashing of the instinct for property among white settlers that caused so much of the violence and misery endured by the Amerindians.[60]

[56] Kent's *Commentaries* vol 2, 265.
[57] Ibid 266.
[58] Ibid.
[59] W Novak, *The People's Welfare: Law and Regulation in Nineteenth-Century America* (Chapel Hill, NC, University of North Carolina Press, 1996).
[60] Cited in Hulsebosch, 'An Empire of Law' (n 16) 392, n 54.

With Murdoch we see yet another version of nation-building, one based on creating a common legal culture, a community of shared civic values. He is more like Blackstone than Kent in this respect, but much more inclusive than Blackstone in defining the relevant community. For Murdoch all Nova Scotians, regardless of race or creed, with one exception, could celebrate the 'simple, elegant and free' code of laws which their ancestors had erected on British and French foundations in the colony. Blacks, according to Murdoch, had long been considered 'free ipso facto upon landing' in Nova Scotia, and possessed full civil rights.[61] There was 'no religious distinction remaining in our Provincial code'.[62] Outside this rainbow coalition were the Mi'kmaq, whom Murdoch treated as barely human in his historical account of the settlement of the province. He undoubtedly knew about both the Royal Proclamation of 1763 and the treaties of the early 1760s which were meant to protect the Mi'kmaq, but failed to mention them and observed that native grievances were now a 'matter for the historian, rather than the jurist'.[63] Later Murdoch had occasion to revise his views, bestowing the ultimate accolade of 'civilised' upon the Mi'kmaq, but in his *Epitome* they were effectively excluded from the Nova Scotian polity.[64]

Property was not at the core of the nation-building exercise, as it was for Kent. As we saw earlier, Murdoch did not include much coverage of commercial law, and he was much more muted about the value of property to mankind, compared to Kent and Blackstone. He was no socialist or leveller, but he believed that the community had the right to impose significant restrictions on the rights of wealth-holders in the common interest. As such restraints could only be imposed via legislation duly enacted by a representative body, Murdoch was not concerned that the rights of the propertied would be unduly trenched upon.

IV. CONCLUSIONS

I have tried to show that the institutional genre was a flexible one that arguably played an enabling and complementary role rather than an antagonistic one vis-à-vis the treatise. The analysis has also shown our three institutists to have had their fingers on the pulse of their respective jurisdictions, although their works were ultimately taken up in ways they could not have imagined. Blackstone's 'baffling' treatment of equity, for example, in fact proved accurate: a century later the fusion of the courts paved the way for the absorption of equitable principles into the common law, proving its dominance. In singling out the common law as the defining feature of the English legal tradition and expressing it in the form of substantive law rules and principles, Blackstone allowed it to be seen as a fit

[61] Murdoch's *Epitome* vol 1, 43.
[62] Ibid 65.
[63] Ibid vol 2, 57–58.
[64] Girard, *Lawyers and Legal Culture* (n 18) 177.

object of legislative reform in the nineteenth century, even though that was not his intention. Particular rules of the common law had of course been altered by legislation for centuries, but Blackstone showed that the common law could be treated as a whole, as a national *system* of law, although he did not use that word. Moreover, his focus on rules and principles and topical arrangement also eased the way for future treatise writers; unlike the alphabetically organised abridgements, one could take almost any chapter of Blackstone and either adapt it for local use, as some Canadian authors did, or write a new book about it.

Finally, at the level of legal culture, Blackstone reflected accurately a sense of insular pride in the common law's Englishness; and even though he addressed himself largely to the elite, the working classes would soon appropriate as their own his encomia to British justice and English liberty.[65] Blackstone's insularity made the common law prima facie unsuitable for inclusion in the wider 'British' identity that was being constructed in the eighteenth century; but the incorporation of some of its fundamentals in the emerging notion of 'British justice' provided a basis for a common legal identity in which all parts of the British Isles could share.[66]

Kent experienced a much more conflictual relationship with his ambient legal culture than Blackstone, trying in his *Commentaries* to create an American common law that could be isolated from democratic influences. The rise of an elective judiciary frustrated his immediate aims but his position that the 'proper' sources for legal authors were judicial decisions rather than legislation proved hugely influential on the emerging treatise tradition. But Kent's erudition and cosmopolitanism did not ultimately serve the rarefied purposes he had intended. Why plough your way through that 850-book library when Kent had already done it for you? Ironically, as Daniel Hulsebosch has noted, Kent's genius for synthesis meant that US lawyers did not feel any need to return to his sources; his very popularity 'contributed . . . to the nativism of [the early Republic's] legal mind'. Lawyers admired the scholarship but went for the usable nuggets of law Kent provided on a myriad of topics, in effect using the *Commentaries* as a treatise.[67]

Kent's focus on judge-made law meant that the *Commentaries* travelled well, both within the US and beyond. Hulsebosch has noted how eagerly lawyers in the new state of Texas embraced Kent.[68] Beyond the US, the Nova Scotian judge Alexander Stewart wrote to Kent that

> [y]our Commentaries are the textbook we put into our students' hands and next to Blackstone . . . are our most esteemed works. At the bar and by the bench 'Kent's Commentaries' are continually cited in company with that of our late much lamented friend Judge Story.[69]

[65] EP Thompson, *The Making of the English Working Class* (London, Gollancz, 1963).

[66] L Colley, *Britons: Forging the Nation, 1707–1837* (New Haven, CT, Yale University Press, 1992). Colley's failure to track the emergence of 'British justice' as a component of the new British identity is a singular omission in this seminal work. *cf* P Girard, 'British Justice, English Law, and Canadian Legal Culture' in PA Buckner (ed), *Canada and the British Empire* (Oxford, Oxford University Press, 2004).

[67] Hulsebosch, 'An Empire of Law' (n 16) 381.

[68] Ibid 407–08.

[69] James Kent Papers, Library of Congress, reel 5, Stewart to Kent, 28 April 1847.

Murdoch's *Epitome* was aimed at his fellow Nova Scotians so we should not be surprised if the work did not attract much attention beyond its borders. But in concentrating on local statutes as his primary source of law, Murdoch virtually ensured that his *opus* would remain tethered to its home jurisdiction. Statutes are tied to locality in a way that the common law is not. But they are also expressive of popular will in a much more direct way than the common law, and herein lies a certain irony. Murdoch, writing in a jurisdiction that had rejected the American Revolution, embraced statute law as containing the essence of Nova Scotian values, while Kent, a supporter of the legacy of the American Revolution, saw legislation as a source of 'fearful experiments'.[70] Kent sought to insulate law from politics via the notion of judicially created 'rights', while for Murdoch governance was the main function of law, with rights ultimately defeasible if the public interest required it.[71]

This focus on statute law, with its intense locality, was not unique to Murdoch. Future Canadian writers also identified statute as the fundamental source of law. In the preface to his 1896 adaptation of Blackstone's law of persons for Ontario, Rupert Etherege Kingsford justified his statement that the Dominion and provincial statutes must be 'always beside any person who wishes to learn the law of this country' with the declaration that '[a]s democracy, with its love of change, is the dominant power on this continent, it must have its way in legislation as in everything else'. He had 'not made many references to cases', he said, because lawyers could look them up in digests.[72] This focus on statute law reflected a key facet of Canadian federalism, in which the provincial legislatures assumed more powerful positions than their US counterparts. Without a revolutionary experience or a civil war to generate a new sense of identity going beyond provincial boundaries, or a powerful judiciary anxious to bind the country in a commercial union, the inhabitants of British North America-Canada long remained attached principally to the colony-provinces they knew, even after Confederation in 1867. No new federal court of general jurisdiction was created in 1867 (a weak Supreme Court of Canada, which long remained in the shadow of the Privy Council, was created only in 1875), leaving the several colonial superior courts to continue as the backbone of Canadian judicature. The provincial legislature came to be seen as the central repository of provincial values, and its statutes the key to local character, as Murdoch had foreshadowed.[73] Canadian identity, legal or otherwise, emerged only fitfully.

While this situation provided the law with a high degree of democratic legitimacy, it also gave it a somewhat parochial, insular character, reflected in Canadian

[70] Ibid. The phrase is Stewart's but he is paraphrasing a statement in a previous letter, no longer extant, from Kent.

[71] See generally, P Girard, 'Liberty, Order, and Pluralism: The Canadian Experience' in JP Greene (ed), *Exclusionary Empire: British Liberty Overseas, 1600–1900* (New York, NY, Cambridge University Press, 2009).

[72] RE Kingsford, *Commentaries on the Laws of Ontario* (n 5) v.

[73] P Romney, 'From Constitutionalism to Legalism: Trial by Jury, Responsible Government, and the Rule of Law in the Canadian Political Culture' (1989) 7 *Law and History Review* 121–58.

legal literature. No one ever completed an institutional work for Canada as a whole, and the treatise literature that eventually developed usually took as its subject a federal statute or a legal topic within the boundaries of a single province. Even though Murdoch successfully situated the Nova Scotia legal tradition within a transatlantic legal culture, and provided a sophisticated analysis of the way British law and local law could interact, his focus on statute law inevitably limited the appeal of his *Epitome*. By treating mostly the common law, Blackstone and Kent created works that were ready-made for export and empire. But all three works were like icebergs from which more specialised studies, treatises or otherwise, might be calved. Institutional works and treatises co-existed profitably for well over a century and a half, until the former, like so much else in the nineteenth century's pantheistic legal culture, finally faded from view after the First World War.

3

Tapping Reeve, Coverture and America's First Legal Treatise

ANGELA FERNANDEZ*

By marriage, the husband and wife are one person in law: that is, the very being or legal existence of the woman is suspended during the marriage, or at least is incorporated and consolidated into that of the husband: under whose wing, protection, and *cover*, she performs every thing; and is therefore called in our law-french a *feme-covert*; is said to be *covert-baron*, or under the protection and influence of her husband, her *baron*, or lord; and her condition during her marriage is called her *coverture*.

William Blackstone, *Commentaries on the Laws of England* (1765)

The husband and wife in legal consideration are one person, her existence is united with and swallowed up in that of the husband [. . .] As the law contemplates the husband and wife as being but one person, it allows them to have but one will, which is placed in the husband, as the fittest and ablest to provide for and govern the family . . .

Zephaniah Swift, *A System of the Laws of the State of Connecticut* (1795)

The law does not view the husband and wife as one person . . .

Tapping Reeve, *Baron and Femme* (1816)

* Angela Fernandez is currently an associate professor at the Faculty of Law, University of Toronto. Her chapter for this collection is material adapted from her JSD Dissertation, supervised by Robert W Gordon at the Yale Law School. Funding assistance for that project was provided by the Social Sciences and Humanities Research Council of Canada Doctoral Award and Lillian Goldman Scholarships provided by Yale Law School. The portions of the work drawn on here owe thanks to then-director of the Rare Book Room at Yale Law School, Harvey Hull, and staff at the Litchfield Historical Society in Litchfield and the Connecticut Historical Society in Hartford, as well as the very sadly now-deceased Morris L Cohen. Sooin Kim and Sufei Xu of the Bora Laskin Library at the Faculty of Law, University of Toronto have been very helpful with the subsequent research that has gone into the piece.

I. INTRODUCTION

TAPPING REEVE WROTE in his treatise on domestic relations the following surprising statement: 'The law does not view the husband and wife as one person'.[1] Surprising because we have come to think of Blackstone's insistence that a husband and wife were one person and the famous passage above from his *Commentaries* about coverture as a final and authoritative statement of the law, grounded as it was on that second bible of English common law in the colonies, *Coke Upon Littleton*.[2] One would have thought that Coke plus Blackstone created firm ground if ever there was any on the point in nineteenth-century American law. It is certainly treated that way by both lawyers and historians of married women's property rights who have taken little notice of Reeve.[3] Tapping Reeve taught students at his school in Litchfield, Connecticut and wrote in his treatise that the language of one-person-in-law was 'metaphorical' only.[4] How could it not be, Reeve asked, when one found that a married woman was 'often an active agent, executing powers, conveying land, suing with her husband, and liable to be sued with him, and liable to punishment for crimes'?[5] Reeve argued that coverture could not mean that the legal existence of a woman was subsumed by her husband or suspended for the term of the marriage since she could still be a guardian and give a receipt. The power to engage in such activities showed that it could not be true that a wife 'has no existence during the coverture, and is destitute of volition'.[6] The maxim that a wife had no will had 'not the least foundation in common sense'.[7] She should, for instance, be allowed to make a will, one of the very basic entitlements of a subject with legal personality.[8]

Why did Reeve take such a surprising position? What hope did this reverse-principle ever have of carrying the day? Lest Reeve's position appear to be some

[1] T Reeve, *The Law of Baron and Femme; of Parent and Child; of Guardian and Ward; of Master and Servant; and of the Powers of Courts of Chancery* (New Haven, CT, Oliver Steele, 1816) 89.

[2] See *Commentaries on the Laws of England, A Facsimile of the First Edition of 1765–1769, vol I, Of the Rights of Persons (1765)* (Chicago, IL, University of Chicago Press, 1979, 2002) 430, n 1 (citing 'Co Litt 112'). See also T Stretton, 'Coverture and Unity of Person in Blackstone's *Commentaries*' in W Prest (ed), *Blackstone and His Commentaries: Biography, Law, History* (Oxford, Hart Publishing, 2009) 111, 115–16 (explaining that the passage in *Coke Upon Littleton* that Blackstone relied on was in a chapter on 'tenure in burgage, one of the most obscure forms of tenure in English law' and that 'Littleton and Coke made reference to unity of person, but neither author relied on it to any great extent').

[3] But see N Basch, *In the Eyes of the Law: Women, Marriage, and Property in Nineteenth-Century New York* (Ithaca, NY, Cornell University Press, 1982) 42–69 (who makes an exception for Reeve in her line-up of largely conservative writers on married women's property law – Blackstone, Kent and Story); H Hartog, *Man and Wife in America: A History* (Cambridge, MA, Harvard University Press, 2002) 107 (calling Reeve's book 'the most important American treatise dealing with marriage during the first half of the nineteenth century' and noting that it 'entirely avoided the language of unity').

[4] Reeve, *Baron and Femme* 129.

[5] Ibid 130.

[6] Ibid 121.

[7] Ibid 64.

[8] This subject occupies two chapters of *Baron and Femme* and will be explored in detail below. See ibid 137–60.

kind of quaint aberration, it must be said that in fact his views had noteworthy effect. The most dramatic evidence of this is a statute Reeve's students passed in the Connecticut legislature in 1809 empowering married women to make wills. Scholars of married women's property law have found it puzzling why this statute appeared so early (especially in Connecticut which was known for being particularly restrictive of women's property rights) when reform enabling married women to bequeath property did not occur in most states until after 1850.[9] Well, evidence suggests that the Connecticut legislature was filled with Reeve's students, who were exposed to his passionate arguments on the issue and were convinced enough by them to pass the law.[10] The other place to look for evidence of influence is subsequent legal commentary. James Kent, while generally keen on Reeve's work, did not agree with Reeve's position on the legal personality of married women and declined to follow it in his famous *Commentaries on American Law*.[11] Kent chose Coke (and impliedly Blackstone) instead.[12] However, Nathan Dane, in his abridgement on American law, did follow Reeve, showing that not only was Reeve's book an important one, Reeve was persuasive to some on this most controversial point, rejection of the one-person-in-law maxim. Relying directly on Reeve, Dane wrote 'the notion that a wife has no will, is a mere fiction without foundation in fact'.[13] Reeve influenced students and early American legal culture more generally through his school and his treatise, a truly didactic or teaching text. The second question, why Reeve put forward the position he did, is more difficult to answer. It relates as we will see to Reeve's religion, his own marriage and conditions that were unique to Connecticut during this period.

The first quarter of the nineteenth century was a time in post-Revolutionary America when many legal issues were up for grabs. In a way, the independence Reeve exhibited in his treatise was simply in keeping with the express legal philosophy that, after the Revolution, Connecticut did not have to follow English common law and, indeed, it should not if that law was wrong or made no sense. Rejection of the Coke/Blackstone maxim was certainly in keeping with this, however out of step it might be with what we have learned about the law of husband and wife in the nineteenth century. However, Reeve did not present his arguments as part of Connecticut's right to go its own way or a continuation of what

[9] See RH Chused, 'Married Women's Property Law: 1800–1850' (1983) 71 *Georgetown Law Review* 1359, 1366.

[10] See text below at notes 81–88.

[11] For reliance on *Baron and Femme*, see J Kent, *Commentaries on American Law*, vol 2 (New York, NY, O Halsted, 1827) 67, 78, 88, 108, 163, 165, 185, 189, 205, 211, 148–49.

[12] See ibid 109 ('[t]he legal effects of marriage, are generally deducible from the principle of the common law, by which the husband and wife are regarded as one person, and her legal existence and authority in a degree lost or suspended, during the continuance of the matrimonial union', citing for support to the same obscure passage in *Coke Upon Littleton* that Blackstone referred to, 'Co. Litt. 112').

[13] Nathan Dane, *General Abridgement and Digest of American Law*, vol 1 (Boston, MA, Cummings, Hilliard, 1823) 371. Dane relied on Baron and Femme to state that a married woman 'is, in no sense, an idiot or *non compos*; nor does the criminal law view her as one . . . [E]ven the laws of property view her as able to convey or devise, and even alone, where her husband has no interest affected thereby, as where she executes a power by trustee, [and] has separate property'.

we will see was a Puritan orientation in the law specific to New England. Rather Reeve called what he wrote in the treatise 'English law' that was of concern to Connecticut and other states in the Union. While he included discussion of some English statutes and cases, we will see that by and large Reeve argued from what I will call 'pure principle', not only ignoring local Connecticut cases (those for and against) but going so far as to ignore positive law like the 1809 statute that actually supported and vindicated him. How are we to understand such odd behaviour in a legal treatise?

When Roscoe Pound lectured in 1936 about the 'taught law' tradition and its connection to Kent's *Commentaries* and treatise writers like Joseph Story and later John Henry Wigmore and Samuel Williston, he used Reeve's *Baron and Femme* to mark the beginning of 'American text writing as a significant force in our legal development', identifying it in effect as the first American legal treatise.[14] It might be something of a stretch to call the work a treatise. Reeve himself did not do so in his title, nor, we should note, did Pound. While *Baron and Femme* is written on a specialised topic, constituting a *treatment* of the law of husband and wife, it is really a collection of Reeve's lectures and might well be judged to be not rigorous or systematic enough in its arrangement or presentation in order to qualify as a treatise. However, we should note that later editors who updated Reeve's text did not hesitate to call it a treatise.[15] And Reeve's book is nothing if not a statement of principle. Indeed, the issue is not a want of principle; it is rather the absence of precedent that makes it an odd legal treatise.

We have come to think of the *legal* treatise as a place where an expert (lawyer, judge, academic) commits to paper explanations of legal doctrine supported by sources of positive law: cases and statutes (at a bare minimum). Such a treatise becomes persuasive and authoritative (if it does) in part because of who the writer is; but that judgment is also based in part on the sense that develops in the relevant legal community that the author can be trusted in his or her use of the positive legal sources. When a treatise writer pushes and wants to move from the descriptive to the normative, there is usually a signal to that effect, a mark to the reader, a 'we might suggest' or 'it seems to us'.[16] What is striking about *Baron and Femme* is that Reeve does not do this. He does not report what the cases say, for instance, and then go on to argue that they were wrongly decided; he simply ignores the cases and statute law and argues for what he thinks the law ought to be. In the case of married women making wills, it makes no sense to say married women have no will and so a default common law presumption that they cannot make a will

[14] R Pound, *The Formative Era of American Law* (Boston, MA, Little, Brown, 1938) 144, 140. See also R Pound, 'Taught Law' (1912) 3 *American Law School Review* 164.

[15] See Preface to T Reeve, *The Law of Baron and Femme* 2nd edn, L E Chittenden (ed) (Burlington, VT, Chauncey Goodrich, 1846) iii; Preface to T Reeve, *The Law of Baron and Femme* 3rd edn, A J Parker & C Baldwin (eds) (Albany, NY, Gould, 1862) iii.

[16] See S Waddams, 'What Were the Principles of Nineteenth-Century Contract Law?' in L Andrew, P Brand and P Mitchell (eds), *Law in the City: Proceedings of the Seventeenth British Legal History Conference, London, 2005* (Dublin, Four Courts Press, 2007) 308.

cannot be correct. No doubt many treatise writers play some sleight of hand with the cases, burying points to the contrary in footnotes no one will follow up on or justifying exclusion of problematic or complicating cases on the grounds that the case is badly reasoned, the court is not of a sufficiently high authority, or the point of view is considered by those in the know as old or out of date.[17] Indeed, '[t]he reader who blinks' might well miss the treatise writer's shift from descriptive to normative, always a slippery line at best.[18] But excluding the most relevant cases and excluding positive law that actually supports the point? This seems to stretch the limit. However, Reeve did just that in *Baron and Femme*. He simply did not seem to feel the need to be bound in his treatise in the ordinary positivist ways. Instead he capitalised on a moment in which a legal scholar could (somewhat surprisingly) actually *invoke* English law as a way to *challenge or contradict* a formulation of that common law in a new environment. This is extremely interesting, creating in effect a version of English law that no English lawyer would agree with, evidenced in this case by rejection of the one-person-in-law maxim. Reeve's treatise was teaching and speaking to lawyers in early America, invoking the authority of the common law while simultaneously challenging and re-creating it. In doing so, he acted as a typical 'fading Federalist', using whatever authority he still possessed (as a judge, teacher and treatise writer) to fashion a new American common law, only loosely connected to England and tied very much to local conditions, despite what it formally claimed and disclaimed.[19]

II. CAN A MARRIED WOMAN MAKE A WILL?

In the preface to *Baron and Femme*, Reeve wrote that 'the governing principle' of each subject must be viewed as the 'pole-star'.[20] In the case of a will, the 'pole-star' was the intention of the testator. In England, married women were expressly prohibited from being testators by statute. A sixteenth-century statute expressly listed married women among those legally incapable of making a will. Connecticut did not formally receive English law after the Revolution. There was no reception statute.[21] And so English statute law, like English common law, did not formally bind the territory. Connecticut jurists like Reeve's own teacher, Jesse Root, stated

[17] Neil Duxbury has written about Frederick Pollock, for instance, that he 'had a crafty knack for slipping his own perspectives into his doctrinal expositions and passing them off as if they were law'. See N Duxbury, *Frederick Pollock and the English Juristic Tradition* (Oxford, UK; New York, NY, Oxford University Press, 2004) 269.

[18] Ibid 222.

[19] See A Fernandez, 'Tapping Reeve, Nathan Dane, and James Kent: Three Fading Federalists on Marital Unity' (Draft in-progress).

[20] Reeve, Preface to *Baron and Femme*.

[21] See C Collier, 'Tapping Reeve, the Connecticut Common Law, and America's First Law School' (2006) 1 *Connecticut Supreme Court History* 13, 19.

that the common law of England was not the common law of Connecticut.[22] And while '[t]he common law of England we are to pay great deference to . . . the rules, however, which have not been made our own by adoption, we are to examine, and so far vary from them as they may appear contrary to reason or unadapted to our local circumstances, the policy of our law, or simplicity of our practice'.[23] As one of Reeve's students put it in the notebook he copied, '[t]he com'[mon] law of Eng. [land] [h]as been accepted so far as it has been considered as applicable to the local circumstances of [this] country; but where it has been considered as inapplicable it has been rejected'.[24] Here then was the opportunity to depart from English common law and English statutory law should there be the desire to do so.

The Connecticut legislature did not speak clearly when it turned its mind to the issue of whether or not married women would be allowed to make wills. When the state revised its laws in 1784, including its statute on testamentary capacity, it added the phrase 'and all others legally incapable' to the list of those who could not make a will.[25] Had the English statute made it notorious that married women were to be included among those 'others' who were rendered legally incapable? Or was it an exclusion that the legislature needed to make explicit? Deviation suggested meaningfulness, Reeve argued, given that the statute was 'in many of its expressions . . . a literal copy' of the English one.[26] Here was a question at least.

The Connecticut Superior Court held in 1786 that the will a married woman made disposing of her own lands was void.[27] This case, *Adams v Kellogg*, was overruled by the Supreme Court of Errors, the state's highest court. Zephaniah Swift wrote in 1795–96, 'the law is now settled, that a married woman may make a devise of her own lands, even to her husband'.[28] Blackstone had written that a married woman could not will lands to her husband as she is 'at the time of mak-

[22] See EG Brown, *British Statutes in American Law, 1776–1836* (Ann Arbor, MI, University of Michigan Press, 1964) 59, n 27. Reeve studied with Root in Hartford from 1770–72, served with him on several political committees, and succeeded to his seat on the Superior Court when Root was appointed Chief Justice in 1798; See CC Goetsch, 'The Litchfield Law School: A Modern View' (unpublished American Society for Legal History paper, 1979) (copies available at the Litchfield Historical Society & Yale Law School Library) 10–11. The creation of 'Connecticut common law' would require reports of Connecticut cases and the cases for an American common law would have to come from somewhere. Root published a collection of Connecticut cases, *Reports of Cases Adjudged in the Superior Court and Supreme Court of Errors, from July A.D. 1789 to June A.D. 1793*, 2 vols (Hartford, CT, Hudson & Goodwin, 1798–1802). He identified one of his motivations as providing an independent nation with its own judicial proceedings. See WW Horton, 'Day, Root and Kirby' (1996) 70 *Connecticut Bar Journal* 407, 413. Litchfield-based Ephraim Kirby produced the first set of print-published American reports in 1789. E Kirby, *Reports of Cases Adjudged in the Superior Court of the State of Connecticut, from the year 1785, to May 1788* (Litchfield, CT, Collier & Adam, 1789).

[23] See Z Swift, *A System of the Laws of the State of Connecticut in Six Books*, vol 1 (Windham, CT, Printed by John Byrne, 1795–96) 144 (relying on *Wilford v Grant*).

[24] *Notebook of Seth Staples*, vol 1 (1798) (Yale Law School Library) 10.

[25] See Reeve, *Baron and Femme* 156.

[26] Ibid 155.

[27] *Adams v Kellogg* (1796) 1 Kirby 195 (Ct. Sup. Ct.).

[28] Swift, *System*, vol 1, 325.

ing it [the will] she is supposed to be under his coercion'.[29] The worry was the usual one that a wife would be pressured by her husband to will her lands to him. Under English law, when a married woman died, her husband was granted 'curtesy' in her lands, a kind of life estate, but only if there were children of the marriage. The husband was never given the fee simple, which stayed with the wife's family. Reeve argued that a husband's curtesy should not depend on the birth of a child despite the rationale for the rule, which was to provide support for children of the marriage.[30] Indeed, Reeve's advocacy for extended rights of curtesy and a married woman's power to make a will, even to her husband, raises the question of whether his was more a case of 'husband's rights' than 'women's rights', particularly for husbands like him from a modest background who married into families of power and wealth like his first wife, Sally Edwards Burr, whose family would have worried about a husband like him.

Zephaniah Swift was another important Connecticut jurist in this period. He too ran a law school but in the northeast part of the state (Litchfield was in the northwest). Swift wrote a number of important legal works, including *A System of the Laws on the State of Connecticut* in 1795–96 (a two-volume set of commentaries on Connecticut law) and a two-volume *Digest of the Laws of the State of Connecticut* in 1822–23. He is sometimes called 'the first American treatise writer' on the basis of this first book despite its Justinian-inspired persons-things-actions structure that made it more like Blackstone's *Commentaries* than a treatise on a discrete and specialised topic.[31] Swift was a Democrat where Reeve was a Federalist. From 1801 to 1815, he and Reeve sat together on the Supreme Court of Connecticut (where both were eligible to sit on the once-a-year session of the Supreme Court of Errors). Not surprisingly, given their rival schools and political backgrounds that were almost literally at war with one another in Connecticut at this time, their views on the bench were 'often divergent'.[32] Swift was much more positivistic in his approach to the law than Reeve was.[33] Swift wrote 'a commentator on the laws must take the laws as he finds them'.[34] As Morton Horwitz put it, Swift 'came as close as any jurist of the age to maintaining that law is what the courts say it is'.[35] On the topic of married women, Swift was also much more

[29] Blackstone, *Commentaries*, vol 1, 432.

[30] See Reeve, *Baron and Femme* 30. Swift criticised the 'born alive' rule, which irrationally excluded children born by caesarean section and included those born who then died. Swift thought that the rule should either be that children were irrelevant (as Reeve desired), or that there should be a simple requirement of children who survive the wife and require support. See Swift, *System*, vol 1, 253.

[31] AWB Simpson, 'The Rise and Fall of the Legal Treatise: Legal Principles and the Forms of Legal Literature' (1981) 48 *University of Chicago Law Review* 632, 669. See also J Cohen, 'Swift, Zephaniah' in AWB Simpson (ed), *Biographical Dictionary of the Common Law* (London, Butterworths, 1984) 499 ('Swift's most important achievements . . . were as one of the earliest American treatise writers').

[32] Horton, 'Day, Root and Kirby' (n 22) 418.

[33] See M Grossberg, *Governing the Hearth: Law and Family in Nineteenth-Century America* (Chapel Hill, NC, University of North Carolina Press, 1985) 22 (describing Reeve's approach as 'political' and 'reformist').

[34] Swift, *System*, vol 1, 292.

[35] MJ Horwitz, *The Transformation of American Law, 1780–1860* (Cambridge, MA, Harvard University Press, 1977) 25. Thanks to Roman Hoyos for pointing me to Horwitz on Swift.

conservative. He opposed separate estates on the grounds that husband and wife could not make a contract with one another and he and Reeve battled over this.[36] Swift accepted Blackstone's maxim that the husband and wife were one person in law. Indeed, his version of the statement replaced Blackstone's emphasis on coverture with an emphasis on 'one will', which was, he wrote, 'placed in the husband'.[37] How then could a married woman make a document purporting to be a reflection of her own will, no longer having one and residing in her husband? Although he must have disagreed with the result in the case, Swift dutifully recorded in his first work, *A System of the Laws*, what *Adams v Kellogg* said the law was – he might not like it but a married woman could make a will of her lands in Connecticut.

This issue, however, did not go away. Reeve and Swift would have found themselves on opposite sides of it as judges in the Supreme Court of Errors in 1805. In this case, *Fitch v Brainerd*, the court reversed itself, declaring that *Adams v Kellogg* 'was not law' after all.[38] After reviewing the relevant statutory and common law history, the court found that there was no established practice in Connecticut of allowing married women to devise. 'For near a century, femes-covert had no estate to devise. The custom for them to devise, if such it may be called, is very recent, as well as very limited – confined, so far as is known, to a few instances, and within the last twenty years'.[39] There is no indication in the report who wrote the decision, but it became known in Connecticut legal circles as the case in which Zephaniah Swift reconsidered how radical the departure from English law should be.[40] Swift's first book, his *System of the Laws*, often argued from principle that the law should be this or that way. His second book in the 1820s is much less likely to start talking about how the law should be. It is a digest and in it he is obviously primarily concerned with gathering together what the state has now said the law is.[41] However, in *Fitch v Brainerd*, Swift could do as a judge (in concert with others) what he did not feel he could do as a legal writer even in 1795–96, namely, reverse a case he thought was bad law. Unlike Reeve, he did not think he could ignore it and say the law was the opposite of what a case from the state's highest court said it was.

Reeve, on the other hand, takes a completely different attitude. His two chapters on the willing issue in *Baron and Femme* do not refer to either *Adams v Kellogg* or *Fitch v Brainerd*. He wrote that he would approach the issue 'independent of any authorities; as if it were a question wholly novel, respecting which there had

[36] The battle resulted in a compromise. Reeve was forced to concede that husbands and wives could not make contracts with each other and women could not have separate estates for their sole separate use and management. However, a married woman could have a separate estate if there was a trustee. See *Nichols v Palmer* (1811) 5 Day 47 (Ct. Sup. Ct. Errors).

[37] Swift, *System*, vol 1, 194 (also quoted at the outset of this paper).

[38] *Fitch v Brainerd* (1805) 2 Day 163 (Ct. Sup. Ct. Errors) 194.

[39] Ibid.

[40] SE Baldwin, 'Zephaniah Swift' in W Draper Lewis (ed) *Great American Lawyers*, vol 2 (Philadelphia, PA, John C Winston, 1907) 101–44 117–18.

[41] Z Swift, *A Digest of the Laws of the State of Connecticut* 2 vols (New Haven, CT, S. Converse, 1822–23).

been no adjudications, and was now to be decided upon principle. In such case, unshackled with precedents, nothing can govern us, in deciding the question, but what is reasonable and right'.[42] He did not say there were no authorities. He said he would treat the question 'as if' there were none.[43] We know that Reeve promulgated this 'as if' approach almost 15 years before he was over-ruled in *Fitch v Brainerd* and he might have been doing it for even longer, strongly suggesting that he did not ignore Connecticut case law simply because it was unfavourable to him. Indeed, the earliest available version of these lectures on a married woman's right to make a will were given in 1791, at a time when he could have relied on *Adams v Kellogg* to support him and did not.[44] Authorities for or against were not determinative. '[I]f the authorities teach a different doctrine . . . nothing more can be inferred from this, than that the law, in this instance, is unreasonable'. While admittedly, '[n]o maxim is of more utility to the community than stare decisis', Reeve wrote, 'we can never fail to decide on that side which is reasonable and right'.[45] A *de novo* treatment, with complete disregard of the cases in the jurisdiction, was a perfectly legitimate way to arrive at a statement of what the law was.

Reeve's reasoning is a remarkable statement of pure principle given the absence of any connection to precedent. The spirit that motivated it seems very similar to the Supreme Court of Errors' blanket pronouncement that *Adams v Kellogg* was no longer (and maybe never was) law. However, a court of law is authorised to issue such statements, make law or over-rule if necessary its previous decisions. In the hierarchy of formal sources of law, a treatise cannot do this, no matter how authoritative its author is. It can recommend that the law be changed (because it is bad, unreasonable, immoral, inefficient, ugly or for any other reason); but a common law treatise ignoring case law and setting out what the law is in opposition to what case law in the jurisdiction says stands in serious danger of simply being characterised as a bad treatise. So, for instance, in 1804, in a case called *Dibble v Hutton*, the Supreme Court of Errors adopted the Coke/Blackstone version of the one-person-in-law maxim in no uncertain terms: 'By the common law, the husband and wife are considered as one person in law, the existence of the wife being merged in that of the husband, or suspended during the coverture'.[46] How could Reeve continue to write what he did in *Baron and Femme* about this issue in the face of such a ruling? This was not just 'law-making by treatise' but over-ruling by treatise.[47]

Some contemporaries did see Reeve's treatise as a bad treatise. One former student, Edward Deering Mansfield, who moved to Ohio, 'the new Connecticut', and wrote his own (extremely conservative) book on married women's property rights, said that 'the lawyers admired [Reeve's treatise on Domestic Relations],

[42] Reeve, *Baron and Femme* 137.

[43] Ibid.

[44] *Notebook of Eliphalet Dyer*, vol 2 (1791) 74, Connecticut Historical Society.

[45] Reeve, *Baron and Femme* 137.

[46] *Dibble v Hutton* (1804) 1 Day 221 (Ct. Sup. Ct. Errors) 235.

[47] M Moers Wenig, 'The Marital Property Law of Connecticut: Past, Present and Future' (1990) *Wisconsin Law Review* 807, 844.

but said [it] was not law, on account, I believe, of its leaning too much to women's rights'.[48] In making this statement, Deering seems to have been politely saying that this is what he thought. I am sure Swift would also have viewed the book that way, both for its disregard for the positive law in Connecticut and for being too progressive on women's issues.

III. WHY DID REEVE ARGUE AS HE DID?

Reeve's promotion of women's rights was almost certainly related to his religion. Reeve was an ardent Congregationalist, the traditional dominant sect of Calvinist Protestantism in New England, and he was very active in a movement known as the 'Second Great Awakening' in Connecticut, a long revival that took place in New England in the 1790s. Women had special roles to play in this kind of evangelical movement. They constituted the greatest number of converts during revivals, and they figured prominently in the organisational efforts of reform organisations, including anti-slavery and temperance groups. Indeed, the era has been called 'an age of female societies' given the importance of women in raising money and organising various charitable and other kinds of institutionally-organised activities.[49] Women moved outside the domestic sphere in order to participate in these activities, raising their prominence and importance in areas that men like Reeve cared about and were impressed by the ability to make achievements in.

High numbers of female participants in religious activity in this period have led some scholars to speak about the 'feminization of Protestantism'.[50] Doctrines like infant damnation – something that caused particular distress to mothers who lost children before they could be baptised – came up for reconsideration.[51] Fear of death in childbirth and fear of losing young children helps explain why women turned in such high numbers to religion and voluntary associations like prayer groups.[52] Participating in religiously organised activities outside the home gave women an opportunity to express their 'moral, intellectual, and physical powers in

[48] See E Deering Mansfield, *Personal Memoirs: Social, Political, and Literary, with Sketches of Many Noted People, 1803–1843* (Cincinnati, OH, Robert Clarke, 1879) 127. Deering supported allowing married women to make wills but in his book, written for women, encouraging them to celebrate the loss of personal independence upon marriage, he provided the one-person-in-law maxim with biblical support and reversed everything Reeve taught him about the powers and independence of married women. See E Deering Mansfield, *Legal Rights, Liabilities, and Duties of Women* (Salem, MA, John P Jewett, 1845) 211, 262–63, 273.

[49] See CR Keller, *The Second Great Awakening in Connecticut* (New Haven, CT, Yale University Press, 1942) 233.

[50] See NF Cott, *The Bonds of Womanhood: 'Woman's Sphere' in New England, 1780–1835* (New Haven, CT, Yale University Press, 1977) 132. See also B Welter, 'The Feminization of American Religion: 1800–1860' in MS Hartman and LW Banner (eds), *Clio's Consciousness Raised: New Perspectives on the History of Women* (New York, NY, Harper & Row, 1974) 137–57; RD Shiels, 'The Feminization of American Congregationalism, 1730–1835' (1981) 33 *American Quarterly* 46.

[51] See Welter, 'The Feminization of American Religion', ibid 139.

[52] See Cott, *The Bonds of Womanhood* (n 50) 144.

other ways'.[53] Piety (and particularly Calvinist self-examination) 'allowed women a sort of holy selfishness, or self-absorption . . . requir[ing] attention to one's own thoughts, actions, and prospects'.[54]

Reeve's first wife, Sally, was actually the grand-daughter of the architect of the 'First Great Awakening', Jonathan Edwards, the religious movement in the 1740s that originally split revivalists and non-revivalists in both Congregational and Presbyterian communities in New England; 'New Lights' accused 'Old Lights' of being asleep in a dead religion.[55] Individuals like Timothy Dwight, Joseph Bellamy and Lyman Beecher created a school in the 'Second Great Awakening' known as 'New Divinity'. These were the descendants of Edwards who, rather than revolting against strict Calvinist doctrines relating to issues like pre-destination as Unitarians did, 'fought for orthodoxy within the church through revivals, modifying it, liberalizing it, rendering it more acceptable by making it more reasonable'.[56] Dwight was related to Reeve by marriage – his mother was another of Jonathan Edwards' daughters.[57] Reeve's brother-in-law, Sally's brother, none other than Aaron Burr, studied theology with Bellamy prior to coming to Litchfield to study law with Reeve.[58] Burr was alone among the founding fathers for holding anything remotely like feminist views, which it is a mistake to try to understand without a sense of his neo-Edwardsean background.[59] Sally and Aaron Burr's father, Aaron Burr Senior, was the first president of the College in New Jersey that would become Princeton, originally organised as a 'New Light' institution. Their mother, Esther Edwards Burr, was an intellectual woman deeply steeped in the traditions of pious self-examination.[60] Beecher was a close associate of Reeve's when Beecher was in Litchfield.[61] Beecher gave a special sermon for Reeve when he died.[62] In it, Beecher claimed Reeve for New Divinity.[63] He also noted that Reeve visited many individuals engaged in the conversion process, saying that no one viewed more people or was more familiar with their conversion experiences.[64] This brought

[53] Ibid 138.

[54] Ibid 140.

[55] See generally WG McLoughlin' in *Revivals, Awakenings, and Reform: an Essay on Religion and Social Change in America, 1607–1977* (Chicago, IL, University of Chicago Press, 1978).

[56] Keller, *The Second Great Awakening* (n 49) 229.

[57] See DH Fischer, 'Dwight, Timothy' in *The Revolution of American Conservatism: the Federalist Party in the Era of Jeffersonian Democracy* (New York, NY, Harper & Row, 1965) Appendix II 286–88.

[58] N Isenberg, *Fallen Founder: The Life of Aaron Burr* (New York, NY, Penguin, 2007) 16.

[59] Ibid 413 (calling Burr 'the only founder to embrace feminism'). Isenberg points out that Burr was a great admirer of Mary Wollstonecraft's *Vindication of the Rights of Woman* and thought there should be an American version. She thinks he thought he was the one to write it. See ibid 240.

[60] See CF Karlsen and L Crumpacker (eds), *The Journal of Esther Edwards Burr, 1754–1757* (New Haven, CT, Yale University Press, 1984).

[61] See B Cross (ed), *Autobiography of Lyman Beecher*, vol 1 (Cambridge, MA, Harvard University Press, 1961) 156, 170–72.

[62] L Beecher, 'Memoir of the Honourable Tapping Reeve' (Feb, 1827) *Christian Spectator* 62.

[63] Beecher described Reeve's views as those 'explained and vindicated . . . by Edwards, and Bellamy, and West, and Hopkins, and Dwight'. Ibid 67. Reeve's list of books included titles like 'Edwards's works', 'Bellamy's Discourses' and 'Dwight's Theology'. See 'Copy of Tapping Reeve's Inventory. Re[ceived] & accepted Feb[ruar]y 14th AD. 1824. F Wolcott, Judge', Litchfield Historical Society.

[64] Beecher, 'Memoir' 66–67. See also *Autobiography of Lyman Beecher*, vol 1, 272–77.

Reeve into exchanges with women in his community who were also active in the movement.[65] He supported a school for girls that some have said offered more than training in the elegant accomplishments.[66]

Revivalist Congregationalism actually contained the seeds of an equality-oriented understanding of women and the husband-wife relation. The idea of marriage as friendship had antecedents in the religious philosophy of New Light Divine, John Witherspoon.[67] One of Reeve's students who sat with him for a time as a judge and would go on to become governor of Connecticut, John Cotton Smith, noted that Reeve allowed Sally to remain in control of the fortune she inherited from her family. Smith remembered that, like his own father, who allowed his mother to retain control of her own property, the two men rejected 'that portion of the old English Common Law which takes away all property rights from married women. Both of them had *shown their faith by their works*'.[68] The religious formulation is no mere adornment. New Divinity deeply informed where these people were coming from. There is probably a connection between it and the rough equality of the sexes that Cornelia Hughes Dayton has found in older Puritan culture.[69] Reeve and Smith were both involved in the Connecticut Bible Society. John Cotton Smith was its first president and Reeve was a local agent.[70] Smith was known as the last Puritan governor, as he was the last Federalist Governor in Connecticut prior to religious disestablishment in the state.[71] The surprisingly progressive views about married women's property rights we find in Reeve's lectures and writing must be understood against this religious background. And his insistence on pure principle is probably motivated in part by how desperate the larger war had become by the time he published the book in 1816.

Federalists lost control of the state in 1817 when the 'Stelligeri' or Democrats challenged the Federalist 'Standing Order' and won. Swift, a Deist, was an early member of this group.[72] Connecticut's first constitution was enacted shortly thereafter, in 1818, and it brought in disestablishment of the Congregationalist religion.[73] It also adopted the Federal Constitution's separation of powers between

[65] See, eg Tapping Reeve to Maria Cushman, [?27?] November 1814, Litchfield Historical Society.

[66] See AM Siegel, '"To Learn and Make Respectable Hereafter': The Litchfield Law School in Cultural Context' (1998) 73 *New York University Law Review* 1978.

[67] Isenberg, *Fallen Founder* (n 58) 72.

[68] H Evertson Smith, *Colonial Ways and Days* (New York, NY, Century, 1900) 304–5 (emphasis added).

[69] See C Hughes Dayton, *Women Before the Bar: Gender, Law and Society in Connecticut, 1639–1789* (Chapel Hill, NC, University of North Carolina Press, 1995); C Hughes Dayton, 'Was There a Calvinist Type of Patriarchy?' in CL Tomlins and BH Mann (eds), *The Many Legalities of Early America* (Chapel Hill, NC, University of North Carolina Press, 2001). See more generally, RJ Ross, 'The Career of Puritan Jurisprudence' (2008) 113 *Law and History Review* 975.

[70] See Keller, *The Second Great Awakening* (n 49) 110–11.

[71] Ibid 58.

[72] See DF Gerardi, 'Zephaniah Swift and Connecticut's Standing Order: Skepticism, Conservatism, and Religious Liberty in the Early Republic' (1994) 67 *The New England Quarterly* 234, 239.

[73] See ML Greene, *The Development of Religious Liberty in Connecticut* (New York, NY, Houghton, Mifflin, 1905).

the legislative, executive and judicial branches of government. This is something Swift had long advocated and it is indeed one of the things he is chiefly remembered for.[74] So, prior to this change, the Supreme Court of Errors was a court that mixed legislative and judicial functions, like the 'General Court' of the colonial period in Massachusetts.[75] To modern eyes, this might explain why Reeve did not show a lot of respect for the cases produced by the Supreme Court of Errors.[76] However, I think that this would not have been grounds for disrespect to Reeve, as he was a staunch proponent of that pre-1818 'mixed' tradition. Indeed, I think, just the opposite, he would have seen himself – literally, in his physical person – as if he were a source of law, whether he was standing lecturing in front of his students, sitting in the state courts or writing his book.

So, for instance, when discussing in *Baron and Femme* the question of seisin and whether 'seisin-in-fact' was required in order for a husband to take curtesy in his deceased wife's land as in England, or whether 'seisin-in-law' would be sufficient, Reeve quoted from the following 1810 case, *Bradley v Bush*: 'our system of law respecting real property, is, in many instances, very different from the English system . . . if we reject our own [rule], and adopt theirs, we shall mar the symmetry of our law'.[77] This is a great example of a classical Connecticut rejection of English common law, consistent with the training and orientation Reeve would have received from Jesse Root. The court held here that actual seisin of a wife's lands was not required for a husband's curtesy. What Reeve does not point out in his discussion of this in the book is that this was in fact one of his own decisions. The words quoted from are actually his own.[78] Here is Reeve blurring the boundaries of his different roles, judge and treatise-writer, so as to achieve persuasive effect in his teaching book. Calling *Bush v Bradley* a case where 'seven of the judges concurred', with not a whisper of his own involvement as he did, sounds a lot more detached, objective and ultimately more convincing than saying, 'as I said in *Bush v Bradley*, this is an important principle, and I got the others to agree'. Like the mixed and blurry legal, political and religious order he was struggling to maintain, Reeve was not going to think too much about a separation of identities or distinguishing between the different capacities in which he was operating. Publication of the book in 1816 of what he had been teaching all those years certainly must be understood as a last hurrah for the world-view that he

[74] See Swift, *System*, vol 1, 28. See, eg EC Goodwin, *The Magistracy Rediscovered: Connecticut, 1636–1818* (Ann Arbor, MI, UMI Research Press, 1981) 1, 95–115.

[75] See CA Desan, 'Remaking Constitutional Tradition at the Margin of the Empire: The Creation of Legislative Adjudication in Colonial New York' (1998) 16 *Law and History Review* 258; 'The Constitutional Commitment to Legislative Adjudication in the Early American Tradition' (1998) 111 *Harvard Law Review* 1381.

[76] See, eg SE Baldwin, 'Historical Sketch of the Supreme Court of Errors of Connecticut' in B Clark (ed), *The Supreme Court of the States and Provinces of North America*, vol 1 (New York, NY, Medico-Legal Journal, 1895) 384 (where Baldwin suggests that this body does not become a real court until 1808).

[77] Reeve, *Baron and Femme* 33.

[78] See *Bush v Bradley* (1810) 4 Day 298 (Ct. Sup. Ct. Errors) 305.

embodied. It was one due to be replaced by Swift's, who did actually replace him as Chief Justice in 1815.[79]

Reeve fought hard against the transfer of ruling power away from the Federalists on a national level. He wrote in one of Litchfield's newspapers against Thomas Jefferson with a vehemence that landed him in a seditious libel prosecution under the *Alien and Sedition Act*.[80] Swift embodied much of the new order – a positivist orientation in law book writing (cases and statutes matter, they cannot simply be ignored); more clearly delineated roles for judges and law teachers writing treatises (you can over-rule a case as a judge but not as a treatise writer); conservatism on married women's property rights; a separation of church and state; and a separation of powers. Swift would win the war and not just in Connecticut. However, there was one battle Reeve won. He got his students to do what *Fitch v Brainerd* said would have to be done in order to allow married women to make wills, namely, pass a statute empowering them to do so.[81]

This remarkable and extremely short statute in 1809 set out simply that 'married women shall have the power of disposing of their estates by last will and testament'.[82] There were at least 15 of Reeve's former students in the House of Representatives when it was passed.[83] Among these was the Speaker of the House, Lyman Law. Law attended the school the same year as another student, Eliphalet Dyer, and Dyer's notebooks show that the students that year were treated to an essay by Reeve entitled 'Can a feme covert by the laws of Connecticut devise her real Estate?' This essay substantially reproduces what was later included in the two chapters of *Baron and Femme*.[84] John Cotton Smith was also a member of the May 1809 legislative session that passed this statute, as were several classmates from his year. We know Smith was ideologically on board, given the comments he made about his own mother and Sally Reeve noted above. He was also a general proponent of Reeve's views, helping in the publication of Reeve's second book

[79] Horton, 'Day, Root and Kirby' (n 22) 418.

[80] See RG Wetmore, 'Seditious Libel Prosecutions in 1806 in the Federal Court in Connecticut: United States *v. Tapping Reeve*, and Companion Cases' (1983) 57 *Connecticut Bar Journal* 196. One study concluded that the prosecution was dropped because Reeve was 'a nationally revered figure'. See CA Heckman, 'A Jeffersonian Lawyer and Judge in Federalist Connecticut: The Career of Pierpont Edwards' (1996) 28 *Connecticut Law Review* 669, 701.

[81] *Fitch v Brainerd* (n 38) 194.

[82] 'An Act in Addition to 'An Act relating to the age, ability and capacity of Persons'', ch VII, 1809 *Connecticut Public Acts* 15 (May Sess. 1809).

[83] Shubael Griswold (1809); Roger Whittlesey (1788); Ezekiel P Belden (1797); Joseph Bulkley (1810); Nathan Smith (1790); Augustus Collins (1804); John Kingsbury (1788); Lyman Law (1791); Samuel Blackman (1796); James Stevens (1796); Aaron Smith (1791); John C Smith (1788); Daniel Brindsmyaide (1803); Phineas Miner (1796); and Noah B Benedict (1789). This list was generated by cross-referencing the names and years of attendance from Samuel H Fisher, Litchfield Law School, 1774–1833. *Biographical Catalogue of Students* (New Haven, CT, Yale University Press, 1946) with the 109-person list of the members of the House of Representatives, May Session, 1809 in *Roll of State Officers and Members of General Assembly of Connecticut 1776 to 1881* (Hartford, CT, Case, Lockwood & Brainard, 1881) 173–175.

[84] *Notebook of Eliphalet Dyer*, vol 2, 74. Comparative analysis on file with the author.

after Reeve's death.[85] Referring to Reeve's 'celebrated pamphlet on "The Domestic Relations"', Smith noted that Reeve's was 'the first voice ever publically raised in our country . . . in [sic] behalf of the property rights of married women'.[86] While he may have 'stood almost alone among the lawyers of his day', Smith recalled, 'in his school he made many disciples'.[87] Another former student wrote that Reeve's treatment of 'the axiom that "a married woman has no will of her own"' caused his students to leave the lecture room 'the very knight errants of the law burning to be the defenders of the right and avengers of the wrong; and he is no true son of the Litchfield school who has ever forgot that lesson'.[88] It stands to reason that these Litchfield sons, disciples, knight errants, changed the law when they had the opportunity to do so.

Swift was forced to write in his *Digest of the Laws*, '[w]hether a married woman can devise her lands is a question that has been much agitated, but the legislature have put it to rest, by giving her that power'.[89] Why would Reeve have failed to take note of this in his own book?

The substantial similarity between Dyer's essay and what ultimately appeared in *Baron and Femme* makes one wonder whether Reeve simply failed to update his lectures before publishing the book. We know he was keen to receive the proceeds from book sales after he was forced to retire from the bench in 1815 and lost that portion of his income.[90] He wrote to one student, 'I have arrived at that time in my life that I can no longer hold a seat on the Bench so that I have to depend on my school and the books I publish for a livelihood'.[91] Perhaps he was in too much of a rush to publish to update. However, he did make one change in the text in response to *Fitch v Brainerd*.[92] This shows that Reeve was not simply dropping the lectures into his text *holus-bolus* with no thought about what had happened to the topic over the 25 years he had been teaching it.

[85] T Reeve, *A Treatise on the Law of Descents in the Several States of America* (New York, NY, Collins & Hannay, 1825); See J Calder, *Life and Times of Tapping Reeve and his Law School* (Paper prepared pursuant to a Master's Degree, University of Vermont & Litchfield Historical Society Internship, 1978) (copies available at the Litchfield Historical Society & Yale Law School) 28.

[86] Smith, *Colonial Ways and Days* (n 68) 304.

[87] Ibid.

[88] DC Kilbourn, *The Bench and Bar of Litchfield County, Connecticut, 1709–1909: Biographical Sketches of Members, History and Catalogue of the Litchfield Law School, Historical Notes* (Litchfield, CT, 1909) 187. This former student was Charles Loring. He attended in 1813.

[89] Swift, *Digest*, vol 2, 39.

[90] A state statute in 1811 brought in mandatory retirement at age 70, which Reeve reached in 1815. See Baldwin, 'Historical Sketch of the Supreme Court of Errors' (n 76) 387.

[91] Tapping Reeve to Samuel Law, 4 March 1817, Litchfield Historical Society, Litchfield, Connecticut. Once he was forced to retire from the school, Reeve's financial situation worsened. See Calder, *The Life and Times of Tapping Reeve* (n 85) 27–28. A letter sent to students to raise money for him in 1822 is reproduced in MC McKenna, *Tapping Reeve and the Litchfield Law School* (Dobbs Ferry, NY, Oceana Publications, 1986) 199–200.

[92] The essay in Dyer's notebook asked: 'Are the rights of an Heir of a feme more [?favoured?] than those of a Baron[']s?' Reeve left this rhetorical question out of *Baron and Femme*, since *Fitch v Brainerd* had made it clear that actually, yes, unless the legislature made it otherwise, the contingent rights of an heir were more favoured than those of a husband. *Notebook of Eliphalet Dyer*, vol 2, 75.

It is possible that Reeve saw legislation as too vulnerable to change to be part of the law *Baron and Femme* described. His students banded together and passed the law; but it could be undone by a future similar campaign in the legislature. I do not think that his failure to discuss the statute, which he must surely have known about given the size of the legal community, his place in it, and his great interest in this subject, was due to a general contempt for statutory law. He discussed English statutes at length but not this local statute. He also included English cases but not local ones. Unlike Swift, who deliberately put Connecticut in the title of his works and showed no hesitancy about describing the law in the state, Reeve set out in *Baron and Femme* to describe the English common law in such a way as 'to render the book, if of any value, equally valuable to all parts of our country'.[93]

Swift's more local focus explains why his work is not more well-known and why it was not included in Pound's speeches on the textbook teaching tradition. Yes, Swift was producing textbooks. Yes, he was even a teacher as well as a judge. However, Swift would not have been thought to have a sufficiently national perspective, a key component of the full-time Harvard Law School model Pound promoted. Reeve, on the other hand, took himself to be describing English common law that could form the basis of an American common law. Here was the orientation fellow-Federalists like Kent (in New York) and Dane (in Massachusetts) would have found appealing, the same one that would have contributed to Pound's choice to place Reeve at the beginning of the 'tough-law' textbook tradition. If it was somehow 'soft' to try to describe local state rules as they were embodied in cases and statutes from a particular jurisdiction that practitioners from that jurisdiction cared most about, this inverted the usual dichotomy between the tough/hard/masculine world of practice and the weak/soft/effeminate academic world. The fact that we know about Reeve but not about Swift is connected to a larger struggle over the professionalisation of law teaching and the triumph of the full-time Harvard model over part-time practitioners and judges in the twentieth century's conception of the best kind of academic legal education. However, this is too large a story to recount here.[94]

It is tempting then to excuse Reeve's failure to discuss the Connecticut cases and statute on the willing issue on the grounds that this was, unlike Swift, simply not his project. Reeve wrote that the 'object' of the work was 'to exhibit the Common Law of England and such of their Statutes as we have adopted in words or principle'.[95] *Baron and Femme* was intended to be a description of English law. However, at the same time, Reeve gave himself the option of referring to

[93] Reeve, Preface to *Baron and Femme.*

[94] Part of it is that Harvard chose Litchfield as the place to trace its intellectual lineage and Simeon Eben Baldwin chose Swift for Yale. I describe this adoption of allegiances and its mapping onto the larger struggle for the professionalisation of legal education in A Fernandez, 'Spreading the Word: From the Litchfield Law School to the Harvard Case Method' (JSD Dissertation, Yale Law School, 2007).

[95] Reeve, Preface to *Baron and Femme.*

Connecticut when it was favourable to do so.[96] This approach, a description of English law that could selectively refer to Connecticut but need not do so, is what allowed Reeve to ignore a case like *Dibble v Hutton* in which a Connecticut court actually said that the Coke/Blackstone maxim was a correct statement of the common law and continue to write as if this was undecided in *Baron and Femme*. He and Swift could fight it out over this in the Supreme Court of Errors and Reeve could lose; yet, this had no effect on how the common law could be formulated in the version of English law imagined and possibly followed by other states. We might think of this as a fictional or mystical notion of English law. It could not be actual English law if it was impossible to find a single English lawyer who would reject Coke and Blackstone on the point. This was a local battle in Connecticut, which Reeve lost. Yet all of this is invisible in the treatise, as was also the larger tectonic shifts of power and authority in the state. However, Reeve was using the book to continue the fight in the only way he could, writing for lawyers in other states, whom he hoped would find his version of the common law persuasive. This is typical of fading Federalist jurists like James Kent who used their law teaching and didactic writings to continue to exert influence that it becomes impossible for them to exert in the political world. As Daniel Hulsebosch has put it:

> Federalists turned to the nonlegislative dimensions of law and legal training, the areas of legal culture that were beyond the reach of electoral politics . . . [I]f they could not control decision making directly, they could try to control the raw material on which decisions were made: the reports, treatises, handbooks, and educational institutions that inculcated law's purpose . . . [resulting in the] painstaking acculturation of lawyers and judges in a supposedly nonpartisan legal culture.[97]

In is unsurprising that Reeve faced with the sea-changes he was tried to exert influence in this way with his book and among his students. Given the connections between Federalism and religion, at least in Connecticut,[98] and Reeve's religion and his views on married women's rights, this is surely an example of a New England scholar using 'scholarly means to evangelical ends'.[99] What we must notice, however, is how paradoxical it is for Reeve to have used English law in the way he did, to harness its authority while at the same time undermining it with a quintessentially Connecticut or Puritan-based jurisprudence that strongly rejected English law and a maxim as fundamental as one-person-in-law.

[96] The way Reeve put it was to say that he has 'seldom mentioned the law of the state in which he lives; unless that difference arises in causes equally operative in all parts of the Union where it differs from the Common Law; or where an explanation of it has, in his opinion, served the purpose of shedding light upon the Common Law'. Ibid.

[97] DJ Hulsebosch, *Constituting Empire: New York and the Transformation of Constitutionalism in the Atlantic World, 1664–1830* (Chapel Hill, NC, University of North Carolina Press, 2005) 278–79.

[98] Keller, *The Second Great Awakening* (n 49) 56 ('Religion must be kept in mind when attempting to explain Federalism – in Connecticut at any rate').

[99] L Stevenson, *Scholarly Means to Evangelical Ends: The New Haven Scholars and the Transformation of Higher Learning in America, 1830–1890* (Baltimore, MD, Johns Hopkins University Press, 1986), referred to in SA Siegel, 'Joel Bishop's Orthodoxy' (1995) 13 *Law and History Review* 215, 252.

IV. CONCLUSIONS

Although Reeve called his book a description of English law, it was struggles in his own state and his involvement in them that made him passionate about married women's property rights and influenced the content of his 'teaching and preaching attitude'.[100] His views were strongly rooted in New England and Connecticut culture and concerns, most notably the equality-oriented idea of marriage underlying his desire to reverse the one-person-in-law maxim. However, by calling his views English law and by leaving out of the book the twists and turns in his battles with Swift, Reeve studiously avoided any sense that his ideas and views were Connecticut-specific. Indeed, given the simple description of what was 'reasonable and right', it was difficult on the basis of Reeve's text to understand what was controversial about allowing married women to make wills or why married women would ever be described as of one will with their husbands. Unlike Swift, Reeve did not put 'Connecticut' in the title of the work. He wanted to provide an account that could be adopted in all states, even if it was informed by New England and Connecticut in its essential aspects. In other words, he was, like a good Federalist, teaching and providing didactic works that could be used to build a common national account, an American common law. This national dimension explains Pound's interest in Reeve and the placement of *Baron and Femme* at the beginning of a 'tough' 'taught law' tradition despite the fact that Reeve's operation was pre-professionalised and very different from the Harvard full-time teaching model Pound was promoting.[101] Reeve was producing an account he was trying to export, in the physical bodies of his students and in their notebooks. In this way and through publication of the lectures in his book, Reeve might manage to 'Connecticutize the world'.[102]

Given the way that Blackstone made one-person-in-law part of the political and legal firmament of the nineteenth century, it is difficult to appreciate in retrospect that here was a moment in which things really could have been different.[103] As Dirk Hartog has demonstrated in his work on the law of husband and wife, in actual fact, coverture was constantly being outweighed by other policies in the courtroom, which provided public recognition of the separate legal identities of

[100] C Grasso, *A Speaking Aristocracy: Transforming Public Discourse in Eighteenth-Century Connecticut* (Chapel Hill, NC, University of North Carolina Press, 1999) 264 (quoting Yale president Ezra Stiles).

[101] These lectures were given two years before the United States Supreme Court ruled that there was no federal common law that federal courts could use when hearing state claims under diversity jurisdiction. However, in 1936, *Swift v Tyson*, Joseph Story's creation of federal common law for the states was still controlling. See *Erie Railroad Co v Tompkins*, 304 US 64, (1938); *Swift v Tyson*, 41 US 1 (1842).

[102] Grasso, 'A Speaking Aristocracy' (n 100) 376 (quoting from a biography of Timothy Dwight by Kenneth Silverman).

[103] Unjustifiably, as scholars like Mary Beard have shown. Beard's argument was that Blackstone completely ignored equity when he stated that husband and wife were one-person-in-law. See M Beard, *Women as Force in History: A Study in Traditions and Realities* (New York, NY, Collier Books, 1962). See also Stretton (n 2) (tracing the older history of one-person-in-law, showing that while it was present in legal writing before Blackstone, Blackstone gave it its most significant force and effect).

wives.[104] The legal fiction, in other words, was often rejected as the fiction it was.[105] Laura Edwards points out that enthusiasm for Blackstone on one-person-in-law was by no means universal.[106] 'Variant readings', of which Reeve was certainly one, 'were very much in evidence in the late eighteenth and early nineteenth centuries'.[107] What looks to us now like a very particular version of the local, Reeve's Connecticut, might well have come to be the generally and nationally shared view. So, for instance, relying on *Baron and Femme*, Nathan Dane wrote in his digest and abridgement of American law in 1823 that because married women can do many of the things that presuppose separate legal existence (eg being liable to punishment for crimes, being a guardian, giving a receipt), the one-person-in-law maxim was 'now almost done away [with]'.[108] That is really quite a remarkable statement. Here was a moment in which what I have argued was Reeve's locally-inspired view powered the resistance of Blackstone at a national level.[109] Yes, Reeve lost to Swift in Connecticut. However, there was still the chance that Reeve's Connecticut-informed view might actually become American common law. The fact that it did not heightens the need to understand how things might have been different, and how they were in fact different at different times and places, both on-the-ground and in-the-books.

[104] See Hartog, *Man and Wife in America* (n 3) 128–31.

[105] See ibid 107.

[106] LF Edwards, *The People and Their Peace: Legal Culture and the Transformation of Inequality in the Post-Revolutionary South* (Chapel Hill, NC, University of North Carolina Press, 2009) 104 ('[S]outherners in the late eighteenth and early nineteenth centuries were decidedly less enthusiastic about Blackstone's version of domestic authority than later generations – and later historians').

[107] Ibid 105.

[108] Dane (n 13), vol 1, 332.

[109] On the importance of the 'local', its connection to public conceptions of the peace, and its contra-distinction to formal sources of state law (cases, statutes, legal treatises), see Edwards, *The People and Their Peace* (n 106). Edwards takes Reeve's *Baron and Femme* to be a typical example of the latter category rather than the former, helping to create universal rules based in individual rights at the state level that excluded localised law. See 251–53.

4

Story'd Paradigms for the Nineteenth-Century Display of Anglo-American Legal Doctrine

G BLAINE BAKER*

IT HAS BEEN said of Joseph Story that when the history of the Anglo-American legal treatise comes to be written, his name will be conspicuous in it.[1] Story's nine texts on American public and private law, written between 1829 and 1845, collectively went through about 75 editions before the turn of the twentieth century.[2] In the two generations that have elapsed since Theodore Plucknett prophesied Story's centrality to accounts of the treatise as a distinc-

* Faculty of Law and Institute of Comparative Law, McGill University. I am grateful to the Toronto Legal History Group, Angela Fernandez, and Rande Kostal for commentary on an earlier version of this chapter.

[1] See TFT Plucknett, *Early English Legal Literature* (Cambridge, Cambridge University Press, 1958) 19. See also P Miller, *The Life of the Mind in America from the Revolution to the Civil War* (New York, NY, Harcourt, Brace and World, 1965) 239–69; R Pound, *The Formative Era of American Law* (Boston, MA, Little, Brown, 1938)) 152–53.

[2] See J Story, *Commentaries on the Law of Bailments, with Illustrations from the Civil and Foreign Law* (Cambridge, MA, Hilliard, Brown, 1832); J Story, *Commentaries on the Constitution of the United States, with a Preliminary Review of the Constitutional History of the Colonies and States Before the Adoption of the Constitution* (Boston, MA, Hilliard, Gray and Company, 3 vols, 1833); J Story, *Commentaries on the Conflict of Laws, Foreign and Domestic in Regard to Contracts, Rights, and Remedies, and Especially in Regard to Marriages, Divorces, Wills, Successions, and Judgments* (Boston, MA, Hilliard, Gray and Company, 1834); J Story, *Commentaries on Equity Jurisprudence, as Administered in England and America (Boston MA, Hilliard, Gray and Company*, 2 vols, 1836); J Story, *Commentaries on Equity Pleadings, and the Incidents Thereof, According to the Practice of the Courts of Equity of England and America* (Boston, MA, CC Little and J Brown, 1838); J Story, *Commentaries on the Law of Agency as a Branch of Commercial and Maritime Jurisprudence, With Occasional Illustrations from the Civil and Foreign Law* (Boston, MA, Little, 1839); J Story, *Commentaries on the Law of Partnership, as a Branch of Commercial and Maritime Jurisprudence, with Occasional Illustrations from the Civil and Foreign Law* (Boston, MA, CC Little and J Brown, 1841); J Story, *Commentaries on the Law of Bills of Exchange, Foreign and Inland, as Administered in England and America: With Occasional Illustrations from the Commercial Law of Nations of Continental Europe* (Boston, MA, CC Little and J Brown, 1843); J Story, *Commentaries on the Law of Promissory Notes and Guarantees of Notes, and Checks on Banks and Bankers: With Occasional Illustrations from the Commercial Law of Nations of Europe* (Boston, MA, CC Little and J Brown, 1845).

tive form of nineteenth-century legal literature, several careful treatments of the North Atlantic treatise tradition have appeared.[3] Those essays have been complemented by a solid biography of Story, and by a handful of shorter works on his extra-judicial writing.[4] There has also been a groundswell of scholarship that deals with specific English, Canadian, and American legal treatises, which has typically drawn on authors or texts that marked the last decades of the nineteenth century as the zenith of Anglo-American treatise-writing in law.[5] Story has been a kind of brooding omnipresence in that secondary literature, which has taken cues from a revitalised history of the book.[6] But his monumental set of treatises has not yet attracted detailed scholarly attention, individually or collectively.

This article is not intended to fill that large historiographical gap. But it will offer a tentative assessment of Story's role in shifting trends in the production of early- and mid-nineteenth-century Anglo-American legal literature, and suggestions about what he intended his treatises to do from epistemological, pedagogical, political and commercial points of view. If there are brooding omnipresences in those accounts, they are natural science, professional consolidation, federalism and economic subsidisation.

[3] See, eg J Davies, 'Aspects of Nineteenth Century Legal Literature' (1998) 29 *The Cambrian Law Review* 22; D Sugarman, 'Legal Theory, the Common Law Mind, and the Making of the Textbook Tradition' in W Twining (ed), *Legal Theory and Common Law* (Oxford, Basil Blackwell, 1986) 26; AWB Simpson, 'The Rise and Fall of the Legal Treatise: Legal Principles and the Forms of Legal Literature' (1981) 48 *University of Chicago Law Review* 632.

[4] See RK Newmyer, *Supreme Court Justice Joseph Story: Statesman of the Old Republic* (Chapel Hill, NC, University of North Carolina Press, 1985). See also GB Baker, 'Interstate Choice of Law and Early-American Constitutional Nationalism' (1993) 38 *McGill Law Journal* 454; G Kegel, 'Story and Savigny' (1989) 37 *American Journal of Comparative Law* 39; HJ Powell, 'Joseph Story's Commentaries on the Constitution: A Belated Review' (1985) 94 *Yale Law Journal* 1285; MH Hoeflich, 'John Austin and Joseph Story: Two Nineteenth Century Perspectives on the Utility of the Civil Law for the Common Lawyer' (1985) 29 *American Journal of Legal History* 36; GL McDowell, 'Joseph Story's 'Science' of Equity' (1979) 153 *Supreme Court Review*; K Nadelmann, 'Joseph Story's Contribution to American Conflicts Law: A Comment' (1961) 5 *American Journal of Legal History* 230.

[5] For English material, see, eg N Duxbury, *Frederick Pollock and the English Juristic Tradition* (Oxford, Oxford University Press, 2004); RA Cosgrove, 'Sir Thomas Erskine Holland and the Treatise Tradition: The Elements of Jurisprudence Revisited' in JA Bush and A Wijffels (eds), *Learning the Law: Teaching and the Transmission of English Law, 1150–1900* (London, Hambledon Press, 1999) 397; RA Cosgrove, *The Rule of Law: Albert Venn Dicey, Victorian Jurist* (Chapel Hill, NC, University of North Carolina Press, 1980). For Canadian material, see, eg RCB Risk, 'Constitutional Scholarship in the Late-Nineteenth Century: Making Federalism Work' (1996) 46 *University of Toronto Law Journal* 427; RCB Risk, 'AHF Lefroy: Common Law Thought in Late-Nineteenth Century Canada' (1991) 41 *University of Toronto Law Journal* 307; RCB Risk, 'John Skirving Ewart: The Legal Thought' (1987) 37 *University of Toronto Law Journal* 335. For American material, see, eg A Kull, 'James Barr Ames and the Early Modern History of Unjust Enrichment' (2005) 25 *Oxford Journal of Legal Studies* 297; W Twining, *Theories of Evidence: Bentham and Wigmore* (Stanford, CA, Stanford University Press, 1986)); SA Siegel, 'John Chipman Gray, Legal Formalism, and the Transformation of Perpetuities Law' (1982) 36 *University of Miami Law Review* 439. See also AWB Simpson, 'The Salmond Lecture' (2007) 38 *Victoria University of Wellington Law Review* 669.

[6] See generally DM Rabban, 'Historiography of The Common Law' (2003) 28 *Law and Social Inquiry* 1161; MH Hoeflich, 'Legal History and the History of the Book: Variations on a Theme' (1998) 46 *The University of Kansas Law Review* 415; DD Hall, 'On Native Ground: From the History of Printing to the History of the Book' in DD Hall (ed), *Cultures of Print: Essays in the History of the Book* (Amherst, MA, University of Massachusetts Press, 1996) 15.

Story himself thought that his 1834 *Commentaries on Conflicts* would be his 'best law work'. His son (and perennial editor) William Wetmore Story reported that 'none of [my father's] works interested him like *Commentaries on Conflicts*', and American Secretary of State Daniel Webster opined that that text was 'regarded by the judicature of the world as the great book of the age'. From beyond the United States, longtime attorney general and premier of Ontario Oliver Mowat said that Story's 'able work on the Conflict of Laws has a world-wide reputation . . . and it will probably have no rival for many years to come'.[7] *Commentaries on Conflicts* will therefore provide a platform for this study. That book's epistemic construction and its style of presentation, together with its author's goals for it, will be emphasised. *Commentaries on Conflicts*' doctrinal content is not a primary subject of this essay, but it is difficult to reflect on the form of Story's texts or that of any other legal treatise without incidental consideration of the principles stored in them and publicised by them.

Broad-brush anticipation of this study's conclusions seems appropriate at the outset. At his best, Story was a master of exhaustive description and of consequentialist reasoning. He was also a gifted technician with a knack for seeing the architectonic structure of legal systems. At worst, Story tended to verbosity and hyperbole, and readily adopted jurisprudential buzzwords of the day despite his apparently incomplete sense of their meanings. Perhaps most relevant for current purposes, Story engaged in limited reported reflection on scientific epistemology in law or the theory of juristic knowledge that his trademark treatises epitomised. His animating insight was that the more abstractly a legal rule was expressed, the more likely that rule was to reflect or promote uniformity of intercolonial, interstate or international practice. That perception effectively led to an instrumentalisation in law by Story of scientific method, terminology and purposes.

I. ABRIDGING, CONSOLIDATING AND CODIFYING

Story came to legal treatise-writing through the production of digests of case law and consolidations of statutes, and by way of private-law codification. He also prepared several derivative English texts prior to his assumption in 1829 of a law school teaching position endowed by Massachusetts abridgement author Nathan Dane that required the production of treatises to facilitate Harvard's emergence as a national institution of professional consolidation. Story therefore lived an accelerated version of the nineteenth-century development of Anglo-American legal literature.

[7] Joseph Story to Richard Peters (24 April 1833), reproduced in WW Story, *Life and Letters of Joseph Story*, vol 2 (Freeport, NY, Books for Libraries Press, 2 vols, 1971) 140–41; 142; *New Jersey Steam Navigation Company v Merchants Bank of Boston*, 47 US 349, 377 (1848); O Mowat, 'Observations on the Use and Value of American Reports in Reference to Canadian Jurisprudence' (1857) 3 *Upper Canada Law Journal* 3, 5.

Story's unpublished 1809 'Digest of Law' was conceived by him as an American supplement to John Comyns' widely-used *Digest of the Laws of England*, an 'institutional work' that was representative of the prevailing seventeenth-and-eighteenth-century British genre of enumerative surveys of common-law information.[8] Several other abridgements of that sort were prepared for use in the North American colonies or states, and that local literature has begun to attract insightful commentary.[9] Those institutional works generally survey juridical information comprehensively, but without significant inductive generalisation, synthesis or other forms of abstraction. Their authors normally aspire to treat the entire sweep of budding 'national' law, and topical divisions are often ones like persons, estates, crimes and courts.[10] Within those divisions the subcategory of property tends to be dominant, and particularistic 'forms of action' or social functions imposed by the operation of law provide a dense array of alphabetically-organised subheadings.[11] That species of Anglo-American legal literature most closely resembles law students' and practitioners' ubiquitous commonplace books, which were sometimes forerunners of published digests or abridgements.[12]

It was therefore a modest step for Story to move from his 1809 'Digest' to the American annotation of three English legal treatises in the next couple of years.[13] As was the norm in that period, those texts dealt with small corners of topical fields,

[8] Compare KH Nadelmann (ed), 'Extract from Joseph Story's Manuscript *Digest* of *Law*' (1961) 5 *American Journal of Legal History* 265 with J Comyns, *Digest of the Laws of England* (London, H Woodfall and W Strahan, 5 vols, 1762–67).

[9] See, eg DJ Hulsebosch, 'An Empire of Law: Chancellor Kent and the Revolution in Books in the Early Republic' (2009) 60 *Alabama Law Review* 377; MH Hoeflich, 'American Blackstones' in W Prest (ed), *Blackstone and His Commentaries: Biography, Law, History* (Oxford, Hart, 2009) 181; CE Shields, 'Chancellor Kent's Abridgement of Emerigon's Maritime Insurance' (2004) 108 *Pennsylvania State Law Review* 1123; S Normand, 'François-Joseph Cugnet et la reconstitution du droit de la Nouvelle-France' (2002) 1 *Cahiers aixois d'histoire des droits de l'outre-mer français* 127; JH Langbein, 'Chancellor Kent and the History of Legal Literature' (1993) 93 *Columbia Law Review* 547; P Girard, 'Themes and Variations in Early Canadian Legal Culture: Beamish Murdock and His Epitome of the Laws of Nova Scotia' (1993) 11 *Law and History Review* 101; A Johnson, 'The Influences of Nathan Dane on Legal Literature' (1963) 7 *American Journal of Legal History* 28.

[10] See generally RB Robinson, 'The Two Institutes of Thomas Wood: A Study in Eighteenth Century Legal Scholarship' (1991) 35 *American Journal of Legal History* 432; JW Cairns, 'Blackstone, an English Institutist: Legal Literature and the Rise of the Nation State' (1984) 4 *Oxford Journal of Legal Studies* 318; A Watson, 'Justinian's Institutes and Some English Counterparts' in P Stein and A Lewis (eds), *Studies in Justinian's Institutes in Memory of JAC Thomas* (London, Sweet and Maxwell, 1983) 183.

[11] See generally W Prest, 'Blackstone as Architect: Constructing the Commentaries' (2003) 15 *Yale Journal of Law and the Humanities* 103; JH Baker, 'English Law Books and Legal Publishing, 1597–1695' in J Barnard and DF McKenzie (eds), *Cambridge History of the Book in Britain*, vol 4 (Cambridge, Cambridge University Press, 4 vols, 2002) 474; JW Cairns, 'Eighteenth Century Professional Classification of English Law' (1987) 33 *McGill Law Journal* 225.

[12] See generally MH Hoeflich, 'The Lawyer as Pragmatic Reader: The History of Legal Common-Placing' (2002) 55 *Arkansas Law Review* 87.

[13] See J Chitty, *Practical Treatise on Bills of Exchange: New Edition, from the Second Corrected and Enlarged London Edition with the Addition of Recent English and American Cases by Joseph Story* (Philadelphia, PA, William P Farrand and Company, 1809 and 1819); C Abbott, *A Treatise Relative to the Law of Merchant Ships and Seamen: Second American from the Third English Edition, with Annotations by Joseph Story* (Newburyport, MA, E Little and Company, 1810, and 1827); E Lawes, *A Practical Treatise on Pleading in Assumpsit, with the Addition of American Decisions by Joseph Story* (Boston, MA, James W Burditt and Company, 1811).

and were organised around principles that were few in number and all-embracing in character. Generalisation and systemisation of the essential characteristics of civil liability into an all-inclusive Anglo-American codal or near-codal treatise literature would not be attempted for another two or three generations. But already in those derivative English texts, Story was engaging the treatise's distinctive features of objective and systematic treatments of limited fields of legal knowledge that were said to have inherent qualities of internal unity, and especially induction from specific events to abstract, black-letter rules.[14] The reproduction of English law books with North American annotations was a lucrative practice for legal publishers and became legion as the nineteenth century advanced, especially in respect of British North America.[15]

Perhaps most significant in Story's transition from technical 'case-law compiler' to abstract 'legal scientist' was his 1812 appointment, with William Prescott and Nathan Dane, to undertake an unprecedented official consolidation of Massachusetts' statutes.[16] That consolidation, which involved much more deletion, regrouping, rewriting, and retitling of legislation than had been attempted in earlier 'revisions' of colonial laws, was used as a model for similar exercises in New York (1828), Nova Scotia (1851) and New Brunswick (1854). The products of those consolidations prompted Chairman René-Édouard Caron of Lower Canada's Civil Code Commission of the 1860s to remark that they 'closely resembled codes of law'.[17] That was so because pioneering North American statute consolidations were typically set up in 'books' and 'chapters', in topical clusters that often followed the nomenclature and sequencing of late-eighteenth and early-nineteenth-century European private law codes. The watchwords of that form of legal-information packaging were order, synthesis and concision, descriptive terms that underline the epistemological similarities of codes to consolidations of statutes and help to emphasise their common roots in the contemporary natural sciences.[18] It is regrettable that little scholarly attention has been

[14] Paraphrasing and merging Simpson (n 3) 633–34 with Plucknett (n 1) 19, a working definition of the treatise as an 'ideal type' of legal literature would be that it first defines its subject matter and then proceeds by logical stages to cover that subject's field. The result of that empiricism and induction is the presentation of law in a framework of principles, with the implication that in work-a-day practice those principles will provide (by deduction) results in a multitude of cases. Treatises are monographs that deal with a branch of the law that is conceived as possessing some quality of unity, and their structure is determined by substantive principles rather than by procedural rules.

[15] See generally EC Surrency, *A History of American Law Publishing* (Dobb's Ferry, NY, Oceana Publications, 1990) 111–27 165–80; HK Jones, *Butterworth: History of a Publishing House* (London, Butterworths, 1980); MW Maxwell, 'The Development of Law Publishing 1799–1974' in J Burke and P Allsop (eds), *Then and Now, 1799–1974* (London, Sweet and Maxwell, 1974) 121.

[16] See generally CM Cook, *The American Codification Movement: A Study of Antebellum Legal Reform* (Westport, CT, Greenwood Press, 1981) 104–06 173–81; EC Surrency, 'Revision of Colonial Laws' (1965) 9 *American Journal of Legal History* 189; HL Stebbins, 'Outline of Massachusetts Statute Law Publications' (1927) 20 *Law Library Journal* 72.

[17] Reported in JEC Brierley, 'Quebec's Civil Law Codification Viewed and Reviewed' (1968) 14 *McGill Law Journal* 521 554–55.

[18] See generally JL Halperin, *The French Civil Code* T Weir (trans) (London, University College of London Press, 2006); G Birtsch, 'Reform Absolutism and the Codification of Law: The Genesis and Nature of the Prussian General Code (1794)' in J Brewer and E Hellmuth (eds), *Rethinking Leviathan:*

addressed to nineteenth-century North Atlantic attempts at legislative consolidation.[19] The treatise was the product in decisional law of epistemological imperatives similar to those that informed early consolidations of statutes.

Story was subsequently appointed chair of the Massachusetts Commission on the Codification of Private Law, a governmental body that was active in 1836 and 1837 (after the publication of four of his treatises), and reported to the state legislature in favour of moderate, nationally-coordinated codification of local law as a way of addressing the issue of domestic legal pluralism.[20] That stance was consistent with Story's longstanding extra-legislative support for codification of the fields he thought ripest for generalisation and systematisation, namely commercial law, criminal law and procedural law.[21] In any case, Massachusetts' abortive codification project was part of an emergent Anglo-American preoccupation with codes as a way of doing legal science.[22] While the work of parallel civil code commissions in neighbouring New York and Lower Canada has attracted considerable academic attention, the efforts of Story and his Massachusetts co-codifiers have not.[23] That difference may be attributable to a measured and

the Eighteenth Century State in Britain and Germany (Oxford, Oxford University Press, 1999) 343; HE Strakosch, *State Absolutism and the Rule of Law: the Struggle for the Codification of the Civil Law in Austria* (Sydney, Sydney University Press, 1967).

[19] But see J Fishman, 'The History of Statutory Compilations in Pennsylvania' (1994) 86 *Law Library Journal* 559; N Larsen, 'Statute Revision and Consolidation: History, Process, and Problems' (1987) 19 *Ottawa Law Review* 321; AH Manchester, 'Simplifying the Sources of the Law: An Essay in Law Reform. Lord Cranworth's Attempt to Consolidate the Statute Law of England and Wales' (1973) 2 *The Anglo-American Law Review* 395.

[20] See J Story *et al*, *Report of the Commissioners Appointed to Consider and Report upon the Practicability and Expediency of Reducing to a Written and Systematic Code the Common Law of Massachusetts* (Boston, MA, Sutton and Wentworth, 1837). See also LS Cushing, 'Codification of the Common Law in Massachusetts' (1836) 15 *American Jurist & Law Magazine* 111.

[21] See, eg J Story, 'Law, Legislation and Codes' in F Lieber (ed), *Encyclopedia Americana*, vol 7 (Philadelphia, PA, Carey, Lea and Carey, 1820–33) 581; J Story, 'Codification of the Common Law' in Story (n 7) 715; J Story 'Address' in J Story, *The Miscellaneous Writings of Joseph Story, LL.D.* (Boston, MA, James Monroe and Company, 1835) 405.

[22] See generally GB Baker, 'Strategic Benthamism: Rehabilitating United Canada's Bar Through Criminal Law Codification, 1847–54' in J Phillips *et al* (eds), *Essays in the History of Canadian Law: A Tribute to Peter N Oliver* (Toronto, ON, University of Toronto Press, 2008) 257; L Farmer, 'Reconstructing the English Codification Debate: The Criminal Law Commissioners' (2008) 18 *Law and History Review* 397; KJM Smith, 'Anthony Hammond: "Mr. Surface" Peel's Persistent Codifier' (1999) 20 *Journal of Legal History* 24; B Rudden, 'A Code Too Soon: The 1826 Property Code of James Humphreys: English Rejection, American Reception, English Acceptance' in P Wallington and RM Merkins (eds), *Essays in Memory of Professor FH Lawson* (London, Butterworths, 1986) 103; NJO Liverpool, 'The History and Development of the St. Lucia Civil Code' in RA Landry and E Caparros (eds), *Essays on the Civil Codes of Quebec and St. Lucia* (Ottawa, ON, University of Ottawa Press, 1983) 303; KM Bindon, 'Adam Thom and the Institution of Order in Rupert's Land, 1839–54' in DH Flaherty (ed), *Essays in the History of Canadian Law* (Toronto, ON, University of Toronto Press, 1981) 43; WB McCash, 'Thomas Cobb and the Codification of Georgia Law' (1978) 62 *Georgia Historical Quarterly* 9; G Dargo, *Jefferson's Louisiana: Politics and the Clash of Legal Traditions* (Cambridge, MA, Harvard University Press, 1975).

[23] But see Newmyer (n 4) 272–81; Cook (n16) 171–81. Compare LA Grossman, 'Langdell Upside-Down: James Coolidge Carter and the Anticlassical Jurisprudence of Anticodification' (2007) 19 *Yale Journal of Law and the Humanities* 149; M Reimann, 'The Historical School Against Codification: Savigny, Carter, and the Defeat of the New York Civil Code' (1989) 37 *American Journal of Comparative Law* 102; SN Lubrin, 'David Dudley Field and the Field Code: An Historical Analysis of an Earlier

diplomatic attitude toward codification on Story's part, a posture that contrasted with the more flamboyant, persistent and controversial approach of leading New York codifier David Dudley Field. It may also have to do with Story's ambidextrous attitude to legal federalism: Story the constitutional-law judge on the First (New England) Circuit Court of Appeal and the Supreme Court of the United States from 1811 to 1845 provided through case law the jurisdictional space for an expansive and uniform federal common law of commerce, admiralty, and diversity of citizenship; Story the publicist capitalised on that opportunity with seminal legal treatises; and, Story the Harvard law professor recruited entering students from Boston's hinterland and spread republican legal values throughout the expanding interior of the United States in the minds, hearts and luggage of returning graduates.[24] It is, therefore, unsurprising that modern students of Story have tended to focus on his judicial and educational activities, rather than on his actions as a legislative delegate on statutory consolidation and private law codification commissions. That work was, however, crucially important to Story's choice of media for the extended expression of his economic and other developmental policies.

II. LEGAL DISCORD

Story's pursuit of the commercially and politically unifying potential of federal common law and national legal treatise literature was directly informed by his involvement in the Anglo-American codification movement. In structure, his treatises are near-codes, written around general principles presented as rules. *Commentaries on the Constitution*, for example, was constructed from 19 maxims of 'codal' interpretation.[25] In one of his more prominent *Encyclopedia Americana* entries, Story provided 21 principles for the application of private law.[26] And *Commentaries on Conflicts* is comprised of 645 consecutively-numbered paragraphs that provide individual choice-of-law rules and thumbnail glosses on them.

Story's models for that organisation were the late-eighteenth century's spate of European doctrinal texts, rather than the legal literature of his own Anglo-American tradition:

Procedural Vision' (1988) 6 *Law and History Review* 311; S Normand, 'La codification de 1866: contexte et impact' in HP Glenn (ed), *Droit québécois et droit français: communauté, autonomie, et concordance* (Cowansville, QC, Blais, 2005) 43; B Young, *The Politics of Codification: Lower Canada's Civil Code of 1866* (Montreal, QC, McGill-Queen's University Press, 1994); J-M Brisson, *La formation d'un droit mixte: l'évolution de la procédure civile de 1774 à 1867* (Montréal, QC, Thémis, 1986) esp 117–62.

[24] See generally GE White, *The Marshall Court and Cultural Change, 1815–1835* (Oxford, Oxford University Press, 1991); RH Newmyer, 'Harvard Law School, New England Legal Culture, and the Antebellum Origins of American Jurisprudence' in D Thalen (ed), *The Constitution in American Life* (Ithaca, NY, Cornell University Press, 1988) 74; R Story, *The Forging of an Aristocracy: Harvard and the Boston Upper Class, 1800–1870* (Middletown, CT, Wesleyan University Press, 1980).

[25] See Story, *Commentaries on the Constitution* (n 2), vol 1, 305–49, 382–83.

[26] See Story, 'Law, Legislation and Codes' (n 21) 583–85.

> There is a remarkable difference, in the manner of treating juridical subjects, between the foreign and the English jurists. The former, almost universally, discuss every subject with an elaborate, theoretical fullness and accuracy, and foreign jurists *ascend to the elementary principles of each branch of the science*. The latter, with few exceptions, write what they are pleased to call 'practical treatises', which contain little more than a collection of the principles laid down in the adjudged cases, with scarcely an attempt to illustrate them by any general reasoning, or even to follow them out into collateral consequences. In short, [*texts by English jurists*] *are little more than full Indexes to the Reports.*[27]

Story also used continental treatises for rhetorical advantage. A single page of *Commentaries on Conflicts*, for example, has three lines of French and six of Latin, together with quotations from Louis Boullenois, Achille Rodemburg, Paul Voet, John Voet, Charles D'Argentré and Ulricus Huberus.[28] The key point, however, relates to Story's desire to 'ascend to the elementary principles of each branch of [legal] science' in order to augment the prevailing Anglo-American practice of scholarship in law which turned out works that were 'little more than full Indexes to the Reports'. It is precisely that penchant for generalisation, synthesis, abstraction or inductive reasoning that is the hallmark of a legal treatise-writer.

All of Story's treatises were written at Harvard Law School as a condition of his occupancy of the Dane Professorship. Dane's endowment stipulated that linkage of pedagogy to scholarship and statesmanship, and Story himself regularly mused publicly about the unhappy implications of a sparse Anglo-American legal literature for 'scientific' education in law.[29] College-based instruction in pre-Revolutionary and antebellum American law had occurred without nationally-oriented texts as teaching tools, and Charles Viner's endowed chair in law-teaching at Oxford University that was initially held by William Blackstone had not emphasised scientific or imperialistic approaches to law.[30] Story's treatises were, however, intended to be more than classroom aids. They were conceived as motivational tracts on a system of political and economic democracy that placed

[27] Story, *Commentaries on Bailments* (n 2) viii–ix (emphasis added).

[28] See Story, *Commentaries on Conflicts* (n 2) 360. See also Story, *Commentaries on Bailments* (n 2) 20, 11, 17. Commentators such as Lawrence Friedman have concluded that Story went too far with those kinds of flourishes, describing them as 'blatant erudition', 'stultifying pedantry' and 'totally mysterious'. LM Friedman, *A History of American Law* 3rd edn (New York, NY, Simon and Shuster, 2005) 247.

[29] See, eg J Story, 'Review of a Course of Legal Study Respectfully Addressed to the Students of Law in the United States, by David Hoffman, Professor of Law in the University of Maryland' in Story (n 21) 223; J Story, 'Discourse Pronounced upon the Inauguration of the Author, as Dane Professor of Law in Harvard University, August 25th 1829' in Story (n 21) 440. See also AJ Johnson, *The Life and Constitutional Thought of Nathan Dane* (New York NY, Garland, 1987) 8–12, 94–114.

[30] See generally JH Langbein, 'Blackstone, Litchfield, and Yale: The Founding of the Yale Law School' in T Kronman (ed), *History of the Yale Law School: Tercentennial Lectures* (New Haven, CT, Yale University Press, 2004) 17; WH Bryson and EL Shepard, 'The Winchester Law School' (2003) 21 *Law and History Review* 393; PD Carrington, 'Teaching Law and Virtue at Transylvania University: The George Wythe Tradition in the Antebellum Years' (1990) 40 *Mercer Law Review* 673; Compare W Prest, *William Blackstone: Law and Letters in the Eighteenth Century* (Oxford, Oxford University Press, 2008) 109–82.

lawyers administering common-law and constitutional protections of private rights at the centre of an American polity closely linked to consolidated commodities and credit markets. The treatises, the Law School, and the federal courts were thus embraced by Dane and Story as sibling institutions that would help to promote uniformity of private law, nurture a nationally-oriented bar, assist in securing a leading, non-partisan role for lawyers and courts in the consolidation of American domestic policy and help to cement the Republic along nationalist lines. Those pursuits became Story's legacy to the Anglo-American legal tradition, a potent but sometimes under acknowledged bequest. His publishers certainly thought that Story's statements of law and conception of its social role remained saleable through much of the nineteenth century, evidenced by their production of more than six dozen editions of his treatises.

Story regarded constitutional divisions of power, intercourt rivalry and inter-jurisdictional legal pluralism as related challenges that existed at the junction of governmental law, judicial law, and public and private international law. It was no accident, therefore, that his *Commentaries on Conflicts* was published on the heels of his *Commentaries on the Constitution* and just before his *Commentaries on Equity Jurisprudence.*[31] Story thought he was dealing as directly with conflicts issues when he adjudicated, taught or wrote about division-of-powers cases under the federal admiralty, commerce, or diversity headings of the Constitution as when he dealt with interstate choice-of-law problems in *Commentaries on Conflicts*, and the private-law lines between states were in many ways as firm as those among nations.[32] The same is true of Story's judicial applications of the federal Judiciary Act of 1789, most notably *Swift v Tyson*, in which he set about reigning in the unco-ordinated activities of state courts.[33]

Interstate choice-of-law doctrine was a complementary aspect of Story's wholistic conflicts thought, and the controversies it spawned in antebellum America were regarded as novel ones. Optimal security, and thus sovereignty, for interstate traders was thought to require that private law be uniform, and

[31] Several reviewers of those books noted the interconnection of one of them that dealt with frictions arising from constitutional delegations of power to federal and state governments, another that distinguished between the jurisdiction of courts of equity (a large part of which related to commerce) and that of courts of law with a view to minimising intercourt conflicts on that frontier, and a third book in that sequence that rounded out treatments of choice-of-forum and intergovernmental conflict-of-laws issues by addressing interstate choice-of-law issues. See, eg (1834) 4 *Legal Examiner & Law Chronicle* 512; (1841) 5 *Jurist (OS)* 562; (1840) 67 *London Quarterly Review* 32; (1835) 17 *American Quarterly Review* 303.

[32] Although scholarship on constitutional provisions relevant to American interstate conflicts issues is immense, D Laycock, 'Equal Citizens of Equal and Territorial States: The Constitutional Foundations of Choice of Law' (1992) 92 *Columbia Law Review* 249; S Jay, 'Origins of Federal Common Law' (1985) 133 *University of Pennsylvania Law Review* 100 and 1231; and WE Nelson, 'The American Revolution and the Emergence of Modern Doctrines of Federalism and Conflict of Laws' in Colonial Society of Massachusetts (ed), *Law in Colonial Massachusetts 1630–1800* (Boston, MA, Colonial Society of Massachusetts, 1984) 419 are especially helpful.

[33] 41 US 1 (1842). See generally W Holt, 'To Establish Justice: Politics, the Judiciary Act of 1789, and the Intervention of the Federal Courts' [1989] *Duke Law Journal* 1421; TA Freyer, *Harmony and Dissonance: the 'Swift' and 'Erie' Cases in American Federalism* (New York, NY, New York University Press, 1981) esp 1–43.

an important step toward the integration of American's common laws involved persuading states to compromise their domestic law when presented with private rights acquired out-of-state. Story's themes in *Commentaries on Conflicts* were therefore the circumscription of local governmental power by private-law unification, the indispensability of choice-of-law rules to commercial nationalism and the role of popular consent in notions of state sovereignty. Sovereignty and vested rights were effectively the controlling topics in a book about legal pluralism and private international law.

In his inaugural lecture as Dane Professor, Story announced that he would:

> . . . venture far more than has been usual with publicists, into an examination of those general principles of jurisprudence which effect the contracts, govern the titles, and limit the remedies of the subjects of independent powers, who acquire rights or contractual obligations, or succeed to property, or are in any measure subjected to the municipal law in a foreign country. This will include a variety of delicate and interesting topics belonging to the operation of foreign jurisprudence or, as it is sometimes called, the *lex fori* and the *lex loci*.[34]

That new attention to the '*lex fori*' and the '*lex loci*' was said to be timely because the Supreme Court of the United States had to cope with 'the jurisprudence of twenty-four states, essentially differing in habits, laws, institutions, and principles of decisions'. Story was similarly concerned about 'systematical legal diversities' that prevailed among the American states.[35] That state of affairs meant that:

> To no part of the world is [choice-of-law doctrine] of more interest and importance than to the United States, since the union of a national government with that of twenty-four distinct, and in some respects independent states, necessarily creates very complicated relations and rights between citizens of these states, which call for the constant administration of extra-municipal principles. This branch of public law may be fitly denominated private international law, since it is chiefly seen and felt in its application to the common business of private persons, and rarely rises to the dignity of national negotiations or national controversies . . . [Q]uestions upon the conflict of laws of

[34] Story, 'Discourse' (n 29). A more-or-less complete listing of pre-Story, Anglo-American conflicts literature, the bulk of which appeared in essay rather than monographic form, would include: H Home, *Principles of Equity* 2nd edn (Edinburgh, Kimlaid, Bell and Miller, 1767) 345–74; J Henry, *The Judgment of the Court of Demerara in the Case of Odwin v Forbes* (London, np, 1823) 1–86; E Cowan, 'Digest of Decisions on Lex Loci' 4 *Cowan* 510 (NY 1825); S Livermore, *Dissertations on the Questions Which Arise from the Contrariety of the Positive Laws of Different States and Nations* (New Orleans, B Levy, 1828); J Henry (ed), 'Wheaton's Restatement of American Conflicts' (1828) 1 *Jurist* 430; J Kent, *Commentaries on American Law* (New York NY, O Halsted, 2 vols, 1832), vol 1, 36, 81–2, 93, 118–22, 419; vol 2, 86, 91–3, 108, 394, 453–63, 515, 522. See generally P Macalister-Smith and J Schwietzke, 'Bibliography of the Textbooks and Comprehensive Treatises on Positive International Law of the Nineteenth Century' (2001) 3 *Journal of the History of International Law* 75 esp 104–14.

[35] J Story, 'The Life of Chief Justice Marshall' (1846) 6 *American Jurist & Law Magazine* 294; Joseph Story to Daniel Webster (4 January 1827), reproduced in Story (n 7), vol 1, 435–37; Story, 'Address' (n 21) 417–25. See also J Story, *A Discourse on the Past History, Present State and Future Prospects of the Law* (Edinburgh, Thomas Clark, 1835) 75, reproduced in J McClellan, *Joseph Story and the American Constitution: A Study in Political and Legal Thought with Collected Writings* (Norman, OK, University of Oklahoma Press, 1971) 325–49; Joseph Story to James John Wilkinson (26 March 1834), reproduced in Story (n 7), vol 2, 165–66.

> different states are the most embarrassing and difficult of decisions of any, that can occupy the attention of courts of justice.[36]

Story concluded that if American common law failed to provide 'scientific', 'precise' and 'symmetrical' choice-of-law rules to govern inter-jurisdictional commerce promptly, it would be:

> Impractical for [states] to carry on an extensive intercourse and commerce with each other. The whole system of agencies, purchases and sales, credits and negotiable instruments, rests on this foundation; and the nation, which should refuse to acknowledge the common [conflicts] principles, would soon find its whole commercial intercourse reduced to a state, like that, in which it now exists with savage tribes, with the barbarous nations of Sumatra, and with the other portions of Asia, washed by the Pacific.[37]

In other words, doctrinally malingering states were at risk of becoming truly alien and uncivilised. Security for interstate traders required that private law be as uniform as possible, and an important step toward that goal involved persuading states to compromise their local law when presented with private rights acquired out-of-state:

> . . . Without some common principles adopted in this regard there would be an utter confusion of all rights and remedies; and intolerable grievances would grow up to weaken all the domestic relations [of the states with each other], as well as to destroy the sanctity of contracts and the security of property.[38]

Judicial protection of 'the sanctity of contracts and the security of property' was a mission Story urged on his fellow jurists so frequently that his use of those catch-phrases literally defies counting. His standard prescription for that task was 'to build our commercial law, as much as possible, upon principles absolutely universal in their application'.[39]

[36] Story, *Commentaries on Conflicts* (n 2) 9, 151. For discussion of early-nineteenth-century American legal diversity, see generally GR Hornaday, 'The Forgotten Empire: Pre-Civil War Southern Imperialism' (2003) 36 *Connecticut Law Review* 225; MS Arnold, *Unequal Laws unto a Savage Race: European Legal Traditions in Arkansas, 1686–1836* (Fayetteville, AR, University of Arkansas Press, 1985); HN Scheiber, 'Federalism and the American Economic Order, 1789–1910' (1975) 10 *Law and Society Review* 57; WE Nelson, *Americanization of the Common Law: the Impact of Legal Change on Massachusetts Society, 1760–1830* (Cambridge, MA, Harvard University Press, 1975). For accounts of eighteenth-century legal pluralism, to which Story was exposed in his Essex County, Massachusetts law practice of the 1790s, see generally AG Roeber, 'He read it to me from a book of English law: Germans, Bench, and Bar in the Colonial South, 1715–1770' in DJ Bodenhamer and JW Ely (eds), *Ambivalent Legacy: A Legal History of the South* (Jackson, MS, University of Mississippi Press, 1984) 202; GL Haskins, 'Influence of New England Law on the Middle Colonies' (1983) 1 *Law and History Review* 238; SB Kim, *Landlord and Tenant in Colonial New York: Manorial Society, 1664–1775* (Chapel Hill, NC, University of North Carolina Press, 1978); SB Presser, 'An Introduction to the Legal History of Colonial New Jersey' (1976) 7 *Rutgers-Camden Law Journal* 262.

[37] Story, *Commentaries on Conflicts* (n 2) 202–03.

[38] Ibid 5.

[39] Joseph Story to Sir William Scott (22 September 1828), reproduced in Story (n 7), vol 1, 559. Distinguishing features of Story's judicial decisions on domestic issues were expansive interpretations of property interests to include fisheries, franchises, inert natural resources, trees and the seabed under tidal waterways. He promoted emerging 'will theories' of contract by permitting common carriers and other bailees to limit their customary liability by agreement, and he suppressed 'just price' notions of

Safeguarding contractual entitlements and property followed directly from Story's valorisation of the sovereignty and vested rights of individuals. Citizens and not states were the building blocks of his Republic, and institutions like the Constitution and the federal courts were said by him to have been conceived as the primary guardians of patrimonial and contractual entitlements.[40] Story's choice-of-law rules echoed the premises that animated his constitutional jurisprudence. The aim of those rules was to secure the rights of individuals operating across state lines in a national market, and the promotion of comity among states was a secondary concern. Story routinely called interstate conflicts problems ones of 'mixed rights' or 'harmonisation', rather than disputes about mixed laws or comity. And he regularly characterised the juristic sources of interstate and international threats to 'private rights and contracts' as 'despotic powers'.[41] In some ways, *Commentaries on Conflicts* is a heuristic, quasi-constitutional tract on the correlative scope of private and public sovereignty, written through distinctive and highly technical legal doctrine. It bears recollection that that book was authored during a period of increasingly virulent states'-rights agitation that nationalists like Story regarded as a threat to the new Republic.[42] Story was, in effect, engaged in the invention of American nationalism through law and, however New Englandesque its commercial and republican ethos, his legal nationalism was extroverted, optimistic and visionary.

III. COMMENTARIES ON CONFLICTS

Commentaries on Conflicts began as a 557-page monograph, in 17 chapters.[43] It is prefaced by a four-page 'bibliographical note' listing 'some of the more important authors whose works have been cited' that includes 42 European scholars and three Anglo-American jurists. Its 'Index to Cases Cited' contains about 300 United States decisions and another 200 English ones (some of which are not

substantive equality in exchange. See generally H Hovenkamp, *Enterprise and American Law, 1836–1937* (Cambridge, MA, Harvard University Press, 1991) 85–113; TA Freyer, *Forums of Order: the Federal Courts and Business in American History* (Greenwich, CT, JAI Press, 1979) 19–98; MJ Horwitz, *The Transformation of American Law, 1780–1860* (Cambridge, MA, Harvard University Press, 1977) 40–120.

[40] See Story, *Commentaries on the Constitution* (n 2) 397–407.

[41] See, eg Story, *Commentaries on Conflicts* (n 2) 3, 4, 6, 25.

[42] See generally RE Ellis, *The Union at Risk: Jacksonian Democracy, States' Rights, and the Nullification Crisis* (New York, NY, Oxford University Press, 1987); JJ Gibbons, 'Federal Law and the State Courts, 1790–1860' (1984) 36 *Rutgers Law Review* 359.

[43] *Commentaries on Conflicts* went through seven subsequent, nineteenth-century editions, the first of which was revised by Story (J Story (ed) (Boston, MA, Little, 1841)); WW Story (ed) (Boston, MA, Little, 1846); WW Story (ed) (Boston, MA, Little, 1852); CH Bennett (ed) (Boston, MA, Little, 1857); IF Redfield (ed) (Boston, MA, Little, 1865); EH Bennett (ed) (Boston, MA, Little, 1872); MM Bigelow (ed) (Boston, MA, Little, Brown, 1883). It was republished twice in Britain within a year of its original release (London, RJ Kennett, 1834 and Edinburgh, T Clark, 1835), and later produced in two Spanish translations (Mexico City, Castillo Velasco, 1880 and Buenos Aires, F Lajouane, 1891). There is also a twentieth-century reprint of *Commentaries on Conflicts* (New York, NY, Arno Press, 1972) and a twenty-first-century one (Stockstadt, Keip, 2007).

conflicts cases), judgments that Story thought were too often 'loose and scattered' or 'provincial and unusual'.[44] But it was important for him to compile that case law exhaustively to showcase legal empiricism at work, and to fortify the doctrinal generalisations that he synthesised from those raw materials. Story's treatise was also intended as a register of interstate and international custom, presumably because those kinds of collections were important products of prevailing methodological practices in the natural sciences.

Bibliographical material is followed in *Commentaries on Conflicts* by brief substantive sections that contain introductory remarks and general maxims. Two succeeding chapters deal with the connecting factor of domicile and the acquisition of juridical personality through the law of capacity. The following nine chapters, the core of Story's interstate choice-of-law scheme, are structured around legal relationships: contractual; proprietary; testamentary; and relationships of agency. That doctrinal architecture was comparatively novel, since most of the European texts to which Story referred were organised by categories like personal, real and mixed rights. His structural reliance on private-law relationships was consistent with his overriding concern about personal sovereignty and entitlements. The last four chapters of *Commentaries on Conflicts* deal with the adjectival law of jurisdiction, foreign judgments and evidence. Statutory and decisional law is treated on all-fours throughout the text, apparently because Story regarded most forms of normativity as will-based and therefore vulnerable to legislative, judicial, contractual and customary variation from one place to another in accord with local preferences.

Story devoted the first two dozen pages of *Commentaries on Conflicts* to a subject that 'properly belongs to a general treatise upon public law' to lay the groundwork for 500-odd pages that follow and that deal with private international law through the medium of approximately 70 code-like choice-of-law rules.[45] It was the 'municipal regulations' of each state or nation expressed in black-letter conflicts rules, rather than maxims of public international law, that were ultimately to be used deductively to determine on a case-by-case basis when and how much out-of-state law would be applied. One might therefore ask why Story prefaced an enumeration of six dozen choice-of-law rules that typically allow forum courts little discretion to ignore prejudicial foreign laws with a discussion of international comity 'which constitute[s] the basis, upon which all reasonings on the subject must necessarily rest' that obliged forum courts to apply out-of-state laws only 'so far as they do not prejudice the power or rights of other governments, or other citizens'.[46] The answer may be found in the fact that that analysis was introduced with sleight of hand by Story through three 'axioms' of public international law:

> every nation possesses an exclusive sovereignty and jurisdiction within its own territory . . . no state or nation can, by its laws, directly affect, or bind property out of its

[44] Story, *Commentaries on Conflicts* (n 2) v, 121.
[45] Ibid 23.
[46] Ibid 19, 30.

> own territory, or persons not resident therein; [and] . . . whatever force and obligation the laws of one country have in another, depends solely upon the laws, and municipal regulations of the latter, that is to say, upon its own proper jurisprudence and polity, and upon its own express or tacit consent.[47]

Folding a pioneering Louisiana essay and a leading Massachusetts judicial decision on the conflict of laws into his axiomatic reasoning, Story then provided a pithy statement of private international law policy, also in maxim form:

> the true foundation, on which the administration of [private] international law must rest, is, that the rules, which are to govern, are those, which arise from mutual interest and utility, from a sense of the inconvenience, which would result from a contrary doctrine, and from a sort of moral necessity to do justice, in order that justice may be done to us in return.[48]

Story's implicit claim was that that maxim, like most others in prominent North Atlantic legal traditions of-the-day, was generalised from widespread state practice.[49] But he had to acknowledge governmental sovereignty as an overarching value, however strategically or obsequiously, before proceeding to its modification through conflict-of-law rules.

Consensualism played a role in Story's conception of interstate and international relations that was similar to the place contractualism occupied for him in interpersonal affairs. The application of choice-of-law rules involved states waiving a portion of their otherwise exclusive jurisdiction over legal controversies within their territory to courts administering private international law in order to secure, in exchange, protection for the mixed private rights of their citizens doing business across political frontiers. Story's choice-of-law doctrine therefore amounted to a kind of supranational constitution that simultaneously limited the authority of forum courts presented with interstate conflicts, empowered those courts to apply extraterritorial private law and told them how to exercise that extraordinary jurisdiction. Because international sovereignty meant that no nation had an inherent obligation to yield to the laws of another and that none had an intrinsic right to give its laws extraterritorial effect, the express or tacit consent of countries was required for domestic laws to have extrajurisdictional force.[50] That acquiescence to choice-of-law principles was found by Story in the

[47] Ibid 19, 21, 24. For a different but ultimately unpersuasive account of what Story was doing with those axioms, compare A Watson, *Joseph Story and the Comity of Errors: A Case Study in Conflict of Laws* (Athens, GA, University of Georgia Press, 1992).

[48] Story, *Commentaries on Conflicts* (n 2) 34, citing Livermore (n 34) and *Blanchard v Russell* 13 Mass 1 (Mass SJC 1816).

[49] See generally JC Hogan and MD Schwartz, 'On Bacon's Rules and Maximes of the Common Law' (1983) 76 *Law Library Journal* 48; P Stein, *Regulae Juris: From Juristic Rules to Legal Maxims* (Edinburgh, Edinburgh University Press, 1966) esp 153–79.

[50] See generally DM Golove and DJ Hulsebosch, 'A Civilized Nation: The Early American Constitution, the Law of Nations, and the Pursuit of International Recognition' (2010) 85 *New York University Law Review* 932; MW Janis, *The American Tradition of International Law: Great Expectations, 1789–1914* (New York, NY, Oxford University Press, 2004)) 25–116; C Sylvest, 'International Law in Nineteenth Century Britain' (2004) 75 *British Journal of International Law* 9.

articulation by publicists of customary conflicts norms, in the practice of nations evidenced by the work of their courts and 'by silent adoption [of] a generally connected system'.[51] Without such a 'voluntary and mutual annihilation of sovereignty', represented by the adoption of black-letter, choice-of-law rules, 'the most serious mischiefs and most serious conflicts would arise', 'there would be an utter confusion of all rights', and states would have failed to act for their citizens from 'an enlarged sense of national duty'.[52] The concepts of statal and national sovereignty prevented Story from trumpeting the universality of private rights, but circumscriptions of sovereignty in the interest of securing the expectations of cross-border traders could be achieved with appropriate conditional inquiries into interjurisdictional comity, broad state practice, mutual commercial convenience and scientifically-oriented legal uniformity.

IV. PRINCIPLED POLICY IN CHOICE-OF-LAW

Practicability suggests focusing on a cluster of representative choice-of-law rules from *Commentaries on Conflicts*, rather than attempting treatment of all six dozen of them, or even trying for an assessment of a sizeable cross section of those rules.[53] Commercial law was Story's 'favourite department' of legal studies, and he wrote extensively about such special contracts as mandate, partnership, loan, insurance, charter party, hire and bailment.[54] His only scholarly treatment of domestic contract law at-large was a substantial entry for Francis Lieber's *Encyclopedia Americana*, but he assisted his son William in the 1844 preparation and publication of a first comprehensive Anglo-American contracts treatise.[55] In view of those interests, it is unsurprising that Story's chapter on 'Foreign Contracts' (at over 100 pages in length) is the single largest component of *Commentaries on Conflicts* by a substantial margin. When his chapters on real and personal property, which also have to do mostly with contractual exchanges, are added, the conclusion

[51] Story, *Commentaries on Conflicts* (n 2) 4, 25, 32, 36.

[52] Ibid 5.

[53] Since Story did not highlight his rules or otherwise distinguish rigorously justification or comparative textual material from norms, it seems appropriate to locate those rules in his treatise with pinpoint citations. See Ibid 96–9, 103–04, 112, 160–62, 168, 201–04, 213–19, 246, 254, 272, 275, 293, 307, 311, 334, 340, 357, 358, 363, 370, 378, 380, 383, 391, 398, 402–04, 410, 414, 419, 432, 450, 463, 466, 470, 476, 481, 483, 492, 495, 499, 508, 516, 524, 527.

[54] See, eg Story, *Commentaries on Agency* (n 2); Story, *Commentaries on Partnership* (n 2); Chitty (n 13); Story, *Commentaries on Bills of Exchange* (n 2); Story, *Commentaries on Promissory Notes* (n 2); Abbott (n 13); Story, *Commentaries on Bailments* (n 2). See also Lawes (n 13). On his untimely death in 1845, Story had two additional private law treatises in incomplete drafts that dealt with American federal admiralty and maritime law.

[55] See J Story, 'Contract' in Lieber (n 21), vol 3, 503; WW Story, *A Treatise on the Law of Contracts not under Seal* (Boston, MA, CC Little and J Brown, 1844). On Story's participation in his son's writing projects, see generally ME Phillips, *Reminiscences of William Wetmore Story, the American Sculptor and Author* (Chicago, IL, Rand McNally, 1897) 56–87. See also SM Waddams, 'Nineteenth-Century Treatises on English Contract Law' in this volume.

follows that over half of Story's conflicts treatise is about the law of exchange transactions. Indeed, 'Foreign Contracts' in *Commentaries on Conflicts* deals primarily with theoretical issues in domestic contract law and in a complementary fashion with choice-of-law rules. That emphasis strongly suggests that Story's choice-of-interstate-contract rules were extrapolated from Anglo-American law's emerging mandate to enforce promissory expectations by converting them into proprietary entitlements.[56]

The dilemma to which Story's choice-of-law rules in contract were addressed was how to protect personal autonomy and bargains expressive of freely-willed market choices when:

> Persons, capable in one country, are incapable by the laws of another; considerations, good in one, are insufficient or invalid in another; the public policy of one permits or favours certain agreements, which are prohibited in another; the forms prescribed by the laws of one, to ensure validity and obligation, are unknown in another; and the rights acknowledged by one, are not commensurate with those belonging to another . . . Unless some uniform rules are adopted to govern such cases (which are not uncommon), the grossest inequalities will arise in the administration of justice between the subjects of different countries in regard to such contracts . . . Innumerable suits must be litigated in the judicial forums of these countries and provinces, in which the decision must depend upon the point, whether the nature of a contract should be determined by the law of the place, where it is litigated; or by the law of the domicile of one or both of the parties; or by the law of the place, where the contract was made.[57]

Paraphrasing Story's well-known dissenting dictum on the contracts clause of the American Constitution from the *Charles River Bridge* case, he believed that if a state means to invite its citizens to enlarge interstate commerce there must be an implicit pledge by that state in the form of its subscription to uniform conflicts rules that contractual entitlements will be held inviolate.[58] Story was surrounded by evidence that interstate traders balked at the prevailing pluralistic character of the United States' private law, resistance that was apparent in longstanding reliance on contractual choice-of-law and choice-of-forum clauses.[59]

Story's solution to those commercial handicaps was to announce two choice-of-contract-law rules of broad application, and two ancillary rules for special contracts. His controlling principle was that 'the validity of a contract is to be

[56] See generally PS Atiyah, *The Rise and Fall of Freedom of Contract* (Oxford, Clarendon Press, 1979) esp 398–505; AWB Simpson, 'Innovation in Nineteenth Century Contract Law' (1975) 91 *The Law Quarterly Review* 247.

[57] Story, *Commentaries on Conflicts* (n 2) 193–94.

[58] See *Charles River Bridge v Warren Bridge*, 36 US 420 (1837) 636. See generally SI Kutler, *Privilege and Creative Destruction: the Charles River Bridge Case* (New York, NY, WW Norton and Company, 1978) 85–132.

[59] See generally CN Conklin, 'Transformed, Not Transcended: The Role of Extrajudicial Dispute Resolution in Antebellum Kentucky and New Jersey' (2006) 48 *American Journal of Legal History* 39; BH Mann, 'The Formalization of Informal Law: Arbitration Before the American Revolution' (1984) 59 443 *New York University Law Review* esp 456–79; WE Nelson, *Dispute and Conflict Resolution in Plymouth County, Massachusetts, 1725–1825* (Chapel Hill, NC, University of North Carolina Press, (1981) esp 3–43.

decided by the law of the place, where it is made' except 'where the contract is either expressly or tacitly to be performed in any other place, the contract, as to its validity, nature, obligation, and interpretation, is to be governed by the law of the place of performance'. Contracts of loan and those related to real estate were exempted by Story from those rules: 'contracts respecting . . . debts, are now universally treated, as having no situs or locality; and they follow the person of the creditor in point of right . . . though the remedy on them must be according to the law of the place, where they are sought to be enforced'.[60] Conversely, 'any title or interest in land or real estate can only be acquired or lost agreeably to the law of the place, where the same is situate'.[61]

By way of quick contrast with Story's rules, the current 'Restatement of Conflicts' of the American Law Institute does not attempt to provide comprehensive choice-of-law doctrine for an undifferentiated field of exchange transactions. Instead, that Institute is now promoting narrow rules specific to particular kinds of agreements like life-insurance contracts, contracts of loan, contracts of carriage, service contracts and contracts of suretyship.[62] That splintering parallels late-twentieth-century scholarship structured around a local law of contracts, rather than contract, based on prevailing perceptions of dissimilarity among kinds of transactions.[63] The upswing in domestic contracts scholarship alongside which Story worked was characterised by efforts to suppress the particularistic nature of the early-modern law of interpersonal obligations. It therefore seems natural that doctrinal minimalism would have become the reciprocal order-of-the-day for the nascent private international law of contract.

More than resonance with an emerging and generic Anglo-American law of contract was, however, animating Story's architecture for private international law. He was able to say with satisfaction in the second (1841) edition of *Commentaries on Conflicts* that 'the repose and common interest of all nations require each to observe towards all others the principles of reciprocal justice and comity; and those, *as we have seen*, are best subserved by the adoption of the general rule[s] that the laws of the place of contract and [performance] shall govern'.[64] Story apparently thought that he was simultaneously reporting and effecting state practice in ways that went beyond doctrinal parallelism in domestic and private international contract law.

[60] Story, *Commentaries on Conflicts* (n 2) 201, 233, 202, 204.

[61] Ibid 299, 302.

[62] See *Restatement of the Law, Second: Conflict of Laws, 2d. As Adopted and Promulgated by the American Law Institute at Washington, DC, May 23, 1969* (St Paul, MN, American Law Institute, 1971), vol 1, 576–632. See generally GE White, 'The American Law Institute and the Triumph of Modernist Jurisprudence' (1997) 15 *Law and History Review* 1.

[63] See generally R Kreitner, *Calculating Promises: the Emergence of Modern American Contract Doctrine* (Stanford, CA, Stanford University Press, 2003); IR Macneil, *The New Social Contract: an Inquiry into Modern Contractual Relations* (New Haven, CT, Yale University Press, 1980).

[64] Story, *Commentaries on Conflicts*, 2nd edn, (n 43) 306 (emphasis added).

V. A NATURAL SCIENCE OF TREATISE-WRITING

The goal that Story set for himself in *Commentaries on Conflicts* was to compile scientifically and then provide nutshell exposés on choice-of-law rules that would displace choice-of-forum considerations (and the disparate law those fora applied) as governing factors in American interstate conflicts cases.[65] Similar issues were, of course, presented in international settings. But Story had limited interest in genuinely transnational private-law discord, presumably because international legal pluralism did not directly impede New England's commercial aspirations or threaten its political nationalism.[66] He must also have known that neither the Spanish American settlements nor the British North American colonies were significant overland trading partners of the United States in the antebellum period, and that its overseas trade with the West Indies and Europe was largely regulated by international merchant and maritime law.[67] Situating a domestic, private-law problem in the context of international practice and the law of nations was in some measure a rhetorical flourish on Story's part, intended to add appealing classical cachet to choice-of-law rules at risk of being ignored or rejected by parochial state courts.[68] He was thus careful to show in *Commentaries on Conflicts* that the New England choice-of-law rules he applied on Circuit were consistent with the jurisprudence of 'the most polished and commercial states of Europe', reflected 'universality', were in 'perfect coincidence' with continental doctrine and, only when foreign conflicts rules were contradictory, that local rules should be preferred if they 'escaped from those incongruities'.[69]

[65] For indications of the role played by Story's sponsors in the establishment of those scholarly goals see, eg J Quincy, 'Address on the Occasion of the Dedication of Dane Law College' (1833) 9 *American Jurist & Law Magazine* 48; N Dane, 'To the President and Fellows of the Corporation of Harvard University', reproduced in Story (n 7) 2, 3–6. See also AE Sutherland, *The Law at Harvard: A History of Ideas and Men, 1817–1967* (Cambridge, MA, Belknap Press, 1967) 92–139.

[66] Landlocked American states were increasingly connected by roads, bridges, steamboats, and canals in the 1820s and 1830s, and the resulting hum of commerce moved Story to remark repeatedly that inland trade was the principal force to which local law was required to adjust. See, eg J Story, 'Review of a Treatise on the Law of Insurance, by Willard Phillips', reproduced in Story (n 21) 294; J Story, 'Discourse Delivered Before the Boston Mechanics' Institute, at the Opening of their Annual Course of Lectures, November 1829' in Story (n 21) 112.

[67] There are two references to Canadian trade in *Commentaries on Conflicts* (Story (n 2) 242, 469), and none to Spanish American commerce. The traditional rule in respect of international maritime law was that its applicability was determined geographically by the ebb and flow of the tide, but by the mid-nineteenth century the United States Supreme Court had sufficiently blunted that rule that federal courts' admiralty jurisdiction extended to commerce on such fresh waters as the Great Lakes, the Erie-Hudson system, and the Ohio–Missouri–Mississippi network. See generally SL Snell, *Courts of Admiralty and the Common Law: Origins of the American Experiment in Concurrent Jurisdiction* (Durham, NC, Carolina Academic Press, 2007).

[68] Compare C Winterer, *The Cultures of Classicism: Ancient Greece and Rome in American Intellectual Life* (Baltimore, MD, Johns Hopkins University Press, 2002) 99–151; MH Hoeflich, *Roman and Civil Law and the Development of Anglo-American Jurisprudence in the Nineteenth Century* (Athens, GA, University of Georgia Press, 1997) 9–102.

[69] Story, *Commentaries on Conflicts* (n 2) 118, 121, 354, 282.

The primacy and appropriateness of official law was, for Story, 'to be measured neither by moral law alone, nor by universal law alone, nor by the laws of society alone, but by a combination of the three'.[70] Unlike the formalistic law of many later nineteenth-century writers, Story's common law was not a discrete body of knowledge removed from other normative orders like economics, ethics or politics.[71] Its principles were, however, discoverable empirically and frameable abstractly in a wholistic scheme intended to replicate the geographically unbounded character of the natural sciences of astronomy, botany, and zoology. The patina of universalism provided by the reconciliation of European sources with English and American ones helped to buttress Story's assertions about the global essence of his choice-of-law rules.

Story's claims about the universal character of private law also found expression in the insights that underlay his contemporaneous recasting of Harvard Law School as a national institution. As Kent Newmyer has noted, Story thought that the prevailing apprenticeship system of law training often aggravated centrifugal tendencies in American law and politics because law-office study typically taught the local and state law that most supervising lawyers practised. Treatise-based, systematic instruction, supported by an eclectic law library in a metropolitan university, was his response to parochial, politically and commercially-fragmenting legal apprenticeships. Harvard's cosmopolitan library was not only assembled aggressively by Story and made part of that school's culture, it was also used heavily by him for research and writing projects.[72] And, like Story's eight other treatises, *Commentaries on Conflicts* soon became a keystone of classroom instruction, in Harvard's foundational commercial and property-law courses. That internal deployment of the treatises was central to the school's national aspirations.[73]

More generally, inductive synthesis in legal generalisation, the essence of what Story claimed to be doing as an author of treatises about law, went hand-in-hand with his juristic capacity to present juridical information in an objective fashion. Together, those skills cemented his claim to competence in respect of a particular type of 'legal science'.[74] Prevailing styles of organising raw informa-

[70] Story, *Commentaries on the Constitution* (n 2), vol 2, 249.

[71] Compare AJ Sebok, *Legal Positivism in American Jurisprudence* (New York, NY, Cambridge University Press, 1998); WM Wiecek, *The Lost World of Classical Legal Thought: Law and Ideology in America, 1886–1937* (New York, NY, Oxford University Press, 1998).

[72] The contents of that collection, together with those of Story's personal library, are described in: MH Hoeflich and KS Beck, *Catalogues of Early American Law Libraries: the 1846 Auction Catalogue of Joseph Story's Library* (Austin, TX, Jamail Center for Legal Research, 2004); and 'A Catalogue of the Law Library of Harvard University' (1841) 26 *American Jurist & Law Magazine* 254.

[73] See Newmyer, (n 24); C Warren in *History of the Harvard Law School and of Early Legal Conditions in America* (New York, NY, Da Capo Press, 2 vols, 1970) vol 1, 413–533; vol 2, 80, 92–139. For indications that the essential premises of Story's legal pedagogy persisted and spread over time, see generally EA Farnsworth, 'Casebooks: Contracts Scholarship in the Age of Anthology' (1987) 85 *Michigan Law Review* 1409.

[74] Although detailed discussions of legal science in its various early-modern and modern representations are beyond the scope of this study, helpful work of that kind can be found in JR Hackney, *Under Cover of Science: American Legal-Economic Theory and the Quest for Objectivity* (Durham, NC, Duke University Press, 2006); RS Berkowitz, *The Gift of Science: Leibniz and the Modern Legal Tradition*

tion about nature gave a central role to taxonomic divisions of knowledge, and so did Story. Through the vehicles of his nine treatises, Story marched across the terrain of bailments, constitutional law, conflicts of law, equity, procedural law, agency, partnership, bills of exchange and promissory notes, a template that was said to have been as inherent in state-law and its constituent subject matter as their internal taxonomies were for astronomy, botany and biology. Story's first treatise, *Commentaries on Bailments*, followed structurally and content-wise William Jones' half-century-old English staple on the same subject (reproduced in three editions before Story wrote), his agency text built on Samuel Livermore's contemporary Maryland treatise on that topic, *Commentaries on Bills of Exchange* expanded his 1809 and 1819 Americanisations of Joseph Chitty's English bills and notes text, and *Commentaries on Conflicts* had a head-start with the choice-of-law cases collected for his 1809 'Digest of Law'.[75] In addition to that companion treatise literature, Anglo-American law journals had begun to augment their standard repertoire of case law, book reviews and social notes by including short essays on legal doctrine whose authors often deployed in condensed form the methodology that underpinned monographic legal treatises.[76] Story was plainly not the inventor of the treatise, methodologically or substantively, but he publicised that format tirelessly and he thereby helped to restructure juristic knowledge pervasively by parting it out into many fewer subdivisions than did the institutional works with which his treatises co-existed and by which they were sometimes facilitated.[77]

The abstraction, orderliness, and compaction that characterised Story's treatises was presumably learned and practised in his statute consolidations and codal research, and was in harmony with prevailing methods of epistemic presentation in the companion Anglo-American natural sciences.[78] Story's style deliberately approached one of 'absence', in which he effaced himself from the legal events, rules and policy stockpiled and displayed in his texts. The techniques of collecting,

(Cambridge, MA, Harvard University Press, 2005); H Schweber, 'The Science of Legal Science: The Model of the Natural Sciences in Nineteenth Century American Legal Education' (1999) 17 *Law and History Review* 42.

[75] See generally D Ibbetson, 'Sir William Jones as Comparative Lawyer' in A Murray (ed), *Sir William Jones, 1746–94: A Commemoration* (Oxford, Oxford University Press, 1998); RA Ferguson, 'The Emulation of Sir William Jones in the Early Republic' (1979) 52 *The New England Quarterly* 3; S Livermore, *A Treatise on the Law of Principal and Agent and of Sales by Auction* (Baltimore, MD, Samuel Livermore, 1818); Chitty (n 13); Nadelmann (n 8).

[76] See generally S Vogenaur, 'Law Journals in Nineteenth-Century England' (2008) 12 *Edinburgh Law Review* 26; J Fishman, 'An Early Pennsylvania Legal Periodical: The Pennsylvania Law Journal 1842–1848' (2001) 45 *American Journal of Legal History* 22; S Normand, 'Profil des périodiques juridiques québécois au XIXe siècle' (1993) 34 *Cahiers de droit* 153; EL Shepard, 'The First Law Journals in Virginia' (1987) 79 *Law Library Journal* 33.

[77] Compare Z Swift, *A System of the Laws of the State of Connecticut* (New York, NY, Zephaniah Swift, 2 vols, 1795–96); N Dane, *A General Digest and Abridgement of American Law* (Boston, MA, Cummings, Hilliard and Company, 9 vols, 1823–29); Kent (n 34).

[78] See generally J Endersby, 'Classifying Sciences: Systematics and States in Mid-Victorian Natural History' in MJ Daunton (ed), *The Organization of Knowledge in Victorian Britain* (Oxford, Oxford University Press, 2005) 61; MJ Nye (ed), *The Cambridge History of Science*, vol 5 (Cambridge, Cambridge University Press, 8 vols, 2003) 21-215; E Mayr, *The Growth of Biological Thought* (Cambridge, MA, Harvard University Press, 1982).

categorising and abstracting legal information helped writers like Story pose as a kind of neutral medium through which scientifically-processed law passed to readers. Since universality and continuity are among the watchwords of treatise-writing, potential differences in representation were collapsed into sameness.[79] And because Story the commentator purported to be merely discovering and reporting empirically-given, doctrinal 'facts', he could claim the methodological expertise to write tomes on nine discrete areas of Anglo-American law in 16 years. Authorial effacement in service of scientific neutrality and permanence also helps to explain why it was thought appropriate by publisher Little, Brown to engage six unrelated and subsequent nineteenth-century editors of 'Joseph Story's' *Commentaries on Conflicts*.[80] In his emphasis on technique, Story foreshadowed analogous integration of antebellum scientific method into the writing and practice of other fields of human action like design, business and public administration.[81]

It bears repetition that *Commentaries on Conflicts*, like several of Story's other treatises, is a book about the sovereignty of individuals, vested private rights, and consent-based normativity. As such, that text echoed his ongoing work on other fronts like management of two of New England's financial institutions (executive positions that Story retained throughout his time at Harvard and on the Supreme Court) and leadership of the American Unitarian Association.[82] Self-reliance, self-improvement, civility and enterprise were the qualities most closely associated with his libertarianism.[83] The state's primary role, in that scheme of things, was to promote and protect the sanctity of contracts and the security of ownership. Reconciling or merging natural law and Cartesian inheritances with the dictates of neo-classical political economy through inductive method was intended by Story, artfully, to produce a more broadly-based *jus commune* of private international proprietary and contractual rights than the authoritative injunctions of naturalism, logic and Roman law had been able to achieve. 'Artful' seems like a fitting descriptive term because Story's interstate choice-of-law rules were a facsimile *lex mercatoria*, buttressed by the techniques and metaphors of science.

[79] CompareParker in this volume.

[80] See n 43. Compare TA Baloch, 'Law Booksellers and Printers as Agents of Unchange' (2007) 66 *Cambridge Law Journal* 389; L Daston and P Galison, *Objectivity* (Cambridge MA, MIT Press, 2007).

[81] Compare MF Guillen, *The Taylorized Beauty of the Mechanical: Scientific Management and the Rise of Modern Architecture* (Princeton, NJ, Princeton University Press, 2006); J Yates; *Control Through Communication: the Rise of System in American Management* (Baltimore, MD, Johns Hopkins University Press, (1989); HL Schacter, *Frederick Taylor and the Public Administration Community: A Reevaluation* (Albany, NY, State University of New York Press, 1989).

[82] See generally GT Dunne, 'Joseph Story: The Salem Years' (1965) 101 *Essex Institute Historical Collections* 307; GT Dunne, 'Mr Justice Story and the American Law of Banking' (1961) 5 *American Journal of Legal History* 205; DW Howe, *The Unitarian Conscience: Harvard Moral Philosophy, 1805–1861* (Cambridge, MA, Harvard University Press, 1970).

[83] See Story, 'Natural Law' in Lieber (n 21), vol 9, 150. See also Story, *Commentaries on Conflicts* (n 2) 71; Story, *Commentaries on the Constitution* (n 2), vol 2, 249; vol 1, 397–407. For discussion of the local impact of Story's idol in political theory, William Paley, see generally FW Smith, *Professors and Public Ethics: Studies of Northern Moral Philosophers Before the Civil War* (Ithaca, NY, Cornell University Press, 1956).

The lengths to which Story went, in the form of nine plump treatises, to bolster the patina of scientific authority for law is very nearly the best evidence for which one could hope of his closely-related commitment to the autonomy of individuals and their capacity to engage in willed, consensual exchanges. The roles of free choice and determinism in American legal doctrine of the antebellum and reconstruction periods have been shown in recent scholarship to have been complicated.[84] But the grist that Story provided for those reflective mills lies more in a pattern of behaviour and in passing remarks than in explicit pronouncements. Likewise, he did not have much to say about the treatise's relationship as a trope or idiom to commercial custom, personal expectations, economic exigency or general judicial practice. Story was a prolific writer in a talky age who used words like 'science' and 'scientific' volubly, but without great regard to the pedigree, definition or implications of those terms' use. He did not write often about the form of legal literature that his treatises epitomised, and he said little about 'legal science' that is especially revealing or profound. Organisations for the study or promotion of the natural sciences and natural history abounded in the North Atlantic community during the second and third quarters of the nineteenth century, and their membership lists often read in part like a 'who's who' of local lawyers. Story does not appear to have been active in those kinds of associations, where significant methodological cross-pollination between science and law apparently occurred and quickly came to saturate elite legal culture.[85] He was plainly consumed by an increasingly prominent species of legal science and he was a dyed-in-the-wool legal instrumentalist, but Story's epistemological commitments in law are accessible mostly by observation or through ad hoc remarks in his correspondence and speeches.[86]

VI. CONCLUSIONS

Joseph Story was a federally-oriented, commercially-savvy nation builder who plainly thought that judicial decisions, legal doctrine, legislation and constitutions

[84] Compare SL Blumenthal, 'The Mind of a Moral Agent: Scottish Common Sense and the Problem of Responsibility in Nineteenth-Century American Law' (2008) 26 *Law and History Review* 99; LA Grossman, 'James Coolidge Carter and Mug-Wump Jurisprudence' (2002) 20 *Law and History Review* 577; SA Siegel, 'John Chipman Grey and the Moral Basis of Classical Legal Thought' (2001) 86 *Iowa Law Review* 1513.

[85] See generally RE Kohler, *All Creatures: Naturalists, Collectors and Biodiversity, 1850–1950* (Princeton, NJ, Princeton University Press, 2006) 47–136; SJMM Alberti, 'Placing Nature: Natural History Collections and Their Owners in Nineteenth-Century Provincial England' (2002) 35 *British Journal for the History of Science* 291; C Rosenberg, 'Science and Social Values in Nineteenth Century America: A Case Study in the Growth of Scientific Institutions' in C Rosenberg (ed), *No Other Gods: On Science and American Social Thought* (Baltimore, MD, Johns Hopkins University Press, 1997) 135.

[86] For indications that Story was not always so taciturn about things that mattered to him, compare SM Silverman, 'Joseph Story and Death in Early-19th-Century America' (1997) 21 *Death Studies* 397. Story lost most of two families at a relatively young age, which helps to explain the time he had available for fast-paced writing, judging, and teaching.

could play instrumental roles in the United States' social development. Commerce, transportation and national security were said by him to be especially relevant to American progress, and therefore particularly eligible for legal promotion:

> Let us extend the national authority over the whole extent of power given by the Constitution. Let us have great military and naval schools; an adequate regular army; the broad foundations laid of a permanent navy; a national bank; a national system of bankruptcy; a great navigation act; a general survey of our ports, and appointments of port wardens and pilots; Judicial Courts which shall embrace the whole Constitutional powers; national notaries public and national justices of the peace, for the commercial and national concerns of the United States. By such enlarged and liberal institutions, the Government of the United States will be endeared to the people, and the factions of the great States will be rendered harmless. Let us prevent the possibility of a division, by creating great national interests which shall bind us in an indissoluble chain.[87]

The centripetal sentiment apparent in those acutely programmatic remarks played itself out not only in Story's approach to internal improvements and the institutions of American commerce, but also in his attitudes toward the political division of constitutional powers, the institutional relationship of federal to state courts and, most notably for current purposes, the economic problem of interstate private-law discord. Story and other discriminating observers of-the-day regarded *Commentaries on Conflicts* as the most ambitious and influential of his nine treatises, and it has therefore been treated in this chapter as emblematic.

By packaging *Commentaries on Conflicts* as a treatise, Story traded on the antebellum natural sciences to appeal to juristic sentiment and thereby garner national, professional support for universal choice-of-law rules. That treatise consisted of generalisations from collectable judicial results in individual cases, rather than discoveries of norms divinely given in nature, attention to the commands of a sovereign or enumeration of those norms and commands. Doing legal science on that model, like comprehension of the natural sciences, was said to offer antebellum Americans heightened control over their environment as law was deployed diligently in service of humanly-posited, progressive goals. Indeed, public opinion of-the-day was increasingly reluctant to accept grounds of authority other than rigorously scientific ones.[88] Logical deduction from empirically-derived abstract principles enabled science to get things done in the physical world, and so it would be with reflections of that methodology like synthesis and *stare decisis* in the socio-legal world.[89]

[87] Joseph Story to Nathaniel Williams (22 February 1815), reproduced in Story (n 7), vol 1, 253–54.

[88] See generally RH Drayton, *Nature's Government: Science, Imperial Britain, and the Improvement of the World* (New Haven, CT, Yale University Press, 2000); BV Bruce, *The Launching of Modern American Science, 1846–1876* (Ithaca, NY, Cornell University Press, 1987); SE Zeller, *Inventing Canada: Early Victorian Science and the Idea of a Transcontinental Union* (Toronto, ON, University of Toronto Press, 1987).

[89] Compare N Duxbury, *The Nature and Authority of Precedent* (Cambridge, Cambridge University Press, 2008); FG Kempin, 'Precedent and Stare Decisis: The Critical Years, 1800 to 1850' (1959) 3 *American Journal of Legal History* 28.

One large issue with which Story has left his early-twenty-first-century readers is how he could have been an empirical researcher and an abstract generaliser at the same time that he was a social engineer. Expressed more bluntly, a residual problem is how legal doctrine could have been thought to have had the truth-value of empirically-verifiable generalisations while being humanly-adaptable to social needs.[90] Story dreamed of designing a comprehensive, international law of private rights, and in the meantime his *jus commune* of choice-of-law doctrine was offered as a stopgap measure to help make 'science of cacophony'.[91] But he provided few hints for a reconciliation of legal empiricism with social planning through law. Story has also been an appropriately favourite subject of instrumentally-minded historians who have, however, devoted comparatively little energy to the tenets of legal science that made his treatises epistemologically credible but at the same time called the possibility of humanly-managed economic progress through law into theoretical question.[92] If asked about that seeming incongruity, Story probably would have said that his objective descriptions of state law were themselves normative, and that it was coincidentally a good thing that the norms implicit in his empirical collections of legal facts conduced to commercial progress.

The Anglo-American legal treatise-writing project would not reach its peak during Story's lifetime. Comprehensive generalisation and systematisation of common-law principles in a homogenous and all-inclusive treatise literature was, instead, a phenomenon of the last third of the nineteenth century.[93] The Storyesque goals that underlay that later consolidation included demonstration to sibling academics, practising lawyers and lay-people that legal knowledge was an orderly object, its principles were universal, it could only be acquired through methods characteristic of the contemporary study of nature, and that it therefore constituted a field eligible for learned reflection in university settings.[94]

Private production of magisterial treatises, and a related embrace of the deductively-based doctrine of precedent, has sometimes been said to have deflected

[90] Compare H Hovenkamp, 'Evolutionary Models in Jurisprudence' (1985) 64 *Texas Law Review* 645; P Stein, *Legal Evolution: the Story of an Idea* (Cambridge, Cambridge University Press, 1980).

[91] That apt expression was borrowed from Newmyer (n 4) 38, who used it in a slightly different context.

[92] See, eg DJ Hulsebosch, 'Debating the Transformation of American Law: James Kent, Joseph Story, and the Legacy of the Revolution' in DH Hamilton and AL Brophy (eds), *Transformations in American Legal History: Essays in Honour of Morton J Horwitz* (Cambridge, MA, Harvard University Press, 2009)) 1; R Harris, 'The Encounters of Economic History and Legal History' (2003) 21 *Law and History Review* 297 esp 324–45; P Karsten, *Heart Versus Head: Judge-Made Law in Nineteenth Century America* (Chapel Hill, NC, University of North Carolina Press, 1997) 47–143.

[93] Although, and perhaps enigmatically, traditionally-structured legal treatises have continued to be produced in a minority of Anglo-American jurisdictions into the late-twentieth and early-twenty-first centuries.

[94] See generally BA Kimball, *The Inception of Modern Professional Education: C.C. Langdell, 1826–1906* (Chapel Hill, NC, University of North Carolina Press, 2009) 84–232; RW Gordon, 'The Ideal and the Actual in the Law: Fantasies and Practices of New York City Lawyers, 1870–1910' in GW Gawalt (ed), *The New High Priests: Lawyers in Post-Civil War America* (Westport, CT, Greenwood Press, 1984) 51; D Sugarman, 'The Legal Boundaries of Liberty: Dicey, Liberalism and Legal Science' (1983) 46 *The Modern Law Review* 102.

Anglo-American codification initiatives that promised an even purer expression of system, abstraction, and compaction in law. Story's leading biographer concluded, for example, that:

> Codification confronted the problem of domestic [legal] conflict, as did Story in his treatises. But codification was dead [in New England by the 1830s] and the unifying impact of treatise education was long-range at best . . . Story the publicist [therefore] took over where Story the codifier left off.[95]

And in the sweeping words of one of Story's Harvard successors, Roscoe Pound:

> . . . the doctrinal writing of the formative era delivered us from the danger of premature, crude codification. Lay discussions of American law in the first quarter of the nineteenth century abound in demands for an American code . . . Had such men as [James] Kent and [Joseph] Story allowed their good sense to be overcome by the Continental philosophers of law, whom they undoubtedly admired, the future of American law might have been very different. I doubt if our judges would have been strong enough to withstand the movement for codification . . .Doctrinal writing preserved unity in our law when its unity was sorely threatened.[96]

Parodying the American intellectual historian Perry Miller, another modern commentator concluded simply that common lawyers beat down their codifying opponents with an awesome array of legal treatises.[97]

Other observers have taken different views of the interface among codes, treatises, and digests as competing, complementary, or sequential products of scientific methodology in modern law:

> After private law (or indeed any branch of law) has been systematized, the obvious next step is codification, which will confer a special authoritative status upon a particular succinct statement of the principles of the law. This happened in France, for example. There the indefatigable [Robert-Joseph] Pothier, after spending many years on the task of putting Justinian's *Digest* into a methodological scheme and some more on a redaction of the customs of Orléans, set about writing treatises . . . that made the French code possible, and of course the code supplanted the treatises. The similarity between the ideal of the treatise writer and that of the codifier is well illustrated by a remark of [Jean-Etienne-Marie] Portalis on the aim of codifying legislation: 'The function of statutory law is to determine, in broad perspectives, general legal maxims, to establish principles from which inferences can be drawn, and not to involve itself in the particulars of individual areas'.[98]

[95] Newmyer (n 4) 296, 281.

[96] Pound, (n 1) 152–53.

[97] See RW Gordon, 'Review [of Cook (n 16)]' (1983) 36 *Vanderbilt Law Review* 431–56, citing Miller (n 1) 239–54. See also A Masferrer, 'Defense of the Common Law Against Postbellum American Codification' (2008) 50 *American Journal of Legal History* 355; H Schweber, *The Creation of American Common Law, 1850–1880* (Cambridge, Cambridge University Press, 2004).

[98] Simpson (n 3) 675. See also JW Cairns, 'Attitudes to Codification and the Scottish Science of Legislation, 1600–1870' (2007) 22 *Tulane European and Civil Law Forum* 1; M Moran, 'Portalis v Bentham: The Objectives Ascribed to Codification of the Civil Law and the Criminal Law in France, England and Canada' in Law Commission of Canada (ed), *Perspectives on Legislation: Essays from the 1999 Legal Dimensions Initiative* (Ottawa, ON, Law Commission of Canada, 2000) 125; D Lieberman, *The Province of Legislation Determined: Legal Theory in Eighteenth-Century Britain* (Cambridge, Cambridge University Press, 1989).

Legislative enactment is, on that view, a capital difference between codal and treatise packaging of legal doctrine. The elite bar's trust in local legislatures to avoid manhandling of draft codified texts in parliamentary or congressional debate and to confide ongoing supervision of enacted law to lawyerly managers keen about social change seem, therefore, to be important factors in the collective professional assessment of whether 'democratic' codes or 'jurisconsults' treatises should be preferred as scientific warehouses or exhibitions of legal information.

This chapter and several other recent assessments of transnational experience suggest that the relationship among various literary expressions of nineteenth-century legal science was more often dialogical than sequential or adversarial.[99] Those literary forms shared methodological and idiomatic roots in the natural sciences, a feature that was regularly emphasised for public relations advantage. And they were all routinely and perhaps ironically turned in service of the pursuit of a kind of ethnic nationalism through law as the nineteenth century shaded into the 20th.[100] That later process of stoking political identity with legal artifacts gave rise, in turn, to the spectrum of very modern legal traditions that are now more-or-less taken for granted.[101] But that distinctive series of events, which often deployed the treatise in aid of nativistic goals different from the goals that Story had in mind, is a *problématique* for another day.[102]

[99] See text at notes 8–25. See also Girard and Wright in this volume; KGC Reid, 'From Text-Book to Book of Authority: The Principles of George Joseph Bell' (2011) 15 *Edinburgh Law Review* 6; M John, *Politics and the Law in Nineteenth Century Germany* (Oxford, Clarendon Press, 1989) 15–41, 73–104; S Normand, 'Une analyse quantitative de la doctrine en droit civil québécois' (1982) 23 *Cahiers de droit* 1009; N Crystal, 'Codification and the Rise of the Restatement Movement' (1979) 54 *Washington Law Review* 239.

[100] See generally B Young, 'Overlapping Identities: The Quebec Civil Code of 1866, Its Reception and Interpretation' in R Beathier and I Rorive (eds), *Le Code Napoléon: un ancêtre vénéré? Mélanges offerts à Jacques Vanderlinden* (Bruxelles, Bruylant, 2004) 259; N Kasirer, 'The Annotated Criminal Code en *Version Québécoise*: Signs of Territoriality in Canadian Criminal Law' (1990) 13 *Dalhousie Law Journal* 520; GB Baker, 'The Reconstitution of Upper Canadian Legal Thought in the Late-Victorian Empire' (1985) 3 *Law and History Review* 219.

[101] See generally HP Glenn, *Legal Traditions of the World* 4th edn (New York, NY, Oxford University Press, 2010).

[102] For indications of how that account might unfold, see, eg RA Macdonald, 'Understanding Civil Law Scholarship in Quebec' (1985) 23 *Osgoode Hall Law Journal* 573, esp 585–604; E Veitch and RA Macdonald, 'Law Teachers and Their Jurisdiction' (1978) 56 *Canadian Bar Review* 710. See also NEH Hull, 'Restatement and Reform: A New Perspective on the Origins of the American Law Institute' (1990) 8 *Law and History Review* 55.

5

A Province of Jurisprudence?: Invention of a Law of Constitutional Conventions

ROMAN J HOYOS*

> The plague is met by order; its function is to sort out every possible confusion . . . Against the plague, which is a mixture, discipline brings into play its power, which is one of analysis.
>
> Michel Foucault, *Discipline and Punish*, 1977

IN HIS BRIEF essay on the treatise literature, Morton Horwitz suggested that the first appearance of legal treatise marked the 'crystallisation' of an area of law.[1] Horwitz did not develop either the idea of crystallisation or first-ness in any depth, and these ideas remain under-theorised. But they do suggest something important about changes in legal consciousness. Even understood in terms of legal consciousness, though, the parameters of crystallisation are not entirely clear. What does it mean, for instance, for an area of law to crystallise? What exactly is being crystallised? And what are the purposes and consequences of crystallisation? There are also important questions about first-ness worth examining. What, for instance, qualifies as a 'first' treatise? Does it entail developing a new area of law, an area implicit or inchoate within a larger subject, or something else entirely? Were first treatises simply 'firsts', or was there something more significant at work? In this chapter I want to suggest a way to begin to conceptualise this idea of crystallisation, one that centres around the idea of 'order'.

To get at this idea, I start by examining some first treatises through the lens of Joel Bishop's *The First Book of the Law* (1868). Bishop was described by some of his contemporaries as 'the foremost law writer of the age' because of his prolific writing.[2] But his method and theory of treatise writing was concentrated

* Associate Professor, Southwestern Law School, Los Angeles, California.

[1] M Horwitz, 'Treatise Literature' (1976) 69 *Law Library Journal* 460, 461. See also AWB Simpson, 'The Rise and Fall of the Legal Treatise: Legal Principles and the Forms of Legal Literature' (1981) 48 *The University of Chicago Law Review* 632, 652.

[2] S Siegel, 'Joel Bishop's Orthodoxy' (1995) 13 *Law and History Review* 215, 220 (inner quotations omitted).

in *The First Book*, a treatise that was simultaneously about legal education and jurisprudence. By 1868 the treatise had become a major component of American law. Just how important this development was can be seen in a brief comparison between Bishop's work and David Hoffman's. Hoffman's *A Course of Legal Study* (1817) was the first attempt to offer guidance to legal study.[3] Hoffman, writing just before the flowering of the treatise tradition in the United States, urged students to range wide in their studies, from moral and political philosophy to works on civil law to constitutions. But it was 'folly' 'to hope from them particular and definite knowledge' of law.[4] By contrast, Bishop, writing in the midst of decades of treatise writing, emphasised the treatise as the central tool for the study of law, as treatises were written by a 'class of legal persons' whose special role it was to impose order on the law by identifying the reasons that constituted law. Treatise writers made law legible and understandable to both students and practitioners by 'rationalising' and 'systematising' it. That is to say, they sorted through cases and doctrines to identify major principles undergirding the law.

This process of 'rationalisation' and 'systematisation' entailed what Mark Neocleous has called, in a somewhat different context, the 'fabrication of order'.[5] Two things are important to note about Neocleous' idea. First, 'order' refers to the central concern of police. Second, Neocleous emphasises the older, constructive definition of 'fabrication'. Conceived as fabrication, policing appears 'as an *activity* rather than an institution, shaping order rather than passively responding to disorder: the fabrication of order'.[6] Neocleous was interested in a particular form of order, or more precisely a form of order within the larger sphere of civil society, which he sees as lacking the motive power to be self-generating. Police is thus a tool by which 'the state fabricates order within civil society' to prevent its collapse. A police power, then, does not merely maintain order, it has a '*productive* and *creative* force'.[7]

But we should not be too quick to dismiss or ignore the more common imaginative definition of 'fabrication', as it has a productive and creative force as well. Treatise writers fabricated order in both senses; they were both making law appear as if it was orderly and attempting to make it so. Importantly, the fabrication of order depended first upon the fabrication of 'disorder'. As part of the construction of their authority, treatise writers had to portray the state of the existing law as disorderly or chaotic. Given the fast growing number of cases, often going in different directions, it was relatively easy for writers to identify drift. But disorder, like order, is at least as much about consciousness as fact. Indeed, the

[3] P Miller, *The Life of the Mind in America from the Revolution to the Civil War* (New York, NY, Harcourt, Brace, Javanovich, 1965) 141.

[4] Quoted in ibid.

[5] M Neocleous, *The Fabrication of Social Order: A Critical Theory of Police Power* (Sterling, VA, Pluto Press, 2000); Neocleous, 'Theoretical Foundations of the "New Police Science"' in MD Dubber and M Valverde (eds), *The New Police Science: The Police Power in Domestic and International Governance* (Stanford, CT, Stanford University Press, 2006).

[6] Neocleous, 'Theoretical Foundations', ibid 26–27.

[7] Ibid 28–29.

'fundamentally irrational' nature of the common law could be seen as a strength rather than a weakness.[8] To see it as irrational, or disorderly, was the epiphany that led to crystallisation. It was this process of the fabrication of dis/order that is, I think, a potentially useful conception of 'crystallisation', and should help us to understand more fully the significance of treatises, especially first treatises. Neocleous' idea of the fabrication of order allows us to see the treatise not only as a text to understand the 'underlying metaphysics' of a juridicalised police, but as an act of that police as well. The first treatise, then, was the creation of a field to be policed.

This idea of crystallisation is on full display in John Alexander Jameson's *Constitutional Conventions*, which I take up in the second part of the chapter. Jameson's treatise, the most interesting of the century's first treatises, has gone largely unexamined by modern historians, lost in the shadows of some of his more famous contemporaries like Thomas Cooley, John Dillon and Christopher Tiedeman. Yet for the 20 years – at least – in which his treatise went through four editions, it was enormously important. My interest in Jameson's treatise stems from a larger project that I am working on dealing with the history of the constitutional convention, where it plays an important role. But his treatise has much to tell us about the history of the treatise literature as well, particularly as it concerns the themes of crystallisation, first-ness and dis/order. Dis/order in fact was a prominent theme in Jameson's work. It could hardly be said that there was a 'law' of constitutional conventions prior to the publication of Jameson's treatise. Until the mid-nineteenth-century, there was little thought of the convention as a *legal* institution at all. In fact, the idea that a constitutional convention was or could be a legal institution would have been deeply controversial prior to Jameson's treatise. If there was a law of constitutional conventions at all, it was a localised or particularised law, not universal and systematic. This was precisely what made the convention so important; it was an extra-constitutional institution that lay beyond law, one that embodied the people and their sovereignty. Jameson's success in inventing a law of constitutional conventions was not merely the product of his eloquence or labour, but was due in large part to its timing as well. Written both after and in consequence of the Civil War, Jameson's work highlights the significance of the first treatise and the fabrication (in the dual sense) of dis/order, and suggests that rationalisation and systematisation must be understood historically. In this case, the use of the convention by the southern states to secede from the Union raised problems about the convention that could be taken seriously in ways that it could or might not 20 years earlier or later. Secession also induced Jameson to be more explicit about his aims than the typical treatise writer, in particular about his goal of imposing law's authority on the convention, and ultimately the people. Jameson's treatise then suggests that a great deal more was at stake in treatises than simply the rationalisation and systematisation of law.

[8] Miller, *The Life of the Mind* (n 3) 121.

I

According to Perry Miller, the common law as it existed in the eighteenth century was no 'construction of systematic reason: it was a haphazard accumulation of precedents, quirks, obscurities . . . fundamentally irrational by its inherent nature'.[9] But it was only after the American Revolution that Americans began to consider seriously the common law's irrationality. This concern grew out of a number of factors, including a desire to establish an indigenous jurisprudence, one that rested on republican principles, the devolution of a new plenary judicial power on the former colonies, the rapid, often overwhelming, increase in litigation, the multiplicity of jurisdictions, and the publishing of judicial opinions.[10] This new legal environment seemed to be outpacing lawyers' ability to digest or even understand the law. How to organise and make sense of this material was one of the chief legal questions of the nineteenth century. A number of different forms of legal literature emerged to address this issue, including case reports, digests, legal journals, codes and treatises. But by the second quarter of the nineteenth century, the treatise had emerged as the principal tool of organising the law and educating lawyers. This was important as the treatise form gave the writer a great deal more individual authorial freedom to determine the course and content of the law, even as he claimed to be simply 'stating the law as it is'. This freedom enabled treatise writers to transcend the cases they relied upon to derive general principles upon which law rested, which they did through the fabrication of both order and disorder. In this process, the first treatise was key; it was the moment in which disorder came into legal consciousness to congeal an area of law. By bringing legal drift into view, it could be segmented, regulated and ordered. It is here that Joel Bishop's work offers a useful starting point, as he offered one of the clearest statements of the treatise's role in American law and legal development.

Bishop authored treatises on criminal law and procedure, family law, statutory interpretation, contracts and torts. But it was in his treatise on the study of law, *The First Book of Law*, that he offered a theory of the treatise and treatise writer. 'There is', Bishop wrote,

> a class of legal persons, whose especial duty it is to give reasons. These are the writers of those textbooks which are called legal treatises, or commentaries on the law. And we have already seen, that the law itself consists, not in the points decided by the judges in the causes coming before them, but in the legal reasons. These textbooks become, therefore, under certain circumstances, authority; and under other circumstances, they are a sort of *quasi* authority; while, under still other circumstances, very little weight is given them.[11]

[9] Ibid.

[10] Ibid; GE White, *The Marshall Court and Cultural Change, 1815–1835* (New York, NY, Macmillan, 1988); R Pound, *The Formative Era of American Law* (New York, NY, Little, Brown, and Co, 1938); J Goebel, *Antecedents and Beginnings to 1801* (New York, NY, Macmillan, 1971).

[11] JP Bishop, *The First Book of the Law, Explaining the Nature, Sources, Books, and Practical Applications of Legal Science, and Methods of Study and Practice* (Boston, MA, Little, Brown & Co, 1868) 132.

Bishop's construction of treatise writers as a 'class of legal persons' was an attempt to deal with the problem of authority that confronted treatise writers. As AWB Simpson has described, 'the text-writer, unless he himself is a judge, possesses as an individual no authority derived from the office'.[12] His authority lay only in 'the truth which any such treatise bears'.[13] And this 'truth' rested on the writer's ability both to identify disorder in the law and to provide clarity through the development of broad principles. This was not unique to treatise writing. Thomas Haskell has described a similar phenomenon occurring around the same period in the social sciences. 'Once freed of the dead weight of the marginal practitioner', Haskell has written, social scientists believed that 'the general level of science would rise. The authentic man of science would reach his audience without distraction and be able to speak with the authority that he deserved and the truth required'.[14] The 'marginal practitioners' that were the targets of treatise writers were the lawyers and judges who were responsible for the irrationality of the law.

As a 'class of legal persons', treatise writers were particularly engaged in crafting a scientific approach to law, which involved the 'systematic derivation and application of general principles to make law more intelligible, predictable, and in harmony with republicanism and a market economy'.[15] As Bishop explained,

> A legal treatise or commentary is an orderly statement of those principles in which the law consists, whether drawn from the reports of law cases, from natural reason, or from any other source; accompanied by such illustrations and references to authorities to render them plain in their application and accurate in their outlines, and settle to the inquiring mind the fact that they are truly the law.[16]

Importantly, Bishop pointed out, this was the particular domain of the treatise writer, and it was what separated the writer from other legal actors, including judges in particular. In fact, it was in contrast to the judge that Bishop was able to identify the treatise writer's role and authority. Of course, both judges and treatise writers were engaged in the similar project of giving reasons. And *reasons*, Bishop reminded his readers, were law. '[L]learned and lucid reasons' may come from judges, in which case, the treatise writer merely quoted and attributed the judge. But in most cases it was a process of 'weav[ing] what is partly original with him, and partly taken from others, into the fabric of text law'.[17] In fact, Bishop doubted judges' abilities to give good or even sufficient reasons. Whether because they were involved in the day-to-day administration of law or simply lacked the capacity, judges' opinions were not necessarily dispositive as reasons.

[12] Simpson, 'The Rise and Fall of the Treatise' (n 1) 638.

[13] Bishop, *The First Book* (n 11) 154.

[14] TL Haskell, *The Emergence of Professional Social Science: The American Social Science Association and the Nineteenth Century Crisis of Authority* (Urbana, IL, University of Illinois Press, 1977) 66.

[15] White, *The Marshall Court* (n 10) 94. See also Miller, *The Life of the Mind*; Simpson, 'The Rise and Fall of the Legal Treatise'; CF Stychin, 'The Commentaries of Chancellor Kent and the Development of an American Common Law' (1993) 37 *American Journal of Legal History* 440.

[16] Bishop, *The First Book* (n 11) 137.

[17] Ibid 142.

To differentiate the treatise writer from the judge, Bishop devised the point-principle distinction. Judges decided 'points', which filled the volumes of reports and digests. But 'points adjudged' were only 'deemed by legal idiots to be the law'.[18] They were merely historical artifacts, and could never control future cases. The treatise writer, by contrast, with the cases before him, as well as 'natural reason . . . or any other source', looked at the law as a whole to discover principles. A 'principle', in contrast to a point, was 'universal'; it governed past and future cases, and could never be controverted by a case.[19] This difference between point and principle was the difference between darkness and truth. Where the judge 'often grop[ed] in darkness', the treatise writer, 'by long and laborious methods', derived the principles that governed the cases.[20] It was this labour that constituted treatise writers as a class and defined their authority. In a world of disorderly law, 'time and labour' became crucial to the construction of the treatise writer's authority. Identifying law as a 'chaotic mass', as Horace Gray Wood had put it,[21] meant that only someone willing to invest the 'time and labour' to sort through it could claim to be an expert on the law. Bishop described the process in the following way:

> The writer of a textbook, by long and laborious methods, has brought the cases together, has collected out of them and out of the works of preceding authors such principles as had been already discovered, has himself added such principles as he was able to discover also, has applied his practised mind to the arranging and stating of the principles in the clearest way possible to him . . .[22]

It was only the treatise writer who took the time to sort through the common law's irrationality and conjure up order. As an illustration, in his treatise on family law, Bishop included an index entry for 'Not thought of', consisting of cases in which the judges had failed to identify principles that Bishop himself had discovered.[23]

Even a merely competent treatise could elevate a jurist's status within the profession. Thomas Cooley's aim in writing his first treatise, for instance, was informed by the fact that he saw 'the chance to gain in reputation and income by competently performing a necessary job'.[24] Yet even a competent job required a great deal of labour. Cooley's treatise was 'massive', 'pervading the hundreds of cases, principles, and illustration', which helped both to create a field of law and to establish his authority by putting his erudition on display.[25] It was through their labour that treatise writers became 'discoverers' of the law, and in that sense

[18] Ibid 127.

[19] Ibid 148–49.

[20] Ibid 151–52.

[21] HG Wood, *A Treatise on the Law of Master and Servant. Concerning the Relation, Duties and Liabilities of Employers and Employees* (Albany, NY, J D Parsons, 1877) iii. I would like to thank my colleague Gowri Ramachandran for pointing me to this treatise.

[22] Bishop, *The First Book* (n 11) 151–52.

[23] Siegel, 'Joel Bishop's Orthodoxy' (n 2) 231.

[24] AR Jones, *The Constitutional Conservatism of Thomas McIntyre Cooley: A Study in the History of Ideas* (New York, NY, Garland Publishing, 1987) 140.

[25] Ibid, 122. See also PS Paludan, *A Covenant with Death: The Constitution, Law, and Equality in the Civil War Era* (Urbana, IL, University of Illinois Press, 1975) 249.

'just as much entitled to the credit of discovery, as was Sir Isaac Newton for the *discovery* of the law of attraction in nature'.[26]

Bishop could not quite bring himself to say explicitly that a treatise made or was law. 'The true theory', he wrote, 'is not that a text-writer can create law'. But the idea was implicit in the point-principle distinction. As Stephen Siegel has explained, 'Bishop maintained that all decisions not only are limited by their facts, but to their facts'.[27] The treatise writer was not burdened by cases and their facts. Indeed, the best writers kept cases in the footnotes, neatly sealed off from principles, preventing them from becoming textual authority. This view was not unique to Bishop. George Ticknor Curtis described the process in similar terms.

> It is not the province of any writer to make law, and he must certainly state the law as it is, if he means to have his book respectable and respected. But while his text should exhibit clearly the actual state of the law, he should never forget that he is dealing with principles; that it is his task, to exhibit the doctrine of the law, which is its life; and that unless he does this, his work, however accurately he may have strung the cases together, will be a mere collection of husks, the shell without the germinating principles that lies wrapt in the meat. If, then, he essays in eliminating [illuminating?] the principle of a rule or a decision, tracing it in all its bearings and following it by the thread of analogy into other systems of jurisprudence, in order to ascertain whether it be really part of the general science, and not a local idea, he cannot avoid the expression of his own opinion, to some extent. The study of law is the pursuit of truth; and he who undertakes to express and embody such truth, must occasionally express his own convictions.[28]

The study of law was not only 'illuminating' labour, it was 'the pursuit of truth'. Perhaps these were synonyms for 'crystallisation'. But crystallisation was not restatement. If truth was to be obtained, the writer must at some point transcend the cases, and, even if modestly, 'express his own convictions' about the true nature of the law.

The fabrication of disorder was an important component of treatise writers' labour, and the first step in the creation of truth. It was particularly important in first treatises, where the fabrication of disorder was most apparent. Theodore Sedgwick, for example, explained that the 'variance of opinion' within courts on issues of damages was so great 'that it is with great difficulty in many cases that I have been able to do more than state the doubts as they exist'.[29] Thomas Cooley explained the relationship between order and disorder in his, the first, treatise on taxation: 'The decisions in this country on the subject of taxation have become so numerous, that it would be impossible to give abstracts of them all, within any

[26] Bishop, *The First Book* (n 11) 141.

[27] Siegel, 'Joel Bishop's Orthodoxy' (n 2) 227.

[28] GT Curtis, *A Treatise on the Law of Copyright: In Books, Dramatic and Musical Compositions, Letters and Other Manuscripts, Engravings and Sculpture, as Enacted and Administered in England and America* (Boston, MA, Little and Brown, 1847) vi.

[29] T Sedgwick, *A Treatise on the Measure of Damages; or, An Inquiry into the Principles Which Govern the Amount of Compensation Recovered in Suits at Law*, 2nd edn, rev and greatly enl'd (New York, NY, JS Voorhies, 1852) vii.

reasonable compass'.[30] Thus, he wrote, '[t]here are, or should be, general principles underlying all the cases; and an understanding of these will enable one to make use of decisions under the various tax systems, without confusion'.[31] Similarly, in his influential treatise on state constitutional law, he wrote that 'the rapid multiplication of judicial decisions on matters of constitutional law [demanded] some work bringing together those principles in a manner that would enable them to be examined as a comprehensive system. . . .'[32] John F Dillon also bemoaned the drift that seemed to characterise the law of municipal corporations that he saw first hand as a judge.

> The necessity for a work upon the subject of the present Treatise was so seriously felt by the author when holding a seat on the Supreme Bench of a state where questions relating to the powers, duties, and liabilities of municipalities were presented at almost every term, that he resolved, eight years ago and more, to undertake to supply the want. Although the subject is one of unsurpassed practice importance, since nearly every considerable city and town in the United States is incorporated, no American work upon it has ever appeared. A careful examination of the English treatises satisfied the authority that they were, in a great measure, inapplicable here, and that they fail to cover a large portion of the existing field of the law upon the subject as enlarged by American legislation and practice.[33]

Dillon used that disorder to subordinate municipal corporations to state authority. Variance, multiplicity and confusion were different forms of disorder that needed policing.

The imaginative side of the fabrication of disorder can be seen in Theophilus Parsons' maritime law treatise. Parsons explained that '[l]ong ago I had become satisfied, that the boundless affluence of existing legal authority, and the rapid increase of the reports of English and American courts, and of other repositories of the law, made it with every passing year, more difficult for a lawyer to possess the means of a thorough investigation, and impossible for him to give the time and labor necessary for such investigation, to the many questions which arise in practice'.[34] There had been other treatises on maritime law, one in fact published just a few years before Parsons', but they were 'still open to the objection, that they treated severally and disconnectedly, topics which in themselves were closely connected and needed the mutual illustration they could give each other'.[35] But the fact is that there had been previous treatises on maritime law that had not made the connections between shipping and marine insurance that Parsons thought so important.

[30] TM Cooley, *A Treatise on the Law of Taxation* (Chicago, IL, Callaghan, 1876) iii.

[31] Ibid.

[32] TM Cooley, *A Treatise on the Constitutional Limitations Which Rest upon the Legislative Power of the States of the American Union* (Boston, MA, Little, Brown & Co, 1868) iii.

[33] JF Dillon, *Treatise on the Law of Municipal Corporations* (Chicago, IL, J Cockcroft, 1872) v.

[34] T Parsons, *A Treatise on Maritime Law: Including the Law of Shipping; the Law of Maritime Insurance; and the Law and Practice of Admiralty* (Boston, MA, Little, Brown & Co, 1868) vii.

[35] Ibid.

Having first fabricated disorder, treatise writers then set out to fabricate order, to crystallise law. This was the treatise writers' authority at its apex. Disorder freed the writer to 'discover' principles, and then claim that those principles were universal and had always governed law. This circularity meant that judges and lawyers subsequently would be confined by the rules and doctrines developed by treatise writers. This made the effect of a successful first treatise powerful. While it may not be law itself, a writer's identification and development, or invention, of an area of law made it nearly automatic in becoming law, as 'the judges, by a law of the mind over which they have not even themselves control, bow more and more to its views'. It was through the treatise writer's labour and the judges' mindlessness that the treatise 'becomes practically an authority, though it is never such in the very strictest of terms'.[36] Perhaps one example of this process is the emergence of the at-will rule in employment contracts. Horace Wood used the 'chaotic mass' of employment law to his advantage in his *Master and Servant* treatise, deeming it necessary only to offer the 'gist' of the law. But his most important innovation was in developing the idea that employment-at-will was the 'inflexible' American rule governing employment contracts. He did so, however, 'in the absence of valid legal supports'.[37] Despite this lack of support, the doctrine took off after the publication of Wood's treatise.

The fabrication of order, then, as Neocleous argues, was creative, and meant that treatise-writing was not simply a statement of the law as it had been 'settled', as so many writers claimed. The oft-repeated claim of treatise writers that they were simply 'stating the law as it has been settled' thus cannot be taken at face value. 'Stating', 'the', 'law' and 'settled' are all problematic terms. This was apparent in Bishop's subtle shift from 'stating the law as it has been settled', to 'settl[ing] to the inquiring mind the fact that they are truly the law'. Indeed, in first treatises it could hardly be said that the law had been settled at all; its unsettledness, its disorder, was precisely the reason for the treatise in the first place. Rather, the success of a treatise writer in providing an 'orderly statement of the law' began to bridge the divide between the source of law and law-making. Through his labour in both discovering a field of law (or at least elaborating it), and the orderliness of the principles he enunciated, a treatise writer both acquired his authority, and created law. This was how treatise writers became more than simply commentators on the law. Treatise writing was instead a way of policing the enormous growth of law occurring in the nineteenth century, of taming it, domesticating it. The treatise was not simply a statement of or a commentary on the law (as treatise writers themselves reluctantly acknowledged), but law itself, a body of rules governing the behaviour of legal actors, like justices of the peace, judges, legislators or convention delegates. As law, treatises blurred the distinction between manuals, treatises and codes, as well as the distinctions between law and source of law. When these distinctions begin to break down, treatises begin to appear not only as

[36] Bishop, *The First Book* (n 11) 157.

[37] JM Feinman, 'Development of the Employment at Will Rule' (1976) 20 *The American Journal of Legal History* 118, 126.

texts that provided the 'underlying metaphysics' of law (and police),[38] but as positive acts of law-making and police as well. Through the fabrication of dis/order, treatises not only made law, they also disciplined and policed law and legal actors. The treatise writer, as part of 'a class of legal persons', was thus simultaneously creating and exercising authority, determining the boundaries between legitimate and illegitimate. The effect of this authority can be seen clearly in Jameson's treatise on constitutional conventions.

II

That John Jameson's treatise was the first ever published on constitutional conventions was appropriate as the constitutional convention was a uniquely American invention, indeed one of 'the most characteristic of the political institutions in the United States'.[39] However, unlike most treatise writers in the nineteenth century, Jameson did not state as his aim to simply state the law as it existed. Rather, he was explicit that his aim was to develop a particular view of constitutional conventions, that the constitutional convention was a legal or governmental institution. He was, however, like treatise writers more generally, deeply interested in developing legal principles to guide the convention. Jameson's explicitness thus highlights the themes of fabrication of dis/order, and enables us to witness the transformation of consciousness at work, a consciousness that extended well beyond legal doctrine. Prior to the Civil War, the constitutional convention was understood as an institution that provided for an orderly change of the system of government. Only after the war could it be challenged effectively as an institution, if left unrestrained, that produced disorder. This was precisely Jameson's task.

Jameson's stated purpose was seemingly innocuous, 'to inquire into the history, powers, and modes of proceeding' of the convention.[40] But there was a basic first question that Jameson had to treat that other treatise writers in the nineteenth century, first or otherwise, typically did not have to: 'Is this institution . . . *subject to any law, to any restrictions*?'[41] Jameson, then, first had to deal with whether the convention even lay within the province of jurisprudence. This question immediately changed the nature of the inquiry for Jameson from what it had been for previous treatise writers. For the most part, treatise writers did not venture explicitly into questions about the nature of law, or attempt to answer so frontally the question, 'What is law?'[42] Generally, they dealt with topics that were

[38] W Novak, *The People's Welfare: Law and Regulation in Nineteenth-Century America* (Chapel Hill, NC, University of North Carolina Press, 1996) 25.

[39] JA Jameson, *The Constitutional Convention; Its History, Powers, and Modes of Proceeding* (New York, NY, C Scribner and Co, 1867) 1.

[40] Ibid.

[41] Ibid 2 (emphasis added).

[42] Notable exceptions include, JC Hurd, *The Law of Freedom and Bondage in the United States* (Boston, MA, Little, Brown & Co, 1858); JC Gray, *The Nature and Sources of the Law* (New York, NY, Columbia University Press, 1909).

firmly within the scope of common law. Here, it was clear that the convention was an important political institution and worth a full-scale study; it was less clear that it was or should be the object of a *legal* study.

Importantly, previous treatise-level discussions of the convention had treated the institution as beyond law. Even Francis Lieber, by no means a radical on this issue, characterised the convention as 'extra-constitutional'.[43] It is significant as well that Lieber discussed conventions in his *Manual of Political Ethics*, that is, as part of a discussion about civic virtue, not of law. In terms of limits of conventions, the electoral nexus was crucial, as it framed the ethical duties of the delegates. While delegates often believed that they were at leave to act according to their conscience, and thus were not necessarily bound by their constituents' views, they nevertheless understood quite well that their actions were subject to the approval of those they represented. There was even at times a sense of obligation to posterity. Ethics, then, not law, governed conventions and delegates. As the 'institutional embodiment of the people', the convention lay beyond law's horizon.[44]

But conventions should not be confused for something they were not. They were often controlled by the same people who controlled the legislatures, the reform of which so often the object of conventions. Leaders of the bench and bar often served as delegates. John Marshall, Joseph Story, James Kent and Lemuel Shaw were just some of the more notable jurists to serve as delegates to nineteenth-century conventions. Conventions were also often apportioned to privilege the geographically dominant section of a state, and often failed to achieve the reforms for which they were called, leaving reformers enormously dissatisfied. Rhode Island's experience in the 1830s and 1840s was only the most notable and dramatic of an experience that can be seen throughout the Union.[45] And yet, Americans continued to clamour for conventions. If one failed to achieve the desired reforms, another would be called a few years later. And if that failed, still another after that. Louisiana, for instance, held a series of conventions within a handful of years of one another in the late 1840s and early 1850s. Illinois, Jameson's adopted home state, held three conventions within a 20-year span.

Jameson understood well this aspect of the convention. 'To any society, far enough advanced in civilization to demand as well the ascertainment as the protection of its civil and political rights,' he wrote, 'no institution could be of more interest than one charged thus with the *role* of both founder and restorer of its social machinery'. This was an institution of no little importance, an institution that could both make and remake the social or political order. For Jameson this meant that the convention 'obviously exhibits more features that are menacing to

[43] F Lieber, *Manual of Political Ethics, Designed Chiefly for the Use of Colleges and Students at Law*, 2 vols (Boston, MA, CC Little and J Brown, 1838).

[44] M Peterson, *Democracy, Liberty, and Property: The State Constitutional Conventions of the 1820s* (Indianapolis, IN, Bobbs-Merrill, 1966).

[45] P Conley, *Democracy in Decline: Rhode Island's Constitutional Development 1776–1841* (Providence, RI, Rhode Island Historical Society, 1977).

republican liberty than any other in our whole political structure'.[46] 'Menace to republican liberty', however, was a curious way to phrase the significance of the convention in light of its ubiquitous presence in nineteenth-century American public life. For much of the nineteenth century to that point the convention had been seen as the exact opposite, as the embodiment of republican liberty. It was the means by which 'the people' maintained control of their government and exercised their liberty. As an Indiana court explained, '[a] constitutional convention of eminent citizens is the substitute for the armed mob of other countries'.[47] The convention was the tool through which the people exercised their right to alter or abolish government, the right that protected every other right.

But after the Civil War, things had changed, and Jameson explained why: 'To the interest attaching to the Convention, thus, from abstract considerations, has been added a greater, resulting from the connection of that institution with recent political events. The desolating war of secession, which has just closed, could hardly have been inaugurated but for the use made by the revolting faction of that institution'.[48] The use of the constitutional convention as the device by which the states of the Confederacy seceded from the Union had brought the idea of an extra-constitutional institution as the embodiment of the people into question. And that question was, what, if any, are the limits of a convention? For much of the nineteenth century this had been something of an academic question. Conventions had pushed the boundaries somewhat, but had never put the question in so stark a form before secession. Rhode Island had come close in the 1840s in the Dorr War. But even the constitution the Dorrites produced was a moderate one.

The full-scale destruction brought about by the Civil War, however, raised the question in a way that could no longer be avoided. The long-standing criticisms of the convention could now be taken seriously in a way that they could not before the war. Again, Jameson saw this clearly. '[I]t had become a maxim', he wrote, 'that whatever had been done by a Constitutional Convention, had been done by the people, "in their primary and sovereign capacity", and was therefore absolutely unquestionable, on legal or constitutional grounds'. The Civil War, though, had brought that 'disorganising' maxim into question in a powerful way. There had been arguments both during and after the war, that pro-secession elements had taken control of the secession conventions and had led an otherwise pro-Union populace out of the Union against its will. Jameson adopted this view himself. Secession, he wrote, was the result of 'a vote of a few conspirators, sitting as a Constitutional Convention, pretending to utter the voice of the people, and refusing to submit their ordinances to the test of a popular vote, under false pleas that neither the theory of the Convention system nor the practice of the fathers made such a submission necessary'. It was a 'picture of treachery and cunning, playing upon popular ignorance

[46] Jameson, *The Constitutional Convention* (n 39) 2.
[47] *Beebe v State*, 6 Ind. 501 (1855).
[48] Jameson, *The Constitutional Convention* (n 39) 2.

for their country's ruin'. The factual accuracy of this claim was always open to question, but its ideological value was powerful. For Jameson, the value was in the ability to attack the maxim that equated the convention with the people. Secession, he argued, had demonstrated that 'there were not wanting those who arrogated to that ill-defined assembly, as by an extension to it of the absurd maxim, that "the voice of the people is the voice of God", – an omnipotence transcending that higher law, to which ordinary legislative assemblies acknowledge themselves at all time subject.'

These ideas regarding popular sovereignty and the constitutional convention were not epiphenomenal. They were constitutive of the action taken in their name. Without these ideas, 'there could have been no victories won by the armies of treason'.[49] Secession and civil war had thus destabilised the connection between the convention and the people.

The distinctiveness of Jameson's treatise should, I hope, be becoming clear. This was not an ordinary legal treatise. This was not going to be a case of simply stating the law, as he fully acknowledged, but the creation of an entirely new field of law. In inventing a field of law, Jameson was bringing an institution within the ambit of law for the first time, which raised a methodological problem: how does one invent an area of law? Certainly, a great deal of conceptual and theoretical work was required. Just how distinctive Jameson's treatise was can be seen in comparison with some of his contemporaries. The year following the first edition of Jameson's treatise, Cooley published his more well-known treaties on state constitutional law. Cooley's volume began with 'Definitions'. The definitions were simply a series of declarative statements. For example, 'Sovereignty . . . imports the supreme, absolute, uncontrollable power by which any state is governed. A state is called a *sovereign state* when this supreme power resides within itself . . .' Or, 'A *constitution* is sometimes defined as the fundamental law of a state . . .'[50] Such terms were presented as unproblematic.[51] Cooley then turned to a discussion of the federal constitution, then the formation of state constitutions before getting into the bulk of his discussion about the specific limitations of the legislative power. Christopher Tiedeman similarly started with definitions in his treatise on the police power, and John Dillon began his treatise on municipal corporations with a historical survey before also turning to definitions. These works were not particularly theoretical; they were more traditionally centred on case law and its development, and the systematisation of legal doctrine being developed by the courts. Cooley's method, in fact, has been described as 'anti-metaphysical,' and one that 'evad[ed] big questions'.[52]

Two things explain Jameson's more theoretical or conceptual bent. One is that he simply had little case law to rely on, and that which existed was of little help. The weight of authority stood firmly opposed to the idea that the convention was

[49] Ibid 2–3.

[50] Cooley, *Constitutional Limitations* (n 34) 1, 2.

[51] AR Jones, *The Constitutional Conservatism of Thomas McIntyre Cooley: A Study in the History of Ideas* (New York, NY, Garland Publishing, 1987) 156.

[52] Ibid.

a legal institution. Courts before the war generally eschewed venturing into the thicket of convention power. When they did they usually deferred to the convention. This meant that Jameson could not follow the patterns set by so many other first treatises, most of which involved issues that had been dealt with in detail by the courts. Rather, he first had to find a way of understanding the convention as a legal or governmental institution. He understood that he could not blithely define the convention and move on. It would have been too easy to dismiss. For his work to have any influence, for it to become 'authority' in Bishop's terms, he had to reconceptualise the constitutional convention. This was why he devoted the bulk of his treatise to broad theoretical questions, such as, what is a constitutional convention? What is sovereignty? What is a constitution? But these were not questions posed in the abstract, as part of a philosophical treatise. The goal was far more practical and precedential. Jameson, after all, was not a philosopher, but a lawyer and judge. Indeed, he lacked the philosophical pedigree of writers like John Codman Hurd and John Chipman Gray, though this probably helped the reception of his work. But given its deep historical links to popular sovereignty, this would necessarily entail reconceptualising the entire structure and nature of American government.

The elements to construct an area of law existed, and had been around for years. Most of the ideas Jameson developed had been more fully articulated in and around conventions than in cases. Jameson's originality lay in bringing them together under one roof. That he chose the treatise form as opposed to the pamphlet, digest, law journal article or newspaper editorial is significant. The treatise had a much different mode of authority, as Bishop would point out the next year. As the primary tool of 'legal science', it depended on ostensibly 'objective' methods of both deduction and induction to 'systematise' and 'rationalise' law. This enabled Jameson to move, at least rhetorically, beyond mere political debate. The authority of the treatise as a form of legal literature operated in tandem with the labour of the treatise writer that helped to shift Jameson's ideas from mere political opinion to legal authority.

The lack of case law meant that Jameson's labour lay more in conceptualisation than in organisation. His main task was to answer definitively a question that had long been central to the constitutional convention. 'Is this institution', he asked, 'subject to any law, to any restriction? What claims does it itself put forth, and what do the precedents teach, in relation to its nature and powers? When called into existence, is it the servant of the master, of the people, by whom it was spoken into being?'[53] It was here that Jameson revealed the similarities between his project and John Austin's. Austin had argued that the sovereign is 'incapable of *legal* limitation'.[54] If the convention was sovereign, then Jameson's project was at an end. It was here that Jameson had to fabricate disorder. The problem, as Jameson saw it, was that the convention was an 'ill-defined assembly', which had led to the 'prevailing maxim' that the convention was the embodiment of 'the people', and that what-

[53] Jameson, *The Constitutional Convention* (n 39) 2.

[54] J Austin, *The Province of Jurisprudence Determined* in WE Rumble (ed) (New York, NY, Cambridge University Press, 1995).

ever it had done the people had done.[55] This 'maxim' meant that Jameson would have to deal with many of the same questions that Austin had dealt with, although as applied to a specific institution rather than in the abstract. To answer this question, Jameson would have to determine where sovereignty lay. The conceptual work Jameson did here was enormously important, and easy to gloss over. But it was crucial to imposing law on both the convention and the people.

Jameson's first step was to develop a taxonomy of conventions. Unlike other writers, Jameson developed his taxonomy not from abstractions, but from the ways that conventions had been used historically. Jameson organised conventions from the 'lower species of conventions', the spontaneous and ordinary legislative, to the revolutionary, and each had its own type or mode of authority. At the most basic level were the spontaneous conventions, 'voluntary assemblages of citizens, which characterize free communities in advanced stages of civilization'. Their importance was chiefly as 'manufactories of public opinion', as they were 'wholly unofficial' bodies that could only form opinion; they had no legal authority. The ordinary convention, the legislature, on the other hand, was wholly official: 'it can do nothing except by the authority contained in the [constitution]'.[56] It could act, but only under certain conditions.

The more important distinction to be made, however, was between the revolutionary and the constitutional convention. Revolutionary conventions, Jameson explained, were bodies that wielded considerable, essentially illimitable, power. These conventions were essentially the people writ small. It was the institution by which the people exercised their revolutionary power, or their right to alter or abolish government. This was an enormous power, and was tolerable only because they were temporary, ad hoc bodies. Jameson referred to them as 'a bridge' from one political order to another, whose authority was derived from necessity. As an 'apparatus of revolution', the convention helped to guide the commonwealth through it, providing a semblance of governmental authority in the interim between the old order and the new. At one level, this taxonomy may seem obvious. But Francis Lieber had discussed conventions in his *Manual of Political Ethics* without distinguishing between them.[57]

Jameson's separation of revolutionary from constitutional conventions was thus crucial to the separating of sovereignty from the convention, because he could then reimagine a *constitutional* convention, as an institution 'subaltern' to the constitution. 'If a Constitutional Convention step outside the circle of the law', he wrote, 'it does not continue to be a Constitutional Convention, but, so far, becomes that whose powers or methods it assumes, – a Revolutionary Convention. It leaves the domain of law, which is one of specified and restricted powers, and enters upon that of arbitrary discretion, within which law is silent, and where he is master who wields the greater force'.[58]

55 Jameson, *The Constitutional Convention* (n 39) 3.
56 Ibid 4–5.
57 F Lieber, *Manual of Political Ethics* (n 45) 467–71.
58 Ibid 11.

By contrast, a revolutionary convention was a 'body which can, *violently and without law*, uproot all existing institutions'.[59] This taxonomy helped to mark the boundaries between legitimate and illegitimate by identifying 'usurping' conventions, which started as constitutional and assumed revolutionary powers. Instead of 'restoring the social machinery', the constitutional convention simply reformed a constitution.

Jameson's idea of a constitution was a narrow one. It referred to a specific text, not to the organisation of the body politic. By 'constitution' Jameson meant an 'objective fact'. This conception enabled Jameson not only to dispute the compact theory that underlay arguments about the constitutionality of secession, but also to develop a theory of legalised or juridicalised constitutional change. As objective facts, he wrote before James Bryce's more famous formulation,[60] written constitutions were 'rigid' documents requiring periodic change. 'Written constitutions are liable, if not frequently amended, to become inadequate, an evil inseparable from all attempts to define the powers of that which is in a state of transition or growth'.[61] The constitutional convention, then, was necessary to *prevent* a state of emergency, not an exercise of an emergency power. 'To render a written Constitution safe', Jameson wrote, 'it must embrace efficient machinery for its own amendment'.[62] The constitutional convention was now simply the 'machinery' for amending a constitution. This was how it could be 'subaltern' to the constitution. The constitutional convention was no longer an institution through which the people organised and policed the state. Instead, they were institutions that exercised a limited, delegated function, to amend a state constitution.

While Jameson's discussion thus far had gone a long way toward separating the constitutional convention from sovereignty, and bringing the convention within the domain of law, two other questions remained. It was here that Jameson went beyond discussing the institutional aspects of the convention, and began to interrogate more directly the idea of sovereignty and its locus. This was also where he changed methods. To understand sovereignty, Jameson began deductively with John Austin's famous formulation, the idea of a sovereign as a 'determinate and common superior' to which is owed 'habitual obedience'.[63] Why he began deductively here is curious. He did not explain the methodological shift, if he was even aware of it. But to look for it inductively may have led him down a path that had long bedeviled American political thinkers, who became mired in discussions about who gave whom which powers, and which powers were more sovereign than others. The division of power had of course been explained by popular sovereignty, but that was still problematic for Jameson. Relying on Austin enabled Jameson to transcend these debates at least momentarily, debates

[59] Ibid (emphasis added).

[60] J Bryce, *Studies in History and Jurisprudence* (New York, NY, Oxford University Press, 1901) 124–215.

[61] Jameson, *The Constitutional Convention* (n 39) 79.

[62] Ibid 81.

[63] Ibid 18, citing John Austin, *The Province of Jurisprudence* (n 54).

that had led at least in part to the Civil War. With Austin at his side, Jameson could now face these issues on his terms, and claim the mantle of philosophical erudition, and hence objectivity as his authority. Jameson, though, held an uneasy relationship to Austin, largely because Austin himself had located sovereignty in America in the people of the states. Jameson fleshed out this particular disagreement with Austin in a posthumously published article.[64] But he did address it in his treatise in a couple of different ways. First, he argued that within a federal system the political organisation capable of determining its powers and that of the others, but not vice versa, was sovereign. Moreover, he continued in another methodological shift, and this was a direct attack on secession and the doctrine of state sovereignty, 'Whatever, *historically considered*, may have been the original relations of the two political bodies at present distinguished from each other by the mark indicated, the powers wielded by the inferior must be conceived as delegated by the superior'.[65] In other words, whatever had obtained before the war, the power of state governments was now to be understood as a power delegated by the federal government, or more precisely the federal constitution.

This still did not answer the question of where precisely sovereignty lay in the United States, only that it did not lie in the convention. Jameson certainly adhered to the doctrine of popular sovereignty, observing that 'the people is in reality the sovereign', and that 'no theory of sovereignty but that of the people as a whole is in harmony with the facts of American political life'.[66] For Jameson, though, this meant that *no institution* was capable of embodying the people. Rather, 'the pressure of public opinion consciously brought to bear upon the electorate, although inarticulate, is a clear and legitimate exercise of the sovereign power'.[67] This was an important shift. Although public opinion had long been an important component in American politics and political theory, Jameson was now arguing that it was sovereign. More specifically, national public opinion was sovereign. This was what Jameson called 'the doctrine of national sovereignty'.[68] Jameson was one of the earliest postbellum treatise writers to develop this idea.[69] According to this doctrine, elections were the primary means of expressing this opinion, as electors were the 'immediate' representatives of the people. 'In ninety-nine cases in every hundred', he wrote, 'the action of the nation as the sovereign will be taken through the states' electorates as its ministers'.[70] This was a peculiar form of sovereignty, however.

Jameson's notion of an 'inarticulate' public opinion hints at a transformation in both the authority of the convention and American political theory. 'The people' in Jameson's scheme were reduced to a moral force, acting mostly through

[64] JA Jameson, 'National Sovereignty' (1890) 5 *Political Science Quarterly* 193.
[65] Jameson, *The Constitutional Convention* (n 39) 18 (emphasis added).
[66] Jameson, 'National Sovereignty' (n 64) 213.
[67] Ibid 200.
[68] Ibid 213.
[69] CE Larsen, 'Nationalism and States' Rights in Commentaries on the Constitution After the Civil War' (1959) 3 *American Journal of Legal History* 360.
[70] Jameson, 'National Sovereignty' (n 64) 202.

the generation of public opinion, or, only rarely, through 'organic movements'. As a moral force this action was directed toward influencing representatives. They could thus command but not enact as they could when the convention was their institutional embodiment. Now, the people delegated the power to enact to various institutions. In fact, the people could barely even command, depending on who read the election tea leaves and how. 'In our government', Jameson explained, 'the sovereign has allowed the establishment of a certain system by which its multifarious powers are, so to speak, farmed out, in state and nation, to representatives; and what it allows, it enacts'. Enactment by the sovereign was now achieved through acquiescence. A subsequent treatise writer, Roger Sherman Hoar, made the 'doctrine of acquiescence' an important element of convention law, especially as a curative for legal defects. But he went even a step further, holding that: 'It is the acquiescence of the sovereign community, clearly manifest and continuous, that is alone effectual'.[71] Manifest acquiescence as a sovereign (non-) act signalled a new era of both popular sovereignty and constitutional conventions. This was a natural extension of Jameson's project.

By de-institutionalising and disembodying the people, Jameson could now rethink the structure of government, further reducing the status of constitutional conventions. Specifically, he identified five branches of government. First, was the electorate, the branch of government that chose the 'functionaries'. The electorate was the closest to the people, representing them 'immediately'. It was the branch that constituted 'the people', although it did so only in a 'qualified' sense. The distinguishing characteristic of the electorate was that it acted but did not assemble. Jameson skipped over the next three branches of government because they were so well known – the legislature, executive and judiciary. The 'fifth branch of government', however, was 'unknown abroad', it was a 'special legislature',[72] the constitutional convention. The latter four branches were all 'mediate' representatives of the people. Jameson made sure to emphasise that none of the branches was actually sovereign; it was instead a question of proximity. The relative authority of each was determined by the extent of the sovereign powers possessed and/or the proximity to the sovereign, the newly-disembodied people. According to these determinants, Jameson ordered the branches, listing the constitutional convention third behind the electorate and the legislature. Not only, then, was the convention no longer sovereign, it was no longer even the most sovereign institution. It was now merely another branch of government, to which was delegated a specific, narrow task: the drafting of a constitution.[73]

Jameson's taxonomies fundamentally reconceptualised both the constitutional convention and the people. After he had reduced the convention to a legal institution, or 'a fifth branch of government', the rest of the treatise was an application

[71] RS Hoar, *Constitutional Conventions: Their Nature, Powers, and Limitations* (Boston, MA, Little, Brown and Co, 1917) 255.

[72] Jameson, *The Constitutional Convention* (n 39) 23.

[73] Ibid 24.

of these schemes to particular aspects of the law of conventions. The two most important elements of this law were the convention act and ratification, both of which made the convention and its work 'legitimate and safe',[74] or legal and well-regulated. In other words, law disciplined the convention, imposed order on it, policed it. This was not simply the fabrication of an orderly convention, but of an orderly people as well. By 'domesticating' the convention and the people, Jameson was putting to bed that 'disorganizing maxim' *vox populi vox dei* and its association with the convention, making democracy safe for itself.

III

Jameson's treatise illustrates nicely the stakes involved in first treatises. They were more than simply firsts, and entailed a great deal more than mere synthesis of legal doctrine. The first treatise more than any other marked the boundaries of legitimacy and illegitimacy, of what lay within law's domain and the province of jurisprudence and what did not. The doctrines and distinctions that they made mattered. They were often picked up and deployed by judges and by subsequent treatise writers. Jameson's treatise is exemplary. During Reconstruction, courts were frequently pressed to make a statement on the scope of convention power. Before 1867, the year Jameson's treatise was published, courts shied away from the question. It was only in 1867 that they began to hold that conventions were subject to limitations. In 1873, two of the most important cases on the nature of the convention were handed down. Although there was a line of cases challenging Jameson's construction of convention authority, they were clearly in the minority. Even subsequent treatise writers who were critical of Jameson's work never challenged his most important innovation, that the convention was a legal institution.[75] Jameson thus successfully stretched the domain of law so as to impose its logics on a governmental institution previously subject to its own internal and distinctive logics. Not only was the constitutional convention, post-Jameson, subject to a juridicalised police, 'the people' were as well. Jameson's treatise thus marked both the emergence of new ideas of freedom, and a new role for law and the people within that new order of liberty. Formerly, the institutional embodiment of the people, the people themselves, became objects of law, subject to the state, subject to the techniques of power, of governance, regulation, police, that Foucault opened our eyes to. It is significant that Jameson chose the legal treatise as the medium to press such views. The authority of the treatise meant that legal actors – lawyers, judges, delegates – would have to account for Jameson's ideas in ways they would not had he chosen a different form of literature.

[74] Ibid 106.

[75] RJ Hoyos, 'The Rise and Fall of Popular Sovereignty: Constitutional Conventions, Law and Democracy in Nineteenth Century America' (PhD Dissertation, University of Chicago, 2010) ch 5.

6

Nineteenth-Century Treatises on English Contract Law

STEPHEN WADDAMS*

BLACKSTONE'S *COMMENTARIES ON the Laws of England* (1765–69) allowed no explicit place for contracts as a distinct part of English law.[1] Blackstone likened his work to a map, writing that 'an academical expounder of the laws . . . should consider his course as a general map of the law, marking out the shape of the country, its connexions and boundaries, its greater divisions and principal cities'.[2] Blackstone's map gave no definite place to contract law, though he mentioned contracts in several places. A definition of 'contract' was offered in Book 2 (rights of things) as part of a chapter (entitled 'Of title by gift, grant, and contract') dealing with methods of acquiring rights to property.[3] In Book 1 (rights of persons) contracts were mentioned as part of the law of master and servant, and of husband and wife, and in Book 3 (private wrongs) assumpsit was mentioned as providing a remedy for breaches of promises, considered as wrongs. In respect of husband and wife, Blackstone wrote that 'our law considers marriage in no other light than as a civil contract'.[4] The comment shows that Blackstone did not visualise contracts as a body of controlling principles from which legal obligations were derived: if he had thought in those terms, he would have given contract law a place on his map, and a different place from matrimonial law. It was not that Blackstone thought contracts unimportant – he referred to marriage as 'the most important contract of any'[5] – and contracts were an important means of transferring property rights, and an important aspect of the law of private wrongs. But he did not think of legal issues as 'part of' an independently existing contract law. It would be more accurate to say that he thought of contracts as 'part of' several different areas of the law – a means of effecting various legal consequences – and hence to be found in several different places on his map.

* University Professor, Faculty of Law, University of Toronto.

[1] W Blackstone, *Commentaries on the Laws of England* 4 vols (Oxford, Clarendon Press, 1765–69).

[2] Ibid, vol 1, 35.

[3] Ibid, vol 2, ch 30.

[4] Ibid, vol 1, 433.

[5] Ibid 436.

With the changing view of contracts in the nineteenth century, Blackstone's treatment of the subject came to seem inadequate. Joseph Chitty, who published an edition of the *Commentaries* in 1826, wrote of Blackstone's definition in volume 2:

> It will be remarked that the observations of the learned Commentator in the text, contain but a very small part of the law of Contracts, which has so greatly increased since his work was published. The more ancient books and present abridgements are very defective in information upon this subject; and the student must therefore resort to the modern elementary works . . .[6]

In a note in Book 3, Chitty took the opportunity to be even more critical of Blackstone's treatment of the subject:

> This subject is not so well arranged or considered, as most parts of this work. Indeed it is observable that contracts, and the remedies for the infraction of them, are by no means, in any part of this work, well discussed. In the second volume, contracts are cursorily considered, as one of the means by which a title to personal property may be acquired. In the present volume, which professes to describe injuries and their remedies in general, it is inexpedient to consider the action of contracts more particularly.[7]

About 60 years before Blackstone's *Commentaries*, Jeffrey Gilbert, later Chief Baron of the Exchequer, wrote an essay headed 'Of Contracts'. This work was never printed and remains unpublished. The word 'treatise' has sometimes been used in connexion with Gilbert's writings, but it is by no means clear that Gilbert intended 'Of Contracts' to be a free-standing work, or, if he did, that it is complete.[8] It consists of 56 double-sided folios containing a detailed discussion of particular topics, notably consideration. Like Blackstone in his second book, Gilbert envisaged contracts primarily as a means of transferring property. His opening words were:

> Contracts are twofold: verbal and solemn. Now contract is the act of two or more persons concurring, the one in parting with, and the other in receiving some property right or benefitt. The most notorious way of transferring of right from one to the other is this by contract for all men by their labour and industry did first acquire to themselves a property so they may by other acts of their own transferr that property where they please, and all laws have allowed it as a settled maxim that the right of disposall must of necessity follow the rights of absolute dominium, for certainly as a man may be industrious for himself he may be so also for another and therefore the establishment of the propriety must be in his hands to whom the disposition is made and no doubt as the notion of propriety was begotten from humane necessity so was also this of contract.[9]

Publication of an annotated edition of Gilbert's work, when it appears, will probably shed new light on the question, but meanwhile it may be tentatively

[6] J Chitty (the elder), *Commentaries on the Laws of England by the late Sir W Blackstone: a new edition by Joseph Chitty*, 4 vols, (London, William Walker, 1826), vol 2, 442 (fn).

[7] Ibid, vol 3, 154 (fn).

[8] See M Macnair, 'Sir Jeffrey Gilbert and his Treatises' (1994) 15 *Journal of Legal History* 142.

[9] J Gilbert, Of Contracts, (about 1710), British Library, Hargrave 265, f 39 (some punctuation added, abbreviations expanded, and capitalisation removed).

suggested that Gilbert, like Blackstone, regarded contracts as important legal instruments, but not as an independent source of obligations.

In 1761 the great French jurist, Robert Joseph Pothier, published his treatise on obligations, which appeared in an English translation by Sir William Evans in 1806.[10] So unfamiliar to English readers was the idea of a law of obligations that the translator found it necessary to add to the title, calling it A Treatise *on the Law of Obligations* or Contracts.[11] The modern reader might naturally suppose that the purpose must have been to enlarge the meaning of 'contracts', but the translator explained that his purpose was rather to enlarge the meaning of 'obligations' beyond the restricted meaning (ie penal bonds) that it had in contemporary English legal usage:

> To an English reader the name of the principal treatise would have conveyed a more extensive idea, if the term *Contracts* had been substituted for that of *Obligations*, as we are familiar with the latter term, in a more confined application of it; but the object of the treatise is, to comprize the general doctrines which relate to the obligations between one individual and another, as well for the reparation of injuries, as for the performance of engagements. The principles applicable to obligations resulting from contracts, however, constitute the leading subject of the author's attention, and the reference to other topics may be considered as subordinate and incidental.[12]

Pothier did indeed devote the vast bulk of the treatise (573 pages of 578 in Evans' translation) to contractual obligation, but he was concerned that his account should be conceptually complete. He divided obligations into 'contracts' and 'other causes of obligations', and though he devoted only five pages to these 'other causes', he took care to divide them in their turn into 'quasi contracts' (one page and a half), 'injuries and neglects' (two pages and a half) and a residual class called 'of the law' (one page), consisting of obligations derived directly from natural or positive law. Pothier's works were greatly admired in England.[13] Sir William Jones, in his *Essay on Bailments*, had given high praise to Pothier, writing:

> [At this time] the learned M Pothier was composing some of his admirable treatises on all the different species of express and implied contracts; and here I seize, with pleasure, an opportunity of recommending those treatises to the English lawyer, exhorting him to read them again and again; for if his great master Littleton has given him, as it must be presumed, a taste for luminous method, apposite examples, and a clear manly style,

[10] There had been an earlier American translation: *A Treatise on Obligations considered in a Moral and Legal View, Translated from the French of Pothier*, by F-X Martin (Newburn, NC, Martin & Ogden, 1802).

[11] RJ Pothier, *A Treatise on the Law of Obligations or Contracts*, translated by WD Evans (London, Butterworths, 1806). The words 'treatise' and 'contracts' appear in italics on the title page, allowing for 'Law of Obligations' to be read as the main title.

[12] Ibid 82 (translator's introduction).

[13] AWB Simpson, 'Innovation in Nineteenth Century Contract Law' (1975) 91 *Law Quarterly Review* 247, repr in *Legal Theory and Legal History* (London, Hambledon Press, 1987) 171; D Lieberman, *The Province of Legislation Determined: Legal Theory in Eighteenth-Century Britain* (Cambridge, Cambridge University Press, 1989) 110; G Samuel, *The Foundations of Legal Reasoning* (Maastricht, Maklu, 1994) 72; D Ibbetson, *Historical Introduction to the Law of Obligations* (Oxford, Oxford University Press, 1999) 220.

> he will surely be delighted with works, in which all these advantages are combined, and the greatest portion of which is law at Westminster as well as at Orleans.[14]

This praise was echoed by Best J (later Chief Justice of the Common Pleas), who went so far as to say, in 1822:

> The authority of Pothier is . . . as high as can be had, next to the decision of a Court of Justice in this country. It is extremely well known that he is a writer of acknowledged character; his writings have been constantly referred to by the Courts, and he is spoken of with great praise by Sir William Jones in his Law of Bailments and his writings are considered by that author equal, in point of luminous method, apposite examples, and a clear manly style, to the works of Littleton on the laws of this country.[15]

Addison, in the preface to his *Treatise on Contracts* (1847), took a similar view, comparing English writings, to their disadvantage, with 'the elaborate and elegant works of Pothier'.[16] Later in the century, however, Pothier's opinion on an important point of contract formation was severely criticised by three English writers (Leake, Benjamin and Pollock) and was decisively rejected by two judicial decisions in 1880.[17] In the twentieth century, Pothier was rarely cited as an authoritative source of English law.[18]

The first published book on English contract law (Powell, 1790) had given some measure of conceptual unity to contracts as a subject,[19] and this conceptual unity was extended by Evans' translation of Pothier, and by at least 12 nineteenth-century English books.[20] The demarcation of contract law had far-reaching implications, including a division between property and obligations, and divisions among various classes of obligations. Some writers also implied, as we shall see, that English contract law was a manifestation of a universal order.

Lord Mansfield had said that precedents served to illustrate principles,[21] but he did not say that precedents could be dispensed with as mere surplusage. Precedents may illustrate principles, but the interrelation of the ideas runs in both

[14] W Jones, *An Essay on the Law of Bailments* (London, Charles Dilly, 1781) 29.

[15] *Cox v Troy* (1822) 5 B & A 474, 480–81.

[16] C Addison, Preface to *A Treatise on the Law of Contracts and Rights and Liabilities Ex Contractu* (London, Benning, 1847) vii.

[17] SM Leake, *The Elements of the Law of Contracts* (London, Stevens & Sons, 1867) 20, note; JP Benjamin, *A Treatise on the Law of Sale of Personal Property with References to the American Decisions and to the French Code and Civil Law* 2nd edn (London, 1873) 58; F Pollock, *Principles of Contract at Law and in Equity . . .* (London, Stevens & Sons, 1876) 11; *Byrne v Leon van Tienhoven* (1880) 5 *CPD* 344; *Stevenson v McLean*, (1880) 5 QBD 357 (Lush J, May 25). See S Waddams, 'What *were* the Principles of Nineteenth-century Contract Law?' in Andrew Lewis, Paul Brand & Paul Mitchell (eds), *Law in the City: Proceedings of the Seventeenth British Legal History Conference, London, 2005* (Dublin, Four Courts Press, 2007) 305.

[18] Pothier was referred to on the question of mistake of identity, but expressly rejected by the English Court of Appeal in *Lewis v Averay* [1972] 1 QB 198, 206 (Pothier's statement 'no part of English law' and 'has given rise to such refinements that it is time it was dead and buried [al]together').

[19] JJ Powell, *An Essay upon the Law of Contracts and Agreements* (London, Johnson and Whieldon, 1790).

[20] See AWB Simpson, 'Innovation in Nineteenth Century Contract Law' (1975) 91 *Law Quarterly Review* 247, repr in *Legal Theory and Legal History* (n 13) 171.

[21] *Jones v Randall* (1774) *Cowp* 37, 39.

directions: the principles of English contract law could not themselves be formulated, or articulated, without reference, express or implicit, to decided cases. Cases have been both a source of principle and evidence of it; principle has been simultaneously *derived from* past cases, and *imposed upon* them as a criterion of their authenticity and validity. Any advocate, addressing Lord Mansfield or his successors on a point of contract law, would have been ill-advised to dispense entirely with reference to past cases, and the same may be said of students seeking to satisfy examiners, and of writers purporting to offer an accurate account of the law at any point in its history.

This last proposition was put to the test by Henry Colebrooke, who published in 1818 a remarkable book entitled (echoing Pothier and Evans) *Treatise on Obligations and Contracts.*[22] Colebrooke, like Sir William Jones, had spent much of his life in India. He was an eminent Sanskrit scholar, had written a digest of Hindu law, and had held office as a judge in India.[23] His book on contract law contains no preface, but the whole approach shows that it was founded on the assumption that the law of contracts depended on and manifested universal principles, and that a satisfactory account could be offered of English contract law without reference to English cases. A note stated that 'the preface, with other preliminary and introductory matter, will be published with the second part of the volume', but the second part never appeared. The book is replete with references to Roman law, to the French Civil Code, to Hindu law and to civilian writers, including Barbeyrac, Pufendorf, Godefroy, Grotius, Domat, Pothier and Erskine. Marginal notes refer also to English writers, including Blackstone, Powell, Comyns and Newland, but there is scarcely a reference to any decided English case.

The book was not a success, either commercially or intellectually. It was privately printed, and the projected second part never appeared. 'The second portion', his son wrote in his biography, 'was considerably advanced; but he received little encouragement to pursue his task'.[24] His son offered an explanation for the failure, which probably reflected comments made to him and to his father by English lawyers and judges, or rather, the Colebrookes' *perception* of the significance of those comments, that 'the work is perhaps too succinct, and it is wanting in practical examples and illustrations'[25] – probably a polite way of suggesting that an account of English law required reference to decided cases. Colebrooke's approach had the effect of abstracting, or detaching, his account from the English law of contracts as a real historical and social phenomenon, and his book, interesting as it is from several perspectives, offered little usable guidance to the actual content of English law in 1818. That such a book was unlikely to succeed in the legal marketplace may seem obvious in retrospect, but to Colebrooke himself it was evidently a disappointment. In 1823 he wrote in a private letter:

[22] HT Colebrooke, *Treatise on Obligations and Contracts, Part I* (London, Printed for the Author, 1818).
[23] *Dictionary of National Biography*, Leslie Stephen (ed) (London, Smith, Elder, 1885–1900).
[24] TE Colebrooke, *Miscellaneous Essays [of H.T. Colebrooke] with the Life of the Author by his Son* (London, Trubner, 1873) 279.
[25] Ibid.

> Nothing has been published by me on the law of Contracts, nor any other topic of jurisprudence, since the treatise on Obligations, which I published a few years ago, as the first part of a larger work. Shortly afterward, while I was preparing the sequel of it for the press, I became involved in [a troublesome lawsuit] . . . I have neither health nor spirits for the undertaking, and cannot bring myself to make the effort of setting about it . . . I have it in contemplation to prepare a preface and introduction to the Treatise on Obligations, as a single work, and give it with the notice of my final relinquishment of the greater work. The treatise is complete in itself, wanting nothing but a preface.[26]

Colebrooke's son wrote of the *Treatise*,

> Testimonies to its value have been repeatedly given by those who have followed the same path, and I think it was a matter of some disappointment to its author that it was not more generally appreciated. He had devoted to the subject much time and attention, and had compressed into the space of 250 closely printed pages an elaborate compendium of legal principles derived chiefly from the Roman jurisprudence, and had made considerable progress in a second volume.[27]

The fate of Colebrooke's book must have been known to every subsequent nineteenth-century writer on English contract law. Chitty (1826), though he referred at several points to the civil law, gave priority to English cases. Addison wrote in his preface (1847) that English contract law was founded 'upon the broad and general principles of universal law' and that 'the law of contracts may justly indeed be said to be a universal law adapted to all times and races, and all places and circumstances, being founded upon those great and fundamental principles of right and wrong deduced from natural reason which are immutable and eternal'. He went on, as has been mentioned, to compare English writings on contract law, to their disadvantage, with 'the elaborate and elegant works of Pothier'.[28] Following such a preface, the reader might have expected a book like Colebrooke's, but the text of Addison's treatise turned out to consist almost entirely of somewhat pedestrian discussion of decided English cases, reflecting in part, no doubt, commercial considerations, but also the genuine impossibility of attempting to formulate principles of English contract law without regard to their formulation and reformulation in past judicial decisions.

Almost all the nineteenth-century writers claimed to discern principles, but principle is an elusive concept, varying in meaning according to what is contrasted with it. Sometimes it appears to mean a stringent legal rule that demands absolute obedience, but at other times the word seems to signify an ideal objective, desirable in general terms, but liable to be outweighed by countervailing considerations, which are themselves apt to be called principles.[29]

[26] Ibid 345–46 (letter to Sir Thomas Strange).

[27] Ibid 315.

[28] C Addison, Preface to A Treatise on the Law of Contracts (n 16) iv–v, vii.

[29] See L Farmer, 'The Idea of Principle in Scots Criminal Law' in J Chalmers, FL Keverick and L Farmer (eds), *Essays in Criminal Law in Honour of Sir Gerald Gordon* (Edinburgh, Edinburgh Studies in Law, 2010); S Waddams, *Principle and Policy in Contract Law: Competing or Complementary Concepts?* (Cambridge, Cambridge University Press, 2011).

Attempts were made to discern principles in tort law, as well as in contracts. Addison, in addition to his treatise on contracts, also published a treatise on torts. He wrote in the preface, perhaps rather too confidently, that with the abolition of the forms of action 'the pathway to legal science . . . has been rendered comparatively easy and inviting'.[30] Arthur Underhill, who himself wrote a book on torts in 1873,[31] was not favourably impressed. He said of Addison's book that it was 'a huge volume, a compendium of case law, a "wilderness of single instances" with no attempt to distinguish principles from examples'.[32] Of his own book, Underhill said: 'My object, on the other hand, was to trace out the principles of the law and to use decided cases merely as examples of comparatively few principles'.[33] Pollock also wrote a treatise on torts, invoking the concept of principle, saying in the preface that 'the really scientific treatment of principles begins only with the decisions of the last fifty years', and of his own book that 'this is a book of principles if it is anything'.[34] But the object proved elusive. He wrote of the strict liability torts that 'as a matter of history such cases cannot be referred to any definite principle'.[35] About 20 years later he wrote that 'the classification of actionable wrongs is perplexing, not because it is difficult to find a scheme of division, but because it is easier to find many than to adhere to any one of them'.[36]

Contract law appeared to offer a more promising area for the discernment of principles. As we have seen, Pothier was cited by many nineteenth-century English writers. Pollock (1876), though mentioning Pothier at several points in his treatise, gave even greater prominence to the German writer Friedrich Carl von Savigny (1779–1861), calling him 'a man of true scientific genius'.[37] In a footnote to the second paragraph of the first chapter, he explained the fundamental concept (in Pollock's account of English law) of 'agreement' as equivalent to '*vertrag* as used by Savigny, whose analysis . . . we follow almost literally in this paragraph', quoting Savigny in German because 'a perfectly literal translation is not practicable'.[38] This is remarkable. Pollock was writing a book for English readers on English law, but on the most fundamental concept at the very beginning of his book he found it necessary to give such deference to a German writer that the German text (the subtleties and nuances of which can hardly have been thoroughly understood by most of Pollock's readers – the crucial word seems to have been *Willenserklaerung*) was given priority over any possible English translation.

[30] CG Addison, *Wrongs and Their Remedies: Being a Treatise on the Law of Torts* (London, Stevens, 1860) vii.

[31] A Underhill, *A Survey of the Law of Torts or Wrongs Independent of Contract* (London, Butterworths, 1873).

[32] A Underhill, *Change and Decay* (London, Butterworth & Co, 1938) 74.

[33] Ibid 74–5.

[34] F Pollock, *The Law of Torts: a Treatise on the Principles of Obligations Arising from Civil Wrongs in the Common Law* (London, Stevens & Sons, 1887) vii–viii.

[35] Ibid 393.

[36] *Encyclopaedia Britannica*, 11th edn, 29 vols (Cambridge, Cambridge University Press, 1910–11) vol 27, 64.

[37] Pollock, *Principles of Contract* (n 17) 2 (fn).

[38] Ibid 1 and 2 (fns).

In the third edition (1881), this passage disappeared, and Pollock began gently to distance himself from Savigny, saying in the Introduction that the treatment, in Pollock's earlier editions, of offers in advertisements 'was the result of overmuch deference to a passing opinion of Savigny's, which must be allowed to have been hardly worthy of his usual judgment and insight'.[39]

In his first edition, Pollock gave a central place to the concept of consent: 'A contract is before all things a transaction in which two or more parties consent'.[40] In the preface to the third edition, however, and more prominently in subsequent editions, Pollock emphasised the idea of reasonable expectations. In a letter to Holmes in 1920, Pollock, commenting on recent American writings, said, 'It is rather amusing to see your new lights trumpeting reasonable expectation as the real fundamental conception in contract. I agree, of course, having put it in my 3d edition, *ad init*, nearly forty years ago, only without a trumpet obligato'.[41] This comment reveals that Pollock was conscious that his views of 'the real fundamental conception in contract' had altered in the five-year period between the dates of the first and third editions (1876 and 1881). It also shows that reasonable expectation was, in Pollock's mind, an aspect of reliance, and that protection of the one was the natural corollary of protection of the other.[42]

It is doubtful whether Pollock would have used the phrase 'real fundamental conception' in this context in 1881, the date of his third edition, but it is significant that, when he looked back 40 years later, he then thought that his insight on this point dated from that time. The fact that a concept seen later as 'the real fundamental conception' should have eluded the author during the years of work he put into the first edition of a treatise on general principles is revealing. Also revealing is Pollock's reference to the absence of 'trumpet obligato'. It certainly is true that the passages in question were introduced without fanfare. Buried as they were in a long introduction (not exactly, therefore, *ad init.* [at the beginning]), they could hardly have been less conspicuous in the third edition, and they were only gradually promoted, first to the beginning of the preface in the fourth edition, and then to real prominence in the fifth, and subsequent, editions. This suggests that Pollock was by no means sure of his ground in 1881, and was not ready to commit himself fully to a rejection of the idea that contractual obligation depended on consent.

Pollock was anxious in 1920 to claim credit with Holmes for anticipating American scholars on this point, and Pollock's next published edition (ninth edition, 1921) gave very prominent approval to 'the modern tendency to look to "the realization of reasonable expectations" as the ground of just claims rather than an artificial equation of wills or intentions', with reference to Roscoe Pound, and

[39] Pollock, *Principles of Contract* (3rd edn, 1881) vi.

[40] Pollock, *Principles of Contract* (n 17) 2.

[41] Emphasis in original. A later letter (vol 2, 53–54) shows that the reference was to the Wigmore Celebration Volume (*Celebration legal essays to mark the 25th year of service of John H Wigmore* (1919)), and especially to Roscoe Pound.

[42] See Fuller and Perdue, 'The Reliance Interest in Contract Damages' (1936) 46 *Yale Law Journal* 52 52.

the work mentioned in Pollock's letter to Holmes of 1920.[43] The express rejection here of 'an artificial equation of wills and intentions' indicates, as Neil Duxbury has pointed out, a marked departure from continental theorists, particularly Savigny,[44] and Pollock's open recognition that the concept of intention could not, on its own, supply a complete explanation of contractual obligation. The contrast with Pollock's first edition could scarcely have been more striking.

English reference to continental writers was closely connected with the search for a principled, reasoned, ordered and 'scientific' approach to law. '[I]f LAW be a *science*', Sir William Jones had said in 1781, 'and really deserve so sublime a name, it must be founded on principle, and claim an exalted rank in the empire of *reason*'.[45] Civilian writers were often invoked by English writers, but this does not establish the actual influence of civil law. A number of historical and comparative law difficulties arise. Pothier and Savigny were writing in different centuries, in different jurisdictions, and in different languages. They may have over-generalised, or may not have accurately described the law in their own jurisdictions in their own times as it operated in actual practice. English writers may have misunderstood the civilian writers, and may well have underestimated the diversity of civil law systems and failed to appreciate aspects of them that affected their practical operation. Modern observers may make the same mistakes. Moreover, the invocation by English writers of the names of civilian writers, intellectually fashionable as they were in the middle of the century, does not establish their actual influence. As we have seen, Pollock gradually distanced himself from Savigny's views on intention. On the influence of civil law more generally, he wrote in his fifth edition (1889), that 'for my own part I have found myself, as time goes on, rather less than more disposed to make Romanistic elements bear up any substantial part of the structure of the common law'.[46] There is a note of personal and nostalgic sense of loss in this comment ('for my own part . . . found myself . . . as time goes on'), for the attraction of the civil law lay in its close connection with a search for order, elegance and a 'scientific' approach to the study of English law, ideas that Pollock could not abandon without regret. What may be safely concluded, however, is that nineteenth-century English writers were influenced by an *idea* or ideal of civil law, closely associated as it was with order, science, elegance, logic and principle.

Almost all the English nineteenth-century writers on contract law took, as their conceptual point of departure, the idea of agreement, or mutual assent. This idea, often dignified by the Latin phrase *consensus ad idem* (agreement to the same thing), was usually called a principle and was frequently accompanied by a direct or indirect reference to civil law. But even a cursory examination of English law,

[43] Pollock, *Principles of Contract*, (9th edn, 1921) 1, fn (a).

[44] N Duxbury, *Frederick Pollock and the English Juristic Tradition* (Oxford, Oxford University Press, 2004) 194.

[45] W Jones, 'An Essay on the Law of Bailments' (n 14) 123 (emphasis in original). Every coherent subject of intellectual inquiry was supposed to have principles. See W Paley's much cited The Principles of Moral and Political Philosophy (1885), Lord Kames [H. Home], Principles of Equity (1760), and many titles of eighteenth-century books on scientific and religious subjects.

[46] Pollock, *Principles of Contract*, (5th edn, 1889) 698.

as it actually worked in practice, shows that proof of mutual assent, in the ordinary sense of those words, was not a requirement for the imposition of contractual obligation. One eminent legal historian has gone so far, indeed, as to suggest that the 'mysterious phenomenon of agreement' was an 'organizing myth' that encouraged 'the suspension of disbelief'.[47]

On a number of important issues, the effect of the treatises, particularly that of Anson, has been to oversimplify complex questions. English law had much trouble with privity of contract and third party beneficiaries. Early cases had accepted that a contract might in some circumstances be enforceable by a third party, but in *Tweddle v Atkinson*[48] the earlier cases were rejected as inconsistent with the doctrine of consideration as understood in the nineteenth century. Pollock's initial reaction (1876) was to point out that *Tweddle v Atkinson* was a common law decision, and to imply that the result might be different in equity. Pollock wrote that 'the rule is distinctly established *so far as any common-law right of action is concerned*'[49] adding pointedly that 'the doctrines of equity are not so free from doubt',[50] and discussing at some length a case (*Gregory v Williams*[51] indicating that equity would permit a third party to join with the promisee as co-plaintiff. Pollock wrote, in a rather convoluted sentence, that 'it is impossible to say with confidence that the question how far third persons can acquire equitable rights under contracts and independent of trust is not to some extent unsettled',[52] and these words were repeated in the second edition.[53] This complex assembly of qualified and counter-qualified double negatives reveals Pollock's uneasiness on the question: he was conscious that, after the Judicature Acts, equity ought to prevail over a conflicting common law rule,[54] but he was reluctant to grapple with the consequences of this line of thinking. This was the line of thinking that led Professor Corbin 50 years later to conclude that equity, and therefore a modern court, would permit enforcement by a third party wherever justice required it.[55]

Anson in his first edition (1879) followed Pollock on this issue paragraph by paragraph, but where Pollock tended to be cryptic and tentative, Anson was plain and dogmatic. Anson wrote, without limiting his conclusion to the common law, that the old doctrine permitting actions by third parties was 'finally overruled in the case of *Tweddle v Atkinson*'.[56] Having mentioned one of the old cases, he said:

But there is no modern case in which this proposition has been accepted. On the contrary, it is now established *that no stranger to the consideration can take*

[47] AWB Simpson, 'Raffles *v.* Wichelhaus and Busch' in *Leading Cases in the Common Law* (Oxford, Oxford University Press, 1995) 156–57.
[48] (1861) 1 B & S 393.
[49] Pollock, *Principles of Contract* (n 17), 190 (emphasis added).
[50] Ibid 191.
[51] *Gregory v Williams*, (1817) 3 Mer 582.
[52] Pollock, 'Principles of Contract' (n 15) 193.
[53] Pollock, *Principles of Contract*, (2nd edn) 198.
[54] Judicature Act 1873 s 25 (11); Supreme Court Act 1981 s 49(1).
[55] AL Corbin, 'Contracts for the Benefit of Third Persons' (1930) 46 *Law Quarterly Review* 12.
[56] WR Anson, *Principles of the English Law of Contract* (Oxford, Clarendon Press, 1879) 200.

advantage of a contract, although made for his benefit.[57]Anson dealt with the equity cases as follows:

> Until very recently there was no doubt that a third party could not sue alone in equity for benefits intended to be conferred upon him by the contract, although there is authority for saying that he could join as co-plaintiff in a suit brought by the actual promisee.[58]

Gregory v Williams was cited in the side note to this paragraph, without discussion.

This treatment was calculated to marginalise, in the reader's mind, the effect of the equity cases. The proposition 'that no stranger to the consideration can take advantage of a contract, although made for his benefit' was printed in italics, signifying its high importance. Reference to *Gregory v Williams* was consigned to a concessive subordinate clause, and for Anson to say that a third party could not sue 'alone' and to mention in passing that he could sue as co-plaintiff in a suit brought by the promisee, without pointing out that the court would, if necessary, compel the promisee to lend his name to the action, conceals the real extent of the beneficiary's right and suggests that the matter was of merely technical or procedural significance. In Anson's second edition (1882), *Gregory v Williams* disappeared altogether.

Pollock's third edition (1881), probably influenced in its turn by Anson, also marginalised *Gregory v Williams* by explaining it as amounting to a declaration of trust of property,[59] and by adding a generalised conclusion, following discussion of another case, that 'the result is that there is no real and allowed authority for holding that rights can in general be acquired by third parties under a contract, unless by the creation of a trust'. The equity cases were further marginalised in the fourth edition (1885) by the insertion of the words 'at first sight', so that the introduction to the discussion of equity was amended to read 'the doctrines of equity are *at first sight* not so free from doubt'.[60]

One aspect of the separation of law from equity in the English legal system was that the common law judges were able to lay down legal rules in rather absolute terms, knowing that another court had the power to mitigate the application of the rules in cases of severe injustice. After the Judicature Acts, equity was, in case of conflict, supposed to prevail, but, in respect of several issues in contract law, the opposite occurred, and, oddly enough, equity was marginalised because it came to seem inconsistent with common law rules and principles. This was a curious irony, not only because the Judicature Act provided that, in case of conflict, equity was to prevail, but because the common law rule might never have been asserted in absolute terms had it not been for the existence of the mitigating

[57] Ibid 201 (emphasis in original).

[58] Ibid.

[59] Pollock, *Principles of Contract* (3rd edn, 1881) 220. The report of the case, 3 Mer at 590, makes it clear that it was the *benefit of the promise* that was held on trust for Gregory, not any tangible property. Corbin discusses this aspect of the cases (n 55).

[60] Pollock, *Principles of Contract* (4th edn, 1885) 220 (emphasis added).

power of equity, and because it was the very inconsistency with the common law that had justified the Court of Chancery in taking the position it did in the first place.[61] A similar process of marginalisation, much assisted by Pollock and Anson, can be discerned in the rules relating to other aspects of contract law, particularly mistake and unconscionability.

The topic of mistake has caused considerable difficulty.[62] If contractual obligation depended on consent, it would seem to follow that a material mistake on any matter that induced the consent would prevent the formation of a contract. It was by application of this principle that Pothier asserted that 'error is the greatest defect that can occur in a contract, for agreements can only be formed by the consent of the parties, and there can be no consent when the parties are in an error respecting the object of their agreement'. He did not hesitate to spell out the far-reaching consequences of this line of thinking: 'error annuls the agreement, not only when it affects the identity of the subject, but also when it affects that quality of the subject which the parties have principally in contemplation, and which makes the substance of it', adding, as an illustration, 'therefore if, with the intention of buying from you a pair of silver candlesticks, I buy a pair which are only plated, though you have no intention of deceiving me, being in equal error yourself, the agreement will be void, because my error destroys my consent; for my intention was to buy a pair of silver candlesticks'.[63] Even where there was reasonable reliance by one party on the apparent consent of the other, as in the case of an artist commissioned to paint a picture by a person privately mistaken as to the artist's identity, Pothier thought that the mistaken party could not be liable on contractual principles, though he might be liable on a non-contractual principle: 'in this case I am obliged not by the agreement, which was void, and therefore could not produce any obligation; the reason of my obligation is the principle of equity which obliges me to indemnify the person whom I have imprudently led into an error'.[64]

Despite Pothier's reputation, this line of thinking could not be assimilated by nineteenth-century English law. The idea that any material mistake destroyed consent and made the contract void would have seemed too wide, because almost every case of a disadvantageous contract might be analysed as having been caused by a mistake. Notably in cases of mistake of quality of goods sold, as in Pothier's candlestick example, the English law was that the contract was enforceable, a result that might be explained (or perhaps merely restated) by saying that, in the absence of warranty or misrepresentation, the buyer takes the risk of the error. Moreover, the idea that reliance might be protected, as in Pothier's painter example, by a non-contractual principle having the same result as though there were a contract but depending on principles of equity, could not be assimilated to English legal thinking. It would have seemed convoluted and artificial to deny that

[61] See *Tomlinson v Gill* (1756) *Amb* 330, and Corbin's discussion (n 55) 18.
[62] See C MacMillan, *Mistakes in Contract Law* (Oxford, Hart Publishing, 2010).
[63] Pothier (n 11) 1,1, III, 17 and 18, Evans' translation, 12.
[64] Ibid 1, 1, III, 19 (Evans, 13).

there was a contract and then to create an equivalent obligation derived from a non-contractual source. And no such source was available in nineteenth-century English law: no tort liability existed in such a case, and English equity could not have imposed such an obligation (to pay money as compensation for loss caused by imprudence) as Pothier contemplated.[65]

Pollock's first edition (1876) included a chapter on mistake, which, though lengthy,[66] was rather discursive, inconclusive, and, at times, self-contradictory. He wrote that 'mistake does not *of itself* affect the validity of contracts at all' adding in a footnote that 'as fear is to coercion so is mistake to fraud',[67] words that imply that mistake is irrelevant without fraud. He then added: 'But mistake may be such as to prevent any real agreement from being formed; in which case the agreement is void both at law and in equity . . .'[68] These words indicate an attempt to assimilate law and equity under a single principle of contract formation, and this theme was reflected in the principal sub-heading of the chapter, 'Mistake as excluding true consent'.[69]

The danger of adopting a test that is too wide, which, when rejected, causes a swing to the opposite extreme of a very narrow test is illustrated by Pollock's treatment of consent. In his first edition, Pollock cited, with full approval,[70] the following proposition, from the Indian Contract Act: 'Where both parties to an agreement are under a mistake as to a matter of fact essential to the agreement, the agreement is void'.[71] This proposition was too wide to be an accurate description of English law in 1876, or to be acceptable as a test for the future, and Pollock must soon have realised this for, by degrees, he distanced himself from the proposition. In the third edition it was introduced with the words, 'The Indian Contract Act gives the rule in *rather wide* language . . .'[72] and in the fifth edition (1885) it was relegated to a footnote.

Another fundamental aspect of contract law is relief on the ground of unfairness or unconscionability, and here it is the granting (not the withholding) of relief that is difficult to reconcile with the idea of consent as the sole test for creating an obligation. Since the nineteenth century, writers on English contract law have emphasised the enforceability of contracts, and have tended to marginalise the instances in which contracts have been set aside for unfairness. In dealing with consideration, it has been common to point out that inadequacy of consideration is not, in itself, a defence to contractual obligation, and from this 'elementary principle', as Pollock called it, it has been inferred that, if there is sufficient

[65] Pothier made a somewhat similar suggestion, discussed in Waddams, 'What *were* the Principles of Nineteenth-century Contract Law' (n 17) 307–08, that an uncommunicated withdrawal of an offer could give rise to non-contractual liability, again based on equity.

[66] 88 pages, in a book of 577.

[67] Pollock, *Principles of Contract* (n 17) 357.

[68] Ibid.

[69] See C MacMillan, *Mistakes in Contract Law* (n 62) 153.

[70] Pollock (n 17), 397, 'We cannot do better than begin with the rule and illustrations as given in the Indian Contract Act . . .'

[71] Ibid.

[72] Pollock, *Principles of Contract* (3rd edn, 1881) 455 (emphasis added).

consideration to meet the test of contract formation, the contract must be enforceable. Pollock in his first edition (1876) wrote that it was:

> a distinguishing mark of English jurisprudence that the amount of the consideration is not material. 'The value of all things contracted for is measured by the appetite of the contractors, and therefore the just value is that which they be contented to give'. It is accordingly treated as an elementary principle that the law will not enter into an inquiry as to the adequacy of the consideration.[73]

Anson (1879) followed the same line, and made the point more forcefully:

> So long as a man gets what he bargained for Courts of law will not ask what the value may be to him, or whether its value is in any way proportionate to his act or promise given in return. This would be 'the law making the bargain, instead of leaving the parties to make it'.[74]

As both writers were aware, however, this was not the whole story, because courts of equity had often set aside contracts on a variety of grounds related, in general terms, to unfairness. Pollock mentioned this aspect of English law with a somewhat awkward side note in his chapter on consideration (chapter IV), 'Inadequacy *plus other things* in Equity: see chap. XI'. In the text, he wrote:

> Inadequacy of consideration coupled with other things may however be of great importance as evidence of fraud, &c, when the validity of a contract is in dispute: and it has been considered (though, it is believed, the better opinion is otherwise) to be of itself sufficient ground for refusing specific performance. This subject, which is by no means free from difficulty, will be examined under the head of Undue Influence, Ch XI., *post.*[75]

Anson, closely following both the form and the substance of Pollock's work, but with less nuance, dealt with the matter as follows:

> Equity so far takes adequacy of consideration into account in dealing with contracts, that if a contract is sought to be avoided on the ground of Fraud or Undue Influence, inadequacy of consideration will be regarded as strong corroborative evidence in support of the suit. [Reference followed to what Anson, like Pollock, considered the doubtful power of the court to deny specific performance on this ground.][76]

English courts, after 1875, administered law and equity together, and one of the principal stated purposes of Pollock's book was to consider English law and equity as a whole. However his approach to this question, followed in starker form by Anson, tended to marginalise the power of the court to set aside disadvantageous contracts. The statement of the general principle of law, followed by mention two pages later of a power to set aside contracts in 'equity', suggests that the power is exceptional. The categories of 'fraud, &c.' and 'fraud or undue influence' suggest rare and closely defined instances, scarcely affecting the

[73] Pollock (n 17) 154, quoting Hobbes, *Leviathan*, (1660) pt 1, ch 15.

[74] Anson, *Principles of the English Law of Contract* (n 56) 63, quoting Alderson B in *Pilkington v Scott* 14 M & W 657, 660.

[75] Pollock, *Principles of Contract* (n 17) 156.

[76] Anson, Principles of the English Law of Contract (n 56) 65.

general principles of contract law. The reference to inadequacy of consideration as a matter only of *evidence* tends to suggest that it has little effect on substantive law, and the emphasis of both writers on the power of the court of equity to refuse specific performance (leaving the promisee with a right to full damages) tends to distract the reader from the far more significant power of the court to *rescind* the contract (leaving the promisee with no remedy at all). The postponement of the subject to a later chapter also tends to suggest that it is not directly relevant to the most basic principles of contract law, and that relief on the ground of unfairness is conceptually exceptional. The tendency to marginalise the issue reached a peak in Halsbury's Laws of England (1907–15) where unconscionable contracts were excluded altogether from the article on Contract, and dealt with, anomalously, in a different volume in the article on Fraudulent and Voidable Conveyances (a quite separate topic).

The question of the direct influence of public policy on enforceability of contracts is another important issue that presented difficulties to Pollock, who sought to minimise the power of the courts to decline to enforce contracts on grounds of policy,[77] Pollock being closely followed on this point by Anson.[78]

Before 1876, the usual way of referring to the subject of contract law was the 'law of *contracts*' (plural), but in that year Pollock, followed in 1879 by Anson, adopted in his title the singular ('law of *contract*'), and this usage was followed by most English writers in the twentieth century. The change was significant in a number of respects. The use of the singular suggests a high degree of conceptual unity. It lends itself more readily to a deductive approach: 'law of contract' tends to suggest the prior existence of a body of principles, of which individual decisions are mere applications, whereas 'law of contracts' is a phrase more amenable to the idea that principles may be derived from a multiplicity of individual instances. The singular also suggests that one unified and coherent body of principles governs all contracts, whatever their nature, whereas the plural lends itself more to a view that there might be very substantial differences between one kind of contract and another.

Frequent reference has been made in the preceding paragraphs to Anson's *Principles of the English Law of Contract* (1879). Anson, like other English writers, sought order and precision, but found difficulty in attaining it. In a letter presenting a copy of his book to Lord Justice Thesiger he said:

> Writing as I have done for students and beginners I have ventured on a definiteness of statement as to the results of the cases which would have been presumptuous in a book of practice. I took a good deal of trouble to arrange the various parts of the subject in due proportion and order, but it was not till I began to fill in my outline that I realised how much labour was needed and how much more learning than I possessed. Some parts of the subject are very interesting, and here and there it seems, though I may be wrong, that the law is still unsettled even on rudimentary points, and in such matters

[77] Pollock (n 17) 251–52.
[78] Anson (n 56) 173.

> one feels the excitement of an explorer. I can only hope that I have not done discredit to your chambers.[79]

This letter is revealing in a number of ways. It reflects the deference, in part assumed but in part real, that English academic writers of the period paid to judges as to the only authoritative sources of legal principles. It shows that Anson was conscious of having over-simplified his account of the law, and that he had found it difficult to match a logical outline of the subject with the mass of English law as he found it. It is significant that he found the law 'still unsettled even on rudimentary points', a phrase that implies recognition both of a need for change and of confidence in future progress. Anson likened himself to an explorer, but the image suggested is not only of one who maps pre-existing territory, but also of one who assists in bringing about improvements: coloniser as well as surveyor. In his published preface, Anson also recognised that 'I have often run the risk of seeming to dogmatise', offering the weak explanation that, if too many references were given, students would be discouraged from verifying them.[80]

In the Introduction to his third edition, Pollock included some interesting comments on two of his contemporary treatise writers. 'Since the second edition of the present work was published', he wrote, 'there have been some important additions to the literature of the subject'. Pollock then referred to Leake, calling his first edition 'his excellent book', but expressing reservations about the recast and enlarged form of the second edition, which Leake called a 'Digest',[81] Pollock saying that

> its value as a comprehensive book of reference is doubtless much increased; but one cannot help fearing that the gain to practitioners is a loss to students. In its original form it was a work which they might with profit not only consult but read through. A student could now hardly be recommended to attack the thirteen hundred pages of the 'Elementary Digest', except under very careful guidance and selection.[82]

This comment draws attention to an emerging divergence between books aimed at practitioners (with comprehensive citation of cases, but little sustained analysis), and those aimed at student readers (with longer commentary but fewer cases). Pollock attempted, with considerable success during his lifetime, to fill both roles, but, by the mid-twentieth century his book had been outflanked on the one side by Chitty (for practitioners) and on the other by Anson (for students).[83]

As appears from the examples discussed here, Anson's book was very closely based, both in its title and its contents, on Pollock's (first edition, 1876). It seems that Anson must sometimes have had Pollock's book open in front of him as he wrote, for on several issues he followed Pollock paragraph by paragraph, though,

[79] Anson to Lord Justice Thesiger, 20 March 1879, slipped into (and now bound into) a copy of the first edition at the Institute of Advanced Legal Studies in London.
[80] Anson (n 56) vii.
[81] SM Leake, *An Elementary Digest of the Law of Contracts* (London, Stevens & Sons, 1878).
[82] Pollock, *Principles of Contract* (3rd edn, 1881) x–xi.
[83] See the discussion by Lindsay Farmer of criminal law treatises and textbooks, in Chapter 7 of this volume.

as we have seen, usually with less subtlety and nuance. Pollock probably had mixed feelings about Anson's book. Immediately following his comments on Leake, Pollock wrote:

> In 1879 Sir WR Anson brought out his 'Principles of the English Law of Contract' (Clarendon Press), of which it is hardly too much to say that it is not only the best elementary book on its own subject, but the best elementary book yet in existence on any topic of English law. Several valuable criticisms and suggestions which I have derived from it are mentioned in their proper places.[84]

These words, though laudatory on their face, contain a hidden sting, for they may be read to suggest that the chief merit of Anson's book lay not so much in its original contribution to its subject as in its skill in reducing the work of others [sc Leake and Pollock] into elementary form. And to speak of Anson's book as 'the best elementary book yet in existence on any topic of English law', repeating the word 'elementary' in the same sentence, is to imply that the book fell into a separate class of *elementary* law books, somewhat below the level of treatises or serious academic works, rather like those books later disparagingly called 'nutshells' or 'hornbooks'. The words 'on any topic of English law' also imply that the merits of Anson's work were to be judged by comparison not with other books on contract law, but with elementary books on other legal subjects. It may be noted that Pollock, having described the first edition of Leake's book as 'excellent', does not say the same in the following paragraph of Anson's book. Pollock entered into a somewhat unnecessarily prolonged and slightly acrimonious debate with Anson, lasting over several editions of the works of both, on the issue of tacit revocation of offers.[85] From the perspective of 130 years later, each may be said to have had a different kind of success: Anson's book has been republished in more editions than Pollock's, became the standard student textbook for much of the twentieth century, and has lasted into the twenty-first,[86] but Pollock, in his successive editions, offered to his readers a more thoughtful discussion of the difficult questions, frankly admitting, on several points, changes in his own opinion.

Anson's first edition (but not the later editions) was published in a smaller format than the standard octavo size of legal books. This distinction marked the book as something different – a student handbook rather than a practitioner's text or treatise. Anson also avoided footnotes, confining his references, with very few exceptions, to marginal sidenotes. He recognised this practice as an innovation that required comment, and felt it necessary to offer an 'excuse for a departure from the ordinary arrangement of references in footnotes'.[87] The elimination of footnotes drastically restricted the number of references, and wholly precluded

[84] Pollock, Principles of Contract (n 82) xi.

[85] See Waddams, 'What *Were* the Principles of Nineteenth-Century Contract Law' (n 17) 310–11.

[86] 28th edn by J Beatson, 2002; the last edition of Pollock was the 13th, by PH Winfield, 1950.

[87] Anson (n 56) vii. FH Lawson, *The Oxford Law School 1850–1965* (Oxford, Clarendon Press, 1968) 41–2, indicates that Anson wrote the book primarily for 'passmen', as opposed to honours undergraduates. Parts of this paper are based on Stephen Waddams, Principle and Policy in Contract Law: Competing or Complementary Concepts? (n 29).

any secondary discussion of complexities, or any qualification of the somewhat dogmatising (to use Anson's own word) assertions in the text.

Both Pollock and Anson were to some degree responsible for the over-simplification of English contract law. Simplicity might, all else being equal, be regarded as a merit in a treatise, but over-simplification of complex legal questions is not a merit: it risks lending support, through undue rigidity, to unjust results, and it is ultimately self-defeating, because courts tend to invent complex devices to avoid results perceived to be unjust. Anson himself recognised in his letter to Thesiger and in his preface that he had over-simplified. Pollock, from his third edition in 1881, openly changed his views on many fundamental questions as he grappled with complexities that had escaped his first edition. But the approach of Pollock's first edition had meanwhile been, in even more simplified form, crystallised by Anson. The nineteenth-century writers were strongly attracted by the idea of principle, and this ambition may be counted to their credit, but the simplicity, order and elegance that they sought remained always just out of reach. The idea of principle was by no means alien to English contract law, but it proved difficult either to derive precise, unvarying and controlling principles from the past, or (in the absence of any authoritative external source, such as a code) to impose them upon the future, without at the same time undermining the historical and pragmatic aspects of the law that were also characteristic of English legal thought.

7

Of Treatises and Textbooks: the Literature of the Criminal Law in Nineteenth-Century Britain

LINDSAY FARMER*

I. INTRODUCTION

MUCH OF THE analysis of nineteenth-century criminal law has focused on the question of codification – for fairly obvious reasons – but from the perspective of the literature of the criminal law this might produce a rather distorted picture, with its focus on a particular kind of architecture of criminal law and on the clarification of the meaning of concepts of responsibility. This literature typically traces a trajectory that goes from Blackstone through Bentham's critique of the *Commentaries*, to the 1833–45 Criminal Law Commissioners to Stephen's codification project of the 1870s, in which the failures of successive codification projects are balanced against the gains of an increasing sophistication in the conceptual structure of the law.[1] In this chapter I shall argue that this is of secondary importance to the development and practice of the criminal law in the nineteenth century, although it was to become of great importance in the twentieth century with the rise of criminal law as a university discipline and the rise of subjectivism (focusing on the mental element in crime), phenomena which drew heavily on the existing codification literature.[2] Instead I shall argue that by focusing on the practical literature of the criminal law in England and Scotland – and in particular by tracing the rise of a treatise literature

* University of Glasgow, UK. I would like to thank Markus Dubber, Angela Fernandez, Gwenael Guyon, Niki Lacey, Sylvain Soleil and Barry Wright for their comments.

[1] See eg the overarching narrative of KJM Smith, *Lawyers, Legislators and Theorists. Developments in English Criminal Jurisprudence 1800–1957* (Oxford, Oxford University Press 1998).

[2] This is to some extent a revision of my own earlier claims about the impact of the codification debate. See L Farmer,'Reconstructing the English Codification Debate' (2000) 18 *Law & History Review* 403 and critical discussion by M Lobban, 'How Benthamic Was the Criminal Law Commission?' (2000) 18 *Law & History Review* 427–32.

on criminal law over the course of the century – it is possible to begin to develop an alternative history of nineteenth-century criminal law, one in which the failures of codification must instead be seen as being eclipsed by the increasing successes of the formalisation of doctrine and the consolidation of the central role of the legal profession in the criminal justice system.[3] This focus then offers a new perspective on the question of why codification failed in England in the nineteenth century, as I shall argue that the treatise addressed some of the problems that codification was intended to solve, thus rendering more formal codification to a certain extent unnecessary.[4]

This chapter is divided into three main sections, and while mainly focused on literature of criminal law, it will say something in passing about criminal procedure. In the first section I will review the forms of legal literature at the turn of the nineteenth century (a period roughly from 1780 to 1820). This was a period during which there was an extraordinary level of public interest in the criminal law as the reform movement gathered momentum. Some of the literature of this period is well known to historians of the criminal law, but I shall also note some of the lesser and more obscure forms in order to draw attention to the sheer variety of ways of writing about and ordering the law sometimes neglected by legal scholarship.[5] In the second section, I shall examine the history and structure of the most enduring of the nineteenth-century treatises in England and then Scotland, which were first published in the early nineteenth century. In the final section, I will say something briefly about the emergence of the university textbook, which has come to rival the treatise as the dominant form of legal literature. While both treatise and textbook systematised the law in some way, and indeed might share a similar structure, they were intended for different audiences. The textbook was aimed at students as law was increasingly taught as a university course, while treatises, I shall argue, were primarily written by and for practitioners. This is not intended as a hard-and-fast distinction, but I want to avoid some of the definitional problems in this area – what is a treatise? – by looking at the audience and function of the different forms of literature on criminal law. I will go on to argue that the treatise emerges as the dominant form of legal writing, defining and organising the field of criminal law over the course of the nineteenth-century. However, contrary to claims made by Simpson about treatises in other areas of law, criminal law treatises were overwhelmingly practical in focus, aimed at

[3] cf Smith, *Lawyers, Legislators and Theorists* (n 1) 67: 'Resting at the right hand of both judges and lawyers over the centuries, treatises have exercised steady and extensive, if often unspoken, influence.' See also KJM Smith, 'Criminal Law' in W Cornish *et al*, *The Oxford History of the Laws of England*, Vol XIII 1820–1914 *Fields of Development* (Oxford, Oxford University Press, 2010) 179–83 which goes further than his earlier work in acknowledging the role of treatises.

[4] This paper should be read together with that of Wright, chapter 9 in this volume, who looks by contrast at the reasons why codification had greater success as an imperial project.

[5] See, eg L Farmer, '"With all the impressiveness and substantial value of truth": Notable Trials and Criminal Justice 1750–1930' (2007) 1 *Law and Humanities* 57–78; L Farmer, 'The Criminous and the Incriminating' (2000) *The Juridical Review* 285–304, looking at the role of popular trial narratives in Scotland as a form of literature of criminal law.

practitioners and largely unconcerned with the matters of principle and structure that are often taken to be the defining features of treatise literature.[6]

II. EARLY NINETEENTH-CENTURY LITERATURE

Writings on the criminal law in early-nineteenth-century Britain took a wide variety of forms, and were intended for a range of different audiences, and I want to place the emergence of the modern treatise in this particular context. In England, in particular, there was a large number of different types of criminal law texts, written for different purposes, and organised according to a range of classificatory schemes. There were a number of handbooks and dictionaries aimed at magistrates and others involved in law enforcement; 'institutional' texts such as Blackstone's *Commentaries* which were aimed at the student of law and the educated gentleman; and there was a profusion of texts aimed at law reformers and a wider popular audience. I shall look at three main categories of text – those concerned with elucidating principle, those aiming at reform, and practical handbooks – as a means of illustrating this diversity.[7]

A. Principles

The most important books in this category, the 'high' literature of the criminal law, were the so-called 'institutional' writers on criminal law – Hale, Hawkins and Foster – whose writings were focused on the Pleas of the Crown. The major text was Sir Matthew Hale's *History of the Pleas of the Crown* (1736). This was published posthumously in two volumes (Hale died in 1676), the first of which concerned the substantive law and the second criminal procedure.[8] It was not a complete digest of the law, but dealt only with the most serious criminal offences – varieties of treason, homicide and theft. It largely followed the pattern of Coke's *Institutes*, but was much more systematic, treating issues relating to criminal capacity in a separate chapter and following a clear hierarchy of offences.[9] In

[6] See AWB Simpson, 'The Rise and Fall of the Legal Treatise: Legal Principles and the Forms of Legal Literature' (1981) 48 *University of Chicago Law Review* 632–79, http://dx.doi.org/10.2307/1599330 citing Plucknett who defined the treatise in terms of a deductive method, presenting a single branch of law that is conceived of as having a quality of unity (633–34). See also M Lobban, 'The English Legal Treatise and English Law in the Eighteenth-Century' (1997) 13 *Iuris Scripta Historica* 69–88. cf institutional writings, on which see K Luig, 'The Institutes of National Law in the Seventeenth and Eighteenth Centuries' (1972) *The Juridical Review* 193–226; JW Cairns, 'Blackstone, an English Institutist: Legal Literature and the Rise of the Nation State' (1984) 4 *Oxford Journal of Legal Studies* 318–60.

[7] These classifications are not intended to be mutually exclusive, but are simply a way of showing the range of different writings.

[8] *Historia placitorum coronæ, The History of the Pleas of the Crown, by Sir Matthew Hale . . . Now First Published from His Lordship's Original Manuscript, and the Several References to the Records Examined by the Originals, with Large Notes, Sollom Emlyn* (2 vols) (London, np, 1736).

[9] From treason to homicide to grand and petit larceny then other felonies. See Proemium for an explanation a plan of the work. See also Simpson, 'Treatise' (n 6) 640 on Hale.

the words of Andrew Amos, the importance of the work was that it established a 'standard of orthodoxy',[10] going through four editions in the eighteenth century with later editors adding discussion of recent case law and statutes.[11] A work of similar standing and importance was Hawkins' *Treatise of Pleas of the Crown* (1716–21), which went through seven editions in the eighteenth century, with the last edition being published in 1824.[12] Like Hale, the work was divided into two parts, dealing with substantive law and criminal procedure. This largely followed the schema laid down by Hale, though with more extensive treatment of offences against religion, together with more detailed discussion of the substantive law.[13] According to the Preface, the aim was to 'vindicate the Justice and Reasonableness of the Laws concerning Criminal Matters' against their critics by reducing and presenting them under a single scheme.[14]

The most direct successor to these works was East's *A Treatise of Pleas of the Crown* published in 1803 in two volumes.[15] Edward Hyde East was an MP and had also edited reports of cases from the King's Bench before publishing the first edition of his treatise in 1803. He was later made Chief Justice of Bengal (1813–25), before returning to England and a career as an MP, which ended with the reform of Parliament in 1832.[16] The text itself was an 'up to date, fairly comprehensive, and accessible statement of the substantive law.'[17] The subject matter, pleas of the crown, followed in the footsteps of Hale and Hawkins. East claimed some innovation in arrangement: 'In drawing the outline of this treatise I have endeavoured as much as possible to class together kindred offences', leading to departure from the arrangement of Hale and Hawkins.[18] Notwithstanding this, the plan was fairly conventional. The first volume dealt with offences against religion, morality and the church; treason; offences against coin and bullion; homicide; assaults and maiming; rape and marriage; and sodomy. The second volume was largely concerned with offences against property (burglary, larceny, piracy, forgery, arson and malicious mischief). It was thus broader in coverage than its predecessors,

[10] A Amos, *Ruins of Time Exemplified in Sir Matthew Hale's History of the Pleas of the Crown* (London, V & R Stevens & GS Norton 1856) 1. He went on to describe Hale as a 'Pope of Criminal Law' (1) installed so as to exonerate the community from a multitude and diversity of opinions.

[11] The last edition was published in 1800, with annotations on new statutes and cases 'appended at the bottoms of pages . . . like barnacles adhering to the bottoms of ships' (Amos (n 10) xxv).

[12] *Treatise of Pleas of the Crown: or a system of the principal matters related to that subject, divided under the proper heads* (2 vols) (London, np, 1716–21). See also M Foster, *Crown Cases* (Oxford, Clarendon, 1762).

[13] Later editions became increasingly unwieldy, as annotations were added, with the fourth edition running to four volumes.

[14] Hawkins (n 12) Preface, i. See Simpson, 'Treatise' (n 6) 653 commenting on the 'generally defensive' tone of Hawkins' Preface.

[15] EH East, *A Treatise of Pleas of the Crown* (2 vols) (London, Butterworths, 1803).

[16] HJ Spencer, 'East, Sir Edward Hyde, First Baronet (1764–1847)' in *Oxford Dictionary of National Biography* (Oxford, Oxford University Press 2004); online edn; January 2008 www.oxforddnb.com/view/article/8408, accessed 2 Oct 2010.

[17] Smith (n 1) 69.

[18] Preface, x.

and in drawing extensively on unpublished judicial notes it provided the practitioner with access to recent case law.[19]

It is also important to note the classification provided by William Blackstone in his *Commentaries* (1765–69).[20] Although he was not a criminal lawyer, his account, based on a conceptualisation of criminal law as public wrong, had an impact on writings in this area.[21] Blackstone began with a discussion of the requirements of criminal liability in relation to exculpatory conditions, and then restructured exposition of the substantive law in terms of a hierarchical ordering of interests infringed (offences against religion, the state, justice, public order, person and property). This was both influential and innovative, though it is also widely acknowledged that it was not aimed at practising lawyers. The 1824 edition of Hawkins was recast by its editor according to a Blackstonian schema, and Baron Hume also followed this in his *Commentaries* on Scots criminal law.[22] More broadly, the importance of Blackstone was less in terms of its practical utility to lawyers than the attempt to establish that the law had an underlying conceptual coherence. This was of significance in a context of mounting criticism of criminal law and punishment at the end of the eighteenth century. While Bentham's critique of Blackstone is best known, a number of other works inspired by philosophical writings on law and punishment criticised penal law and practice through an examination of the principles underlying the law.[23] William Eden and Henry Dagge both published works which took a largely Beccarian account of punishment, based on natural right and public utility, and applied it to the analysis and critique of English criminal law and practice.[24] From a different perspective, inspired by the historical analysis of Lord Kames, Bicheno sought to link his analysis of English criminal law to laws of social and moral conduct and their development through particular sets of institutions.[25] The significance of these works for our purposes lies in the diversity of approaches to the question of principle and in the debate that was opened up over the scope of principles of criminal

[19] Smith (n 1) 69–70. He used 11 sets of judicial notes, see A Amos, *Ruins of Time* (n 10) 5.

[20] *Commentaries on the Law of England* (4 vols) (Oxford, Clarendon Press, reprinted 1966 University of Chicago Press).

[21] Given the extensive discussion of Blackstone elsewhere, I do not propose to dwell on this. See discussion in Smith, ibid 68. See also D Lieberman, 'Blackstone and the Categories of English Jurisprudence' in N Landau, *Law, Crime and English Society, 1660–1830* (Cambridge, Cambridge University Press, 2002) for a discussion of the underlying understanding of crime and law.

[22] Smith (n 1) 68, noting the limited success of this venture. On Hume see discussion below.

[23] See discussion in TA Green, *Verdict According to Conscience. Perspectives on the English Jury Trial* (Chicago, Chicago University Press, 1985) 288–310; D Lieberman, *The Province of Legislation Determined. Legal Theory in Eighteenth-Century Britain* (Cambridge, Cambridge University Press, 1989); see also Smith (n 1) 25–28.

[24] W Eden, *Principles of Penal Law* (London, B White & T Cadell, 1771); H Dagge, *Considerations on Criminal Law* (3 vols) (Dublin, H Saunders, 1772).

[25] JE Bicheno, *Observations on the Philosophy of Criminal Jurisprudence* (London, R Hunter, 1819). Lord Kames (Henry Home), *Historical Law Tracts* (1758) 4th edn (Edinburgh, Bell & Bradfute, 1792). Kames is discussed in Lieberman (n 23) ch 7. See also H Arnot, *A Collection and Abridgement of Celebrated Criminal Trials in Scotland from AD 1536 to 1784* (Edinburgh, W Smellie, 1785), discussed in Farmer, 'Notable Trials' (n 5).

law and the nature of their connection to social and political institutions for an audience which went beyond the legal profession.

B. Reformers

This was also a programmatic literature, but in a different way from the discussions of principle. In these texts, structure was generally less important than the aim, which was to expose the defects of the law – particularly the statute law.[26] A good example of this type of book is Tomlins' *Digest of the Criminal Statute Law of England* (1819).[27] Tomlins claimed that 'No work . . . has ever yet appeared containing the whole Criminal Statute Law of England; and as the various Acts relating thereto are dispersed (necessarily without any uniformity) through the numerous volumes of printed Statutes, the Search for particular Acts frequently becomes arduous even to Professors of the Law.'[28] The design of the book was thus to bring together all of the criminal statutes of England so as to show the present state of the law. The first volume contained statutes from those on admiralty and ambassadors up to Larceny; the second volume from malicious injuries and manufactories to Wales. Each title would then list the principal statutes on a topic and digest or paraphrase the provisions of the relevant statutes, with little further authorial comment.[29] What made this more than a practical handbook, however, was that Tomlins went on to argue that, by bringing them together, it could then be shown that different statutes had been passed on the same subject, creating similar offences but with widely differing punishments or other inconsistencies. He went on to say 'In not a few cases, also, latter Statutes re-enact, verbatim, the Provisions of former Acts, without noticing the existence of the first Statute.'[30] The purpose then, it becomes clear, is to demonstrate the severity and disorder of the criminal statutes, and to present an argument for reform through digesting the law into a single code.

A similar plan was followed in Evans' *Collection of the Statutes* (1817), though this was not confined to criminal or penal statutes.[31] This covered the whole of the law as might be connected to professional or magisterial practice – with the final four volumes of eight relating to crimes and justices of the peace. The aim was in part to include and digest statutes that were not readily available elsewhere, but more broadly to suggest alterations to the law or to illustrate the principles which

[26] One could obviously include Bentham here for his critique of the common law, though Bentham's work clearly cuts across these first two categories. For a discussion of Bentham, see Lieberman, *Province* (n 23) and Smith (n 1) 30–42.

[27] HN Tomlins, *A Digest of the Criminal Statute Law of England, Alphabetically and Analytically Arranged* (2 vols) (London, H Butterworth, 1819).

[28] Preface, vol II, iii.

[29] Unusual titles include *Buonaparte Napoleon* (56 Geo. III c23), conies, hawks, lace, proclaiming false news, swans, wool and swearing.

[30] Preface, vol I, vii. Citing 35 Geo. III c66 and 37 Geo. III c46 (on forgery) as examples of this.

[31] WD Evans, *A Collection of the Statutes Connected with the General Administration of the Law, Arranged According to the Order of Subjects, with Notes* (8 vols) (London, J Butterworth, 1817). See also G Ensor, *Defects of the English Laws and Tribunals* (London, J Johnson & Co, 1812).

might be applied to reform – 'to counteract the tendency of an excessive dread of innovation'.[32] The part on criminal law dealt with crimes under the familiar broad heads – treason, coin, homicide, etc – but then dealt with statutes chronologically within each section. A model for these types of works was Barrington's influential *Observations on the Statutes* (1766).[33] This book had aimed to identify examples of poor and oppressive law-making with a view to arguing for the repeal of certain statutes, within the broad political context of the recognition of the constitutional freedom of the subject. It was thus not an argument for codification, but an argument for reform that recognised the strengths of the existing system of administration of justice.[34] That said, it is not clear who works such as this or Tomlins were aimed at: too specialised to be aimed at a popular audience, their programmatic character and reforming impulse clearly differentiates them from more practical handbooks and manuals.

This appetite for reform of the penal statutes also inspired a number of initiatives advocating a more wholesale codification of the criminal law, either in the form of draft codes or in a growing literature discussing the most appropriate method of criminal law reform.[35] There were also, finally, more overtly polemical and political attacks on the Bloody Code and the administration of justice, which might address the substance or structure of the law to a greater or lesser degree. Notable here are works such as Samuel Romilly's *Observations on the Criminal Law of England* (1810).[36] This book, based on his celebrated speech to the House of Commons in February 1810, was a wide-ranging attack on the use of capital punishment, and in particular on the ideas of Paley. This argued for a more general system of criminal jurisprudence based on certainty and proportionality in laws and punishment.[37] The rapid republication of parliamentary speeches and review articles in book form suggests that there was a popular appetite for such works.

[32] Preface, vol I, vi. The 8th vol contained an appendix on Observations on Amendment of the Law by A Hammond, see below.

[33] D Barrington, *Observations on the Statutes, Chiefly the More Ancient, From Magna Charta to the Twenty First of James I ch xxvii, With an Appendix; Being a Proposal for New Modelling the Statutes* (London, Bowyer, 1766). The first edition was published anonymously, the third edition (1769) was published under author's name.

[34] See, eg Appendix, 337.

[35] See, eg J Miller, *An Inquiry into the Present State of the Statute and Criminal Law of England* (London, John Murray, 1822); JTB Beaumont, *Essay on Criminal Jurisprudence* (London, 1821); See also Anthony Hammond's Criminal Code, published as the Report of the Select Committee on Criminal Law (1824). See generally Smith (n 1) 72–83; KJM Smith, 'Anthony Hammond, Mr Surface Peel's Persistent Codifier' (1999) 20 *Journal of Legal History* 24–44, http://dx.doi.org/10.1080/01440362008539584.

[36] S Romilly, *Observations on the Criminal Law of England as It Relates to Capital Punishments, and on the Mode in Which It Is Administered* (London, T Cadell & W Davies, 1810). This prompted a further literature see eg Anti-Draco (J Disney), *Five Letters to Sir Samuel Romilly MP on the Subject of his Motion Respecting the Penal Laws* (London, W Clarke, 1810). Disney later contributed a draft code, published under his own name: *Outlines of a Penal Code on the Basis of the Laws of England* (London, R Hunter, 1826).

[37] See also R Peel, *Substance of the Speech of the Right Hon. Robert Peel on Bill for Amendment of Criminal Law* (London, J Hatchard & Son, 1826); H Brougham, *Present State of the Law* 2nd edn (London, H Colburn & H Butterworth, 1828).

C. Handbooks and Other Texts

A final class of texts to note are those handbooks prepared for magistrates who were actually involved in the administration of the criminal law. These texts generally aimed to be as comprehensive as possible, to cover all aspects of law which a magistrate might expect to encounter. The principal text in this area was Burns' *Justice of the Peace*, first published in 1755, which went through 30 editions by 1869 and which covered the full range of law relating to civil and criminal matters to which a magistrate might have to refer.[38] A number of these texts covered only criminal law. Addington's *Abridgement of Penal Statutes* (1775), for example, was presented as a guide for the magistrate because of the difficulties in discharging his duties because the laws were dispersed through so many statutes.[39] This was an index of statutes, presented in tabular form. In spite of the author's claim to be imposing some sort of order on the mass of criminal legislation, this is not apparent to the reader. Some 1532 separate offences were listed over 558 pages, classified by definition, penalty, mode of recovering penalty, and the number of witnesses and justices necessary to convict.[40] In a similar vein was Clark's *Penal Statutes Abridged* (1777).[41] This was aimed at both the magistrate and the individual, for knowledge of the laws is necessary to 'the maintenance of a proper subordination', the preservation of order, security of rights and the manifestation of justice.[42] Like Burn's *Justice of the Peace*, it was organised alphabetically by subject, with cross-referencing and referring also to common-law writers where necessary. A different approach was taken in Nares' *Summary of the Law on Penal Convictions* (1814) which was essentially a book of instructions to magistrates on summary convictions, ordered broadly chronologically from arrest to conviction.[43] What the texts had in common though was that all were intended to be the sole or principal source of reference for a Justice of Peace, who might not have access to any other law books or reports, allowing them to find a simple and up-to-date account of the law on any matter within their jurisdiction, and direct them on the exercise of their powers.

* * *

[38] See Phillips, in this volume, for a discussion of these manuals and the 'low law' they covered. See also JA Conley, 'Doing It by the Book: Justice of the Peace Manuals and English Law in Eighteenth-Century America' (1985) 6 *Journal of Legal History* 257, http://dx.doi.org/10.1080/01440368508530846.

[39] W Addington, *An Abridgement of Penal Statutes* (London, Strahan and Woodfall, 1775) Preface. Went through 4 editions; dedicated to Sir John Fielding.

[40] cf Simpson (n 6) 639 who notes the earlier use of alphabetical abridgements as a means of dealing with the complexity of the common law.

[41] G Clark, *The Penal Statutes Abridged, and Alphabetically Arranged. Calculated to Serve the Desirable End of an Alphabetical Common Place Book of the Penal Laws* (London, Fielding & Walker, 1777).

[42] Preface v.

[43] J Nares, *Summary of the Law on Penal Convictions* (London, J Butterworth & Son, 1814).

The variety of texts suggests wide public interest in the matters relating to crime and penal law. However, while much of this literature speaks to a general concern that the law was complex and in need of some kind of organisation, it is not clear that there was yet either any settled understanding of criminal law as a distinct body of rules or of the best or most practical scheme for ordering the law.[44] For some writers the law was conceived of in traditional terms as Pleas of the Crown, though this was stretched some distance from its original meaning (as actions at common law in which the Crown formally appeared as the prosecutor), to include all serious crimes.[45] Otherwise the terms penal law and criminal law were used interchangeably. In addition, a large part of what we might call the 'practical' literature was aimed at the practising magistrate and dealt largely with misdemeanours, recognised as penal, but not formally as part of the law of crimes. Above all, though, we might ask about the audience for the different forms of literature. Until the late eighteenth century there was only a very small criminal bar as defence counsel were not formally permitted until 1836.[46] Legal education was conducted on an ad hoc basis through the Inns of Court with the result that no systematic or 'scientific' literature was being developed.[47] This, then, can be understood as a practical literature for a system in which the local lay courts were dominant, and in which the defence lawyer was, for the most part, absent from the criminal trial. As this began to change over the course of the eighteenth and early nineteenth centuries, there was a need for a new kind of literature of criminal law, one which addressed the problems of the disorganisation of the sources of law in a form that made it readily accessible to the emerging national criminal bar.

III. THE RISE OF THE TREATISE

The first modern treatises on criminal law, criminal procedure and evidence were published early in the nineteenth century, aimed primarily at an audience of lawyers. They were written by practising lawyers, often early in their legal careers.[48] They are thus not necessarily the fruit of long study or experience in the law, but were often written to pass the time usefully or earn money at a time when

[44] See Lieberman, 'Blackstone' (n 21) 140–42. See also A Amos, *Ruins of Time* (n 10) ch 5 for a discussion of the classification of offences in English criminal law. Cf Waddams, in this volume, making a similar point about the law of contract at this time.

[45] See Lieberman, ibid 153–56.

[46] J Langbein, *The Origins of the Adversary Criminal Trial* (Oxford, Oxford University Press, 2003); AN May, *The Bar and the Old Bailey 1750–1850* (Chapel Hill, University of North Carolina Press, 2003) 76–7; J Beattie, *Crime and the Courts in England 1660–1800* (Oxford, Clarendon, 1986).

[47] See D Lemmings, *Professors of the Law: Barristers and English Legal Culture in the Eighteenth Century* (Oxford, Oxford University Press, 2000); P Polden, 'The Education of Lawyers' in W Cornish *et al*, *The Oxford History of the Laws of England* XI 1820–1914 *English Legal System* (Oxford, Oxford University Press, 2010) 1175–85.

[48] See Simpson (n 6) 664 on the backgrounds of treatise writers. See also the remarks of Cornish in W Cornish (n 47) 59–61.

the young lawyer did not have many clients. These works have normally been either disregarded by historians, or seen as slightly disappointing, because they were not as innovative as the codification projects advanced during this same period. However, my argument here is that the treatises under discussion not only provide a dominant framework for understanding the criminal law, but that in the absence of detailed case reports and other sources, they are the law for the developing legal profession. I should also note that I am not suggesting that these wholly replace the other literature – there is extensive publication of books on criminal law throughout this period, but a full survey of this literature must be beyond the scope of this paper.

A. England

Russell's *Treatise on Crimes and Misdemeanors* was first published in two volumes in 1819.[49] Russell himself was a practising barrister. He was called to the Bar in 1809 and became a Serjeant-at-Law in 1827. Russell (like East) was in 1832 appointed to the post of Chief Justice of Bengal, but died in 1833 shortly after taking up the post.[50] The book went through 12 editions in total, six of which were published in the nineteenth century, the final edition being published in 1964. The first two editions were prepared by the author in his lifetime, and most of the later editions were edited by practitioners, though the final three editions were edited by JWC Turner, an academic.[51] Russell's other publications were limited to two series of case reports: one on the practice of the Carmarthen Circuit (1816), and more substantially (with Edward Ryan) a report of Crown Cases Reserved between 1799 and 1824 (1825).[52] The latter was dedicated to Sir Robert Peel, and Peel returned the favour when presenting his criminal law reform programme to Parliament, praising Russell for having rendered an important service to the law through his clarity and proposals for reform.[53] The Preface to the second edition (1828) then comments favourably on Peel's reforms, and the book also contains the full text of Peel's Acts reforming capital punishment.

While, as Smith notes, Russell's *Treatise* breaks ranks with earlier treatments in respect of the hierarchy of offences, through the exclusion of treason and religious offences, it is not clear that it warrants the claim that it is 'innovatory both struc-

[49] WO Russell, *A Treatise on Crimes and Indictable Misdemeanors* (London, J Butterworth, 1819).

[50] KJM Smith, 'Russell, Sir William Oldnall (*c*.1784–1833)' in *Oxford Dictionary of National Biography* (Oxford, Oxford University Press, 2004) www.oxforddnb.com/view/article/24354, accessed 2 October 2010].

[51] 2nd edn (WO Russell) 1828; 3rd edn (CS Greaves) 1843; 4th edn (CS Greaves) 1865; 5th edn (S Prentice) 1877; 6th edn (H Smith & APP Keep) 1896; 7th edn (W Craies & L Kershaw) 1909; 8th edn (R Ross & GB McClure) 1923; 9th edn (R Ross) 1936; 10th edn (JWC Turner) 1950; 11th edn (JWC Turner) 1958; 12th edn (JWC Turner) 1964. There were also seven American editions between 1824 and 1853.

[52] WO Russell and E Ryan, *Crown Cases Reserved for Consideration; and Decided by the Twelve Judges of England from the Year 1799 to the Year 1824* (London, J Butterworth & Son, 1825).

[53] Peel, *Hansard* 2 1826 14.1238 quoted in DNB entry (n 50).

turally and substantively.'[54] The Treatise itself was divided into five books. Book I dealt with persons capable of committing crimes and principals and accessories (70 pp); Book II with offences against government, public peace and public right (550 pp); Book III with offences against the persons of individuals (290 pp); Book IV with offences against public or private property (850 pp); and Book V dealt with offences which could affect the persons of individuals or property (principally, subornation of perjury and conspiracy) (100 pp). The short treatment of criminal capacity, while dealt with at the start of the book, is then dwarfed by the lengthy sections on offences against government and property, cataloguing the vast compendia of early-nineteenth-century common law and legislation. However, what is striking about the arrangement is that while the order of treatment is broadly similar to earlier works, Russell adopts the method of grouping offences together under the broader heads of government, person and property. This allows for the combination of both system and detail, as the particular offences can then be treated under the broad heads, reflecting the practical orientation of the book. Its other main strength is in clarity of exposition.

The work covered all indictable offences with the exception of treason, which was excluded on the grounds of space and because prosecutions were so infrequent as to leave time to consult the other authorities. He did not attempt to cover minor (summary) offences, except where these might explain or were connected to offences of a higher degree. He claimed in the Preface originally to have intended to include a chapter on evidence, but had excluded this on grounds of space.[55] The subject of procedure was excluded on the grounds that it had recently been dealt with in the work published by Chitty.[56] However, the detailed discussion of each crime included extensive observations on procedure in relation to that crime. In terms of sources, Russell acknowledges his debt to the earlier institutional works of Hale, Hawkins, Foster and Blackstone, and East's more recent *Treatise*, while including much in the way of recent case law, drawing on unpublished judicial manuscripts. Many cases are cited, and at great length, but virtually without comment. However, what is significant about this is that, in the absence of reliable case reporting, the Treatise actually becomes a source of case law. In the Preface to the third edition, for example, the editor commented that he had aimed to follow the system of Russell and in particular his method of citing case law so as to provide a clear view of the facts and the decision. He went on to say: 'Particular attention has been paid to this point, in order to render the work useful on occasions where a question suddenly arises in the course of a trial, or where there may not be the means of referring to the Reports from which the cases are taken.'[57] The

[54] Smith, DNB (n 49). The exclusions reflect the declining practical and symbolic importance of treason for English law. See Russell, Preface to 1st edn. See discussion in L Farmer, *Criminal Law, Tradition and Legal Order* (Cambridge, Cambridge University Press, 1997) 105–06, 112.

[55] 2nd edn (1828): chapter (book) added on evidence (130 pp) by Vaughan Williams.

[56] J Chitty, *A Practical Treatise on the Criminal Law, Comprising the Practice, Pleadings and Evidence Which Occur in the Course of Criminal Prosecutions Etc.* (London, Butterworth & Son, 1816).

[57] CS Greaves (3rd edn) (1843) Preface. Greaves, the editor of the 3rd and 4th edns, was also the main drafter of the Criminal Law Reform Acts of 1861.

work thus provides an invaluable resource for the practitioner: comprehensive and up-to-date, accurate and accessible, but without unnecessary discussion or commentary. This sense of Russell's treatise becoming, if not the source of the law, at least the main point of access to the sources of the law, is confirmed in a letter by Mr Justice Coleridge to the Lord Chancellor:[58]

> At present, the student reads his Russell, or, it may be, East: he refers to Hale and Hawkins: he studies the Crown Cases Reserved which have been published since the last edition of Russell; and he easily keeps up, and notes in his Russell the two or three numbers which may come out in a year of the decisions of the Court of Criminal Appeal. This is no very laborious or expensive course.

There are two other significant English texts that I wish to note here. The first is Archbold's *Summary of the Law Relative to Pleading and Evidence in Criminal Cases* (1824).[59] This, in the judgement of Simpson, was both the most successful of all the nineteenth-century treatises and 'possibly the worst of the lot'.[60] It was successful because it went through 21 editions in the nineteenth century alone and its twentieth-century successor remains a standard work on criminal practice – but it was a work that placed comprehensiveness above questions of style or structure.[61] The second is Joseph Chitty's *Practical Treatise on the Criminal Law* (1826).[62] Both of these works were notable for the fact that they were aimed at the criminal practitioner, and comprised detailed accounts of procedures, forms and precedents. Their popularity and practical utility may readily be measured by the fact that both went through many editions in both England and the US. Neither book offered much by way of conceptual or structural innovation, but they were comprehensive, practical and accessible, and for this very reason clearly met the needs of the criminal practitioner.[63]

[58] Cited in A Amos, *Ruins of Time* (n 10), xxiv. See also May, (n 46) 77–8. Though as Smith notes, what was a useful quality in early editions of Russell became a positive hindrance in later editions, as editors merely added authorities without pruning previous ones or modifying the structure of the work: Smith, DNB (n 49).

[59] Archbold, *A Summary of the Law Relative to Pleading and Evidence in Criminal Cases : With Precedents of Indictments &C. And the Evidence Necessary to Support Them* (London, Pheney, 1824).

[60] Simpson, 'Treatise' (n 6) 664.

[61] EI Carlyle, 'Archbold, John Frederick (1785–1870)', rev M Lobban, *Oxford Dictionary of National Biography* (Oxford, Oxford University Press, 2004) [www.oxforddnb.com/view/article/614, accessed 2 October 2010].

[62] Chitty, (n 55). For biographical details see M Lobban, 'Chitty, Joseph, the Elder (1775–1841)', in *Oxford Dictionary of National Biography* (Oxford, Oxford University Press, 2004) [www.oxforddnb.com/view/article/5336, accessed 4 October 2010].

[63] See also T Starkie, *A Treatise on Criminal Pleading* (London, W Clarke & Sons, 1814) which covered similar ground to Archbold and Chitty. There were also books on particular statutes, see eg EE Deacon, *A Digest of Criminal Law of England As Altered by the Recent Statutes for the Consolidation and Improvement of It* (London, Saunders & Benning, 1831) (alphabetical); R Matthews, *Criminal Law As Altered By Various Statutes of William IV & 1 Victoria* (London, 1837); HW Woolrych, *A Treatise on the Criminal Statutes of 7 Wm IV & 1 Vict* cc 84–91 (London, A Maxwell, 1837).

B. Scotland

A similar pattern can be seen in the development of the modern Scots criminal law following the publication of the first edition of David Hume's *Commentaries on the Law of Scotland Respecting Crimes* in 1797.[64] Published in two volumes, the first of which dealt with the substantive law and the second with procedure and evidence, this was rapidly accepted as the leading work on criminal law. It went through four editions in total, three in his lifetime, and the fourth edition was published in 1844, a few years after his death in 1838. This was a systematic and comprehensive account of the law that shaped the works that followed.

While Hume's *Commentaries* is unique amongst the works considered here in having been written by a professor of law, he nonetheless saw his purpose as that of educating the young lawyer in 'the Elements of our Criminal Practice'.[65] Crimes were treated in order of their practical importance, beginning with a discussion of crimes against property, before moving to crimes against the person, rather than the more traditional focus on crimes against the state. There is a degree of innovation here and also in his short chapter on criminal capacity which begins the work.[66] In general, though, he laid a great deal of stress on the fact that his primary source was case law and practice.[67] This further led him to define crime according to what he took to be the ordinary meaning of the term, going on to say that he would 'consider every act as a crime for which our practice has appointed the offender to make some satisfaction to the public, besides repairing, where that is possible, the injury sustained by the individual.'[68] In this, he suggested, 'the law always supposes that the delinquent has infringed, in some respect, those duties which he owes to the community' either by setting a dangerous example of violence, dishonesty and so on, or by trespassing with respect to the matters of 'wholesome discipline' or 'wise oeconomy' which affect the public welfare or are a matter of general concern.[69] His main aim was that of completeness – to include all relevant crimes discussed in relation to all relevant cases – though by stating and clarifying the law he undoubtedly articulates normative standards or tests capable of being applied by the courts. The measure of his success here was

[64] D Hume, *Commentaries on the Law of Scotland Respecting Crimes* (Edinburgh, Bell & Bradfute, 1797). References are to the 4th edn 1844 (reissued with Introduction by DM Walker, 1986); He was nephew to the celebrated philosopher. For biographical details see JW Cairns, 'Hume, David (*Bap.* 1757, *d.* 1838)', in *Oxford Dictionary of National Biography* (Oxford, Oxford University Press, 2004) [www.oxforddnb.com/view/article/14142, accessed 16 June 2011].

[65] *Commentaries*, ibid I, 13.

[66] The schema essentially follows Blackstone, as the title *Commentaries* might suggest, though Hume does not directly acknowledge this debt. For further discussion see JW Cairns, 'John Millar's Lectures on Scots Criminal Law' (1988) *Oxford Journal of Legal Studies* 364–400.

[67] He remarked that he had gone through the Books of Adjournal (records of the case law) to develop an authoritative statement of the practice of the law. *Commentaries* I (n 64) 3, 18.

[68] Ibid 21.

[69] Ibid, cf Blackstone's view of criminal law as police power, discussed in MD Dubber, *The Police Power. Patriarchy and the Foundations of American Government* (New York, Columbia University Press, 2005) ch 2.

to be his faithfulness to the practice of the law. Indeed, the rapid acceptance of the *Commentaries* by the profession – and the adoption of its schema by later works (notably Alison and Macdonald) – is testimony to his success in this respect.[70]

Hume did not seek to identify general principles of law, but rules which might govern the application of the law in specific areas or in relation to specific issues, and which at most could be understood as shaping the definitions of particular offences. The source of principle was thus understood as a combination of the proper nature of things and the practice of the law. This practice was described as a 'general spirit' of the law.[71] Practice was a way of settling principle, of avoiding strained and artificial rules of law.[72] The most important point here, though, is that the principle is the practice. The radical opposition between the two that is almost axiomatic for modern legal thought did not exist for Hume, and this was a view that continued to be held by his successors.

Alison's *Principles of Criminal Law* (1832) was written as a stopgap after the author – a high Tory – lost his position as Advocate Depute.[73] While he was subsequently to resume his legal career as Sheriff of Lanarkshire in 1834, his immediate response to his loss of position and income was to turn to writing, and he drew on his eight years of experience as Advocate Depute in writing the *Principles.*[74] His immediate justification for writing the book was to provide a work which was 'of more immediate application to the business which actually comes before the Court' than Hume's *Commentaries.*[75] He argued that the years since 1814 had seen a vast increase in criminal business coming before the courts, and that this should be reflected in the new work which, if not superseding Hume as the acknowledged foundation of Scottish criminal jurisprudence, would at least be more up-to-date.[76] The key for Alison, like Hume, was in establishing the link between practice and principle. Here he argued that:

> Practice had sufficiently shown me that there was principle in every part of the law, and that it was the power of reaching and applying that principle which constituted the great characteristic of a profound lawyer.[77]

[70] See Walker, Introduction (n 64) 7 for citations.

[71] *Commentaries* I, (n 64) 2, 13.

[72] For other examples see ibid 38 (on insanity): 'Our practice has always been governed by the general precept . . . which admits of no defence, short of absolute alienation of reason . . . The same principle governed in the trial of Thomas Gray . . .'; 177 (on fraud): 'The instances which have been given may serve as an illustration of the settled principles of our practice, and a ground of inference to other cases of the like cozenage and circumvention.'

[73] A Alison, *Principles of the Criminal Law of Scotland* (Edinburgh, W Blackwood, 1832), covering the substantive criminal law as opposed to the practice, which was the subject of a second volume published in 1833 covering evidence, procedure and punishment.

[74] He was to become much better known to his Victorian audience as the author of a popular multi-volume history of Europe. M Michie, *An Enlightenment Tory in Victorian Scotland. The Career of Sir Archibald Alison* (East Linton, Tuckwell, 1997), Chs 2 & 5; M Fry, 'Alison, Sir Archibald, First Baronet (1792–1867)', in *Oxford Dictionary of National Biography* (Oxford, Oxford University Press, 2004) [www.oxforddnb.com/view/article/349, accessed 16 June 2011]

[75] Alison, Principles (n 73) Preface, v.

[76] He also claimed that the book contained over 1000 unreported cases and more than 500 decisions on analogous points of English law. Ibid, 'Preface, vi'.

[77] A Alison, *Some Account of My Life and Writings* (Edinburgh, Blackwood, 1883) 299.

The problem, however, was that the rapid increase of legal business had 'rendered it impossible for judges in whose minds principle has become matured to give it to the world, except in detached fragments in the decision of particular cases'.[78] Accordingly he claimed to have adopted the plan 'of which Heineccius had given an example in his Institutes and Pandects of the Civil Law, of giving the principle on every subject in a single proposition, and deducing from it a variety of cases of which the particulars were given in the paragraph which followed'.[79] While this then was ostensibly a deductive method, it is in fact inductive, as the principles were extracted from the case law and other authorities which are set out in the following paragraph. The effect, though, is to present the criminal law as a series of free-standing propositions or principles.

The last important nineteenth-century treatise was Macdonald's influential *Practical Treatise* which was first published in 1867. This was written by the young lawyer in his free time as he sought to establish his practice at the Bar.[80] He went on to become an influential legal practitioner, as Lord Advocate and later on the bench as Lord Kingsburgh and this no doubt contributed to the continuing success of the book.[81] While generally following Hume with respect to the organisation and content of the law, the *Practical Treatise* treats principles in a way more akin to Alison. His brief discussion of general conditions of criminal liability, for example, proceeds by stating a series of general principles which are taken to be well-established in the law, but which might be departed from in particular instances. He notes, for example, the 'well-established principle, that the law of Scotland makes no distinction between guilt by direct commission and guilt by accession', before going on to detail a series of specific rules and qualifications.[82] Thus principles are understood as general rules which have been established by the practice of the law, but which can be formulated as independent propositions which can act as a guide to future action. Generally, though, the book was aimed squarely at the practitioner, reducing the law to a series of terse and easy to understand propositions, backed by the authority of recent decisions.

* * *

Certain features of this literature can clearly be identified on the basis of this survey. Simpson's definition is useful as a measure, though the treatises discussed

[78] Ibid 300–1.

[79] Ibid.

[80] JHA Macdonald, *A Practical Treatise on the Criminal Law of Scotland* (Edinburgh, W Paterson, 1867); References are to the 1st edn. This went through five editions between 1867 and 1948, the first three under his direction. For Macdonald's own account of the origins of the work see, *Life Jottings of an Old Edinburgh Citizen* (London, Foulis, 1915).

[81] On his career, see Macmillan, 'Macdonald, Sir John Hay Athole, Lord Kingsburgh (1836–1919)', rev Robert Shiels, *Oxford Dictionary of National Biography* (Oxford, Oxford University Press, 2004) www.oxforddnb.com/view/article/34708, accessed 16 June 2011; *Life Jottings* ibid.

[82] Ibid 4. This is followed by a discussion of the general principles on which individuals are to be held responsible, looking at non-age, alienation of reason and compulsion, where it was argued that the general rule is that a person is answerable unless he falls within one of the exceptions: 14ff.

here largely lacked the features that Simpson takes to be the distinctive characteristics of this literature. Each of the books had the 'quality of unity' that Simpson notes, treating the criminal law as a distinct field and thereby defining this area of law.[83] This, however, was less a matter of conceptual refinement or definition, than a broad positivist assumption that the criminal law is that which is dealt with by the criminal courts. It was not, therefore, a scientific literature. In this there was a clear difference with either the approach of Blackstone, who sought a conceptual definition of crime in terms of public wrong, or earlier writers on Pleas of the Crown, who took a procedural feature as the defining factor. The practical treatises could exclude unimportant offences such as treason, but in the interests of practical utility could also include misdemeanours where necessary. This stress on practice, however, did produce some interesting differences in scope, as the different writers struggled with the question of whether and how to include procedure.[84] Russell excluded procedure, but (from the second edition) included coverage of evidence; Chitty and Archbold were both framed wholly by procedure and saw the substantive law through procedural issues. The Scottish treatises all included discussion of both procedure and rules of evidence, perhaps also reflecting the fact that there was no standard work on criminal procedure until the early twentieth century. Overall, though, criminal law was conceived of primarily as a practical subject, and utility to the practitioner was the organising principle both in terms of structure and substance. This also shapes the idea of principle and the use of authority in the works. With the exception of Alison, it is hard to see these treatises as seeking to identify principles of law which might then be applied to organise the rules and authorities.[85] Principle was instead understood as a quality of the rules which emerged from decided cases, and which might allow the development of the law by analogy and inductive reasoning. This points, finally, to the importance of case law to these treatises. If authorities were not moving from the text into the footnotes in these works, as Simpson suggests, it was because of the importance of these works as a form of law reporting, where the authorities could be identified and transmitted.[86] Finally, it is worth noting that, particularly in the case of the English treatises, the authority of the text was greater than that of the author – a somewhat paradoxical claim as treatises such as *Russell on Crime* were identified by the author's name. In most cases, the original author remains a somewhat shadowy presence, about whom little is known, and with no strong authorial voice or style. However, rather than being an obstacle to the

[83] Simpson, 'Treatise' (n 6) 633.

[84] Ibid 634 excludes from consideration those works whose structure is determined primarily by procedure.

[85] See Ibid, 641–44 for a discussion of the history of the idea of principle, relating it in particular to the form of literature of maxims in the 17th & 18th centuries. For a discussion of Scots law, see L Farmer, 'The Idea of Principle in Scots Criminal Law' in J Chalmers *et al* (eds), *Essays in Criminal Law in Honour of Sir Gerald Gordon* (Edinburgh, Edinburgh University Press, 2010).

[86] Simpson, ibid 640, though at 665 he distinguishes between a treatise written in the self-consciously methodising and selective spirit based on reason, and those based on authority. On law reporting in the 19th century see Polden, (n 47) 1211–22.

achievement of authoritative status, this facilitates it as a succession of later editors update and renew the work. The criminal law treatise, then, is a primarily a means of transmitting a law which is being defined by practice.

IV. THE TEXTBOOK

Criminal law education, as with legal education in general throughout the century, was primarily practice-based in the early part of the century, with teaching at the university law schools largely moribund.[87] There were, however, many critics of this system, and repeated attempts to put legal education on a more formal and systematic basis, both through the professional organisations and the universities.[88] This pressure began to bear fruit towards end of the century as the older universities began to teach law courses – even if this was still piecemeal and dependent on the initiatives of individual professors and scholars. This new style of law teaching, as Sugarman argues, was aimed at building professional legitimacy through the conception of the discipline of law as a special kind of knowledge. On this view law was more than just a practical vocation or an aggregation of authorities, but had a kind of internal coherence or underlying rationality which required a new kind of legal science to understand it.[89] This led to the emergence of a new kind of literature, the legal textbook. Textbooks in the UK took up and modified the treatise tradition, developing a scientific literature, written by academics for law students rather than practitioners, and published by university presses rather than professional law publishers. The pragmatic aim of utility through comprehensiveness was replaced by a pedagogical simplification, which sought to identify principles and eventually present a more programmatic and conceptual understanding of the law.[90]

In criminal law the first work of this new type is CS Kenny's *Outlines of Criminal Law*. First published in 1902, this had already gone through nine editions by 1918, and was to go through 19 in total.[91] He also published one of the first casebooks

[87] A law degree was not a pre-requisite of entering the profession. See generally Polden, (n 47) 1175–1222; CW Brooks and M Lobban, 'Apprenticeship or Academy? The Idea of a Law University, 1830–60' in JA Bush and A Wijffels (eds) *Learning the Law: Teaching and the Transmission of Law in England, 1150–1900* (London, Hambledon Press, 1999) 353–82; D Sugarman, 'Legal Theory, the Common Law Mind and the Making of the Textbook Tradition' in W Twining, *Legal Theory and Common Law* (Oxford, Blackwell Publishing, 1986); W Twining, *Blackstone's Tower. The English Law School* (London, Sweet & Maxwell, 1994) ch 2, making the point that university law teaching was mainly a post-war creation.

[88] Witnesses to the 1846 Select Committee on Legal Education criticised lack of scientific literature as compared with the teaching of law on the European continent: Polden (n 47) 1181. Law reports were seen as encouraging a memory-based system: Brook & Lobban ibid 370–71.

[89] Sugarman (n 87) 29–33, 44–46 also noting the influence of German legal science, in particular through the influence of John Austin, on English legal thought.

[90] See Waddams, chapter 6 in this volume, on the emergence of textbooks in the law of contract.

[91] *Outlines of Criminal Law* (Cambridge, Cambridge University Press, 1902). See also Smith (n 1) 156–57. Kenny was Downing Professor of English Law at the University of Cambridge from 1907 to 1918.

for students on English criminal law.[92] Both the *Outlines* and the *Cases* had two important features which drew on his experience of teaching law in a university. The first was a focus on case law, and the second a clarity and accessibility in organisation and style. In respect of the first, the important differences from the earlier treatises were a reduction in the number of cases cited, and a clearer focus on the principles they represent.[93] This focus on cases, though, also served to promote a view of the criminal law as being based around a core of common law principles.[94] In terms of organisation and content, though, the books represented a clear shift from the earlier treatises. The first section of the book was devoted to discussion of general principles of responsibility, covering the mental element in crime, exemptions from liability, and forms of accessorial and inchoate liability, as well as discussing the purpose of criminal punishment.[95] This was followed by a long section on the definitions of particular crimes (beginning with homicide and crimes against property), as well as shorter sections introducing criminal evidence and procedure. The *Outlines* then concluded with a brief discussion of contemporary developments in criminology. The book thus combines the case law focus of the treatise tradition with a more modern sense of legal and penological science.

A second key figure in this development, though slightly outwith the time period covered by this paper, was JWC Turner, also at the University of Cambridge, who from the 1930s onwards began to promote the idea of subjective fault, drawing on sources such as the Criminal Law Commissioners of 1833–45.[96] Interestingly, the vehicle that Turner chose for his project was new editions of the classic treatises of Russell and Kenny, which were restructured and rewritten to include longer sections on subjective fault.[97] In an important shift of emphasis, he also wrote from a more avowedly 'censorial' perspective, criticising authority where it did not accord with the pre-established principles of fault. This textbook movement was to reach its apotheosis with the publication of Glanville Williams' *Criminal Law: The General Part* in 1953.[98] This work, for the first time in English law, focused exclusively on the general part, and in particular issues of *mens rea* and subjective fault. It was not aimed at practitioners but at law students, and presented a

For biographical details, see AL Goodhart, 'Kenny, Courtney Stanhope (1847–1930)', rev RA Cosgrove, *Oxford Dictionary of National Biography* (Oxford, Oxford University Press, 2004) [www.oxforddnb.com/view/article/34287, accessed 9 October 2010].

[92] CS Kenny, *A Selection of Cases Illustrative of Criminal Law* (Cambridge, Cambridge University Press, 1901).

[93] 'Elementary students who read the Reports under their own guidance are prone to reverse the true order of things, by attending to the names of cases rather than their facts, and to the facts rather than to the principles decided' ibid, Preface.

[94] cf Sugarman (n 87) 34–35 noting the hostility of the textbook tradition to legislation as a source of law.

[95] The first section of the book also start and ends with chapters on the definition and classification of crime. See also Smith (n 1) 152–57 on precursors to Kenny.

[96] JWC Turner, 'The Mental Element in Crimes at Common Law' (1936) 31 *The Cambridge Law Journal* republished in Radzinowicz and Turner, *The Modern Approach to Criminal Law* (London, Macmillan, 1945). See Smith, Lawyers (n 1) 297–304.

[97] See Smith, ibid 301–04 describing Turner's 'conceptual colonisation' of Russell and Kenny.

[98] G Williams, *Criminal Law: the General Part* (London, Stevens, 1953).

view of criminal law in abstract terms to be deduced from principles identified in advance.[99] In a final historical twist these new textbook writers and their works were also a major influence on the English codification initiatives of the late twentieth century, which in turn revived interest in earlier systematising initiatives from the nineteenth century, further eclipsing the impact of the treatise.

V. CONCLUSION

The nineteenth-century criminal law treatises represent a distinct achievement in English and Scots law, one that has often been overlooked because of the absence of obvious conceptual innovation – at least by comparison with the grand codification initiatives of the nineteenth century. They adopted a common classificatory schema and understanding of the criminal law which was enduring and met the needs of the developing legal profession. This discarded the emphasis on crimes against religion and the state which had dominated earlier institutional works, and the movement in scope away from pleas of the crown to indictable offences broadened the coverage of the works while increasing their practical appeal. This in part reflects the more settled state of the criminal law. The combination of the reduction in the number of penal statutes in 1827 and the consolidation of the criminal law in 1861, however imperfect, had the effect of restoring the legitimacy of the criminal law, which had been challenged by reformers in the early part of the century, and then reducing its complexity. It also reflected changes in criminal practice as the treatise writers met the need for a practical literature that was a guide to this new field. What was achieved, then, was a kind of de facto codification of the criminal law as the treatises addressed and resolved the same problems of legitimacy and complexity as the more ambitious political codification initiatives.[100]

As I suggested at the start, this argument can shed light on the history of the failure of codification in England. As Wright notes in his chapter, Benthamite codification was essentially an imperial project both in the literal sense that it was primarily taken up as part of a project of imperial governance, and in terms of its systematising impulse.[101] While domestic resistance to this project from lawyers and judges is normally attributed to an inherent conservatism, what has not been recognised is that the legal profession was at this time developing an alternative project of systematisation of the criminal law through the vehicle of the treatise. On this view, then, the treatise is less a step on the road towards formal

[99] JC Smith and B Hogan, *Criminal Law* (London, Butterworths, 1965) arguably played the role of presenting Williams' subjectivist project in a form that was accessible to both practitioners and students. The scope of this book was much more comprehensive. See also GH Gordon, *The Criminal Law of Scotland* (Edinburgh, W Green & Son, 1967), which was conceived of by the author as Glanville Williams for Scots law. For further discussion, see Farmer, 'The Idea of Principle' (n 85).

[100] Co-ordination and legitimacy are discussed in N Lacey, 'In Search of the Responsible Subject' (2001) 64 *The Modern Law Review* 350–71.

[101] Wright, in this volume. See also Farmer, 'Reconstructing' (n 2).

codification than an alternative.[102] This is to some extent recognised in Stephen's more pragmatic 'common law-based' codification project but where, as Wright points out, this succeeded in places like Canada in the absence of a developed legal profession, with its own methods for transmitting professional knowledge, it foundered in England.[103]

This points, finally, to the role played by treatises in developing and supporting the legal institutions. The eighteenth century criminal law was largely based on local institutions dependent on forms of informal understanding and the personal authority of judicial figures.[104] As the number of courts and cases increased with the rise of organised policing, and as lawyers 'entered' the criminal trial, there was a clear need for some sort of common understanding to replace the localised understandings that had given form to the criminal law up to that point. The importance of the treatise literature here was as a form of de facto codification of the criminal law, as a means of solving the coordination problems and ensuring that the law was applied according to the same standards and using the same authorities across the country. The publication of these texts and the availability of more systematic law reports, even if these were still fairly limited, allowed for the more abstract formulation of legal doctrines of general application. These works then played an important, and unacknowledged, role in synthesising the criminal law and provided a means of transmitting knowledge about an increasingly formalised criminal law and procedure as they went through multiple editions in the course of the century. The consequence of this was that criminal law came to be viewed primarily as a practitioners' subject, with the books explicitly eschewing the kind of elegant structure developed by those such as Blackstone, in favour of an emphasis on the practical importance of certain topics. The achievement of the treatise, then, is the codification of practical knowledge, and of the idea of criminal law as a practical subject.

[102] cf Simpson, 'Treatise', (n 6) 666 who sees treatises as a step in the process towards formal codification.

[103] As Wright notes, the common law culture was weaker in the colonies where codification succeeded, in part because of the absence of a treatise tradition, and the constitutional impulse was stronger.

[104] See Beattie, *Crime and the Courts* (n 46); Langbein, *Origins* (n 46); D Hay, 'Property, Authority and the Criminal Law' in D Hay *et al*, *Albion's Fatal Tree* (Harmondsworth, Allen Lane, 1977).

8

Truth and Privilege: Libel Treatises and the Transmission of Legal Norms in the Early Nineteenth-Century Anglo-American World

LYNDSAY CAMPBELL*

I. INTRODUCTION

THIS CHAPTER DISCUSSES the appearance of treatises on libel law in the early nineteenth-century Anglo-American world and the transmission of ideas within them into two different places, Nova Scotia and Massachusetts. As the eighteenth century gave way to the nineteenth in Britain and the United States, newspapers multiplied, and governments attempted to control expression that challenged political orthodoxies. In courtrooms, on streets, in pamphlets and in newspapers themselves, the rights to freedom of expression and of the press were claimed. Although expression could be disciplined in various ways (consider profanity, for example), it was in the context of prosecutions for 'libels' that the debates over the proper limits of political critique and the place of the press in society took place. Many English writers weighed in, but two key texts ultimately made the trip across the Atlantic. The first editions of these texts, by Francis Ludlow Holt and Thomas Starkie, were published in London in 1812 and 1813 respectively. As this chapter shows, though, the views of the law that they promulgated were not universally or wholly accepted. I aim here to explore the issues of reading and influence and how purportedly coherent, comprehensive scholarly texts were deployed or ignored after they left London and ventured out across the

* Assistant Professor, Faculties of Law and Arts, University of Calgary, Calgary, Canada. For their guidance and support with my dissertation, from which this paper emerges, I am in debt to Harry Scheiber, David Lieberman and the late Thomas Garden Barnes. This paper benefited from being presented, in a preliminary form, at the Atlantic World seminar at Harvard in the summer of 2010. It developed further after a treatises workshop in Toronto in October 2010 arranged by Angela Fernandez and Markus Dubber. I wish to thank all of the workshop participants and especially Chris Tomlins, Simon Stern, Philip Girard, Wes Pue, Barry Wright and Angela Fernandez for their helpful feedback.

Atlantic. I begin the chapter by discussing the provenance of these texts. I then compare the uptake of defences to charges of criminal libel in Nova Scotia and Massachusetts. The last part of this paper posits that socio-cultural factors made one particular defence – qualified privilege – arguable in Nova Scotia but basically unarguable in Massachusetts, where the defence of truth was preferred. One factor was legal publishing practices: Nova Scotia, lacking the domestic publishing industry that had emerged in the United States by 1830, relied on the importation of texts; as a result the second English edition of Thomas Starkie's libel treatise was available to and relied on by Joseph Howe in his famous prosecution for libel in Halifax in 1835. American law took a different direction. I argue that as Americans worked through the implications of basing sovereignty in the people, not only did privilege seem objectionable in principle, but using the law to protect individuals' reputations from injury started to seem troubling, at least when those injured had a 'public' role and had, from some perspective, suffered from no more than the speaking of the truth. However, the distinction between public and private was under pressure as well, more so in Massachusetts than in Nova Scotia, causing different kinds of expression to be problematic. In effect, then, I suggest that we must look to a combination of factors in understanding the reading and interpretation of – at least – a troublesome body of law such as the one that purported to establish the proper limits on expression. The factors that affected how a text was absorbed into a particular legal culture included not only qualities of the text itself but also the material conditions under which it made its appearance, the political situation in which it was interpreted, and the legal traditions already in operation.

II. EARLIER WRITING ABOUT LIBELS

The origins of libel as a 'field' of law lie very far back in time.[1] Texts on 'scandalous words', 'seditious writings' and actions on the case for slander have survived from the seventeenth century. The Star Chamber and the changing jurisdiction of the ecclesiastical courts, not to mention increasing literacy and changing print technologies, are important components of the development of the English law. Highly theorised ideas about what was actionable, what was excusable, and why, formed in the later eighteenth and particularly the early nineteenth centuries. AWB Simpson has emphasised the natural-law thinking that made it possible for treatise writers to see a coherent structure in an area of law, which could be represented in an authoritative, analytic text.[2] Before the nineteenth century, most defenders of libel prosecutions espoused a commitment to preserve a hierarchic-

[1] In Horwitz's terms, the 'crystalisation' process was long: see M Horwitz, 'Part III – Treatise Literature' (1976) 69 *Law Library Journal* 461.

[2] AWB Simpson, 'The Rise and Fall of the Legal Treatise: Legal Principles and the Forms of Legal Literature' (1981) *University of Chicago Law Review* 632.

ally arranged 'peace'; after the revolutionary period, with an engaged political press a reality, freedom of expression had to be thought through. If there is conceptual coherence in these later books, it springs from their authors' need to make sense of these two commitments.

Many writings on the legal regulation of offensive written or pictorial expression – 'libels' – have survived from the eighteenth century.[3] Most addressed particular cases or debates over the substantive law or procedure that arose from them. Some, from their titles, sound like treatises in the sense in which we normally use that term, but upon closer examination, they turn out to be long essays whose purposes were narrower: to intervene in political controversies of the time.[4] Like the later treatises, they often sought principles to balance the reputational interests of the state and individuals against the expressive interests of their critics. These principles, grounded in an understanding of history and politics, would then allow the author to sort the correctly decided cases from the wrong ones, of which there could be many, given the history of political prosecutions in England, new controversies and changing norms around the press and its regulation.

The author of one anonymous text published around 1730 observed that although most other 'heads in the Law' had already been 'copiously and variously handled', 'upon Libels, nothing can be found collected, except a short Chapter or two in some general Treatises'. He (presumably 'he') considered his text an argument for the 'Liberty of the Press', since it suggested the lack of necessity for restraining it and a practice, among those in power, of being lenient toward their detractors.[5] The author's scope was broad, but one particularly important question needed answering: 'Whether a witty Man may not write and publish Things of a scandalous Import, yet so glossed over and disguised, so wrapp'd up in Implications and Allegories, as not to come within Reach of the Laws, nor be construed a Breach of them' – a fair question in the age of Jonathan Swift. The answer, by the way, was no.[6] This discussion thus framed libel law as a response to the question 'what are the proper limits on a free press?' Later treatise writers, as well as most other commentators, asked the same question.

The foundations upon which the early nineteenth-century treatises were constructed included such older texts as Hawkins' *Pleas of the Crown* and Bacon's *Abridgement*. One precursor with treatise-like ambitions was *A Digest of the Law Concerning Libels*, by 'A Gentleman of the Inner Temple'. The author's impetus for writing appears to have been the Wilkes affair in the early 1760s. The text canvassed all matters relevant to proceedings for 'libels' – it contained a chapter on outlawry, among other things – and it carefully cited case authority. However, spoken defamation – slander – was outside the scope of the project. The cases

[3] A search for 'libel' in titles in the Early Eighteenth-Century Collections Online database reveals over 100 documents. Searching for 'libel' in the text results in well over 10 000 hits.

[4] See, eg James Adair's *Discussions of the Law of Libels as at Present Received* [etc] (London, printed for T Cadell, 1785).

[5] Preface to Anon, *State Law: Or, the Doctrine of Libels, Discussed and Examined* [etc] (London 1730 [?]), np.

[6] Ibid 135–36.

digested were arranged in groups under topics rather than being footnoted as illustrating particular principles, as later authors would do. The overarching purpose of libel law, its author indicated, was protecting the peace.[7]

Appearing in the late 1760s, Blackstone's *Commentaries* have their place in this tale. Among the wrongs to an individual, Blackstone included written and pictorial 'libels' as well as spoken words and malicious prosecutions.[8] The public wrongs were organised according to the rank of the person or body wronged, based on the logic that '[a]ll crimes ought . . . to be estimated according to the mischief they produce in civil society'.[9] Accordingly, Blackstone began with offences against God and religion.[10] He went on to discuss offences against the law of nations, the king and branches of government, the public peace and trade, public health, and then individuals, in their persons and property. Offences committed through expression appeared intermittently throughout the text. The sort of offensive texts referred to explicitly as 'libels' were addressed among the offences against the public peace, on the theory that they promoted violence.[11] Blackstone observed that freedom of speech meant that no 'prior restraints' – no licensing, in particular – would be imposed on expression, but individuals could still be prosecuted or sued for what they published, to protect the public welfare.[12]

Books on pleadings and process from the 1790s and the first decade of the nineteenth century, when they addressed offences committed through expression, often echoed Blackstone's assumptions and overall organisation, sometimes explicitly emulating it. The 1793 Dublin edition of John Tremaine's *Pleas of the Crown*, for example, was organised according to who had been wronged. The editor of the 1795 edition of William Hawkins' *Pleas of the Crown* explicitly noted his intention to use Blackstone's taxonomy. Hawkins observed that there were some kinds of verbal expression that would not found a libel, including petitions to committees of Parliament, articles of the peace given to justices of the peace, and submissions to any other court.[13] Eventually these exceptions were reformulated into privileges.[14]

[7] 'A Gentleman of the Inner Temple' [John Rayner], *A Digest of the Law Concerning Libels: Containing All the Resolutions in the Books on the Subject, and Many Manuscript Cases* [etc] (London, printed for the author by H Woodfall and W Strahan, 1765) 16.

[8] W Blackstone, *Commentaries on the Laws of England* (5th edn) (Oxford, Clarendon Press, 1773) 3, 123–27.

[9] Ibid vol 4, 41.

[10] Ibid vol 4, 41–65.

[11] Ibid 150–51. People were to use legal processes rather than weapons to redress reputational injuries. Malicious prosecution was linked to slander and libel because of the possibility that some people would misuse legal processes in order to damage reputation.

[12] Ibid 151–53.

[13] Thomas Vickers (ed) and John Rice (tr), *Tremaine: Pleas of the Crown in Matters Criminal and Civil Containing a Large Collection of Modern Precedents* [etc] (Dublin, printed by H Watts, 1793); T Leach (ed), *Hawkins: A Treatise of the Pleas of the Crown; Or A System of the Principal Matters Related to that Subject Digested Under Proper Heads* (7th edn) (London, printed for GG and J Robinson and J Butterworth, 1795) vol 2, 127–29.

[14] Blackstone's taxonomy was also adopted in EH East, *Pleas of the Crown* (London, printed for J Butterworth, & Dublin, printed for J Cooke, 1803) (reprinted London, Professional Books Limited, 1972) and East, *A Treatise of the Pleas of the Crown* (Philadelphia, PA, P Byrne, 1806).

III. HOLT AND STARKIE

In Britain, the tumult of the late 1700s and early 1800s included many prosecutions of the press.[15] Writers commented, obliquely or otherwise, on aspects of these developments. They wrote in highly critical terms about such matters as the role of juries, the oppressive pre-trial power that the Crown wielded through the *ex officio* information, the role of intent, the place of truth in criminal proceedings and the partiality of the special jury.[16]

In 1812 and 1813, two texts appeared that ultimately passed across the Atlantic and made their way into libraries and cases there. These texts, by Francis Ludlow Holt and Thomas Starkie, communicated not just procedural rules or digests of cases but frameworks for understanding these cases as a body of law.[17] The appearance of the word 'treatise' in the title of Starkie's seems to signal that such a project was afoot. These texts adopted different organisational schemes, suited to their purposes. These schemes were by no means inevitable: a third libel 'treatise' published around the same time adopted still another.[18] Initially Holt's seems to have had a greater audience; a second edition appeared in 1816. Ultimately, though, Starkie's influence surpassed Holt's; editions continued to appear until the early twentieth century.

Holt was clearly responding to popular attacks on libel law. He observed:

> The law of libel has been for a long time rather a theme of declamation than a topic of legal argument. – The subject, indeed, lies so near the confines where politics encroach upon the science of law, that it is difficult to avoid stepping from one to the other; and the learning upon this question, if any it could be called, had so strayed into pamphlets and popular harangues, that all the precision of a legal subject was lost in the loosest generalities.[19]

[15] For an overview, see D Thomas, *A Long Time Burning: The History of Literary Censorship in England* (New York, NY, Frederick A Praeger, 1969) 95–207.

[16] See, eg Adair, *Discussions* (n 4); G Dyer, *An Address to the People of Great Britain, on the Doctrine of Libels, and the Office of Juror* (London, self-published, 1799); A Highmore, *Reflections on the Distinction Usually Adopted in Criminal Libel Prosecutions for Libel* [etc] (London, printed by T Farnworth for J Johnson, 1791); Francis Burdett, *Speech of Sir Francis Burdett, Bt. Delivered in the House of Commons On the 28th March, 1811* [etc] (London, J Morton, 1811). In 1792, Fox's Libel Act – or An Act to Remove Doubts Respecting the Functions of Juries in Cases of Libel 1792 (32 Geo III, c 60), also known as the Declaratory Act – determined that the jury could determine the outcome of the whole case, rather than being confined to answering certain questions related to publication. Rayner in 1785 observed that such was indeed the law: 'Gentleman', *Digest of the Law* (n 7) 70. See also Thomas, *Long Time Burning* (n 15) 175–76.

[17] FL Holt, *The Law of Libel in Which Is Contained a General History of This Law in the Ancient Codes* [etc] (New York NY and London, Garland Publishing, 1978; orig. London and Dublin, 1812); T Starkie, *A Treatise on the Law of Slander, Libel, Scandalum Magnatum, and False Rumors* [etc] (London, printed for W Clarke & Sons, 1813).

[18] John George's *Treatise on the Offence of Libel: With a Disquisition on the Rights, Benefits and Proper Boundaries of Political Discussion* (London, Taylor and Hessey, 1812) conceptualised the material as a field of law. George asked what was a libel, who was a libeller, what kind of intent was problematic, and what the proper boundaries of political discourse were.

[19] FL Holt, *The Law of Libel in Which Is Contained a General History of This Law in the Ancient Codes* [etc] 2nd edn (London, J Butterworth & Son, 1816) vi–vii.

It was time for a masterly, professional intervention.

The second edition began with about 60 pages of general matters. Holt provided a history of the law of libel, objections to it and a view of the liberty of the press that echoed Blackstone's. Holt distanced contemporary law from its oppressive heritage but insisted on the importance of libel law to preserve reputation and the peace. Next came about 180 pages that presented the law, arranged according to Blackstone's logic: offences against God first and ordinary people last, with enormous footnotes in some places, especially where more recent cases were discussed. The book concluded with another 60 pages on procedure, evidence and punishment. There are many fairly subtle but important differences between the two editions that suggest contemporary events in the background. For example, the second edition had additional passages on the correctness of the doctrine that truth could not be a defence to a charge of criminal libel (true libels might provoke people to break the all-important peace even more than false ones) and on how far parliamentary privilege protected members who published their speeches.[20] Instances in which liability or guilt had not been found were scattered among the instances in which it had.

It is in Thomas Starkie's first two editions that Paul Mitchell has located the origins of the modern law of libel.[21] Starkie was concerned with the necessary limits placed on the freedom of discussion as far as it extended to the reputations of individuals or to the interests of the public.[22] Explicitly taking on Blackstone, Starkie asserted, '[t]here is a wide difference between an open press, that is, a press not subject to the previous control of a licenser, and a free press; and yet it is remarkable, that these are treated by a very eminent writer upon our constitution, as identical'.[23] Unlike Holt, Starkie carefully articulated not only the elements of the case for the plaintiff or the public but also, as Mitchell observes, the grounds for attributing – or not – the injury to the defendant. In the first edition, Starkie devoted a chapter to cases involving exemptions from liability for literary critics and for employers who gave unfavourable character references for servants.[24] In the second edition – published in London in 1830 – these cases formed the basis for a much broader 'privilege' for a writer who owed the reader a duty to disclose what he or she knew about a matter in which both had an interest. This privilege was 'qualified', as it could be defeated by evidence of actual malice.[25]

[20] Ibid 38–48, 191–96.

[21] P Mitchell, *The Making of the Modern Law of Defamation* (Oxford and Portland, OR, Hart Publishing, 2005).

[22] See Starkie, *Treatise on the Law of Slander* (n 17) 12.

[23] Ibid 10.

[24] Ibid 255–74.

[25] T Starkie, *A Treatise on the Law of Slander and Libel, and Incidentally of Malicious Prosecutions* (2nd edn) (London, J and W T Clarke, 1830) 1: lxxv-lxxxviii, 1: cxli–cxliii, 2: 255–57. Mitchell observes that Starkie drew from John Borthwick, *The Law of Libel and Slander, as Applied, in Scotland, in Criminal Prosecutions, and in Actions of Damages* [etc] (Edinburgh, printed for W and C Tait, and London, printed for J and WT Clarke, 1826), which in turn responded to Starkie's 1813 text.

IV. NOVA SCOTIA

By 1820, Nova Scotia was a small colony of around 100 000, whereas Massachusetts had passed the half-million mark.[26] Nova Scotia had an elected assembly, which was increasingly at odds with the lieutenant governor and his selected council, who regularly used their power of disallowance to stymie the assembly's efforts. The province had a small legal elite composed of men trained in England and the United States. There was a large American population in Halifax and in certain other areas, and there was a substantial flow of people, books and newspapers back and forth between the two places. Nova Scotia had no legal reporting and few newspapers, so our knowledge is incomplete, but the court records that exist suggest there were also few libel cases.

The number of newspapers in the province began to increase in the late 1820s, and calls for governmental reform began to be heard. A political crisis in 1830 over the assembly's right to pass a money bill was the harbinger of greater conflict to follow. In 1835, Joseph Howe, an aspiring politician and the well-known editor of the Halifax newspaper, *The Novascotian*, published an article attacking the magistrates who governed that city, accusing them of irresponsibility, incompetence and self-interestedness in the conduct of their official duties. The magistrates got the attorney general to initiate a prosecution.

The case has been discussed at length elsewhere,[27] and I wish to make only two main points about it here. The first is that it picked up the trajectories of the English libel debates. Howe, who defended himself, focused on the jury, encouraging these men to act independently to determine guilt on all elements of the case, pursuant to Fox's Libel Act, which the attorney general agreed they were entitled to do. The attorney general, likewise, emphasised that he had proceeded fairly, by indictment, rather than by *ex officio* information. In defending himself, Howe told the jury that intent was now the jury's province to decide, and, as Lord Erskine had done in defending Thomas Paine, Howe told the jury that the nature of the intent that the Crown had to prove was broader – more malicious – than the intent simply to publish the article (the Crown put forth the opposing view).[28]

[26] The Nova Scotia figures are interpolated from JS Moir, 'To Fertilize the Wilderness: Problems and Progress of the Synod of Nova-Scotia in its First Quarter-Century' in P Laverdure (ed), *Early Presbyterianism in Canada* (Gravelbourg SK, Laverdure & Associates, 2003) 56; 'A Statistical Return of the Province of Nova-Scotia, Up to the 31st Day of December 1827' (12 April 1828) *Colonial Patriot* [Pictou NS] 153; and Editorial (8 April 1828) *Free Press* [Halifax, NS] 59. The Massachusetts figures come from the Historical Census Browser from the University of Virginia, Geospatial and Statistical Data Center (2004) fisher.lib.virginia.edu/collections/stats/histcensus/index.html, accessed 28 February 2007.

[27] See, eg J Murray Beck, '"A Fool for a Client": The Trial of Joseph Howe' (1974) 3: 2 *Acadiensis* 39; B Cahill, '*R. v Howe* (1835) for Seditious Libel: A Tale of Twelve Magistrates' in FM Greenwood and B Wright (eds), *Canadian State Trials* vol 1: *Law, Politics, and Security Measures, 1608–1837* (Toronto, ON, University of Toronto Press, 1996); LM Campbell, 'Licence to Publish: Joseph Howe's Contribution to Libel Law in Nova Scotia' (2006) 29 *Dalhousie Law Journal* 79.

[28] T Paine, *The Trial of Thomas Paine, for a Libel, Contained in the Second Part of Rights of Man* [etc] (Boston MA, printed by I Thomas and ET Andrews and sold by D West and E Larkin, 1793) 20;

The second point is that Howe claimed the defence of qualified privilege articulated and elaborated in the 1830 second London edition of Starkie. Thus, asserted Howe:

> Starkie, an eminent authority on the Law of libel, says: 'The occasion and circumstance of a communication may supply a qualified defence, dependent on the actual intention to injure. The constituting [*sic*] a large and extensive barrier for the legal protection and immunity of those who act bona fide and sincerely according to the occasion and circumstances in which they are placed, is not only just in a moral point of view, and advisable in a measure of policy, but is absolutely necessary for the purposes of civil Society.'[29]

Howe argued that, as a newspaper editor and as one who had been on the grand jury in 1832 (blocked by the magistrates in its efforts to gain information about Halifax's finances), he had a responsibility to the public to disclose what he knew about the governance of Halifax. He asserted that although no truth defence was available to him, he had 'the privilege of explaining to the Jury anything which might illustrate the motives and intentions by which he was influenced, to satisfy them, that so far from wishing to provoke a breach of the peace – so far from incurring the guilt of which he [stood] accused, that his motive was praiseworthy, his actions honourable, and his act demanded by the circumstances in which he was placed.'[30]

Explaining his intent and what he knew – the grounds for the privilege claim – at great length, Howe also told the jury that only evidence of his actual malice would rebut the claim of privilege. The attorney general and the chief justice disagreed, telling the jury that only the intent to publish was in question and that qualified privilege was unknown to law. The jury acquitted Howe anyway. The qualified privilege defence was not, therefore, accepted into Nova Scotian law, but it was articulated, and it was a significant factor in making it possible for Howe to present the jury with the evidence necessary for an acquittal. I have argued elsewhere that newspaper editors – especially Howe himself – seem to have been emboldened by the trial, and to have responded to its outcome by beginning to engage far more confidently in public debate.[31] The course of defending against a charge of criminal libel in Massachusetts, however, ran on a different track.

V. MASSACHUSETTS

As is well known, the 1790s were a tempestuous period in the history of the young republic. Theories of federalism and sovereignty were contested, and partisan

'Supreme Court. Hilary Term. The King vs. Joseph Howe. Trial before the Chief Justice and a Special Jury, for a Libel on the Magistrates of Halifax' (12 March 1835) *Novascotian* 81.

[29] 'Supreme Court. Hilary Term', ibid 86.
[30] Ibid 82.
[31] Campbell, 'Licence to Publish' (n 27).

politics took hold. The libel treatises of Starkie and Holt arrived and were taken up in a place with a history of efforts to use criminal libel to regulate expression.

The qualified privilege defence had no purchase in Massachusetts. By the 1820s, the debates around the criminal law of libel revolved around the possibility of introducing evidence of the truth of the allegedly libelous statement as part of the defence's case. The argument made was that, in a republic, it was the right, or even the duty, of citizens to speak the truth about office-holders and the structure of government. The common law's concern to preserve the peace and protect reputations could not be fully accepted alongside the right to seek improvement in political institutions and to ensure that government was properly conducted.

Massachusetts judges, however, were wary of permitting truth to be a defence to charges of defamation. At common law, truth could be a defence in a civil case, on the theory that a person should not be able to recover damages for a reputation that was undeservedly good. Truth had to be specially pleaded, though, and Massachusetts followed this practice. Apparently unlike other American jurisdictions, however, Massachusetts also permitted a plaintiff to use any admissions contained within the plea of truth to rebut the plea on the general issue. A defendant pleading truth would explicitly assert that the plaintiff had done whatever it was that had been alleged in the defamatory statements and that was why the defendant had spoken or published the words in question, 'as s/he lawfully might'. In effect, therefore, a defendant both generally denied defaming the plaintiff at the place and time and in the manner alleged, and then, in the plea of truth, admitted to doing so on the basis that the plaintiff truly had done whatever the discreditable thing was. Unlike other jurisdictions, Massachusetts courts ruled that, unless the court gave permission to 'plead double', the plaintiff could treat the second plea as an admission of liability with respect to the first. Contemporary commentary suggests that in other kinds of suits these special pleas were treated separately; defamation was different. Questions about, say, reference to the plaintiff or knowledge, publication or innuendo, which might have been part of the general denial, would thus be pushed off the table, and the defendant would be stuck with the truth defence alone.[32]

In 1826, by statute, the legislature decreed that the plea of truth would not be taken as evidence that the defendant had written or spoken such words, or made such a charge; nor would an unproven plea of truth be proof of malice. It would be for the jury to decide, upon the whole case, whether the plea was made with malicious intent.[33] Judges, however, limited the reach of the statute and continued to make pleading truth risky for civil defendants, until special pleading was finally abolished in the 1830s.[34]

[32] See *Coffin v Coffin*, 4 *Mass* 1 (1808); *Jackson v Stetson*, 15 *Mass* 48 (1818); *Alderman v French*, 18 *Mass* 1 (1822); *Hix v Drury*, 22 *Mass* 296 (1827). Long editorial footnotes attached to *Jackson v Stetson* and *Hix v Drury* indicated the bar's unhappiness with the rulings in these cases and compared the situation in Massachusetts with the law on the same point elsewhere.

[33] *Jackson v Stetson*, ibid, *cf* St 1826, c 107, s 2.

[34] St 1836, c 273. My dissertation explores these events in greater detail: LM Campbell, 'Truths and Consequences: The Legal and Extralegal Regulation of Expression in Massachusetts and Nova Scotia, 1820–1840' (PhD dissertation, University of California, Berkeley, 2008).

Massachusetts judges were uneasy about a truth defence and were concerned to keep the law of libel, and especially criminal libel, at hand as a useful tool to protect not simply the reputations of the 'best men', in Norman Rosenberg's formulation,[35] but the sanctity of the private, patriarchal household. The story is a long, complex one, but its outline is this.

The first criminal libel case in which evidence of truth made an official appearance in Massachusetts was *Clap*, in 1808.[36] Massachusetts legal practice however, was following that of New York, where the truth defence had been raised in a common-law libel prosecution in 1804, in a case called *Croswell*, a Republican prosecution of a Federalist newspaperman. At Croswell's trial in circuit court, the judge instructed the jury to determine only the issues of publication and the meaning of any innuendoes in the impugned article. The judge would determine whether or not the publication was libellous. The jury could not consider the defendant's intent or whether or not the publication was true. Upon conviction, Croswell appealed to the Republican-dominated appellate court where James Kent sat, the only Federalist. Defending Croswell, Alexander Hamilton argued that the jury could decide both fact and law in criminal cases, and that while truth was not a defence to criminal libel, intent to harm the complainant was an essential part of the prosecution's case. The common-law practice of imputing malice based on the defamatory nature of the publication was unacceptable in a free republic. Hamilton argued that the exclusion of truth was repugnant to republican principles of justice. Accordingly, he argued, the liberty of the press 'consisted in publishing with impunity, truth with good motives, and for justifiable ends, whether it related to men or to measures'. According to Hamilton (though not counsel for the state), truth was relevant to the key question of criminal intent.[37] At this point, the American common law diverged from the English. Shortly thereafter, New York enacted a bill to permit the jury to decide the whole matter in issue and to make truth a defence, as long as the matter was published with 'good motives and for justifiable ends'.[38]

In *Clap* in 1808, the Massachusetts Supreme Judicial Court partly followed Hamilton's lead, ruling that actual malicious intent had to be proven. A defendant could therefore prove 'that the publication was for a justifiable purpose, and not malicious, nor with the intent to defame any man. And there may be cases, where the defendant, having proved the purpose justifiable, may give in evidence the truth of the words, when such evidence will tend to negative the malice and intent to defame'. Evidence of truth could be adduced to rebut the presumption of malice drawn from the fact of publication, given good motives and justifiable ends. However, the Massachusetts court stipulated that this evidence of truth was

[35] NL Rosenberg, *Protecting the Best Men: An Interpretive History of the Law of Libel* (Chapel Hill, NC, University of North Carolina Press, 1986).

[36] The arguments in the decision indicate that the practice had been accepted before the case was decided: *Comm v Clap*, 4 *Mass* 163 (1808).

[37] *People v Croswell*, 3 Johns Cas 337 (NY, 1804).

[38] Ibid. See also LW Levy, *Emergence of a Free Press* (New York, NY, Oxford University Press, 1985) 339.

only admissible in cases of 'public' libels, where the complainant was a holder of or a candidate for a public office and the allegations pertained to that person's suitability for office. Evidence of truth could not be admitted outside this limited domain.[39]

The door had budged, but the problem of how to protect 'private' reputations, and ultimately the privacy of households, remained. Between 1822 and 1833, a series of cases modified the Massachusetts position in two ways. First, between 1822 and 1826, the kind of person whose conduct could be subjected to public scrutiny broadened to include an itinerant Methodist minister who was suspected of becoming unduly close to his female followers,[40] but not the Russian consul[41] or an innkeeper in whose premises someone had died.[42] A ball attended by 200 or 300 people was not properly of public interest,[43] but 'gross swindling' or an apothecary vending poison as medicine might be.[44] Responding to the first of these cases, regarding the minister, Harrison Gray Otis (who had in fact defended Clap 14 years earlier) argued that admitting evidence of truth in such a case was highly dangerous: the truth defence, Otis argued, had to be applicable only to critiques of men who occupied or sought public stations, and it should only be relevant to qualities that pertained directly to their fitness for office. He cautioned against letting actual malicious intent become the core of a criminal case, since doing so would leave it open to would-be moral censors to disclose harmful information – true or false – about others in the name of the public good.[45] This peril was key to the development of the truth defence for the next decade.

During this period, moral and social reformers – crusaders against alcohol, gambling, freemasonry and indeed slavery – and representatives of upstart religious groups found themselves in court far more frequently than their numbers would seem to warrant, either facing charges of criminal libel for allegations they had made against others or defending their own reputations.[46] Truth was made a defence in criminal cases in 1826 by the same statute that modified its role in civil cases.[47] Moral reformers and religious crusaders involved in such cases thereafter often tried to rely on the truth defence or else found others relying on it against them. Things went badly for them either way. In a case against an anti-gambling crusader in 1834, Chief Justice Lemuel Shaw ruled that a criminal defendant pleading truth could be required by the prosecution to set out the instances in

[39] *Comm v Clap* (n 36) 169.

[40] *Comm v Joseph T Buckingham* (Mun Ct Boston, Dec 1822).

[41] *Comm v Buckingham, Thacher's Criminal Cases* 29 36 (1824).

[42] *Comm v Blanding* (1825) *Mass LEXIS* 74, 8.

[43] *Comm v Buckingham, Thacher's Criminal Cases* 51 53–56 (1824).

[44] *Comm v Blanding*, 20 Mass 304, 320 (1825).

[45] A Member of the Suffolk Bar [HG Otis], *A Letter to the Hon. Josiah Quincy, Judge of the Municipal Court, in the City of Boston, on the Law of Libel, as Laid Down by Him in the Case of Commonwealth vs. Buckingham* (Boston, Wells and Lilly, 1823) 31–32.

[46] This statement arises from an extensive examination of the reported and unreported civil and criminal cases of Massachusetts, particularly the counties of Suffolk and Worcester, for the 1820s and 1830s.

[47] *St* 1826, c 107.

which the complainant had supposedly misbehaved, so that the prosecution could meet the defendant's case.[48] The same year, in another prosecution of the same man, Shaw terminated the intent defence. The defendant had pleaded, not truth, but that he had received the information from the best possible source, had reasonably believed it true, and ought therefore to be excused from liability. Shaw insisted that the defendant's philanthropic aims were irrelevant if what he had published was not absolutely true: his intent (to publish) would be inferred from the fact of publication.[49]

What of privilege? One explicit effort was made to argue it, in an address to the Supreme Judicial Court by a Congregationalist minister and temperance crusader (and, for a short time, abolitionist) named George Cheever. Cheever had by this point declared his intention not to contend with the Commonwealth, but he addressed the Court anyway. Since the objectionable text presented the complainant hiring demons to work at his distillery, the truth defence was not viable. Instead Cheever cited Thomas Starkie's treatise on evidence to make a qualified privilege argument, in which he framed the evils of alcohol and his own awareness of it as creating a situation in which he was justified in speaking out. There is no indication that Chief Justice Shaw paid any attention to it.[50]

VI. INTENT AND THE TRUTH TRACK

I have argued elsewhere[51] that one reason why the qualified privilege defence went unused and practically unconsidered in Massachusetts was that by the time the 1830 London edition appeared, an 'American edition' of Starkie already existed – essentially a reprint of the 1813 edition with footnotes to American cases.[52] It and an 1832 American edition were the versions of Starkie that were for sale in Boston and mainly appeared in libraries there in the 1830s, as the antebellum American book trade began to flourish.[53] These seem to be the editions of Starkie that were

[48] *Comm v Snelling*, 32 *Mass* 321 (1834).

[49] Ibid 337.

[50] *Comm v George B Cheever* (CP, Essex, Jun term 1835, pleaded no contest at SJCt Essex, December 1835); George B Cheever, *Defence in Abatement of Judgment for an Alleged Libel in the Story Entitled 'Inquire at Amos Giles' Distillery'* [etc] (New York, NY, Leavitt, Lord, & Co, 1836) 12.

[51] LM Campbell, 'Starkie's Adventures in North America: The Emergence of Libel Law' in H Foster *et al* (eds), *The Grand Experiment: Law & Legal Culture in British Settler Societies* (Vancouver, BC, UBC Press, 2008).

[52] ED Ingraham (ed), *Starkie: A Treatise on the Law of Slander, Libel, Scandalum Magnatum, and False Rumours* [etc] (1st Amer edn) (New York, NY, George Lamson, 1826). MH Hoeflich refers to this publishing practice as one of those available to law booksellers who wanted to sell English books in American markets, and he underlines the considerable cost savings to American publishers and buyers. Adding notes by an American citizen to an English book also made the text subject to copyright protection in the United States, as well as more useful for American lawyers: Hoeflich, *Legal Publishing in Antebellum America* (New York, NY, Cambridge University Press, 2010) 43, 59, 60.

[53] T Huntington (ed), *Starkie: A Treatise on the Law of Slander, Libel, Scandalum Magnatum, and False Rumours* [etc.] (New York, NY, Collins and Hannay, 1832). No libel texts appear in the 1814 estate catalogues of the libraries of Samuel Sewall and Theophilus Parsons: *Catalogue of the Library of the Late*

referred to in courtrooms.[54] The evidence from Nova Scotia is scarce. At least one of the editions of Holt existed,[55] but there is no sign of any edition of Starkie other than the second English edition of 1830.[56] The lack of access to the books would, one assumes, have rendered the arguments in them less likely to be made.

I suspect, though, that it would not have made much difference even if the 1830 edition of Starkie had been available in Massachusetts. 'Privilege' had been described as an 'odious plea' in an earlier case.[57] Legal minds in Massachusetts were committed to working through the relationship between truth and republican political theory.

The moment when truth became the key concept in debates around libel law is hard to pin down. Certainly it found a secure foothold in the political prosecution of John Peter Zenger in New York in 1735. Zenger's counsel was prevented from introducing evidence of truth, but he did argue that for criminal liability to stand, the libelous allegations had to be false. He asserted that a free people had a right to criticise their government and that juries were the bulwark of that freedom. The jury acquitted Zenger.[58]

Bernard Bailyn has observed that Zenger's counsel drew on the radical Whig critique offered in the 1720s by British writers John Trenchard and Thomas Gordon.[59] Grounding sovereignty in the people, 'Cato' argued for the vital importance of political criticism in public life and for disclosing the bad deeds of those who wielded political power. Cato, however, drew a line between the

Chief Justice Sewall, to be Sold at Auction Sept 2 1814 (Cambridge, Hilliard & Metcalf, 1814); *Catalogue of the Library of the Hon. Theophilus Parsons. To be Sold by Auction March 1 1814* (Boston, MA, Francis Amory, 1814). One 1823 Boston book catalogue had only Blackstone's *Commentaries*: *Catalogue of Books to be Sold at Auction On Thursday, March 13 1823* (Boston, MA, Blake & Cunningham, 1823). By 1826, the Harvard law library catalogue had the 1818 American edition of Holt's treatise: *Catalogue of the Library of the Law School of Harvard University* (Cambridge University Press – Hilliard & Metcalf, 1826). Massachusetts booksellers seem not to have started selling libel treatises until around the time when the first American edition of Starkie was published: see Joseph Cunningham, *Catalogue of Law Books. To be Sold on Thursday, June 13 1827* (Boston, MA, Cunningham, 1827) and *Boston Trade Sale. Catalog of Books to be Sold to Booksellers Only, on Tuesday, August 7 1827* (Boston, MA, 1827). These lists of books for sale in Boston are kept by the American Antiquarian Society in Worcester, MA.

[54] I have examined the reported cases and the extensive pamphlet literature associated with libel prosecutions in Massachusetts in the 1820s and 1830s. Citations to Holt and Starkie – always by counsel, never by judges – began before 1826 but were uncommon until the mid-1830s, by which point Starkie was cited more often than Holt. Where it is possible to tell which edition was being cited, the answer is always the American one. The evidence, such as it is, suggests that the American editions of Starkie were the ones most commonly used by the Massachusetts bar.

[55] *Catalogue of Books, in the Law Library at Halifax, Michaelmas Term, 1835* (Halifax, NS, JS Cunnabell, 1835). William Young had both Holt and Starkie: personal communication from William Laurence, referring to the catalogue of the library of William Young, Nova Scotia Archives and Records Management MG2, vol 757.

[56] This edition was also included in the estate of attorney general Richard Uniacke, who died in 1830: *List of Books Belonging to the Estate of the Late Hon. RJ Uniacke to be sold this day, Monday at 11 o'clock* (Halifax, NS, WM Allan, nd).

[57] *Coffin v Coffin* (n 32).

[58] For a description of the trial, see P Finkelman (ed), *A Brief Narrative of the Case and Tryal of John Peter Zenger: Printer of the New York Weekly Journal* (St James, NY, Brandywine Press, 1997) 45–52.

[59] B Bailyn, *The Ideological Origins of the American Revolution* (Cambridge, MA, Belknap Books of Harvard University Press, 1967) 52.

kind of critique that was relevant to improving political institutions and the kind of airing of private vices that damaged the private reputation of an individual.[60] Although the importance of disclosing truths about political chicanery was certainly a key premise of this critique, Cato made no consistent, ringing appeals to truth as a pure good in itself and therefore a primary justification for absolving people from criminal liability for their expression, whether seditious or otherwise. Nonetheless, Pennsylvania, in 1790, became the first state to constitutionalise principles regarding criminal libel prosecutions. Truth was made admissible if the matter alleged to be libelous was suitable for public comment.[61]

Truth's primacy seems to have arisen alongside partisan politics in the 1790s, and it may have emerged first in some places (New York seems likely) and then spread to others. The importance of a right to publish truth seems seldom to have been insisted upon among those who discussed the 1792 London trial (*in absentia*) of Thomas Paine over *The Rights of Man*, Paine's response to Burke's critique of the French Revolution. Thomas Erskine, in defending Paine, asserted not that Paine's assertions were true but that his intentions were good and political critique was vital to the nation.[62] Erskine's arguments were widely excerpted and published in the United States. My sample of American commentary, however, suggests that even those who approved of Paine did not speak of him as having been prosecuted for publishing the truth. Many of the Massachusetts papers were not even troubled by Paine's conviction.[63] Certainly in 1793 the merits of the new France were unclear, and reasonable people could have disagreed. Nevertheless, it must be said that in Massachusetts confidence in the truth defence as the hallmark of free speech did not dominate the arguments around *The Rights of Man*.[64]

The American commitment to the truth defence seems to have emerged in the later 1790s, alongside the conflicts between Federalists and the emerging Democratic-Republican party. Leonard Levy has argued that it was during this period that the libertarian understanding of the First Amendment arose as well. David Rabban argues that American libertarianism's pedigree is older than Levy credits. Nonetheless, as Levy acknowledges, a defence based on truth is a kind of compromise between an unfettered press and the earlier common-law position. Its rise during a period of dramatic conflict between these views makes sense.[65]

[60] See *Cato's Letters: Essays on Liberty, Civil and Religious, and Other Important Subjects* (New York, NY, Da Capo Press, 1971; Reprint of 6th edn, London 1755) 250.

[61] Rosenberg, *Best Men* (n 35) 61–66; Levy, *Emergence of a Free Press* (n 38) 290–91.

[62] Paine, *Trial of Thomas Paine* (n 28) 20.

[63] Using the Eighteenth Century Online database, I searched for 'Paine and libel' and got about 290 hits between 1790 and 1798, most of which were on point. Newspapers from all over the eastern seaboard were represented. I then read most of the articles published in 1792 and 1793 in Massachusetts and a smaller sample from the other New England states and elsewhere, reasoning that the newspapers were probably more favourably inclined toward Paine before *The Age of Reason* was published.

[64] Levy detected no outpouring of libertarian sentiment in connection with this event: *Emergence of a Free Press* (n 38) 290–91.

[65] Levy, *Emergence of a Free Press*, ibid 297–349; DM Rabban, 'The Ahistorical Historian: Leonard Levy on Freedom of Expression in Early American History' (1985) 37 *Stanford Law Review* 795. See also Rosenberg, *Best Men* (n 35) 71–100.

The federal Sedition Act of 1798 criminalised only 'false' or 'malicious' statements against the president, Congress or the government.[66] As is well known, despite this fact and such niceties as the whole case being decided by the jury, the statute was still used by Federalists to persecute Jeffersonians. When it expired in 1801, Jeffersonians, now finally in power, turned to the federal common law of seditious libel to control the federalist press.[67] They also enthusiastically conducted common-law seditious libel proceedings – such as *Croswell* – in state courts.[68] Federalists, formerly the oppressors, were cast in a new role: defenders of the right to freedom of expression. As Rabban has noted, the difficulties with sedition in a republic were evident.[69]

Prosecutions for seditious libel thereafter became seriously impolitic, but criminal defamation could still be employed in the name of protecting reputations and private lives. Logically, the compromise was that matters relevant to public affairs could be freely discussed, but private lives were off limits. Where the line ought to lie, though, was harder to determine. The debate around the extent of the truth defence was about when, if ever, it was legitimate to publish something that was both true and hurtful.

One other observation needs to be made in connection with truth during this period. Kristin Olbertson has noted the importance of being seen as truthful in an eighteenth-century gentleman's reputation.[70] In the context of discussions of expression in the eighteenth century, it seems to me, though, 'true' and 'false' were applied at least as often to people as they were to facts. A true friend or a true subject was one who was loyal. Indeed, Francis Ludlow Holt observed, 'The epithet *false* is not applied to the propositions contained in the libel, but to the aggregate criminal result – the libel'.[71] The purported falseness of Paine's allegations lay partly in their being an attack by a subject, and not merely in factual misstatements. The rise of political factions and of the shift in the notion of sovereignty in the United States, though, seems logically to make this kind of thinking incongruous, since no longer did disagreeing with political positions render a person disloyal, or 'false'. It seems to me that the claims for the importance of truth in public debate shifted such that they now attached mainly to facts, no longer to people. I would suppose that the Second Great Awakening also played a role in elevating the rhetorical power of truth, as it exhorted individuals to seek out their own relationships with God as a way to know 'the way, the truth, and the life'.

The Massachusetts criminal defamation prosecutions of the 1820s and 1830s did not, with one definite exception and one possible one, involve 'public men'

[66] I *US Statutes at Large*, c 75, 596–97.

[67] Eventually the Supreme Court decided that there was no federal common-law jurisdiction over crime: *US v Hudson and Goodwin*, 7 Cranch 32 (US, 1812).

[68] Rosenberg, *Best Men* (n 35) 105.

[69] Rabban, 'Ahistorical Historian' (n 65) 826–27.

[70] K Olbertson, 'Criminally Impolite: Speech Transgressions & Social Order in Massachusetts, 1690–1776' (PhD dissertation, University of Michigan 2005) 280–346.

[71] Holt, *Law of Libel* (n 19) 276.

in the classic sense.[72] Many were, however, deeply political, involving abolitionists, temperance crusaders, antimasons, Universalists and others. Sometimes they attempted to rely on the truth of what they had published as a kind of justification. Sometimes they complained about attacks on their own reputations that made it more difficult for them to convince others of their point of view. In both situations, they tended to lose. 'Good motives and justifiable ends' was not an unreasonable compromise for a republic to make with its past: republics require political critique, and truthful statements about, say, graft in national finances, do need to be aired. In Massachusetts, though, where individuals complained of libel, goodness of motive and justifiability of ends were in the eye of the judicial beholder. Moral and social reformers, aided by a growing national press, spread their views into the private reaches of households, regardless of the wishes of the family patriarch, sometimes disclosing damaging facts about prominent men.[73] Good intent, the foundation of the qualified privilege defence, could not be a justification for libel in Massachusetts. Moreover, the legal tradition of focusing on how much truth the polity required was strong. Nova Scotia during this period was only starting to see the beginnings of temperance agitation. Its religious life was structured around political conflicts among Anglicans, Presbyterians, Baptists and Catholics, but the doctrinal differences among them did not threaten the power structures of Nova Scotia the same way during this period. Developments in English legal traditions could find room instead. The choices and trajectories adopted in these jurisdictions related in part to the movement of ideas through legal texts, but they also related to political, legal and historical commitments already in play. Legal ideas had to adapt to the tumultuous social events of the period, to the growing sense that alcohol was a scourge, that abolitionists were a threat to social order (as indeed they were), to the conspiracy theories of the antimasons, to the challenge that religious disestablishment posed to the social order in Massachusetts. A treatise's place depended on the stakes it raised and the power of the tradition it purported to affect.

[72] The definite exception was *Comm v Theodore Lyman* (SJCt Suffolk, November 1828). The probable exception was *Comm v Child*, 30 *Mass* 198 (1832). David Lee Child, however, was already marking himself as a social reformer. He was one of the earliest Boston supporters of William Lloyd Garrison.

[73] The apprehension of intrusion into the private sphere is clear from commentary in several of the cases and echoes remarks made by Mary Ryan and Leonard Richards regarding advice literature for women and the rationales for antiabolitionist mobs: MP Ryan, *The Empire of the Mother: American Writing About Domesticity 1830–1860* (New York, NY, Institute for Research in History and Haworth Press, 1982) 16–8; LL Richards, '*Gentlemen of Property and Standing*': *Anti-Abolition in Jacksonian America* (New York, NY, Oxford University Press, 1970) 60–62.

9

Renovate or Rebuild? Treatises, Digests and Criminal Law Codification

BARRY WRIGHT*

WHAT IS THE place of the treatise in the narratives of nineteenth-century criminal law reform and codification? Codification, at least in its Benthamite conception, rejected the common law and attempts to conceive and present it in modern form. Jeremy Bentham's critique of William Blackstone's *Commentaries* was a springboard for his injunction to reformulate the criminal law entirely anew by legislative means. The ambitious utilitarian code seems antithetical to nineteenth-century treatise projects inspired by Blackstone. Yet the influence of the treatise can be found in all the British jurisdiction codifications of that century, implicitly so in Thomas Macaulay's India Penal Code (IPC), and more openly in those that followed, including the Canadian Criminal Code.

Bentham coined the term 'codification', a sweeping reform based on his critique of the common law and his ambitious science of legislation. All existing criminal laws were to be replaced by comprehensive provisions set out in rational, consistent and accessible form, anchored in the principles of utility, and amenable to efficient administration and minimal judicial discretion. Such a code held out the promise of a universal jurisprudence, applicable, as Bentham put it, to places as diverse as England and Bengal.[1] Soon after his death in 1832, imperial authority in India was reconstituted by his utilitarian colleague, James Mill, and Macaulay was appointed legal representative on the Governor-General of India's new Legislative Council. His code, drafted by 1837, was not only the first in the British Empire, but also came closest of all the nineteenth-century criminal codes to a practical implementation of Bentham's ideas. Enacted in 1860 in the wake of the Mutiny, it was the basis for codes enacted in British colonies throughout

* Professor of Law, History and Criminology, Carleton University, Ottawa, Canada. I would like to thank KJM Smith, Desmond Brown, Stanley Yeo and Lindsay Farmer for their comments and help with various aspects of this chapter.

[1] 'On the influence of time and place in matters of legislation' (1782) in J Bowring (ed), *The Works Of Jeremy Bentham* (11 vols) (Edinburgh, 1838–43, repr New York, NY, Russell & Russell, 1962) vol 1, 169–94. Bentham's prescient comment about India appears in vol 10.

South Asia and an important reference point for Robert Wright's draft Jamaica Code (1877), a model for those enacted elsewhere in the West Indies and beyond. Criminal law codification was never realised in England and Wales, despite its central place in nineteenth-century law reform debates there. Notwithstanding the Law Commission's recent effort (1968–2008), Fitzjames Stephen's Draft English Code, a cautious effort that reflected accommodation with the common law, came closest to success. The bill died with the fall of the government in 1880, but Stephen's draft became the main external reference for the first wave of British self-governing jurisdiction codes beginning with Canada.

This chapter explores the connections between the modern treatise and codification in England, India and Canada, and, in particular, the shift from Bentham's injunction to draft criminal law entirely anew to the codifiers' increasing reliance on a modern synthesis of existing laws inspired by Blackstone, the very exercise rejected by Bentham in his critique of the *Commentaries*. A broad approach to the treatise is adopted here, suggesting fluid boundaries between it and other modern forms of legal literature such as digests and law commission reports. All share the characteristics of assimilating, abstracting and lending rational order to existing laws, with reference to traditional and modern purposes. There are differences, such as variation in descriptive and prescriptive elements, audience, private and public uses, but such a broad approach helps to illuminate the dynamic relationships between these legal forms, their role in the production of legal knowledge, and connection with social scientific and public policy practices.[2]

The modern treatise and code were Enlightenment-inspired projects, concerned about the rational systematisation of the law and the enticing possibility of approaching law as a science. Brian Simpson portrays codification as the next logical step beyond the discursive treatise, a more concise statement of law, and one of the most interesting developments of the treatise form.[3] Morton Horwitz suggests treatises were a defensive response to the threat codification posed to judicial power, led by legal scholars committed to assumptions about the logic and internal consistency of legal doctrine.[4] The generalisations capture some elements found in my examples but the patterns and intersections are more complex. Simpson accurately portrays the later nineteenth-century English scene but

[2] See Introduction and Christopher Tomlins' chapter on the intertextuality of legal literature. More orthodox understandings of the treatise focus on the common law and the influential *Commentaries* are seen to represent a separate institutes genre. See also n 10.

[3] AWB Simpson, 'The Rise and Fall of the Legal Treatise: Legal Principles and the Forms of Legal Literature' (1981) 41 *University of Chicago Law Review* 632 at 666.

[4] Morton Horwitz, *The Transformation of American Law, 1870–1960: the Crisis of Legal Orthodoxy* (New York, NY, Oxford, 1992) 117–23; See Philip Girard's chapter on the influence of Kent's Commentaries and reliance on English law as intellectual ballast for unified American common law. The American codification movement, particularly ante bellum, is seen by some as an extension of the Revolution, a means of breaking from the continuing influence of English legal tradition, see, eg CM Cook, *The American Codification Movement: A Study of Antebellum Legal Reform* (New York, NY, Greenwood, 1981); A Masferrer, 'Defense of the Common Law Against Postbellum American Codification: Reasonable and Fallacious Argumentation' (2010) 50 *The American Journal of Legal History* 355, and n 41.

neglects Bentham's earlier rejection of the treatise form as means to modernise the law. Horwitz is more applicable to the US, which is not examined here, although the defensive legitimacy question does arise.

The Macaulay and Stephen codes are very different, the former aspiring to break decisively from the common law, the latter seeking accommodation with it. Yet despite drafting the most Benthamite code enacted, there are hints of the treatise in Macaulay's reliance on its synthetic approach in his *Examples* and its discursive style in his *Notes.* The treatise is openly embraced by Stephen, who displaced Bentham as the primary influence on the late nineteenth-century codes. His *General View of the Criminal Law* (1863) and *Digest of the Criminal Law* (1877), important steps towards his 1878 draft code (basis for the failed 1880 bill at Westminster), built upon Robert Peel's criminal law consolidations and the work of Henry Brougham's criminal law commissioners, developing a synthesis of existing laws that was only loosely utilitarian-inspired. Rather than a defensive response to codification, the treatise was deployed to enhance the legitimacy and prospects of codification. Bentham's radical legislative agenda was moderated in the face of mounting opposition by the bar and bench guardians of the common law, and as legal scholars built upon Blackstone's legacy, while the positivists among them sought to make Bentham's legacy more palatable. Stephen's caution was not enough for domestic success, but his strategy proved successful in other British jurisdictions, followed first in Canada by way of the Dominion consolidations, George Burbidge's *A Digest of the Criminal Law of Canada (Crimes and Punishment) Founded by Permission on Sir James Fitzjames Stephen's Digest of the Criminal Law* (1890), and passage of the 1892 code.

This portrayal of the Indian and Canadian codes as manifestations of different stages of nineteenth-century English criminal law reform debates is not intended to suggest they were essentially products of the metropole, or to diminish the place of local influences on their development. But both codes were informed and shaped by this law reform context and pervasive legal connections within an imperial network. My analysis follows KJM Smith's narrative of this period in which Bentham's critique and the interventions of Macaulay and Stephen figure prominently and codification, despite failing domestically, prompts more conceptually sophisticated law.[5] Lindsay Farmer's chapter presents an alternative narrative that focuses on the practical nineteenth-century criminal law literature in Britain rather than the reform debates in which codification looms large. The narratives are not necessarily at odds. Indeed, they represent different ends of a legal literature spectrum, one theoretically oriented and imperial in reach, the other practical and local in application. The influence of professional power, a legal culture that neglects the criminal law as a branch of public law, to see it as an adjunct of private law primarily about the protections of private interests or hardly rated as law at all, in such contrast with Bentham's outlook, is a common theme.

[5] KJM Smith, *Lawyers, Legislators and Theorists: Developments in English Criminal Jurisprudence, 1800–1957* (Oxford, Clarendon Press, 1998); Smith, *James Fitzjames Stephen: Portrait of a Victorian Rationalist* (Cambridge, Cambridge University Press, 1988).

I. BENTHAM, MACAULAY AND THE INDIA PENAL CODE

The inspiration for Macaulay's India Penal Code was Bentham's science of legislation and universal jurisprudence developed from his critique of Blackstone's *Commentaries*. India became a colonial laboratory for these ideas, James Mill's reorganisation of colonial government there providing the opportunity for Macaulay to become an enlightened utilitarian despotic legislator. It was hoped that the colonial example would inspire codification in the metropole, where rationalising reform beyond Peel's consolidations stalled. The bar and bench defenders of the common law portrayed codification as alien to English legal tradition. But the dismissal of the codification as foreign, or the work of philosophical radical interlopers unversed in the common law, neglects its prominence in nineteenth-century English criminal law reform debates and diminishes the importance of Bentham's influence on the early phase of the debates.[6] It is also myopic, ignoring codes enacted in other British common law jurisdictions.

Bentham developed the term 'codification' to describe his ambitious legislative agenda and radical break from the common law.[7] Bentham's critique of his former teacher began with his 1776 *Fragment on Government* and continued throughout his long life.[8] He acknowledged Blackstone's achievement in technical arrangement and lending rational order to English law.[9] But he concluded that the *Commentaries* were ultimately 'an elegant palliative to the inherently chronic confusion of the common law'.[10] The common law, Blackstone's preoccupation,

[6] See L Farmer, 'Reconstructing the English Codification Debate: The Criminal Law Commissioners, 1833–45' (2000) 18 *Law and History Review 397–400*; also, Smith, *Lawyers, Legislators and Theorists*, ibid; M Lobban, *The Common Law and English Jurisprudence, 1760–1850* (Oxford, Clarendon Press, 1991). The failure of codification is also portrayed as one of the peculiarities of the English, a divergence from what Max Weber called formal legal rationality, the typical legal forms associated with modern authority.

[7] 'View of a Complete Code of Laws', *Bentham's Works*, vol 3, 163; also throughout the Bowring edition of his *Works* and *An Introduction to the Principles of Morals and Legislation* (1789) JH Burns and HLA Hart (eds), (London, Athlone, 1970).

[8] See, eg 'A Comment on the Commentaries and a Fragment on Government' in JH Burns and HLA Hart (eds) (London, Athlone, 1977).) Bentham's obsession with Blackstone continued for a half century, at age 80 adding 300 manuscript pages of critique; see W Prest (ed), *Blackstone and His Commentaries: Biography, Law, History* (Oxford, Hart Publishing, 2009) 63.

[9] *A Fragment on Government*, ibid. W Blackstone, *Commentaries on the Laws of England* (1765–69) (repr Chicago, IL, University of Chicago Press, 1979). See Prest ibid on the *Commentaries*, their significance in generating an understanding of the common law as a system, and as a formative intellectual influence on modern treatises; also, SFC Milsom, 'The Nature of Blackstone's Achievement' (1981) 1 *Oxford Journal of Legal Studies* 1; D Kennedy, 'The Structure of Blackstone's Commentaries' (1979) 28 *Buffalo Law Review* 205. Also, Simpson, 'Rise and Fall' (n 3) 658, crediting Blackstone's European breadth and familiarity with civil law for transcending the messiness of common law, renovating the 'old Gothic castle', a theme explored in Kunal Parker's chapter.

[10] Quoted in Smith, Lawyers, Legislators and Theorists (n 5) 11; see also discussion at 9–12; R Cross, '*Blackstone v Bentham*' (1976) 92 *The Law Quarterly Review* 516. While introducing a continental sensibility, Blackstone did not transform the common law's inherent inductive approach; Simpson, ibid, implies a deductive character in his adoption of Plucknett's definition of the modern treatise. Bentham struggled with inductive and deductive logics (see n 14) but regarded the Gothic castle as a tear down to be replaced by a Georgian villa with modern conveniences.

was beyond the reach of rational reform, its arcane nature and needless complexities the invariable result of random cases and self-serving judges. Blackstone's defence of judicial power, based on the incredible claim that judges exercised little discretion around common-law rules, and his neglect and suspicion of legislation, were nonsense.[11] Blackstone's modern ordering of the common law was futile and the common law should be eliminated.

Bentham's science of legislation, set out in *Introduction to the Principles of Morals and Legislation* and elsewhere, called for legislative reformulation of all laws, informed by the rational principles of utility thought to have universal application. Unlike the treatise, there would be no looking back, reference to obscure archaic purposes, or attempt to marry traditional with modern policy objectives. His *pannomion*, composed of penal, constitutional and civil codes, aimed for nothing less than the comprehensive regulation of social relationships and sovereign power.[12] The criminal code occupied much of Bentham's attention, in contrast to the relatively minor place of criminal law in the *Commentaries*, its neglect in the later treatise literature, and indeed its portrayal as hardly counting as law at all in historical narratives celebrating the genius of the common law.[13] Criminal law entails vital matters of public policy, liberty and individual happiness. It regulates key relations between the state and citizens. It is the most commonplace reflection of the exercise of state power in repressive forms, reflecting its monopoly over the legitimate use of violence. Punishment entails the deliberate infliction of harm. Such matters demanded clearer articulation, modern rational justification and could not be entrusted to the courts.

Bentham's taxonomy of criminal harms, prohibitions and penalties took the rationalising spirit of the Enlightenment much further than Blackstone. He sought to map out and categorise the entirety of the criminal law, all offences, forms of liability and defences set out leaving no *terra incognita*, in provisions expressed so clearly that an average person would understand it, an average judge unable to claim not to. Yet Bentham never completed a working criminal code.[14] And while his criminal institutional proposals were well known, the transformations in the administration of English criminal law in the 1820s and 30 s were influenced by complex factors, more a matter of reform consensus between leading Tories and

[11] See JH Langbein, 'Blackstone on Judging' in Prest (n 8) 65; John V Orth, 'Blackstone's Rules on the Construction of Statutes' in Prest, ibid 79; HLA Hart, 'The Demystification of Law' in Hart (ed), *Essays on Bentham: Jurisprudence and Political Theory* (Oxford, Clarendon Press, 1982) 21.

[12] See Smith, 'Lawyers, Legislators and Theorists' (n 5) 20, 28–29; Farmer (n 6) 423.

[13] See, eg SFC Milsom, *Historical Foundations of the Common Law* 2nd edn (London, Butterworths, 1981) 403: 'Nothing worth-while was created . . . The criminal law became segregated as one of the dirty jobs of society'.

[14] Aiming for a deductive code, Bentham encountered the persistence of inductive reasoning in adversarial processes and judicial applications of the law; see Lobban (n 6) 120–55. Outlines for codes and unfinished drafts are scattered though Bentham's unpublished work and offers to draft went to American (approaching Aaron Burr, President Madison and most state governors), French and Russian law-makers.

Whigs than Bentham's advocacy.[15] As for reforms to the substantive criminal law, consolidation (collection and update of all statutes), digests (organised presentation of the law) and yet more comprehensive rationalisations falling short of Bentham's call were debated. Peel's consolidations of 1827–31, which repealed or modernised hundreds of statutes and scaled back the death penalty from over 200 to a dozen offences, was a modest rather than transformative advance. It was nonetheless an important one, relatively neglected by scholars compared to the new police, professionalisation of the criminal trial and the rise of the penitentiary.

The fall of Wellington's government opened the door to the possibility of wider criminal law reform under Henry Brougham. He was unable to match Peel's political and legislative skills and Lord Chief Justice Ellenborough's defence of judicial powers had set the stage for more aggressive intervention against legislative change.[16] Brougham's criminal law commissioners, appointed in 1833 with a mandate to produce a digest of criminal statutes, another of common law and to consider combining both, were divided over the scope of contemplated reform and indulged in esoteric doctrinal and definitional debates.[17] A series of reports resulted in a combined digest in 1845, followed by more modest reports on indictable offences, but the 1853 bill based on the latter collapsed in the face of judicial criticism in a select committee.[18] Few remnants of the commissioners' work are found in Charles Greaves's 1861 consolidation, an update of Peel. Codification was not abandoned but subsequent efforts were condemned to follow a similar pattern and the project proved more promising in colonial contexts.

India became a utilitarian laboratory where Macaulay explored the possibilities of Bentham's scientific legislation and universal jurisprudence. Smith aptly describes the IPC as an important episode in the development of criminal jurisprudence and nineteenth-century intellectual history.[19] While it was the most Benthamite code enacted, giving form and practical content to Bentham's ideas, and making them work in the context of a specific time and place, proved

[15] Bentham was estranged from the legal profession and judiciary (his disdain for judges was reciprocated) although in 1817 he received an honorary call at Lincoln's Inn. On Bentham's influence, see, eg SE Finer, 'The Transmission of Benthamite Ideas, 1826–1839' in G Sutherland (ed), *Studies in the Growth of Nineteenth Century Government* (London, Routledge, 1972); H Benyon, 'Mighty Bentham' (1981) 2 *Journal of Legal History* 62; R McGowan, 'The Image of Justice and Reform of the Criminal Law in Early Nineteenth Century England' (1983) 32 *Buffalo Law Review* 89.

[16] James Mackintosh's 1819 committee that paved the way for Peel's consolidations avoided the judges, and Peel deftly evoked Bacon to head them off when introducing his bills, but they were routinely consulted on subsequent criminal law reforms; see Smith, *Lawyers, Legislators and Theorists* (n 5) 56–63, 361, 364.

[17] John Austin, still Benthamite, quit in frustration in 1836. Andrew Amos followed Macaulay in India, thought the IPC went too far, and rejoined the commission. Henry Belleden Ker was active throughout and more interested in technical legislative drafting than legal theory; see Farmer (n 6) 404–05; M Lobban, 'How Benthamatic Was the Criminal Law Commission?' (2000) 18 *Law and History Review* 427.

[18] See Smith, 'Lawyers, Legislators and Theorists' (n 5) 136–38; Smith, *Stephen* (n 5) 75–76.

[19] KJM Smith, 'Macaulay's Indian Penal Code: An Illustration of the Accidental Function of Time, Place and Personalities in Law Making' in WM Gordon and TD Fergus (eds), *Legal History in the Making* (London, Hambledon, 1991) 145.

difficult. Macaulay confronted the challenges with a Baconian pragmatism, relying in part on a synthesis that resembles the modern treatise.[20]

Most early commentary dismissed the IPC as the work of a philosophical radical non-lawyer (Macaulay trained as a barrister and knew Peel's consolidations well). The more sympathetic assessments tended to downplay Bentham's influence, Stephen describing it as 'the criminal law of England freed from all technicalities and superfluities . . .'[21] although he acknowledged elsewhere, '[t]o compare the Indian penal code with English criminal law was like comparing *Cosmos* with *Chaos*'.[22] Much more recently Eric Stokes fully illuminated Bentham's considerable influence.[23] Yet there were unresolved issues in his codifying ideas (tensions between inductive and deductive logics, between the abstract and the situational) and his precise impact remains difficult to determine. Macaulay's biography of Bacon, written while drafting the code, was probably inspired by Peel's quotation from Bacon to undercut opposition to his consolidation bills. Bacon's ideas have more affinity with the case by case incremental development of general principles characteristic of the common law than the principled abstraction of Plato or Cartesian identification of first principles and derived implications characteristic of the Roman-civilian legal tradition. Bacon's pragmatism also informed Macaulay's approach.

That Macaulay fell short of Bentham's ideals is unsurprising for modern legal theorists.[24] Unlike Bentham, Macaulay devised working provisions. The IPC remains the groundbreaking British code, the most Benthamite in nature and ambition, and many of its qualities remain as progressive law reform aims in the twenty-first century.[25] At the same time it must be recognised that Macaulay's reform did not occur in a vacuum. A product of a particular time and place, cultural and intellectual context, Macaulay's premises were informed by the limits of his experience, outlook and an intellectual milieu of European Enlightenment rationalism and British liberalism.

[20] Smith, ibid 153, puts it similarly, referring to 'a fusion of utilitarian clarity and rigour with Burkean pragmatism'. See B Wright, 'Macaulay's Indian Penal Code: Historical Context and Originating Principles' in Wing-Cheong Chan, B Wright and S Yeo (eds), *Codification, Macaulay and the Indian Penal Code: the Legacies and Modern Challenges of Reform* (Farnham, Ashgate, 2011) 19 for elaboration of themes in this section.

[21] JF Stephen, *A History of the Criminal Law of England* vol 3 (London, Macmillan, 1883) 300; see also SG Vesey-Fitzgerald, 'Bentham and the Indian Codes', GW Keeton and G Schwarzenberger (eds), *Jeremy Bentham and the Law: A Symposium* (London, Stevens, 1948) 222; MC Setalvad, *The Common Law in India* (London, Stevens, 1960).

[22] Social Science Association, 'Mr Fitzjames Stephen on Codification' (1872–73) 54 *Law Times* 44 at 45.

[23] E Stokes, *The English Utilitarians and India* (Oxford, Oxford University Press, 1959). On the importance of the IPC in Macaulay's life as a politician, law reformer and historian, see J Clive, *Macaulay: the Shaping of the Historian* (Cambridge, MA, Harvard University Press, 1987).

[24] See, eg W Twining, 'Imagining Bentham' (1998) 51 *Current Legal Problems* 1 and especially the legal realists on the limits of legislation and persistent judicial tendencies. On the impact of this in IPC jurisdictions, see n 50.

[25] See chapters in Chan, Wright and Yeo, *Macaulay* (n 20). This assessment of the durable qualities of many aspects of the IPC is shared by Smith, 'Macaulay's Indian Penal Code' (n 19).

Nor was the IPC a disinterested initiative, utilitarian and liberal conceits aside. It was a British imperial policy innovation that responded to concerns about effective colonial governance and challenges to British sovereignty. While it is reductionist to dismiss the IPC as essentially an exercise in power, it was also more than a law reform. It was a quasi-constitutional projection of British authority, designed to make the law more effective and legitimate in a culturally diverse frontier setting thereby better regulating relations between the colonisers and the colonised. The adoption of the IPC by authoritarian legislative decree, the denial of indigenous diversity, and common obligations of citizenship as defined by an external power while substantive colonial difference persisted, reflect the limits of assimilative liberal ideals and contradictions between sovereignty and liberal rationalities.[26] Colonial crises also prompted ambitious law reforms and legal practices that better conformed to British constitutional claims and would engender, it was hoped, greater compliance to British rule.[27] It is more than coincidence that the Mutiny led to the IPC's belated enactment, just as crises led to the Jamaica draft and prefaced the codes of the 1890s.[28]

Macaulay's involvement in such an ambitious reconstitutive project, assuming the role and very image of the utilitarian enlightened despotic legislator, was surprising. He was not part of the tight circle of Bentham and Mill disciples and published criticism of utilitarianism, warning of the threat it posed to British liberties. But shortly after Bentham's death he collaborated closely with James Mill on the reorganisation of India's colonial government. Between contributions to the Reform Act, 1832 and the 1834 legislation to prohibit slavery throughout the British Empire, Macaulay became the main Commons advocate for Mill's Charter Act bill, declaring in parliamentary debate, '[a code] is almost the only blessing, perhaps the only blessing, which absolute governments are better fitted to confer on a nation than popular governments'.[29] After arriving in India as legal repre-

[26] On reforms within imperial networks, see CA Bayly, *The Birth of the Modern World, 1780–1914: Global Connections and Comparisons* (London, Blackwell, 2004); 'Colonial Rule and the "Informational Order" in South Asia' in N Crook (ed), *The Transmission of Knowledge in South Asia: Essays on Education, Religion, History and Politics* (Oxford, Oxford University Press, 1996) 280; P Duara, *Rescuing History from the Nation* (Chicago, IL, University of Chicago Press, 1995). For recent assessments of the IPC, see E Kolsky, 'Codification and the Rule of Colonial Difference: Criminal Procedure in India' (2005) 23 *Law and History Review* 631; V Dhagamwar, *Law, Power and Justice: the Protection of Personal Rights in the Indian Penal Code* (New Delhi, Sage Publications, 1992); R Singha, *A Despotism of Law: Crime and Justice in Early Colonial India* (Delhi, Oxford University Press, 1998).

[27] See, eg N Hussain, *The Jurisprudence of Emergency: Colonialism and the Rule of Law* (Ann Arbor, MI, Michigan University Press, 2003); RW Kostal, *A Jurisprudence of Power: Victorian Empire and the Rule of Law* (Oxford, Oxford University Press, 2005) 3–4.

[28] On the subsequent codes, see ML Friedland, 'R.S. Wright's Model Criminal Code: A Forgotten Chapter in the History of the Criminal Law' (1981) 1 *Oxford Journal of Legal Studies* 307; Friedland, 'Codification in the Commonwealth: Earlier Efforts' (1990) 2 *Criminal Law Forum* 145; B Wright, 'Criminal Law Codification and Imperial Projects: The Self Governing Jurisdiction Codes of the 1890's' (2008) 12 *Journal of Legal History* 19.

[29] 10 July 1833, Parliamentary Debates 3rd Series vol 19. Such were the contradictions of early 19th-century British liberalism. Macaulay's background was the Clapham sect (his father Zachary and Fitzjames Stephen's grandfather were fellow abolitionists). His early critiques of Bentham and Mill appeared in the *Edinburgh* and *Westminster* Reviews. After returning from India (see n 43) he turned

sentative on the Governor-General of India's new Legislative Council, he wrote, 'I have immense reforms in hand . . . such as would make old Bentham jump in his grave . . .'[30] His Press Act (1835) ended press licensing and prior restraint, the Black Act (1836) ended special privileges of European residents in the civil courts, and his education reforms widened accessibility and modernised curriculum, but the IPC, which he largely authored, was by far his biggest project.[31] As he started, he wrote to Mill expressing the hope it would inspire codification at home as Brougham's commissioners grappled with the continuing chaotic state of English law.[32]

Macaulay rejected mere consolidation, arguing for a comprehensive code to replace the existing patchwork of Muslim and Hindu laws overlaid with received English criminal laws and East Indian Company regulations, and a singular standard of justice for all.[33] His 4 June 1835 Minute to Council presented his law commission's codifying principles (paraphrased here):

- It should be more than a mere digest of existing laws, cover all contingencies, and nothing that is not in the code ought to be law.
- Crime should be suppressed with the least infliction of suffering, and allow for the ascertaining of the truth at minimal cost of time and money.
- Its language should be clear, unequivocal and concise. Every criminal act should be separately defined, the language followed in indictment, and conduct found to fall within it.

increasingly to historical scholarship, famously critiqued by H Butterfield (The Whig Interpretation of History, 1931 repr London, Bell, 1950). Stokes (n 23) 191–92 suggests that Macaulay's ambivalence about utilitarian political theory did not extend to Bentham's legal theory. Clive (n 23) 467–73 suggests that Macaulay accepted utilitarian absolutism as a means to an end, an impartial enlightened despotism leading to eventual independence. See also Jennifer Pitts, 'Legislator of the World? A Rereading of Bentham on Colonies' (2003) 31 *Political Theory* 200.

[30] Macaulay to Thomas Flower Ellis, 3 June 1835 in Thomas Pinney (ed), *The Selected Letters of Thomas Babington Macaulay* vol 3 January 1834 – August 1841 (London, Cambridge University Press, 1982) 146 (Bentham's *auto-ikon* was more likely to cackle from its perch at University College London).

[31] A law commission to examine a uniform system of law (envisaged by s 53 of the Charter Act and Mill's December 1834 despatch on its implementation) was created in May 1835 and its mandate to codify the criminal law was approved the following month. A draft was presented to Governor General Auckland in May 1837 and a full version accompanied by the Commissioners' Report to Council on 14 October 1837. See British Parliamentary Papers, 'Copy of the Penal Code Prepared by the Indian Law Commissioners and published by Command of the Governor-General of India in Council' vol 41, 1837–80, 463–587 (paper no 673 Return of the House of Commons, 30 July 1838). Macaulay's fellow commissioners succumbed to the heat and illness and commissioner John Macleod testified in 1848, 'I may state a fact already generally known when I say that Mr. Macaulay is justly entitled to be called the author of the Indian Penal Code' Notes on the Report of the Indian Law Commissioners on the Indian Penal Code (London, 1848) vi.

[32] Macaulay to Mill, 24 August 1835 in Clive (n 23) 436–38.

[33] Applicable criminal laws included Muslim (Bengal, Madras and other parts of the north, east and south) and Hindu laws (Bombay), overlaid with East India Company regulations, while European residents were governed by received English laws, on the basis of the 1773 Regulating Act which established a Supreme Court in Calcutta and confirmed English criminal law in effect in 1726 was binding on all Calcutta residents and European residents throughout India, amended in 1828 with adoption of Peel's first consolidations.

- Uniformity is the chief end; special definitions, procedures or other exceptions to account for different races or sects not included without clear and strong reasons.[34]

These codifying principles of comprehensiveness, accessibility and consistency are a practical rendition of Bentham's legislative aspirations, and indeed, Macaulay's presentation of law in the resulting draft is a radical break from existing English laws. The substantive doctrines are less so. The provisions are accompanied by *Examples* illustrating their application to hypothetical cases. Explanatory *Notes*, which disappeared from the enacted version of the IPC, criticise existing English laws and discuss the conceptual features of key provisions. Macaulay's debt to Bentham is more discernable in conception (drafting principles) and presentation rather than in doctrinal details. The latter derive from existing laws, modernised but not reinvented, falling short of Bentham's call to legislate anew.

The IPC is a comprehensive presentation of criminal law, a taxonomy that precludes the common law, and very different in form from existing British legislation. Macaulay fully embraced Bentham's extension of logic of classification in the natural sciences to law, aiming for a systematic and exhaustive statement of criminal harms and attendant prohibitions, liability standards and penalties (maximums) expressed precisely and consistently.[35] Following Bentham's principles of 'nomography', Macaulay devised concise, direct legal expression, characterised by simplicity, clarity, economy and lack of technicality, within a rationally organised and self-contained legislative whole.[36]

The substantive doctrines reflect wider influences. Precise attribution is difficult but the *Notes* suggest they derived mostly from what Macaulay was familiar with, English laws reworked, simplified and modernised according to more general liberal sensibilities. Most are progressive for the time, indeed a number of the original provisions remain more advanced than current criminal laws in most common-law jurisdictions. Principles of liability are not defined in a general part but there is consistent attention to fault requirements and terms, emphasis on subjective standards, with occasional use of lesser standards of rashness (the Macaulayan term for recklessness) and negligence for endangering offences or where public duties were specified. Offences are accompanied, where relevant, by specified exemptions (the Macaulayan term for defences). The arcane English laws of murder and theft are thoroughly reconstituted. Political offences reflect a libertarian orientation, manifested in Macaulay's narrow definition of treason,

[34] See n 31.

[35] Similar ambitious taxonomies were later attempted in other areas of the law, although Macaulay's was perhaps the widest ranging. This appears to be a characteristic of the 19th-century form of legal literature including the treatise; see, eg B Sherman and L Bently, *The Making of Modern Intellectual Property Law: the British Experience* (Cambridge, Cambridge University Press, 1999).

[36] See Stokes (n 23) 230. As Stephen, *History* (n 21) vol 3, 302–03 put it, 'The Penal Code was the first specimen of an entirely new and original method of legislative expression . . . In the first place the leading idea to be laid down is stated in the most explicit and pointed form which can be devised. Then such expressions in it as are not regarded as sufficiently explicit are made the subject of definite explanations. This is followed by equally definite exceptions . . .'

abolition of seditious libel, and criminal liability for abuse of state and official powers. Innovations appear in offences concerning the exploitation of vulnerable groups, endangering and intangible harms. Punishments follow a utilitarian logic of deterrence, certainty and proportionality. Capital punishment is limited to two offences (Peel's dramatic reduction was to a dozen offences) and corporal punishment is abolished.[37]

Macaulay's illustrative *Examples*, authoritative precedents set by legislators rather than judges, were designed to exhibit a provision's entire meaning and range of application and minimise judicial discretion. Bentham contemplated the device and Edward Livingston's draft Louisiana penal code included illustrations,[38] but the technique was rejected by the English Commissioners (Fourth Report, 1839) and in Wright's Jamaica draft.[39] Clive notes that drafting the IPC honed Macaulay's expressive skills as a writer and historian, drawing parallels between the challenges faced by legislators and historians of capturing both the particular and the general. Examples were generated out of subjecting draft definitions to hypothetical exceptions; if doubts or uncertainties were raised, they were accommodated in revisions to sharpen expression, logical distinctions, comprehensibility and perspicuity.[40] Macaulay's method here is analogous to the approach to synthesis in the modern treatise, although the objective is prescriptive rather than descriptive, and his approach results in more economical expression of the law than the more unwieldy typical treatise style formulations.

Macaulay's *Notes* reveal more connections with the treatise. Indeed, they can be viewed as a succinct critical treatise on English criminal law in the 1830s, warranting recognition as one of the most interesting examples of the form. Incisive critique of existing English laws dominates the text and Macaulay takes obvious delight in pointing out common-law absurdities. But the basic doctrinal ideas build from a background he knew best, Peel's English consolidations, peppered with occasional explicit reference to the 1810 French Code *penal* and the draft Louisiana code.[41] The combination of critique and concise explanation reflects Macaulay's historical sensibilities and skills at theoretical and technical synthesis, but Stokes observes that the separate appearance of the rationales for the laws was

[37] For a further discussion of the substantive provisions and cross-references to the *Notes*, see Wright, 'Macaulay's Indian Penal Code' (n 20), also, Smith, 'Macaulay's Indian Penal Code' (n 19) from 158.

[38] Stokes (n 23) 230.

[39] On the basis that complete expression of a provision rendered illustration unnecessary, see n 65.

[40] Clive (n 23) 461–62.

[41] The *Notes* do not make precise attributions; there are oblique references to Peel, more to Bentham, and about a dozen to the French and Louisiana codes. The 1810 French code derived from the revolutionary 1791 codification, inflected with utilitarianism by Jean-Etienne-Marie Portalis; see M Morin, '*Portalis v Bentham*?: The Objectives Ascribed by the Codification of the Civil and Criminal Law in France, England, and Canada', *The Law Commission of Canada, Perspectives on Legislation* (Ottawa, ON, Queen's Printer 139–217. Livingstone, influenced by Bentham and Portalis, completed his draft in 1826. David Dudley Field became the most prominent 19th-century American codifier, his 1881 New York State Code best known outside the US; see n 4 and Sanford Kadish, 'Codifiers of the Criminal Law: Wechsler's Predecessors' (1978) 78 *Columbia Law Review* 1098; 'The Model Penal Code's Historical Antecedents' (1988) 19 *Rutgers Law Journal* 521.

a departure from Bentham's legislative method.[42] It is an important departure. The *Notes* reveal the significant place of existing laws as Macaulay's starting point and primary reference, prefiguring the more open reliance on the treatise form in subsequent codification efforts.

John Stuart Mill echoed Macaulay's hope that his code would inspire stalled English efforts, observing criticism originated in grievances about ending special privileges.[43] But the IPC encountered what Smith calls 'the great dead weight power of governmental and administrative inertia . . .'[44] The 1857–58 crisis restored the code as a legislative priority, as Stephen noted, '[t]hen came the Mutiny which in its essence was the breakdown of the old system . . . The effect of the Mutiny on the Statute Book was unmistakeable . . .'[45] Governor-General 'clemency' Canning was much criticised after the Cawnpore massacre of English civilians, but the revolt and its suppression underscored how resort to martial law (Guyana/Demerara, 1824, Quebec, 1838 and Ceylon, 1848) and the courts martial of civilians (Ireland, 1798–1800, the Canadas, 1838–39) had become increasingly controversial for the English political classes. Such responses undermined the legitimacy of British rule and associated formal claims of constitutionalism and the rule of law. Enactment helped to address such concerns and would, it was hoped, minimise future need to resort to emergency military expedients to restore public order and uphold imperial rule. Revisions to Macaulay's original draft were finalised in 1858, and the IPC was enacted in October 1860. It included retrograde amendments that reflected professional interests and resistance by European residents to the idea of equal legal status with indigenous subjects.[46] The IPC tended to be dismissed in the metropole, seen as suitable only for backward overseas colonies where it was necessary 'to keep things simple for the native population and magistrates of limited ability'.[47] The Law Times obituary for Macaulay read:

[42] Stokes (n 23) (229–30) notes that Livingston, following Bentham, had attempted to weave rationales into provisions with unwieldy results.

[43] (1838) 31 Westminster Review 395. Macaulay returned to an appointment as Secretary of State for War and Colonies, a difficult portfolio after the Canadian rebellions and Lord Durham's report on colonial responsible government. James Stephen, father of Fitzjames, became Permanent Under Secretary in1836.

[44] Smith, 'Macaulay's Indian Penal Code' (n 19) 160. Utilitarian policies were compromised by military and commercial pressures and the renewal of orientalism. See also, Smith, Stephen (n 5) 126–31; Stephen, History (n 21) vol 3, 299–300; Stokes (n 23) 262; Dhagamwar from p 77 on the reception of Macaulay's draft, from his successor Andrew Amos to the Reports of the Indian Law Commissioners (1846, 1847), Drinkwater Bethune's critique, the House of Lords Select Committee recommendations (1852), and final revisions by Barnes Peacock.

[45] Quoted in Setalvad (n 21) 124.

[46] Implementation was delayed to 1862, until passage of criminal procedure legislation, a retreat from Macaulay's aim of equal status, which allowed Europeans residents not to appear before Indian judges and magistrates and maintained the autonomy of the Princely states. Henry Maine, Stephen's immediate predecessor as law member of council (1862–69) objected to the code's Benthamite hue, claiming 'nobody cares about criminal law except theorists and habitual criminals' (quoted in Smith, Stephen (n 5) 127). Stephen added more procedural changes and an evidence act in 1872, while Courtney Ilbert's attempt to restore Macaulay's aim of uniform criminal jurisdiction sparked the 1883) 'white mutiny'; see Kolsky (n 26) 673–82.

[47] G Parker, 'The Origins of the Canadian Criminal Code' in DH Flaherty (ed), *Essays in the History of Canadian Law* vol 1 (Toronto, ON, University of Toronto Press, 1981) 251.

> [H]is code is . . . wholly worthless . . . [with] scarcely a definition that will stand the examination of a lawyer or layman for an instant, and scarcely a description or provision through which a coach and horses may not be driven. All hope of Macaulay as a lawyer, and also as a philosopher was over as soon as his code was seen.[48]

Such was the depth of the profession's hostility. Stephen's assessment was quite different, as we have seen, but after the demise of Brougham's commissioners, codifiers proceeded with much more caution.

II. STEPHEN, BURBIDGE AND THE CANADIAN CRIMINAL CODE

Macaulay's successors in India were prominent figures in later nineteenth-century English legal theory circles, from Andrew Amos through to Henry Maine and Fitzjames Stephen.[49] Retrograde changes to the IPC continued apace after enactment, and in most cases, after independence as well.[50] In England it had become obvious that Bentham's injunction to reformulate criminal law entirely anew was no longer feasible. Professional and judicial resistance to ambitious legislative reform solidified and defences of the common law became more aggressive. The utilitarian critique was deflected by procedural reforms and appeals, scholars such as Maine and Maitland enhanced the modern legitimacy Blackstone lent to the common law, and treatises prompted more sophisticated criminal law. Legal positivists sought to render Bentham's legacy more palatable, finding common cause with the more conservative legal scholars as law emerged as an academic discipline accompanying modern professional legal education. As Twining observes,

> The story of the displacement of Bentham by Austin . . . has often been sketched, but the puzzle remains: Why this extraordinary misjudgement . . . none makes the case for treating Austin as being a thinker of comparable stature in respect of originality, penetration, breadth, or even readability. The most that can be said for him was that he took analysis of fundamental legal conceptions a bit further, he was more sympathetic to the common law than Bentham, and his simplemindeness was more congenial to practitioners . . . and the first generation of scholar-teachers of law . . .[51]

Subsequent codification efforts proceeded from a rationalisation of existing laws in which Robert Peel's consolidations played a formative role, combined

[48] 7 January 1860, 184.

[49] Smith, *Lawyers, Legislators and Theorists* and *Stephen* (n 5) map these connections.

[50] On the continuing changes to the code in IPC based jurisdictions, the low legislative priority of systematic updating and ad hoc reactive legislative amendments, inconsistent judicial interpretation and added common law inspired constructions and complexities, see Chan, Wright and Yeo, *Macaulay* (n 20).

[51] W Twining, 'Reading Bentham' The Maccabean Lecture in Jurisprudence (1989) 75 *Proceedings of the British Academy* 97 at 138 (Bentham's auto ikon might have groaned). See also eg, Smith *Lawyers, Legislators and Theorists* (n 5); Lobban, The Common Law and English Jurisprudence (n 6); W Rumble, 'John Austin and His Nineteenth Century Critics: The Case of Sir Henry Maine' (1988) 39 *Northern Ireland Law Quarterly* 119.

with abstracted principles developed in treatise forms distanced from Bentham's theories.

The treatise plays an important role in the reformers' search for professional and academic credibility and better political prospects. A shift is discernable in the work of Brougham's Commissioners and Wright but is exemplified by Fitzjames Stephen who praised but helped tame the IPC. For his domestic codification project, the injunction to reformulate criminal law anew was abandoned in favour of proceeding from existing laws and synthesis that followed principles which were only loosely utilitarian and reflected his conservative political and social inclinations. No philosophical radical, wary of conceptual abstraction though interested in speculative jurisprudence and the work of Austin and Maine, he had a much more positive view of the common law and judicial discretion than Macaulay and Bentham.[52] His Draft English Code epitomises the safe new approach. It was preceded by *A General View of the Criminal Law of England* (1863) and *A Digest of the Criminal Law* (1877), important steps to what was, in Benthamite and Macaulayan terms, a cautious codification of indictable offences that left defences and the principles of liability to the common law. Ironically, just as the treatise had lent modern intellectual legitimacy to the common law, it came to be relied upon to lend legitimacy to the idea of codification.

Stephen's 1863 treatise, influenced by the failure of the final 1853 bill from Brougham's Commissioners, is described by Smith as:

> . . . a truly pioneering attempt to bring to legal analysis an approach to which revealed not merely the nature and relationship of the subject's principal theoretical elements but, additionally, succeeded in no small measure in showing the wider social scientific setting in which law might be advantageously studied. Not until thirteen years later with the appearance of Pollock's *Principles of Contract* was any legal text published which sought to treat an area of law in anything like this fashion. And only after nearly forty years, with Courtney Stanhope Kenny's *Outline of Criminal Law* (1902), was a theoretical text on the subject finally published that was remotely comparable to the *General View*.[53]

After returning from India in 1872, Stephen drafted modest codified evidence and homicide bills derived from his India legislation, and was frustrated by judicial opposition, a reminder of the treacherous shoals of Westminster's legislative politics. Smith again warrants lengthy quotation:

> In the vanguard of judicial opposition was Lord Chief Justice Cockburn, whose main objection was that partial codification required the unsatisfactory practice of incorpora-

[52] See Smith, *Stephen* (n 5) esp 44–72: Unlike Bentham and JS Mill, he accepted a denunciatory element in punishment and supported capital punishment, although he was a committed empiricist, opposed natural law and rejected Hegel and Kant, and in many ways his views were similar to Oliver Wendell Holmes. His views of subjective and objective elements of criminal responsibility and constructive forms of liability were coherent, although not as consistent as Macaulay, and he contradicted his views as a judge notably in the 1883 Fenian treason-felony trials.

[53] Smith, *Stephen*, ibid 52–53. See Farmer's chapter on 19th-century predecessors, Russell, Archbold and Chitty.

tion of references to non-code sources of law; an argument fielded by Cockburn as Attorney General to undermine the changes of the wider reforms of the 1850s. But as Stephen was later to point out, the suggested dilemma of codification en bloc or no codification was a false one; a staged transition during which common law concepts could be phased out was quite feasible. Yet the centrepiece of explicit judicial antagonism, as before, was the expectation that codification would remove the valuable flexibility of the common law . . .[54]

These experiences informed Stephen's approach to his *Digest*, begun in 1874 as a systematic treatment of indictable offences derived from legislative and common-law sources. Accompanied by digests on evidence and criminal procedure, it attempted to anticipate judicial objections, boiled down vast quantities of diverse case and statute law to succinct principles, and served as a bridge between his treatise and code.[55] Upon its publication, Stephen pitched codification to Disraeli's Government, convincing Attorney General Sir John Holker and Lord Chancellor Cairns that it was in close reach. An outline based on the *Digest* was sent to a statute law committee, and he was instructed to proceed, despite Robert Wright's reservations.[56]

Stephen's 1878 draft code follows the *Digest* closely, with chapters and sections corresponding to *Digest* articles, a virtually identical index, and many sections reproduced *verbatim*.[57] It was introduced into Commons and went to a Royal Commission that included Stephen for revision. A final version went to Parliament in early 1880 but all momentum was lost with Cockburn's not unexpected hostile intervention and parliamentary preoccupation with the Irish question, and the bill died with the fall of the government. Stephen's cautious middle course and narrow code failed to satisfy the defenders of the common law. The Lord Chief Justice declared, disingenuously, that the proposal was inconsistent with the idea of codification and that no code was better than a half-baked one.[58]

Stephen retrospectively defended his approach in *A History of the Criminal Law of England* published in 1883 with substantial reference to the IPC, the Draft English Code, its reception and Cockburn's critique.[59] *History* is much more than an *apologia* of course. While not a treatise in form and presentation, it came to be relied on as a treatise-style source of law. Ironically, it has less social science than *View* and was criticised on those grounds as a history, while *View*, a treatise

[54] Smith, ibid 77.

[55] As Smith, ibid 53 puts it, the Digest was '[p]rimarily written as a step towards codification . . .' See JF Stephen, 'A Penal Code' (1877) 21 *Fortnightly Review* 367 on his techniques of legislative drafting and distilling definitions from the common law; also; Desmond Brown, *The Genesis of the Canadian Criminal Code, 1892* (Toronto, ON, University of Toronto Press, 1989) 25–26. The Digest at 411 pages, with 6 parts, 46 chapters and 398 articles, plus examples and explanatory notes reminiscent of the IPC, is a significant compression compared to Greaves which is nearly 50 pages longer and is limited to statutes.

[56] Smith, ibid 78.

[57] See Brown, *Genesis* (n 55) 27–30.

[58] Smith, *Lawyers, Legislators and Theorists* (n 5) 143–50; Smith, Stephen (n 5) 78–82. Smith also notes Home and Lord Chancellor's office reservations as the profession contended with new procedures under the Judicature Acts which left little appetite for further big change.

[59] See Stephen, *History* (n 21) vol 3, 283–367.

in form, was criticised in professional circles as having too much social science and theory for practical relevance.[60] The defeat of the Stephen code ended what was probably England's best chance at criminal law codification. The most recent attempt, started by the English Law Commission in 1968, did not come nearly as close to success, its 1989 draft languished as a low legislative priority and was abandoned in 2008.[61]

The prospects of codification were better in other British jurisdictions, including those that developed responsible and self-government and where Stephen's code became a primary external reference.[62] The Colonial Office had promoted the IPC for other colonial settings,[63] and it was adopted in Ceylon and the Straits Settlements and some African colonies, and inspired William Badgley's 1850 proposed code for the Province of Canada.[64] The 1865 Jamaican uprising and Governor Eyre's controversial response prompted the Colonial Office to commission Wright to revise the IPC for other colonial settings.[65] The Jamaica Code, 1877 was not enacted, although versions were adopted elsewhere in the West Indies and further afield.[66] The conditions were favourable for codification in self-governing jurisdictions emerging from colonial status. The complexities of received English criminal laws and subsequent local amendments were compounded by the emergence of new colonies out of the territories of older ones (eg Upper Canada from Quebec, New Brunswick from Nova Scotia, Victoria and Queensland from New South Wales) and by colonial union (Upper and Lower Canada, 1840, prefacing the larger challenge faced by the Dominion of Canada in 1867).[67] Consolidations had simplified the accumulated layers of law and codification appealed as a logical next step, a complete, succinct and portable *compendium* of criminal law attrac-

[60] I am grateful to Jula Hughes for these insights. See also Farmer's chapter on the practical literature.

[61] See C Clarkson, 'Recent Law Reform and Codification of the General Principles of Criminal Law in England and Wales: A Tale of Woe' in Chan, Wright and Yeo, *Macaulay* (n 20) 337; 'RIP: The Criminal Code (1968–2008)' Editorial [2009] *Criminal Law Review* 1.

[62] See Wright, 'Self Governing Jurisdiction Codes' (n 28).

[63] See Colonial Office circulars, eg 'Some Considerations Preliminary to the Preparation of a Penal Code for the Crown Colonies' and Sir Henry Taylor's treatise (later appended to Wright's Jamaica draft), 'Subjects Affecting Colonies Generally, Confidential Print' 20 May 1870, National Archives (UK) CO 885/3/19.

[64] See GB Baker, 'Strategic Benthamism: Rehabilitating United Canada's Bar Through Criminal Law Codification, 1847–54" in J Phillips, R McMurtry and J Saywell (eds), *Essays in the History of Canadian Law: A Tribute to Peter N Oliver* (Toronto, ON, Osgoode Society, 2008) 257.

[65] See Kostal (n 27), Friedland, 'R.S. Wright' (n 28). Influenced by the English Law Commissioners, Wright's code was significantly different from the IPC, defined liability in a general part and abandoned Macaulay's use of examples. Stephen critically reviewed a draft he started on his Digest and his disagreements with Wright continued as his own project advanced; see Smith, Lawyers, Legislators and Theorists, (n 5) 151–52.

[66] After a false start on a replacement for Wright by Fitzjames Stephen's son Henry, Samuel Griffith's 1899 Queensland Code had wide influence, including Albert Ehrhardt's 1925 Colonial Office model code; see RS O'Regan, 'Sir Samuel Griffith's Criminal Code' (1991) 7 *Australian Bar Review* 141.

[67] *Calvin's Case* (1608) 77 ER 377 and imperial instructions governed informal reception. English criminal laws tended to be formally received as the foundation of a jurisdiction's criminal laws when representative legislative institutions and colonial courts were first established, empowered to amend these laws as conditions required, subject to imperial supervision.

tive to a bar and bench more distant from the culture of the common law, faced with formidable practical challenges accessing sources of law.[68] Receptiveness to codification was also enhanced by local struggles for responsible government and criminal law reform, informed by experiences of abuse of executive powers in colonial government and the administration of justice.[69] Codification was associated with constraint on state powers and self-government, giving it a constitutional momentum lacking in England itself.[70] While these jurisdictions were unreceptive to imposed codes written by imperial administrators promoted by the Colonial Office, Stephen's Draft English Code was not burdened with such colonialist baggage. His modest, pragmatic approach was loose enough in conception to combine easily with local consolidations and local developments could be accommodated. Stephen unsurprisingly became the primary external reference for the Canadian (1892), New Zealand (1893) and Queensland (1899) codes.[71] As was the case with the IPC's enactment and the drafting of the Jamaica Code, crisis lent urgency to these big legislative projects.[72]

The first of these codes was given impetus by John A Macdonald's insistence on centralised, uniform criminal law under federal jurisdiction during discussions of the proposed union of the British North American colonies. The decentralised American approach was widely perceived as a contributing factor to the then-raging US civil war. Criminal law was seen in the same vein as national defence, associated with the stability of the new Dominion of Canada, its territorial integrity and the securing of its sovereignty and development priorities over the vast North-West territories.[73] Macdonald, the Dominion's first Prime Minister, retained the justice portfolio to ensure rapid passage of federal consolidations in 1868–69, but codification only became a legislative priority after the 1885 North-West Rebellion.[74] Stephen's Draft English Code proved to be a convenient vehicle for rationalising

[68] Institutional holdings were limited, relevant statutes and legal texts often in very distant locations. See Brown, *Genesis*, (n 55) 42, 71.

[69] See, eg numerous examples of uses of the law to fend off challenges and maintain the authority of local elites in the *Canadian State Trials* series.

[70] Smith, *Stephen*, (n 5) 83–84; Farmer, (n 6) 423–24.

[71] Stephen's renderings of the common law were usually adopted, while most statutory-based provisions derived from local consolidations. His narrow conception of codification and retention of common law characterise the Canadian and New Zealand codes, and while most of Samuel Griffith's external references are to Stephen, his more comprehensive approach, inspired by Zanardelli's 1889 Italian Code, resembles the Macaulay and Wright codes; see Wright, 'Self Governing Jurisdiction Codes' (n 28).

[72] For Canada, see n 74. New Zealand's project started in 1883 during resistance to Maori land confiscations and indefinite detentions and a draft was completed before Canada's, but legislative difficulties delayed enactment to 1893. Queensland's code was prefaced by a general strike, emergence of the Labor Party and perceived threats to federation; see Wright, ibid.

[73] See Peter B Waite (ed) *The Confederation Debates in the Province of Canada* 2nd edn (Montreal, QC, McGill Queen's Press, 2006) 24–25. Macdonald's position on criminal law was widely supported, no opposition to it appears in the records and it is one of the few matters that remained unchanged in successive constitutional drafts; see Brown, *Genesis* (n 55) 59–60.

[74] See DH Brown and B Wright, 'Codification, Public Order, and the Security Provisions of the Canadian Criminal Code, 1892' in Barry Wright and Susan Binnie (eds), *Canadian State Trials Volume 3: Political Trials and Security Measures, 1840–1914* (Toronto ON, University of Toronto Press, 2009) 516.

and rounding out the Dominion of Canada consolidations, and a decade after the failure of the code bill at Westminster, Canada pipped New Zealand at the post to become the first British self-governing jurisdiction to codify its criminal law.

As a former attorney general in the United Province of Canada, Macdonald had experience bringing uniformity to the disparate criminal laws of Upper and Lower Canada, prefiguring the larger challenge faced at Confederation.[75] Rapid assertion of the Canadian Parliament's jurisdiction was more easily achieved by consolidation than codification, but even this more modest project could be delayed. Adoption of one of the earlier British North American consolidations risked acrimonious debate between the provinces while a commission charged with assimilating the best colonial provisions could be as time-consuming as codification. Macdonald's expedient solution was to simply adopt Greaves' 1861 English Consolidations as the basis for the Dominion Consolidations.[76] Twenty amending bills were required in the first five years as some provisions intruded on provincial jurisdiction, others were less advanced than those in earlier colonial consolidations, and new laws were imported that had never been in effect.[77]

During this time, Judge Gowan met with leading English barristers, judges and law reformers (including Lord Thring, Lord Cairns, Sir Henry Taylor and Robert Wright) and advocated codification in his *Canada Law Journal*,[78] returning to London at the end of the decade to witness debate on the Draft English Code. There was little political appetite in Ottawa for such a large legislative project, even when Macdonald returned to power, but momentum began to build in 1883–84 during work on a new consolidation as part of the Revised Statutes of Canada. George Burbidge, the Deputy Minister of Justice, obtained Stephen's *Digest*, along with the Draft English Code and associated reports.[79] Passage of the Revised Statutes was delayed because of the North-West Rebellion, while Ministry officials struggled with the applicable laws and prosecutions, relying on the unwieldy *Archbold*'s *Pleading*.[80] At this point, Burbidge became committed to the idea of a Canadian edition of the *Digest*.

[75] See n 67. Each British North American colony had received English criminal law at a different time and amended it in different ways. For instance, Upper Canada's criminal law was based on law as it stood in 1792 but adopted Peel's consolidations in 1833, reducing capital offences to 11, whereas Lower Canada still had over 200 capital offences from English criminal law as it stood in 1774. Lord Sydenham's administration addressed the most obvious anomalies in 1840–41 but the Province of Canada consolidation project stalled. Badgley's proposal was followed by coordinated consolidations in 1859–60; see Brown, *Genesis*, (n 55) 74–78, 84–85.

[76] Put under tight timelines by Macdonald, minor amendments were made by Hewitt Bernard, Gustavis Wicksteed and Judge James Gowan (who corresponded with Greaves); see Brown, *Genesis*, ibid 92–97; also DH Brown (ed), *The Birth of a Criminal Code: the Evolution of Canada's Justice System* (Toronto, ON, University of Toronto Press, 1995) 28.

[77] Brown, *Birth of a Criminal Code*, ibid 31; Brown, *Genesis*, ibid 103–06.

[78] The most influential legal periodical in nineteenth-century Canada, it followed English developments closely and tended to dismiss American ones. Gowan's advocacy of codification did not appear to meet professional resistance or evoke defences of the common law; see Parker (n 47) 253–55; Brown, *Genesis*, ibid 70, 98–99.

[79] Brown, ibid 110–11.

[80] *Archbold's Pleading and Evidence in Criminal Cases* (London, H Sweet, 1886) published originally as *A summary of the law relative to pleading and evidence in criminal cases* (London, Pheney, 1824),

The 1885 crisis and the Revised Statutes were catalysts, mobilising the bureaucratic and political will to make codification a legislative priority. The appointment of John Thompson as Minister of Justice ended recent political neglect of the department, and he was receptive to arguments from Burbidge and Gowan and further encouraged by British officials during a visit to London in 1888.[81] He was also prompted by Mr Justice Taschereau, a Liberal appointee to the Supreme Court of Canada, who offered to draft a code based on the new edition of his treatise, *The Criminal Statute Law of Canada*, as Burbidge completed his Canadian edition of Stephen's *Digest*.[82] Thompson directed Burbidge, now on the bench, and his successor Robert Sedgewick to begin work on a codification bill after the 1890 Parliamentary session.[83]

Like Stephen's *Digest*, Burbidge's Canadian edition encompasses the common law to present a more comprehensive synthesis than Taschereau's treatise.[84] Burbidge significantly edited the 1877 English edition, adding summary offences and Canadian content. Out of 629 articles, 234 appear *verbatim* from Stephen, the remainder were reworked, some combining Stephen's text with Burbidge's supplements (conveniently indicated by brackets), others were Canadian provisions from the 1886 Revised Statutes. Canadian examples were added and the appendix commentary and tables of cases and statutes were revised accordingly.[85] Burbidge then replicated Stephen's approach to the Draft English Code, his close familiarity with the 1886 revisions, combined with his editing of the *Digest*, assimilating all the relevant legislation and common law, set the stage for the code bill.

Burbidge and Sedgewick drafted, while Thompson set out general guidelines and strategised the bill's introduction to Parliament after studying the Westminster debates.[86] Judge Gowan advised, but perhaps his notable, or notorious, contribution was removal of Lord Chief Justice Cockburn's published criticism of the English code from Ottawa's Parliamentary Library.[87] Thompson's bill

described by Simpson (n 3) 664 'the most successful of all is possibly the worst of the lot . . .', is an immense and disorganised work; see also Farmer's chapter. The 1882 edition provided formulations for charges, informations and indictments, evidentiary and procedural matters to accompany relevant Dominion provisions and other received laws applicable in the North-West Territories for 84 cases. Louis Riel was convicted of high treason and his leading associates pleaded guilty to the non-capital treason-felony offence; see Bob Beal and Barry Wright, 'Summary and Incompetent Justice: Legal Responses to the 1885 Crisis' in Wright and Binnie (eds), *Canadian State Trials Vol 3* (n 74) 353.

[81] See Brown, *Genesis* (n 55) 106–118; *Birth* (n 76) 31.

[82] H-E Tashereau, *The Criminal Statute Law of Canada* (2nd ed) (Montreal, QC, Carswell, 1888). The first post-confederation Canadian criminal law treatise appears to be Samuel Robinson Clarke's *Treatise on Criminal Law* (1872). Dandurand and Lanctot's *Traite theoretique et practique de droit criminel* is another early treatise.

[83] Parker (n 47) 257–59; Brown, *Genesis* (n 55) 119–23; also Brown, *Birth* (n 76) 32 and reproduced correspondence, 52–55.

[84] *Digest of the Criminal Law of Canada (Crimes and Punishment) Founded by Permission on Sir James Fitzjames Stephen's Digest of the Criminal Law* (Montreal, QC, Carswell, 1890; repub1980, forward by Justice Fred Kaufman).

[85] See Brown, *Genesis* (n 55) 121.

[86] The 1880 English bill, the 1886 Revised Statutes and Burbidge's edition of the *Digest* were the primary references; see Parker (n 47) 261–64; Brown, ibid 120–22; Brown, *Birth* (n 76).

[87] Parker, ibid 258.

closely resembles the 1880 English bill in concept and organisation. Stephen's common-law renderings were adopted, but most of the statute-derived provisions came from the 1886 Revised Statutes.[88] It was introduced in the spring of 1891 and copies were distributed to provincial Attorneys General, the bench and leading members of the bar.[89] A slightly revised bill, introduced in April 1892, passed within two months of well-managed committee hearings.[90] Taschereau's belated attempt to emulate Cockburn appeared just after the code was passed and proclaimed.[91]

CONCLUSIONS

Blackstone's modernisation of the common law inspired the nineteenth-century treatise but failed to go far enough for Bentham. The attempted rationalisation was a misguided renovation and only demolition and rebuilding would do. The logic of parliamentary supremacy and the public policy challenges facing the modern state, a fuller embrace of Enlightenment rationality and utilitarian theory, meant abandoning common law altogether in favour of transformative legislation in the form of codes. Yet Blackstone succeeded, the common law gained modern legitimacy and codification failed domestically. Professional and judicial hostility to ambitious Benthamite-inspired legislative reform shifted such projects to colonial settings and, in turn, codification was patronisingly dismissed as appropriate for backward frontier situations and irrelevant to the circumstances of the metropole, the birthplace of the common law.

Common-law culture was weaker in the colonies and codification had more constitutional momentum. A key rationale, the better regulation of the powers of the state, seemed more pressing, particularly for jurisdictions in crisis. Codification enhanced the effectiveness and legitimacy of British rule in India where the Mutiny helped ensure IPC's enactment. In Canada, concerns about the effectiveness of the new Dominion's sovereignty, the challenges of post-colonial nation-building, and the events of the 1880s made codification a legislative priority. The English focus was narrower, the better management of crime, and the institutional transformations, consolidation, procedural and treatise-inspired refinement of substantive doctrine had addressed the most archaic elements of the criminal law. Legal scholars allied to the common law continued Blackstone's renovation, developed the academic discipline and the positivist heirs to Bentham

[88] Brown, *Genesis* (n 55) 123–24 estimates 40% (209 sections) of the substantive provisions derive from the Draft English Code, 60% (321) from Canadian sources. The indictable/summary distinction was fully adopted.

[89] Brown, *Birth* (n 76) 34–35; Parker (n 47) 265–69.

[90] Parker, ibid 271; Brown, ibid 37–41.

[91] See Parker, ibid 273–76. The published critique borrowed heavily from the Lord Chief Justice's. Sedgewick defended the Code in a February 1893 memo, noting that the drafters were fully apprised of Cockburn's critique and agreed with Stephen about inclusion of the common law.

wanted in on this action. Ironically then, the burden had shifted to the codifiers to lend legitimacy to their projects and the treatise helped them do this, as exemplified by Stephen's cautious approach that began with a treatise, moved to a digest and then on to a narrow code that retained common law.

The treatise form and synthesis of law plays a complicated intersecting role in these narratives of codification. The Indian and Canadian codes reflect different phases of the nineteenth-century English criminal law reform debates. Macaulay's inspiration was Bentham, Burbidge's was Stephen, the former rejected the common law and the latter sought accommodation with it, one purported to reinvent and the other openly rationalised existing laws. Macaulay was well-situated to take up Bentham's injunction to legislate criminal law entirely anew and drafted the first and most Benthamite code in the British Empire. Yet in facing the practical challenges of codification, a Baconian pragmatism combined with other influences led to implicit reliance on a synthesis of existing laws. Stephen's approach, entailing an open embrace of the treatise, was appealing for the reformers involved with the first British self-governing jurisdiction code. The revised Dominion of Canada consolidations were assimilated into Burbidge's edition of Stephen's digest and it was a relatively simple exercise to use the vehicle of the Draft English Code to rework digested current laws into the Canadian Criminal Code. Codes and treatises were important nineteenth-century forms of legal literature in the British common-law world, and while they may have been at odds at inception, a complex and dynamic relationship developed between them.

10

A Low Law Counter Treatise? 'Absentees' to 'Wreck' in British North America's First Justice of the Peace Manual

JIM PHILLIPS*

I. INTRODUCTION

THE JUSTICE OF the Peace (JP) Manual was the law book most frequently used by legal officials in the Anglo-North American world, at least until the mid-to late nineteenth century, and certainly the law book that most affected the lives of ordinary people. It dealt with low law, the law of local administration, petty crime and small debts, not with the high law propounded by and administered in superior courts. It was law meted out in often very informal proceedings by men without legal training, without the trappings of 'majesty' and the learned speeches of lawyers.[1] The JP manual thus certainly deserves a place in the history of legal literature.

But is a JP manual a treatise, and if it is not, what is its relationship to the history of the treatise? My answer is no to the first question. Definitions of treatise in legal and other dictionaries abound, and despite their differences they have two things in common. First, all of those which I have found insist that a treatise is a 'methodical', 'formal' and 'systematic' discussion of a particular subject. Many, although not all, of those definitions also claim that a treatise's methodical approach includes an 'exposition of the principles of the subject', is 'concerned

* Professor of Law, History and Criminology, University of Toronto. Editor-in-Chief, Osgoode Society for Canadian Legal History. I thank Blaine Baker, Philip Girard, Brad Miller, Chris Tomlins, Mariana Valverde, and the editors of this volume for comments on previous drafts, and Daniel Girard for research assistance.

[1] For discussions of the distinction between 'high' and 'low' law, see D Hay, 'Legislation, Magistrates and Judges: High Law and Low Law in England the Empire' in D Lemmings (ed), *The British and Their Laws in the Eighteenth Century* (London, Boydell and Brewer, 2005); D Hay and P Craven, *Masters, Servants and Magistrates in Britain and the Empire, 1562–1955* (Chapel Hill, NC, University of North Carolina Press, 2004); D Fyson, 'Introduction' in *Magistrates, Police and People: Everyday Criminal Justice in Quebec and Lower Canada, 1764–1837* (Toronto, ON, Osgoode Society and University of Toronto Press, 2006).

with investigating or exposing the principles of the subject', and has a 'discussion of the . . . principles involved'[2]. Brian Simpson's famous investigation of the rise of the treatise also includes a 'logical and systematic' approach and identification of underlying 'principles' as characteristics. He also argues that a treatise is a book which deals with 'a single branch of the law that is conceived of as possessing some quality of unity, a requirement that eliminates the likes of Blackstone's *Commentaries*'.[3]

JP manuals certainly do not deal with a single unified subject, and do not fit the other aspects of standard definitions either. They were always organised alphabetically, with no attempt to bring together conceptually similar topics. Moreover, they were divided into small topics, some recognisably 'legal' subjects – accessory – and others socio-economic categories – bread, for example.[4] Thus they are unlike modern abridgements, which are also organised alphabetically but around large and clearly 'legal' categories.[5] JP manuals cannot therefore be considered 'systematically' ordered if that word or 'methodical' is to be given any meaning at all beyond 'non-random'. That is, they are more systematically ordered than they would be if topics were arranged neither by concept nor alphabet. But systematic and methodical surely imply some attempt to gather together in different parts of the book conceptually similar matter. Nor does a JP manual meet the second criterion, that of being an 'exposition of the principles' of a subject. Although 'principle' has been and is used to mean a variety of different things in the law, a manual does not seek to expound underlying core values or to elucidate leading cases and doctrines.[6]

[2] See the definitions in the *Oxford English Dictionary* ('A book or writing . . . one containing a methodical discussion or exposition of the principles of the subject') and *Wikipedia* ('a formal and systematic written discourse on some subject . . . concerned with investigating or exposing the principles of the subject'). Similar definitions can be found in *Dictionary.com*, *Merriam-Webster on line*, and *West's Encyclopedia of American Law*. Perhaps oddly given the extensive use of the word in legal literature, neither *Black's Law Dictionary* nor *Yogis' Canadian Law Dictionary* has an entry for treatise.

[3] AWB Simpson, 'The Rise and Fall of the Legal Treatise: Legal Principle and the Forms of Legal Literature' (1981) 48 *University of Chicago Law Review* 632, 633.

[4] The examples used here, although common to almost all JP manuals, are taken from the manual that is the subject of this chapter, JG Marshall, *The Justice of the Peace and County and Township Officer in the Province of Nova Scotia, being a Guide to such Justice and Officers in the Discharge of their Official Duties* (Halifax, NS, Gossip and Coade, 1837) [hereafter *Marshall's Manual*]. I am aware that the line between 'legal' subjects and 'non-legal' ones shifts over time. While subjects such as courts and procedure and tort and contract are always in the former category, others may move from the non-legal to the legal. We now teach courses in things like 'construction law' or 'animal law', for example, which formerly would not have been seen as organising subjects for law. See also the fact that eighteenth- and nineteenth-century manuals invariably include 'horses' as a category, yet in 1908 GH Oliphant was able to publish *The Law of Horses* (London, Henry Sweet, 1882).

[5] See, eg the *Canadian Abridgment*, which has 'Trusts and Trustees' coming after 'Trespass' and before 'Unemployment Insurance', but the topics are large ones and within them the text is arranged by themes defined by the topic itself. Thus 'Trusts and Trustees' starts with 'Nature of Trust', and goes on to deal with the different kinds of trusts, their operation, the powers and duties of trustees, etc. The earliest abridgements were different, organised alphabetically into many more smaller topics: see JH Baker, *An Introduction to English Legal History* 3rd edn (London, Butterworths, 1990) 211–14.

[6] See, for the varied use of 'principle', S Waddams, 'What *Were* the Principles of Nineteenth-century English Contract Law?' in ADE Lewis, P Brand and P Mitchell (eds), *Law in the City: Proceedings of the*

What, then, merits the inclusion of a chapter on a JP manual in this collection? I have called it a counter-treatise, and by that I mean to highlight the fact that legal history throws up many different kinds of legal literature, each serving a different purpose. Treatises properly operated at an elite level, seeking to systematise and justify the law and to propound its principles and underlying values among the legal elite of high-profile lawyers, judges and legal academics. A JP manual did not offer justifications or seek to show the normative bases of legal doctrine. It simply instructed those whose job was to enforce state-sanctioned norms. Like the treatise, it dealt in authority, but its authority was highly positivistic – not the leading case or nostrums of natural law, but the detailed provisions of, largely, statute law. As noted at the beginning of this chapter, far more people were affected by JP manuals, on both sides of the divide between enforcers of the law and those subject to it, than by treatises, encyclopaedias and the like. Comparing the JP manual to the high law treatise, I would suggest, can help us to better understand the latter by thinking about the contrasts with the former.

In what follows I first describe the rise of the JP manual in England and its export to North America. I then examine the context out of which *Marshall's Manual* was written, through looking at the author and his place in the court system of the colony of Nova Scotia. I then analyse the manual itself, including its use and reception in the years after publication. The final substantive section links the manual and the author in a search for the latter's motivations in producing a landmark of Canadian legal literature.

II. THE JUSTICE OF THE PEACE AND JP MANUALS

JP manuals became so important because of the peculiarly English system of local government in which the JP was the jack of all trades. Although the office was originally only concerned with enforcing the peace, as its name suggests, from the fifteenth through the seventeenth centuries JPs acquired vastly increased duties – economic regulation, road maintenance, administering the poor law system, to name but a few.[7] They also tried many minor offences and, while they lost jurisdiction over the more serious ones, they remained responsible for the pre-trial aspects of the criminal process – arrest, initial investigation, remand. As Landau succinctly puts it by the late seventeenth century the justice was both a

Seventeenth British Legal History Conference London 2005 (Dublin, Four Courts Press, 2007).

[7] The best account of the JP in England in this period is N Landau, *The Justices of the Peace, 1679–1760* (Berkeley CA, University of California Press, 1984). What follows on the English commission of the peace is taken largely from this. A useful summary also appears in JA Conley, 'Doing It by the Book: Justice of the Peace Manuals and English Law in Eighteenth-Century America' (1985) 6 *Journal of Legal History* 257. A largely descriptive but voluminous study by T Skryme is also useful: *History of the Justices of the Peace* (3 vols) (Chichester, Rose, 1991). For JPs' criminal jurisdiction sitting as Sessions judges, see JM Beattie, *Crime and the Courts in England 1660–1800* (Princeton, NJ, Princeton University Press, 1986).

judicial and an administrative officer: he insured that alleged miscreants appeared to answer for their offences; sitting either in or out of Quarter Sessions he heard and determined charges of all but the most major offences; he supervised parish government; and he administered county government.[8]

The system of government by JP was introduced into most of the colonies which declared independence from England, and all of those which formed British North America after the revolution. Indeed their trans-Atlantic jurisdiction was broader than at home, for in many places they also dealt with small debt and other civil causes. As prerogative appointments holding office at pleasure, they were the cornerstone of the counter-revolutionary system of colonial governance introduced after the revolution. From the late eighteenth century 'the great object of the imperial authorities was to prevent the rise of a spirit of independence' and thus 'the colonial constitution weighed heavily towards the appointed executive rather than the partly elected legislative branch'[9], and thus towards a preference for governance by JP rather than locally elected bodies.[10]

North American JPs differed from their English counterparts in one very significant respect. By the eighteenth century, English JPs were comprised of the existing social and economic elite, the gentry in the countryside, major merchants in the cities, clergymen and other professionals. They obtained posts of official power because they had social authority, and the former of course only reinforced the latter. British North America generally lacked the same kind of leadership class, and those available to be appointed to the commission of the peace were much more modest in means, educational attainments and, at times, respectability. The authorities did what they could, appointing many seigneurs in Quebec, for example, and elsewhere utilising professional men.[11] But Nova Scotia's JPs were generally from the middling sort, small farmers and traders, school teachers, independent artisans. As the author of the subject of this paper put it, local magistrates 'although in general selected from the most suitable persons' were largely of 'ordinary education and attainments' and as they had to work for a living 'have but little leisure for the acquisition of any particular knowledge of the Laws'[12]. JPs who did devote themselves to the task were often criticised for that – they were ungentlemanly 'trading justices' who relied on their fees for their income, not respectable and independent amateurs.

Even the English JPs, no matter what their status and education, came to require guidance in carrying out their myriad duties. The earliest JP manual appeared in the late sixteenth century, and from its first publication in 1618, Dalton's *Country*

[8] Landau, *Justices of the Peace*, ibid 6–7.

[9] D Bell, 'Maritime Legal Institutions Under the *Ancien Regime*, 1710–1850' in WW Pue and D Guth (eds), *Canada's Legal Inheritances* (Winnipeg, MB, University of Manitoba, 2001) 108.

[10] See, inter alia, DC Harvey, *'The Struggle for the New England Form of Township Government in Nova Scotia'* [1949] CHA Report 15.

[11] See generally S Lewthwaite, 'Law and Authority in Upper Canada: The Justices of the Peace in the Newcastle District, 1804–1840' (PhD Dissertation, University of Toronto, 2001); Fyson, *Magistrates, Police and People* (n 1) esp ch 3; Skryme, *History* (n 7) vol 3, ch 5 on Canada.

[12] *Marshall's Manual* (n 4) iv–v.

Justice became the standard text.[13] It had challengers, notably William Nelson's *Office and Authority of the Justice of the Peace*, published in 1704, which was the first one to arrange its subjects entirely in alphabetical order. From the mid-eighteenth century, the Rev Richard Burn's *Justice of the Peace and Parish Officer* came to dominate the field. First published in 1755, it went through numerous editions and editors, with the last edition, the 30th, appearing in 1869. Burn's manual followed the Nelson innovation of alphabetical listing. The 24th edition of 1825, for example, published a decade before the manual that is the subject of this chapter, began with 'Accessary' and ended with 'Wreck'.[14] Under each subject, common-law principles were explained and statutory references, some cases, and leading works such as Hale, Hawkins and Blackstone were quoted and referenced. Conley argues that Burn and its predecessors were 'sophisticated yet easily digestible books' which were crucial both to the justices' work and to the standardisation of law and its administration. But Burn was the best, 'lucid, comprehensive and accurate. . . . The justice could just open his Burn and follow instructions'.[15]

Versions of the leading manuals were imported into the American colonies and competed with locally produced and more or less 'Americanised' manuals. In the northern and middle colonies, Americanisation came mainly in the form of leaving out topics inapplicable to the colonies, and most manuals were otherwise knock-offs of English ones, even after the revolution. Southern manuals were much more localised, principally because they included much on the laws relating to slavery.[16] No 'localised' English versions of Burn were available in British North America until the 1830s, although major parts of it were translated into French for use in Quebec as early as 1789. But Burn itself was available and reasonably widely used.[17]

Marshall's Manual was the first British North American JP manual, in the sense that it was written locally rather than being a revised version of Burn, was based entirely on local law, and aimed only at JPs, excluding all other aspects of law and legal administration not relevant to the work of the JP.[18] Manuals for some of the

[13] For the history of English and colonial American JP manuals in this period, see Conley, 'Doing it By the Book' (n 7) and Landau, *Justices of the Peace* (n 7) *passim.*

[14] Richard Burn, *The justice of the peace and parish officer, 24th ed with corrections, additions and improvements* by Sir G Chetwynd (5 vols) (London, A Strahan, 1825).

[15] Conley, 'Doing It by the Book' (n 8) 262; Landau, *Justices of the Peace* (n 7) 341.

[16] Useful information on colonial and early national American manuals, especially southern ones, is contained in L Edwards, *The People and Their Peace: Legal Culture and the Transformation of Inequality in the Post-Revolutionary South* (Chapel Hill, NC, University of North Carolina Press, 2009)); J Bush, 'Free to Enslave: The Foundations of Colonial American Slave Law' (1993) 5 *Yale Journal of Law & the Humanities* 417.

[17] See R Burn, *Le juge à pace, et officier de paroisse, pour la province de Québec* in J Perrault, F Montreal and Mesplet (trans) 1789), and Fyson, *Magistrates, Police and People* (n 1) 34 and 122–24.

[18] I have defined the JP manual carefully here because the first British North American manual has heretofore been considered to be William Conway Keele's *The Provincial Justice, or Magistrate's Manual, being a complete digest of the criminal law of Canada and a compendious and general view of the provincial law of upper Canada*, published in Toronto in 1835, two years before *Marshall's Manual.* But *Provincial Justice*, I would argue, was not a JP manual in the sense that that term is normally understood. As the subtitle suggests, it contained much more than instruction for JPs, dealing with many areas which were the preserve of higher courts, especially in criminal law. Indeed the preface begins by stating that substantial change had occurred in this area since the reception of English criminal law in 1791, and that justified

other colonies were produced at about the same time, suggesting that the time had come in the development of distinctive local law for a distinct local product.[19] The following section explains its genesis.

III. JOHN GEORGE MARSHALL AND THE NOVA SCOTIA COURT SYSTEM

John George Marshall was born in 1786 in Country Harbour, Sydney County (now Guysborough County), Nova Scotia, the son of Captain Joseph Marshall, a loyalist *emigré* and something of a local grandee who served as a JP, Member of the House of Assembly (MHA), and judge of the Sydney County Inferior Court of Common Pleas (ICCP).[20] Educated locally and at the Halifax Grammar School until he was 17, in 1804 the younger Marshall entered the law office of Lewis Morris Wilkins Senior at Pictou as an apprentice. A Columbia-educated loyalist, Wilkins was one of the colony's best known, best connected and most able lawyers. He sat in the Assembly for 16 years and was speaker for 11. In 1816 he was appointed an assistant (puisne) judge of the Nova Scotia Supreme Court (NSSC). Marshall finished his apprenticeship and started practising in 1808, and two years later, in the general election of 1811, he succeeded his father as an MHA for Sydney County, a seat he held until 1818 and to which he returned in the 1820 election. He did not live in the area he represented; for some years he practised out of Pictou, and moved to Halifax in 1816 and henceforth practised from there.[21] The change came about as a result of Wilkins' appointment to the bench. Wilkins set Marshall up in partnership with his nephew Martin Isaac Wilkins, who had just been called to the bar, and the two took over the senior Wilkins' practice.[22] Throughout his years at the bar, Marshall

publication of Keele's book. There followed many sections devoted to capital offences. Elsewhere we find discussions of other matters not the preserve of JPs, such as King's Bench and the Court of Appeal, of English doctrines hardly used in Upper Canada such as champerty, and a long section on conveyancing. The 1791 *Constitutional Act* was reproduced and Keele listed all provincial government officials and judges, much as an almanac typically did. It was, in short, as the sub-title indicated, 'a compendious and general view of the provincial law', not simply a manual for JPs. As it was much the same length as *Marshall's Manual* [670 pages compared to 641] it also sacrificed many details of JPs' work.

[19] See P Stubs, *The New-Brunswick Manual: A Compilation of Forms and Information Designed for the Use of Justices of the Peace, Merchants, Mechanics, &c.* (Saint John, NB, D McMillan, 1841), and H Taylor, *Manual of the Office, Duties and Liabilities of a Justice of the Peace* (Montreal, QC, Ramsay Armour, 1843). The former was no more than a collection of forms. A variety of other constables' and JPs' guides were produced in the second half of the nineteenth century.

[20] In addition to the specific references below, what follows on Marshall and his family is based on CE Thomas, 'John George Marshall' *Dictionary of Canadian Biography online* [hereafter *DCB*]; *The Legislative Assembly of Nova Scotia, 1758–1983: A Biographical Directory* (Halifax, NS revised edition, Public Archives of Nova Scotia, 1984, by Shirley Elliott)' 152–53; JG McKinnon, *Old Sydney* (Belleville, ON, Mika, 1973); and three accounts by Marshall himself: *A Brief History of Public Proceedings and Events – Legal, Parliamentary and Miscellaneous, in the province of Nova Scotia, during the earliest years of the present century* (Halifax, NS, Wesleyan Office, c 1825); *Personal narratives – with reflections and remarks* (Halifax, NS, T Chamberlain, 1866); and 'Perils and Preservations' in Nova Scotia Archives and Records Management [hereafter NSARM], JG Marshall Papers, MG1, vol 1283.

[21] Marshall, *A Brief History*, ibid 1, 4.

[22] Marshall, 'Perils and Preservations' (n 20).

also travelled the colony with the NSSC circuit. His practice was in both civil and criminal work, at all levels of court; as a criminal lawyer he acted both as a prosecutor and as defence counsel.[23] Marshall was an active Assemblyman, and his work there reflected his interests in the law, education and, especially, sabbath observance as well as his willingness to pursue local legislation on behalf of his constituents.[24] As we shall see later, this last was a particular passion of Marshall's.

Marshall's legislative career ended with his appointment as the Chief Justice of the inferior courts on Cape Breton Island in 1823. Functioning below the NSSC, Nova Scotia had county or district based lower civil courts – the aforementioned ICCPs – as well as similarly organised Sessions of the Peace, which served as both the principal mechanism of local administration and as the lower criminal court. Both courts were staffed very largely by layman JPs, prominent local residents picked for their loyalty to the central administration and the influence they could wield through their status as successful farmers, businessmen or professionals. Potentially all JPs could sit at Sessions, but the ICCPs were staffed by just five judges named in the relevant commission. Cape Breton Island had been a separate colony from 1780 to 1820, but in the latter year was reunited with Nova Scotia. In the process, its system of administration of justice was transformed. It lost its own Supreme Court, and the island was added to the NSSC circuit in 1820, although in a very limited way, for no more than eight days a year. Lower courts were also established, the ICCP and the Sessions Court to sit simultaneously twice a year at Sydney and twice a year at Arichat, for five days each session.[25]

The distance from Halifax, and especially the difficulty of travel there, meant that the NSSC on circuit was a relatively ineffective institution. The NSSC judges greatly disliked the many days of arduous travel to get there, travel which brought 'a vast increase of labour, expense and peril to us unfortunate Judges'.[26] Local

[23] For appearances in civil cases, see ibid. For his prosecution work, see *Appropriations Act 1816*, S[tatutes] of N[ova] S[cotia] 1816, c 1. For his defence work, see his defence of Sampson Fox at Pictou in c 1817, in G Patterson, 'Old Court Records of Pictou County' in Patterson, *Studies in Nova Scotia History* (Halifax, NS, Imperial Publications, 1940) 55–56. He was asked for as counsel by Walter Lee, tried at Guysborough for murder in 1812, but was unable to attend and Lee had to be content with the assistance of Marshall's brother Joseph, who was clerk of the crown for Sydney County: NSARM, Selections from the Files of Government Officials, RG 1, vol 226, No 16.

[24] In 1823 alone he sponsored five bills. One was to establish schools throughout the colony; it passed in the Assembly but was rejected by Council. He also sponsored bills to reform debtor/creditor law, to allow for road allowances in Guysborough Township, and to consolidate all the Acts relative to the poor. Near the end of 1823, he also introduced a bill 'for the better observation of the Lord's Day', but it was given the three-month hoist in committee of the whole. See *Journals of the Nova Scotia House of Assembly* [hereafter *Assembly Journals*], 1823, *passim*.

[25] Cape Breton Laws Act, SNS 1820–1821, c 5, ss 2, 3 and 4.

[26] James Stewart to Peleg Wiswall, 20 December 1820, NSARM, Peleg Wiswall Papers, MG 1, vol 980, No 76. On Travelling Conditions, see Lewis Wilkins' statement that 'we should allow ourselves at least 15 days to perform the journey' from Windsor to Sydney. He also told his travelling companion to 'bring a good wagon as the road is poor and the way very bad': Wilkins to Wiswall, 5 August 1823, MG 1, vol 979, Folder 6, No 13. For circuit conditions, see generally P Girard and J Phillips, 'Courts, Communities, and Communication: The Nova Scotia Supreme Court on Circuit, 1816–1850' in H Foster, B Berger and AR Bucks (eds), *The Grand Experiment: Law and Legal Culture in British Settler Societies* (Vancouver, BC, Osgoode Society and University of British Columbia Press, 2008).

residents resented both the lack of 'service' represented by only eight days of sittings, and instead preferred to litigate in the ICCP, although they also complained about not having a resident legally-trained judge.[27] Almost as soon as the circuit was inaugurated, proposals for reform came from both the judges and leading island citizens, and after a good deal of debate over money – elements in the Assembly were never keen on paying for new judgeships – the solution was found in the creation of a new position of Chief Justice of the ICCPs on Cape Breton, and President of all Sessions Courts. The appointee was to be a lawyer who had been in practice for at least five years, and he would be paid a salary of £400 (£200 less than NSSC judges) plus fees and a travel expense allowance of £100.[28]

Marshall, who had been a member of a five-person Assembly committee tasked to report on the idea, was appointed to the post at the end of April 1823, beating out Shelburne MHA Jared Chipman, although he did not resign his seat in the legislature until 23 January 1824.[29] He held the position until abolition of the ICCPs in 1841. The establishment of the Cape Breton Chief Justiceship was a relatively uncontroversial matter, much less so than the parallel arrangements made the next year for the mainland.[30] Marshall presided over all the lower courts in the island's three judicial districts, sitting twice annually at Sydney, Arichat and Port Hood.[31]

IV. THE MARSHALL MANUAL

Marshall wrote his *Manual* over several years in the early to mid-1830s,[32] but he required public assistance to get it published. Early in March 1837, he offered the manuscript to the Assembly, asking that it take on the cost of publishing. He offered any profit to the Assembly, and stipulated only that printing 'be commenced during the present year' and be 'under my own superintendence and direction'. An Assembly committee laconically reported that it had read the

[27] See Council Minutes, 6 February 1822, NSARM, RG 1, vol 214.5 A, 110–11.

[28] *Administration of Justice in Cape Breton Act*, SNS 1823, c 36. For debates on the bill, see *Assembly Journals*, 4, 8, 12, 13, 15, and 17–20 March 1823. See also *Acadian Recorder*, 8 March and 12 and 26 April 1823. For fees, see Marshall to Sir Rupert George, 8 December 1837, in Assembly Journals, 1838, Appendix 8.

[29] *Acadian Recorder*, 3 May 1823; Council Minutes, 29 April 1823, RG1, vol 214.5A; James Stewart to Peleg Wiswall, 10 April 1823, MG 1, vol 980, No 86; William Blowers Bliss to Henry Bliss, 27 March 1823, NSARM, Bliss Papers, MG1, vol. 1598, No 237. For his resignation, which the 1823 statute did not require, see MHA Directory 268.

[30] The colony was divided into three divisions, and a Chief Justice of the inferior courts appointed for each. The peculiar problems of Cape Breton were not present elsewhere, and the measure, which passed by just one vote in the Assembly, was widely excoriated as creating plum patronage posts for the legal profession: *Equal Administration of Justice Act*, SNS 1824, c 38. See generally JB Cahill and J Phillips, 'Origins to Confederation' in P Girard, J Phillips and JB Cahill (eds), *From Imperial Bastion to Provincial Oracle: the Nova Scotia Supreme Court, 1754–2004* (Toronto, ON, Osgoode Society and University of Toronto Press, 2004) 90–91.

[31] *Cape Breton Courts Act*, SNS 1823, c 33.

[32] *Marshall's Manual* (n 4) vi.

manuscript 'in part' and hastily, and thought it would be 'useful'. The committee based its recommendation to publish mainly on the fact that Marshall's experience made him the ideal person to write such a manual. The Assembly agreed to publish 500 copies,[33] a notable expenditure in a period when small road grants were continually fought over and given that, a few years earlier, nobody had contemplated offering public assistance for what is a much more profound work, Beamish Murdoch's *Epitome of the Laws of Nova Scotia*.[34] Nor, for that matter, was any public assistance given to another Nova Scotia manual published in the same year as Marshall, Pictou lawyer Daniel Dickson's guide for municipal officials,[35] or to Thomas Chandler Haliburton's 1829 *Historical and Statistical Account of Nova Scotia* – although the latter did receive a laudatory vote of thanks from the Assembly.[36] By February 1838, the *Manual* had been printed and was ready for distribution. The Assembly agreed to pay the printing costs – £289-2-3 – and a committee also suggested that Marshall was 'entitled to a reasonable compensation for the time bestowed in superintending . . . the printing'. It recommended £125, but the Assembly pared this down to £50. Advertisements for it appeared in local newspapers,[37] and copies were to be distributed to all clerks of the peace, the clerks given the job of selling them to JPs and any other interested parties.[38] Almost all of them were distributed, but as it turned out, the Assembly had a lot of difficulty over the next few years collecting on payments from the clerks.[39]

The *Manual* began with a brief seven-page preface, which tells us a good deal about his motivation for publishing the work. He saw the local administration of the law in the hands of the JPs as largely inadequate. The 'greatest civil blessings' which any society could have, he asserted, 'are a wise and just system of Laws' and 'their enlightened and faithful administration'.[40] Nova Scotia had the first, in large measure, but the first alone was not enough. What was required was 'the wise and vigilant application' of the law, which would not only produce a good effect in itself, but would also make the law become 'generally known and most truly appreciated'. The colony lacked such a 'wise and vigilant application',

[33] For all this, see Marshall to Sir Rupert George, 11 March 1837, and Committee Report, *Assembly Journals*, 1837, Appendix 45 and 55; *Assembly Journals*, 18, 23, and 27 March 1837.

[34] *Epitome of the Laws of Nova Scotia*, 4 vols (Halifax, NS, Howe, 1832–33). See P Girard, 'Themes and Variations in Early Canadian Legal Culture: Beamish Murdoch and His Epitome of the Laws of Nova Scotia' (1993) 11 *Law and History Review* 101. See also Girard's contribution to this collection.

[35] *A Guide to Town Officers, Shewing Their Appointment, Duties, Liabilities and Privileges, According to the Laws of This Province* (Pictou, NS, Pictou Bee, 1837). As its name suggests, this was not a JP manual, but a brief, 200-page guide for municipal officials – overseers of the poor, assessors of poor rates, county treasurers, surveyors of highways, fence viewers, pound keepers, inspectors and weighers of beef etc.

[36] *Historical and Statistical Account of Nova Scotia* (Halifax, NS, Howe, 1829); *Assembly Journals*, 27 March 1829.

[37] See *Novascotian*, 8 March 1838.

[38] For all this, see Committee Report, 21 February 1838, *Assembly Journals*, 1838, Appendix 34; *Assembly Journals*, 7, 17, and 22 February, and 11 April, 1838.

[39] See *Assembly Journals*, 1839, Appendix 14, and 1843, Appendix 62; *Assembly Journals*, 30 March 1839, 14 February 1842, 4 and 7 March 1843, and 12 March 1845; *Novascotian*, 3 March 1842, 13 and 20 March 1843, and 24 March 1845; and RG 1, vol 278.5, No 2.

[40] *Marshall's Manual* (n 4) iii. Other quotations in this paragraph and the next are from iv–vi.

and it needed 'a more extended diffusion of the knowledge of the Laws . . . and with regard to many of them, a more extensive and active application'. Its legal system had 'a very prevailing and injurious defect' – that 'the first steps in any criminal procedure, or the summary execution of legislative enactments, depend on persons in the Commission of the Peace, or other local officers'. The JPs were inadequate for this task, although their faults were not, he insisted, due to any 'criminal intention or neglect'. Rather, they lacked the advantages of English magistrates, where 'a knowledge of the laws . . . are perpetuated from one generation to another', and where JPs are either 'persons of good and liberal education' and/or men 'so wealthy and independent in their circumstances, as to be able to afford leisure for acquiring the requisite knowledge'.

A variety of reasons explained why matters were so different in the colony. Immigration and frequent migration meant that the local population was both polyglot and unversed in the traditions of the English law. And it was from this motley collection that JPs had necessarily to be chosen. And, as noted in the introduction, he believed that the problem of their lack of education in the law was compounded by their unwillingness and in some cases inability to develop that knowledge. Even when they were so willing, they had no reference books to work from. There were English works, but they were 'voluminous and expensive', and 'can but rarely be procured in this country'. Moreover, they were not particularly useful, containing no references to provincial statutes. And JPs rarely had a complete collection of those statutes anyway, with volume one especially being very hard to find.[41] The result of all these problems was that magistrates were 'generally uninformed' about their duties, and 'very frequently, when applied to, delay or decline to act' either from ignorance or from fear of making a mistake.

There followed some 600 pages taken up with 135 articles, beginning with 'Absentees' and ending, as did Burn, with 'Wreck'. It was thus a much smaller work than Burn, which in 1825 ran to five volumes and contained 251 titles. Most of the topics were legal terms – assault and battery, clerk of peace, indictment and witnesses. Others were social categories – beef and pork, highways, soldiers and taverns. Some of the entries were as short as one to two pages – absentees, blasphemy, bricks, freestone, lighthouses, partition, thistles and wife – most were three to six pages – accessary [*sic*], carriages, fires, revenue and warrant. Some were much longer; bail occupied 13 pages, rates 15, justices of the peace 20, seamen 21, spirituous liquors and bastards 25 each, evidence 31, poor 36 and summary trials 43. Reflecting the differences between high and low law, the number of pages devoted to a subject reflected its importance to a JP, and to ordinary inhabitants, not necessarily its 'seriousness' as normally measured or assumed. Thus the title 'burning', less than a page, simply reproduced the provincial statutory section on arson, making it a capital offence, and then stated that a JP's duty

[41] By the 'first' volume Marshall was presumably referring to the early-nineteenth-century compilation published by Richard John Uniacke, covering the period from 1758 to 1804 (generally known as *Uniacke's Statutes*). This was supplemented by three further collections, but there was no statutory consolidation until 1851.

when the offence was alleged was simply to take examinations and commit the accused to prison to await the next sitting of the NSSC.[42] In contrast, the title 'Rates', concerning county and district taxation, in which the maximum penalty was a £10 fine, occupied over 14 pages. As voluminous as the *Manual* was, it did not cover JPs' duties when they were sitting as sessions judges. Marshall averred that this was unnecessary, principally because all Sessions Courts were presided over by legal professionals like himself.[43] Ironically, Marshall's criticisms of JPs mirrored aspects of the critique made by many Assemblymen in the later 1830s' debates about whether the ICCPs should be abolished. The lay judges that made up such courts, they complained, were ignorant of the law and adjudication lacked uniformity across the colony as a result.[44]

Marshall summarised the 'plan' of the *Manual*: 'It professes to combine the Common and Statute Law of England, with all our own Legislative Enactments, relating, or in any way referring to the office and duties of a Justice of the Peace in this Province'.[45] The typical arrangement for each article bore this out. Each began with general statements of principle, usually citing Burn and perhaps other leading English authorities – Hale, State Trials, Coke, Hawkins, etc. When the article became more detailed, it referred also to local statutes. Thus the entry on 'Bail', after defining it by quoting Burn, listed offences for which JPs could not give bail, those where they could do so in their discretion, and those where they ought to. There was extensive reference to local criminal statutes, intertwined with English authority for offences which were essentially common law. Some titles referred purely to local sources. The first, for example, on absentees, was about the obligation on absentee proprietors to pay their proportion of local taxes and to perform statute labour. The only references here were to provincial statutes. Indeed the longest title, 'Summary Trials', was entirely based on colonial law, for it covered the JPs' small debt jurisdiction. Nova Scotia had introduced summary jurisdiction for small debts as early as the 1750s, and though no such statute was ever made permanent, the legislation was constantly renewed and at times amended to increase the limits for summary jurisdiction.[46] Until 1837, the year of the *Manual*'s publication, the governing statute was one passed in 1822, which gave one JP jurisdiction in debts up to £3 and two JPs the right to hear a case for as much as £5.[47] A statute of 1837, passed a few weeks after the Assembly had agreed to print the *Manual*, raised the two JPs' limit to £10 and presumably required some immediate editing of the *Manual*.[48] Interestingly, another 1837 statute kept the limits of summary jurisdiction in Cape Breton at the old maximum; whether Marshall had anything to do with this continuing restriction on Cape Breton JPs,

[42] See similarly the entries for 'Burglary', 'Homicide', 'Maim' and 'Rape'.
[43] *Marshall's Manual* (n 4) vii–viii.
[44] See B Miller and J Phillips, 'Too Many Courts and Too Much Law: The Politics of Judicial Reform in Nova Scotia, 1830–1841' *Law and History Review* (forthcoming, 2011).
[45] *Marshall's Manual* vii. Other quotations in this paragraph are from ix.
[46] See generally Cahill and Phillips, 'Origins to Confederation' (n 30) 73 and 93–94.
[47] *Summary Trial of Actions Act*, SNS 1822, c 30.
[48] *Summary Trial of Actions Act*, SNS 1837, c 60.

and consequent extra business for the ICCPs in which he presided, is unknown.[49] The addition of this topic, and the omission of specifically English titles from Burn, such as baron court, carrots, common prayer, egyptians, gleaning, leet, game and shire hall constituted perhaps the largest difference between Marshall and his English model.

Many titles also contained forms – informations, summonses, oaths, recognisances, etc. Overall it was, Marshall insisted, a book on which 'full reliance' may be placed as to 'accuracy', for he had 'again and again, carefully and minutely examined and collated' all relevant local statutes. Such a confident, one might say arrogant, assertion presumably had much to do with the intended audience. It was not its job or within its capabilities to question anything in the guide, but to obey the instructions to the letter.

It is difficult to find large themes in this, or perhaps any other, JP manual. One cannot derive a person's understanding of the nature of law and its taxonomies from an alphabetical organisation. As with encyclopaedia and dictionary, alphabetical organisation is a method of facilitating an otherwise untutored reader's access, and in that sense is about the user, not the author. Like all JP manuals, therefore, Marshall assumed his readers would or could not work from 'large' legal categories, such as 'civil liability' or 'court procedure' but from small and very particular topics. If Burn believed that his English gentry or professional JPs needed this organisation, how much more would it appeal to Marshall given what we have seen of his views on local magistrates? Indeed, in addition to lamenting the lack of knowledge and education of JPs in the preface, Marshall constantly returned to the theme in substantive titles. The longest title, on summary civil process, began by noting that very few justices were 'even generally versed in the various branches of the law'.[50]

A few other points bear mentioning. First, unlike English manuals such as Burn, Marshall's did not expound separately at the beginning of his work on the history of the office of JP, nor discuss the relationship between the JP's power as leader of the community and his power as an officer of the law.[51] Marshall was not much interested in constitutional and political history, his was an instructional guide, pure and simple, written for a class of people desperately in need, in his view, of instruction. 'Justices of the Peace' was simply another title, not a subject dealt with separately and generally in the introduction, as it was in Burn.[52]

Second, and a related point, *Marshall's Manual* left very little to the JPs' discretion. Most titles contained a section on 'Directions', which stressed the mandatory nature of both duties and procedures, and even apart from this he frequently added admonitions on the need to observe all mandatory duties. Marshall de-emphasised discretion as much as possible, and in some cases positively preached against it. In his discussion of JPs' jurisdiction in small debts, for example, he

[49] *Summary Trial of Actions in the Island of Cape Breton Act*, SNS 1837, c 59.

[50] *Marshall's Manual* (n 4) 486.

[51] On the changing image of the JP in English manuals, see Landau, *Justices of the Peace* (n 7) 336–41.

[52] *Marshall's Manual* 259–78.

stressed that they 'are not empowered to determine according to what *they* deem to be equitable, but are to decide agreeably to the same rules of law which govern in the highest Courts'.[53] Third, and perhaps consistently with his personality, discussed in more detail below, *Marshall's Manual* did not limit itself to citing the relevant law, or even to carping constantly on the need to follow procedures to the letter. He also offered his opinions and advice quite freely on matters not limited to law enforcement and which also betrayed his broader political views. The 'Absentee' provision for example, the first in the book, advised JPs that the statute was to be 'universally and strictly carried into effect'. Not only would doing so 'enforce . . . just contribution to public charges', it would 'have a tendency to induce them [absent proprietors] to take more prompt and effectual means for the sale or improvement of their lands'.

By the early 1840s, all of the copies of the first edition had been distributed or otherwise sold,[54] and a second edition was published in 1846, an event which brought Marshall a vote of thanks in the Assembly for 'the very laudable and laborious effort he has made to aid Justices of the Peace'.[55] The second edition was essentially the same as the first, although obviously updated. The only substantial difference was the inclusion in it of a section on the conduct of the Sessions, which were no longer presided over by divisional Chief Justices, those positions having been abolished, as discussed below.

The fact that all first edition copies were taken up and a new edition required indicates that *Marshall's Manual* was considered a valuable document, and the limited evidence we have suggests that it was avidly consulted and used for many decades. I have located 25 copies of the first edition in Canadian and American libraries, and 15 copies of the second.[56] They show that JPs across the colony/province used the manual – in Halifax, in central Nova Scotia (Truro and Horton), in the Annapolis region (Annapolis, Bridgetown and Kentville), on the south shore (New Dublin, Port Medway and Shelburne), in the west (Yarmouth, Digby and Smith's Cove), towards the east (Pictou) and, appropriately, Cape Breton Island. Some descended within families as sons succeeded fathers in the commission, others were passed from one local JP to another, including one with six JPs' names from Lunenburg.[57] Many have quite extensive annotations, underlinings, check marks, etc, although it should also be recorded that two were used as flower presses. One extensively annotated copy of the first edition was still in use in the 1860s, lovingly preserved at the time despite being well thumbed; it remains in excellent condition.[58] At least two were used by lawyers, John Orlando

[53] Ibid 6 (emphasis in original). Other quotations in this paragraph are from 1–2.

[54] *Novascotian*, 3 March 1842; 'Advertisement Concerning the Second Edition' 2nd edn, xi.

[55] *Assembly Journals*, 20 March 1846.

[56] 14 of these copies are in Nova Scotian libraries, 16 in other Canadian locations and the remainder (10) are held in American repositories.

[57] Halifax Public Library. For a 'family' succession, see the copy of the first edition at the Killam Library, Dalhousie University, Special Collection, which has the names of Thomas, Jonathan and WH Moody in it.

[58] Killam, *Library, Special Collections* (Halifax, NS, Dalhousie University).

of Bridgetown and Charles Tanner of Pictou; the former's annotations include references to Murdoch's *Epitome* and other legal texts.[59]

V. CONNECTING THE MAN AND HIS MISSION: MARSHALL AND HIS MANUAL

Marshall devoted a good deal of time and effort to the production of his manual, especially given that its publication was uncertain and probably impossible without legislative support, and he made no money from it. He surely did so in part for the reasons he gave in his preface and in his communications with the Assembly – he wanted to provide a valuable service to the colony by improving the standard of practice of its principal, in number, legal officials. But it is possible that his experience and belief system gave him additional motivation. It must be borne in mind that Marshall wrote the Manual, and penned his words about JPs, after serving for a decade as the Chief Justice of the inferior courts on Cape Breton, and thus after widespread and constant interactions with local JPs. His experience thus likely gave him a very low opinion of the Cape Breton magistrates. He regularly gave, and was asked for, his opinion on who should be made a JP or removed from the commission, or about their performance of their duties.[60] In 1834 he wanted one Norman McLeod removed as unsuitable, 'having sanctioned the illegal and cruel act of mutilating a boy by cutting off a part of one of his ears'. Marshall added that 'His being a Minister of Religion may be considered as a further objection' – presumably an objection to the act of maiming as much as to a place on the commission. Another JP, he noted in the same report, had engaged in 'riotous proceedings' while yet another had married people without authority.[61]

Although his low opinion of JPs was no doubt derived from Marshall's general interactions with these kinds of individuals, we know also of at least one particular case in which he had a long-running feud with a prominent JP and member of the local elite, and this case suggests that, in part, Marshall's project was an effort to establish himself as the major figure on the island. His local disputant was another prominent member of Cape Breton's small elite, Richard Gibbons Junior, the son of his namesake who was Chief Justice of the independent colony, and a barrister and JP residing in Sydney. He had been attorney-general of Cape Breton before annexation, and one of the leaders of the movement to have the colony granted

[59] Held at the Mount Allison University Library, Sackville, NB.

[60] See, for example, RG 1, vol 253, Nos 80, 83; vol 252, Nos 104, 131 and 170.

[61] Report Concerning Justices of the Peace, 12 June 1834, in RG 1, vol 282, No 109. McLeod certainly was a domineering sectarian leader who ruled his followers with an iron fist: see F McPherson, *Watchman Against the World: the Remarkable Journey of Norman McLeod and His People from Scotland to Cape Breton Island to New Zealand* (Breton Books, NS, Wreck's Cove, 1993).

an Assembly.[62] After annexation he was prominent in the local secessionist movement. The first visible manifestation of the animosity between him and Marshall was a dispute between them when sitting at Sessions, over who should address the Grand Jury. A little later the two clashed over a dispute between Gibbons and the local deputy-postmaster, whom Gibbons accused of opening a letter addressed to him. When Marshall wrote a report exonerating the postal official, Gibbons posted notices around the town and on Marshall's front gate deprecating him. Marshall recommended, and the executive concurred, that Gibbons be removed from the commission of the peace.[63] The two crossed swords again, in 1840, when Marshall suspended Gibbons from practising before the Cape Breton inferior courts as a barrister, which led to a further imbroglio.[64]

The dispute with Gibbons, which seems remarkably petty in itself, shows the imperious side of Marshall's character. In his years on the bench, he came to consider himself a kind of unofficial leader of the island, so that a challenge from someone like Gibbons, who was not an 'ignorant' country justice but an educated and influential man, may have been seen as a thorough-going affront to his authority. Within the legal system he dominated all proceedings, not just because he presided over the inferior courts, but also because the Supreme Court on circuit played a very small role in the administration of justice. For a variety of reasons, NSSC dockets on the island were always very light. Civil litigants had a choice of the NSSC on circuit or the ICCP, for the two had largely concurrent civil jurisdiction, and the vast majority preferred the local court. Marshall later claimed that in one seven-year period there was only one civil suit brought in the NSSC on the island. Moreover, he also tried most serious criminal cases. The Sessions did not have jurisdiction to do so, but most such cases were tried on special commission with Marshall presiding.[65] Any community wanting a JP appointed or individual wanting to be on the commission went through him.[66] To all this must be added the fact that he was the only Master in Chancery on the Island, and handled a number of equity cases as well.[67]

[62] See RJ Morgan, 'Richard Gibbons Senior' *DCB Online*, and 'Separatism in Cape Breton' in K Donovan (ed), *Cape Breton at 200: Historical Essays in Honour of the Island's Bicentennial 1785–1985* (Sydney, NS, University of Cape Breton Press, 1985).

[63] See Marshall to Sir Rupert George, 11 June 1834, RG 1, vol 282, No 108; Report concerning Justices of the Peace, 12 June 1834, ibid No 109; Richard Gibbons to Sir Rupert George, 25 June 1834, ibid No 117; and the various documents in RG 1, vol 253, Nos 62–71. Marshall may have been justified if he was correct that Gibbons 'scarcely ever acts as a justice', and was almost deaf. But his main reason for recommending removal was his 'recent conduct towards the President of the Sessions'.

[64] Richard Gibbons to Brenton Halliburton, 16 January 1840, MG 1, vol 334, No 43; Council Minutes, 16 April, 5 May and 5 June 1840, RG1, vol 214.5D, 78, 80 and 84.

[65] For more on the differential patterns of court use, see Miller and Phillips, 'Too Many Courts and Too Much Law' (n 44). See also Marshall to Lord Stanley, 3 Jan 1842, MG 1, vol 1282, No 10. The fact that Marshall handled almost all civil work is borne out in James Stewart to Peleg Wiswall, 28 August 1826, MG 1, vol 980, No 110. For explanations of this pattern of civil litigation, see Girard and Phillips, 'Courts, Communities and Communication' (n 26). For Marshall and special commissions see, inter alia, RG 1, vol 252, No 120; MG 1, vol 1455, No 6.

[66] See RG 1, vol 253, No 80, 83 and 113; vol 252, No 104, 122, 131 and 170.

[67] He was made a Master in Chancery on 30 September 1823: MG 1, vol 1282, No 22. For papers on the various Chancery cases, see ibid No 216–46, 249–51, 255–58 and 260.

In addition, outside the legal system he saw himself as occupying a preferred place in island society. In a later Memorial detailing his services, one intended to secure for himself a seat on the NSSC, he claimed that during his term in office 'many public Matters connected with the local affairs of the Island were referred to him by the Lieutenant Governor, with whom [Marshall] . . . held a continued correspondence both of a public and a Confidential nature'. Judging by the voluminous collection of official and semi-official documents preserved in his private papers, covering a host of general administrative matters such as division of districts into townships, the establishment of post offices, the state of roads, as well, of course, as the appointment of magistrates, this was not an idle boast. He was very much the central government's man on the island. Among other things, he reported extensively on JPs, as noted above, and on particular issues as they arose, such as the seizure of two American schooners in 1839, and the distress suffered by emigrants to Cape Breton in the late 1820s and again in 1836.[68]

Both his dominance of the island's court system, and his connections to the executive in Halifax, made him unwilling to brook any challenges to his authority, a trait fuelled by another facet of his character – his rigid sabbatarianism. He kept a record of his many convictions for sabbath-breaking, acting as a sole JP and in most cases as the only witness.[69] His reputation for such ardency spread wide. As NSSC judge James Stewart put it, 'Marshall will not allow an old woman to chop a stick of wood for her fire on Sunday'.[70] He was, of course, acting within his authority in doing this. As his lengthy title on 'Lord's Day' stated, a conviction could be obtained before just one JP and 'upon view of any' JP.[71]

Marshall was also motivated by a cause which had animated him for some years, that of law reform. The 1820s and early 1830s had seen a number of abortive attempts to 'clean up' the provincial statute book, both to clarify which laws were in force and which were not, and to effect substantive change. The former problem resulted from the fact that while some statutes were passed as perpetual, others were passed with a life of a year, or three, or such. A large amount of the time in any legislative session was given over to passing statutes to continue statutes previously passed, and there was often uncertainty about which were still in force. Indeed Marshall's first venture into legal publishing was an 1826 *Index to the Statutes of the Province of Nova Scotia.* He was proud of this work, which was intended to guide a reader through the statute book until it could properly be 'cleaned up'. Law reformers like Marshall thought they had won their battle in 1832 when the Assembly appointed a reform commission to study both court procedures and substantive law.[72] Although the commissioners – leading

[68] See MG 1, vol 1282. See also the reports in RG 1, vol 253, No 35 and 36; vol 252, No 51, 56, 84, 88, 89, 97–99; RG 1, vol 282, No 51; *Assembly Journals*, 10 March 1829.

[69] MG1, vol 1283, No 468.

[70] James Stewart to Peleg Wiswall, 28 August 1826, MG 1, vol 980, No 110.

[71] *Marshall's Manual* (n 4) 299.

[72] See *An Act for appointing Commissioners to inquire into, and report upon, the expediency of reforming the practice and proceedings of Courts of Law and Equity, and revising and consolidating the Laws of the Province*, SNS 1832, c 42.

lawyers SGW Archibald, William Hill, Beamish Murdoch and James Boyle Uniacke – consulted widely, they produced only minor recommendations on the court system and structure. On substantive law, it recommended more, including consolidation of the criminal statutes and a reduction in the number of capital crimes to those of 'an atrocious nature'. The commissioners also recommended a general statutory consolidation, which, by leaving out repealed and amended statutes, would reduce the statute book from 1559 pages to 977.[73] None of this was acted on in the short or medium term however: the criminal law was not reformed until the early 1840s, and the province's first set of revised statutes came out in 1851.

Marshall's preface reminded his readers of the failure of law reform: 'on several subjects, in which the duties of Justices are involved, our Statutes are in such a defective, or intricate state, that it requires the close application of a person skilled and exercised in legal investigations, to reconcile or rightly understand them'.[74] He had hoped that statutory revision would take place before his manual was published – he claimed he had postponed publication for some time in the hope that it would – but it did not happen. He lamented in particular the state of the criminal law, even though the issue was largely irrelevant to the *Manual*, which dealt with offences well outside the reach of the capital statutes. When he praised the content of provincial law in order to make a disparaging comparison with its administration, he nonetheless added that 'some parts of our Legal Code will admit of considerable correction and improvement'. Later in the preface, in what he admitted was a 'digression', he insisted that reform was especially needed in 'some of the higher branches of our Criminal Code', because in some cases 'the severity of the punishment appears disproportionate to the offence'. He provided examples, and offered one of the standard critiques of capital code reformers in Britain and North America in the early decades of the nineteenth century – that nobody convicted of an offence such as breaking down a dyke would ever actually be hanged, and thus the law both provided no deterrent punishment while simultaneously making itself look ridiculous.

Marshall's Manual can thus be seen as a bid by Marshall to establish himself as a leading legal figure in the colony. In this regard, he took pains to distinguish it from another recent notable publication, Halifax lawyer Beamish Murdoch's *Epitome of the Laws of Nova Scotia*. Although the *Epitome* was 'valuable and generally useful', it was not designed to assist local JPs, because it was 'chiefly an exhibition of our Statutes in general', and unsuitable as a guide for JPs where much of their duties and powers arose from English law, common and statute.[75] This, it must be said, is hardly fair to Murdoch, but Marshall was obviously intent on distinguishing his own work.

[73] See 'Report of Commissioners into Courts and Law, 1834' *Assembly Journals*, 1834, Appendix 59.
[74] *Marshall's Manual* (n 4) v. Other quotations in this paragraph are from iii and vi–vii.
[75] Ibid v.

VI. CONCLUSION AND POSTSCRIPT

I began this chapter by contrasting a JP manual and what we typically think of as a 'treatise'. My analysis here has highlighted another distinction between the two, in the relationship within each between author and reader. A treatise is intended to be authoritative, but persuasively so. The reader needs to be convinced by argument and evidence. A JP manual, certainly in Marshall's conception, does not persuade, it instructs, it does not rely for its authority on argument, but on assertion. It is a strategic production, with the explicit purpose of disciplining and educating the relatively unlettered in one part of the colony while bringing them the rule of law in the form of central statutory authority and direction. Not all legal instruction manuals emanate from a personality as domineering as Marshall, and not all likely have his didactic and peremptory tone. But all are intended to instruct, and almost all are intended to guide and instruct non-lawyers. A remarkable amount of our legal literature historically has been written for non-lawyers, and yet we know relatively little about it.[76] We ought, this chapter suggests, to know more.

As for Marshall, his 'manual period' was probably his best as far as making a mark on the society he lived in was concerned. If indeed he was a kind of 'lord of Cape Breton' in the 1830s, and his JP guide an enduring legacy, his career thereafter was marked by disappointment. In 1841 a radical reform of the colony's court system saw the ICCPs abolished, the four divisional chief justices pensioned off, and all civil cases above those triable by JPs in petty sessions transferred to the NSSC. Marshall very much wanted the extra place on the NSSC bench that was created to take on the additional workload, but the job went elsewhere. He lived out his years in Halifax, writing and speaking a great deal about temperance,[77] sabbatarianism[78] and religion generally.[79] He also travelled widely in North America and Europe lecturing on temperance. He was, said the *Novascotian*, Nova Scotia's 'Temperance Apostle'.[80] His obituary defined his character rather well:

> A Puritan of the Puritans himself, he regarded worldly amusement in general as snares of the devil, and being utterly indifferent to popularity, he attacked right and left with a directness of speech in the cause of morality and righteousness . . . He was a prodigious writer on a multitude of subjects, never hesitating to attack what he thought was wrong. He was stern and uncompromising, nevertheless he contributed of his limited means to all objects of charity and philanthropy, and he died as he had lived, in the midst of a true and noble fight.[81]

[76] For Canada, see only M Leslie, 'Reforming the Coroner: Death Investigation Manuals in Ontario, 1863–1894' (2008) 100 *Ontario History* 221.

[77] *No Bible Sanction for Drinking Intoxicating Liquors, but the Support of the Total Abstinence Cause a Christian Duty: Addressed to Ministers and Members of Churches* (Edinburgh, Armour, 1848). For his lectures, see Novascotian, 24 March 1845 and 2 March 1846.

[78] *The Sabbath and the Bible: Moral law, Permanent Authority* (Halifax, NS, Bowes, 1872).

[79] This was largely pamphlet literature; 11 titles are listed in the Nova Scotia Archives Library, written between 1865 and 1878.

[80] *Novascotian*, 2 March 1846.

[81] *Acadian Recorder*, 7 April 1880, cited in Thomas, 'John George Marshall' (n 20).

11

Commentary: Effects of Scale: Toward a History of the Literature of Law

CHRISTOPHER TOMLINS*

LIKE THE EDITORS of this volume, Angela Fernandez and Markus Dubber, I think it appropriate to begin with the ideas that sparked the October 2010 Toronto Workshop, 'The Treatise in Legal History', where most of the chapters assembled here first saw the light of day.

In 1976, Morton Horwitz offered pithy, pungent observations on 'the importance of legal treatises for research in legal history'.[1] The treatise, he held, was an essential but sadly neglected source for legal history.[2] By comparing successive editions of treatises, scholars could chart transformations in legal doctrine. The first appearance of a treatise in an area of law was a marker of especial significance: 'when the first treatise in a particular field was written . . . is almost always an important clue to when a specific subject area has begun to crystallize'.[3] Hardly known in the Anglo-American legal world before Blackstone's *Commentaries*, the rise of the treatise was attributable to nineteenth-century jurists' 'deep and mystical devotion . . . to the proposition that law was a science and that most of its basic problems could be solved through the intensive application of reason'.[4] Common lawyers' faith in the law's capacity to correct itself led them to use the treatise as a scientific systematising device, a trump played repeatedly to ward off codification's threat to the juridical elite's monopoly of law-making. The decline of the treatise in the twentieth century was attributable to Legal Realism's determined twentieth-century corrosion of that faith. Horwitz's conclusion – that 'a history of legal treatises is the single best way to grasp the structure of growth and decline in various areas of . . . law'[5] – was shaped by his own developing interests in writ-

* Chancellor's Professor of Law, School of Law, University of California, Irvine. My thanks to Angela Fernandez and Markus Dubber for inviting me to participate in this endeavour, and to Angela Fernandez for her comments on the first draft of this chapter.

[1] MJ Horwitz, 'Part III –Treatise Literature' (1976) 69 *Law Library Journal* 460.

[2] But see R Pound, *The Formative Era of American Law* (Boston, MA, Little, Brown and Company, 1938) 138–72 (offering a brief history of 'doctrinal writing' in the nineteenth-century US).

[3] Horwitz (n 1) 461.

[4] Ibid 460.

[5] Ibid 461.

ing legal history as intellectual history, 'the rise and fall of paradigm structures of thought', a project that over the following 15 years would solidly identify 'critical legal history' with the history of legal doctrine.[6]

Characteristically, Horwitz's comments are both keenly perceptive and somewhat narrowly drawn. First and most importantly, they emphasise the functions of the legal treatise rather than its form. The treatise, for example, was a neglected *source* for the writing of legal history, not itself a subject *in* legal history. Second, in so far as they consider the form, Horwitz's comments define the treatise as a rather particular kind of artifact – a work of scholarship produced by scholars motivated by a deep belief in 'the logic and internal consistency of legal doctrine' who engage in the reproduction of that belief through 'compilation, classification, and systematization'.[7] Horwitz evinces both a genial contempt for the belief system that produced the grand treatises of the nineteenth and early twentieth centuries and a certain wistful regret that the contemporary legal scholar could put nothing in the treatise's place other than 'mostly worthless casebooks.'[8] Considered simply as a legal monument, Samuel Williston's 1920 *Treatise on Contracts* (which Horwitz identifies as the last of its kind) appears to haunt its critic.

Many of the individual authors in this collection have been informed by Horwitz's short essay; collectively they have avoided its limitations. Here, the legal treatise has been examined carefully in form as well as function – indeed, the interrelationship of form and function is a key theme. The definition of 'treatise', collectively adopted here, too, is roomy – these essays traverse virtually all forms of legal literature other than case reports. Though considered by some to belong in the genre of 'institutes' rather than treatises, for example, Blackstone's and Kent's *Commentaries* are both here (Parker and Girard). So are classic early nineteenth-century American 'first' treatises like Tapping Reeve's *The Law of Baron and Femme; of Parent and Child; of Guardian and Ward; of Master and Servant; and of the Powers of Courts of Chancery* (Fernandez) and later jewels of the genre on its way to dominance like Story's *Commentaries on Conflicts* (Baker). So are the familiar multi-edition classics of English law, many now well into their second century, such as Pollock's *Principles of Contract at Law and in Equity* and Anson's *Principles of the English Law of Contract* (Waddams). But so are an obscure Justice of the Peace (JP) manual from Nova Scotia (Phillips), Thomas Macaulay's Indian Penal Code (IPC) (Wright), commission reports (Wright), assorted handbooks, digests and abridgements (Farmer) and even a glimpse of a law dictionary (Farmer).

Many of these forms of legal literature have been ruled out of the definition of treatise by earlier commentators (and indeed by some of this collection's authors in their individual capacity; for example Fernandez, Phillips and Campbell). Thus, the late Brian Simpson argued in 1981 that a treatise 'is a monograph, purporting

[6] RW Gordon, 'Critical Legal Histories' (1984) 36 *Stanford Law Review* 57, 116, 117–25 (identifying Critical Legal History with the history of legal doctrine).
[7] Horwitz (n 1) 460.
[8] Ibid.

to deal only with a single branch of the law that is conceived of as possessing some quality of unity', or in other words not comprehensive, and that 'involves mainly substantive principles'.[9] Blackstone's *Commentaries* do not qualify; nor, it goes without saying, does a JP manual or a law dictionary. As Fernandez and Dubber affirm, however, it is advantageous to avoid too precise a definition of the object of our attention, and not simply because breadth accommodates the inevitable catholicity of a collection of essays. Breadth of definition allows us access to the quality of intertextuality that underscores the significance of the treatise as artifact. Treatises, it is clear, are conjoined with a wide variety of legal and other texts – successive editions of themselves, other treatises both foreign and domestic, case reports and statutes, reports of legislative hearings and debates, aids to practitioners and students. They exist in a world of newspapers, pamphlets and broadsides, testimony of local custom and knowledge, and literary works. They interact with a diversity of social and economic circumstances, political and religious movements, and ideologies. Whether in itself or in the companionship it seeks, the legal treatise cannot easily be contained within a single textual genre.

Like all other categories of legal text, treatises are sites for the production of knowledge; legal knowledge primarily, but even the most arid legal knowledge is hybrid – that is, it can be accounted historical, political, sociological, anthropological and economic knowledge too. And like all processes of knowledge production, the production of legal knowledge charts power and simultaneously seeks truth. As Mariana Valverde writes, 'if knowledge is power, so, too, are power relations also knowledge relations, truth relations'. She continues, 'if power works through knowledge, it should prove useful to undertake an examination of . . . legal events and processes that highlight the knowledge dimension.'[10] We discover from these essays that treatises represent a highly refined process of legal power-making and truth-seeking, a process that attempts to strain out as much of the clutter of quotidian discourses and competing knowledge forms as possible in the interests of creating a discrete expertise through which power can work that instructs how legal subjects are to be positioned on a given terrain in order to obtain a particular outcome.[11] We also discover that in enacting the specifically *legal* epistemology that appears to call them forth and to determine the form of knowledge they embody, treatises simultaneously 'act' in a rather different way too, as strategic interventions in the 'constitution, contestation, and circulation of truth in law or in respect to law'.[12] It is this combination of roles – the episte-

[9] AWB Simpson, 'The Rise and Fall of the Legal Treatise: Legal Principles and the Forms of Legal Literature' (1981) 48 *University of Chicago Law Review* 632, 633.

[10] M Valverde, *Law's Dream of a Common Knowledge* (Princeton and Oxford, Princeton University Press, 2003) 1.

[11] Note, for example, the observations of TFT Plucknett, quoted approvingly by Simpson, on the 'method' of the legal treatise. It 'begins with a definition of the subject matter, and proceeds by logical and systematic stages to cover the whole field. The result is to present the law in a strictly deductive framework, with the implication that in the beginning there were principles, and that in the end those principles were found to cover a large multitude of cases deducible from them.' TFT Plucknett, *Early English Legal Literature* (Cambridge, Cambridge University Press, 1958) 19, in Simpson (n 9) 633.

[12] Valverde (n 10) 1.

mological with the strategic – that the editors capture in their description of treatises as 'law books in action'. Collectively, finally, these essays confirm Valverde's contention that '[t]he epistemological workings of law . . . cannot be reduced to any one general thesis. *Different fields and situations exhibit different logics*'.[13] What matters most, we will see, is the scalar point in legal practice and culture at which the intervention that a treatise is designed to make takes place.[14]

We begin with Blackstone's *Commentaries on the Laws of England*, not because the *Commentaries* are the ur-text of the Anglo-American common law world – they are, although chronologically the honour belongs to Thomas Littleton's *Treatise on Tenures* –[15] but because, as Kunal Parker brilliantly demonstrates in his chapter 'Historicising Blackstone', the *Commentaries* have been a lively presence in that world ever since their first appearance in 1765–69. The question is how, and why. Like many of the treatises described in these chapters, the *Commentaries* have lived on after their first appearance and after their author's death in the form of continuous reinvention by successive editors: shaping and reshaping, cutting and replacing, revising, updating, brutally manhandling, retrofitting the original text – each successive iteration cancelling, as it were, the predecessor, attempting to consign it to death, assuming to itself the life-claim of the text, which continues to exist whether as *Argo* or as palimpsest continually erased and rewritten, so as to take over the work's soul. Parker contemplates a history of this process that would be told according to an artifact's transit from a state of active liveliness – as determined, for example, by the artifact's capacity to be of 'use' in the contexts into which it is inserted – to one of passivity, a representative of 'style', measured by its aesthetic rather than its practical qualities. He does not deny the truth of such an account. But he wishes to add to it a more disturbing observation; disturbing, that is, to historians who almost invariably assume that history is about change. He wants us to consider how the *Commentaries* have remained the same over time, and how, by obstinately remaining the same, resisting change, they require that we find ways to incorporate sameness and repetition – recurrence – into the project of writing a history of the legal treatise.

The *Commentaries* did not emerge out of thin air, but given the almost complete absence (apart from Littleton) of anything like them in English common law since the *De Legibus*, it seems worth considering how they came to be written in the first place.[16] Here Simpson assists us, for he points to Blackstone's foreignness to English common law, his civilian training and consciousness, as the

[13] Ibid 3 (emphasis added).

[14] On the significance of scalar variation to legal studies, see B de Sousa Santos, 'Law: A Map of Misreading. Toward a Postmodern Conception of Law' (1987) 14 *Journal of Law and Society* 279; A Riles, 'The View from the International Plane: Perspective and Scale in the Architecture of Colonial International Law' (1995) 6 *Law and Critique* 39.

[15] Simpson (n 9) 634–35.

[16] For the *De Legibus*, see *Bracton: De Legibus Et Consuetudinibus Angliæ* (*Bracton on the Laws and Customs of England attributed to Henry of Bratton, c. 1210–1268*) available at hlsl5.law.harvard.edu/bracton/ (accessed 7 May 2011).

source of Blackstone's extraordinary capacity to 'fly high'.[17] Becoming Vinerian professor, Blackstone the foreigner to the common law wrote the *Commentaries* to take English law into his charge. He could do so, it seems to me, unmuddled by the fears or favours of the common lawyer, which he had not imbibed, and thus produced *Commentaries* breathtakingly free of the common law's messy chaos, a renovation of the old Gothic castle for a new inhabitant (himself). Parker shows that Blackstone's remodelled common law was in its turn successively remodelled, in part regularly to restate it in light of new developments, but perhaps also in the service of reclaiming this civilian-inspired disquisition *for* common lawyers, *by* common lawyers.[18] Hence the cascading encrustations of new material barnacled onto and into Blackstone's spare, lean prose, successive attempts to complete the *Commentaries* by both updating and localising them, each rendered obsolete by the next. In England and in America, the *Commentaries* were turned from civilian institutes into something desperately attempting to be a practice manual.[19]

As obvious, perhaps most obviously in the United States, the *Commentaries* also became the bearer of successive legal-political ideologies, at first of law's progress and plasticity, later in the post-Civil War hands of Cooley and, later, Hammond of what look like 'germ' theories of legal origin and continuity.[20] It is significant, I think, that it was at this point that commentary on Blackstone's *style* began to surface in the United States to moderate the relentless updating of the text. As Parker argues, style was a signifier of sameness – of recurrence rather than difference, of endlessness. To this point the *Commentaries*' primary role as textual artifact had been as utilitarian bearer of successive layers of difference, through encrustation. I should like to propose that style – continuity and sameness – can also be understood as a form of use, one of considerable importance in the Reconstruction/post-Reconstruction United States. The fetishisation of Blackstone's style is a stance *against* a certain kind of plasticity or difference, for a way of understanding history not as change but continuity.[21] At a moment of revolutionary upheaval in the American republican polity, Blackstone becomes Burke. Style becomes useful. In point of fact, Parker argues, Blackstone's style had *always* been remarked upon, the point was always present. The separation of style from utility as distinct phenomena, however, does allow one to raise the ques-

[17] Simpson (n 9) 655, 658.

[18] On this point see P Girard, chapter 2 of this volume, p 44.

[19] This was, as Dirk Hartog has noted, exactly what lawyers wanted. H Hartog, *Man and Wife in America: A History* (Cambridge, MA, Harvard University Press, 2000) 16.

[20] On 'germ' theory, see GM Ostrander, 'Turner and the Germ Theory' (1958) 32 *Agricultural History* 258; P Novick, *That Noble Dream: the 'Objectivity Question' and the American Historical Question* (Cambridge and New York, Cambridge University Press, 1988) 80–84. For legal applications, see H Adams *et al*, *Essays in Anglo-Saxon Law* (Boston, MA, Little, Brown, and Company, 1876). On Cooley and common law continuity, see KM Parker, *Common Law, History, and Democracy in America, 1790–1900: Legal Thought Before Modernism* (Cambridge and New York, Cambridge University Press, 2011) 201–04. On Hammond, see D Rabban, *Law's History: Late Nineteenth-Century American Legal Scholarship and the Transatlantic Turn to History* (Cambridge University Press, forthcoming) Chapter 1.

[21] One might observe that producing the ever-same of the common law requires hard preservative work – pruning, weeding, grafting and so forth. One can think of editing as a form of cultivation – the constant work required to reproduce sameness.

tion, what if we instead thought of them as competing uses representing the tension of sameness and difference, continuity and change constantly at odds with each other – often a competition plainly on display within the same editor (for example, Henry St George Tucker)? In short, Parker's journey from style to style is also a journey from use to use.

Let me make two final points, distinct but related. First, Blackstone's style was of course the measure of his enduring uniqueness; it was grounded in his civilian foreignness, which could not be completed by any common lawyer. Even Bentham could praise Blackstone's style, perhaps confident that no successor common lawyer could perform the same feat. The common lawyer's inability to complete Blackstone helps explain the *Commentaries*' longevity. It may even explain the eventual decision to produce the text anew in its original pristine form.

Second, one of the uses of style in the *Commentaries*, it seems to me, is to achieve sameness in the form of translocality. It is clear that the *Commentaries* have enjoyed an enormous and enduring hold throughout the common law world in good part because of this particular instantiation of sameness, a common template into which the many provincial localities of the Anglosphere could plug their particularities. Philip Girard details precisely this phenomenon in his description of the localisation of Blackstone in the provincial law of late nineteenth-century Upper Canada.[22]

Girard's essay comparing the work of Blackstone, Kent and Beamish Murdoch performs as something of a hinge in this collection, in that it enables us to address the transition from 'institutes' to 'treatises' – or more precisely to register their comfortable intertextual coexistence. Though the first half of the nineteenth century is generally thought of as 'the rise of the treatise' as a distinct form of legal text, Girard contends that lawyers needed both institutes and treatises, and that the 'pantheistic' legal culture of the nineteenth century afforded ample room for both.[23] As I have already noted, the work of other authors here adds multiple additional genres of text to the Anglo-American legal universe.

Girard illustrates the continued salience of the institute genre by discussing three institutional works of marked significance: Blackstone's *Commentaries*, Kent's *Commentaries on American Law* and Murdoch's *Epitome of the Laws of Nova Scotia*. Though institutes and treatises blur at the edges in Girard's account, become interchangeable, in at least one important respect the institute stands out, meeting a 'need' for texts that undertake to call a society's legal character into focus. Institutes, I have argued, fly high. They aspire to convey law 'in its historical, political and cultural context',[24] creating legal knowledge but also embedding that knowledge in legal culture – or in Valverde's terms, in power relations. Girard underscores the strikingly different cultures of power apparent in the three works: Blackstone's common law culture was a national culture embedding the ascendancy of a WASP ruling class; Kent's was a defensive Whig barricade against

[22] On this point see Girard (n 18) pp 44–45.
[23] Ibid p 62.
[24] Ibid p 43.

Jacksonian democracy; Murdoch's a broadly-inclusive settler legal culture that denied the 'barely human' indigenous Mi'kmaq membership in its 'community of shared civic values'.[25] In each case the institute form enables the author to splice law into context in a fashion that creates an identity between them – law fused with the cultural landscape of choice in such a way as to naturalise it.

Girard's conclusions grant the first glimpse of the theme to which I have already adverted, and which other chapters will also allow us to explore, namely that the textual formulation of legal knowledge is also a strategic intervention in the formulation/reformulation of the scale of law. Each of Girard's authors chose a level of legal practice and culture at which to intervene to maximise their effect, the national (Blackstone, Kent), the provincial (Murdoch). In Blaine Baker's chapter we find Joseph Story doing the same. Story, Baker tells us, had a 'knack for seeing the architectonic structure of legal systems'.[26] And like Girard's authors, Story's 'seeing' was an act of creation rather than discovery, for as Baker goes on to recount, Story's legal architectonics clearly valorised a specific vision of legal culture – in his case a national culture built on 'the sovereignty and vested rights of individuals'. For Story, 'citizens and not states were the building blocks of his Republic, and institutions like the Constitution and the federal courts were said by him to have been conceived as the primary guardians of patrimonial and contractual entitlements'.[27] Here was a decidedly strategic intervention, an architecture for legal knowledge that spoke against the 'virulent states'-rights agitation that nationalists like Story regarded as a threat to the new Republic',[28] that marshaled legal science in the service of neutral (self-effacing) presentation of a specific legal culture as if it were a natural occurrence.

Story, says Baker, was not the inventor of the treatise. His nine 'plump' texts (a delightful adjective)[29] nevertheless mark an important moment of innovation in the legal history of the antebellum republic. Unsurprisingly, they included many 'firsts' in their number. First treatises were granted a particular significance by Horwitz in 1976. The subject is taken up again here by Roman Hoyos in his chapter on JA Jameson's 1867 treatise, *The Constitutional Convention.*

Whether intentionally or not, Hoyos slightly modifies Horwitz's theory, as it were, of the first treatise. Horwitz said its appearance was 'an important clue' – a sign – 'to when a specific subject area has begun to crystallize'. Hoyos, more directly, says a first treatise 'mark[s] the crystallisation' of a subject area.[30] I think there is an important difference here, not just of emphasis, but of function. Is the treatise a sign of crystallisation or its seed? Crystallisation may be a useful concept – but what is the precise nature of the phenomenon, and what is the precise relationship between a first treatise and the phenomenon of crystallisation?

[25] Ibid pp 57–58, 59.
[26] B Baker, chapter 4 of this volume, p 84.
[27] Ibid p 93.
[28] Ibid.
[29] Ibid p 103.
[30] Horwitz (n 1) 461; Roman J Hoyos, chapter 5 of this volume, p 108.

Hoyos answers these questions historically. In the American case, the early treatise writers – notably Story – were engaged in a project of '"rationalising" and "systematising"' the common law, reinterpreting it in light of the changes wrought by the American Revolution, and in creating an orderly common law vision, not only of law, but of the republic and its market economy as well.[31] Hoyos employs the pregnant and deeply useful idea that treatise writers created an 'underlying metaphysics'[32] of law – an American legal science – which, through 'the fabrication of dis/order' conjured law into existence in particular configurations and simultaneously disciplined (or policed) its use, 'governing the behaviour of legal actors, like justices of the peace, judges, legislators, or convention delegates'.[33] All this makes a great deal of sense. In particular, Hoyos allows us to pursue further the question at which Girard hints, the question of *scale*. The thrust of Horwitz's formulation notwithstanding, crystallisation of law is not some naturally-occurring process that a first treatise writer observes and records. The treatise writers did the crystallising. They did it to alter law's state – to create translocality and uniformity and rights-bearing individuals in the place of the locality and plurality and community that, Laura Edwards has recently shown, was both the post-revolutionary state of law and its prevailing condition.[34] This is a contest over the scale of law and the locale of authority, a contest that Hoyos demonstrates was consciously recognised by treatise writers, at least if Joel Bishop is any guide in defining treatise writers as that 'class of legal persons, whose especial duty it is to give reasons', and whose product was 'an orderly statement of those principles in which the law consists'.[35] Law, of course, exists at many different levels of scale; and so the issue is not one of rationalising a single domain of action but of exalting (indeed creating) one level of law over, or in place of, another. The underlying metaphysics of crystallisation are metaphysics of removal, almost invariably upward.

The chapters in this collection show that treatise writers had many motives – desires for income, career advancement, professional jealousy and so forth all stimulated the production of treatises. Hoyos suggests that an accumulation of material was an important precondition of their crystallising activity, and that from accumulation emerged a will to create order out of perceived disorder. Disorder, of course, lies in the eye of the beholder: in the American case, disorder was indeed an outcome of rapid accumulation of legal materials, and of a widening circumference of communication, but also of an absence of any systematic record of local or provincial law. What was the law? Only the locality knew. The default was

[31] Ibid pp 109, 112.

[32] Ibid p 117. (The phrase 'underlying metaphysics' is borrowed from W J Novak, *The People's Welfare: Law and Regulation in Nineteenth-Century America* (Chapel Hill, NC, University of North Carolina Press, 1996) 25).

[33] Ibid 110, 116.

[34] L F Edwards, *The People and Their Peace: Legal Culture and the Transformation of Inequality in the Post-Revolutionary South* (Chapel Hill, NC, University of North Carolina Press, 2009).

[35] JP Bishop, *The First Book of the Law; Explaining the Nature, Sources, Books, and Practical Applications of Legal Science, and Methods of Study and Practice* (Boston, MA, Little, Brown, & Company, 1868) 132, 137.

transatlantic – unacceptable to the locality, particularly after the Revolution. But although some writers desired to record locality – George Webb is one example before the Revolution, Zephaniah Swift the main example after – [36] overwhelmingly locality per se was identified with *disorder*. As the chapters by Fernandez, Girard and Baker show, Reeve, Kent and Story all deprecated multiplicity and provincialism and sought generality at a high scalar level of abstraction and interconnection, which they imagined and invented for themselves. In the same vein, Theophilus Parsons deprecated texts on maritime law that 'treated severally and disconnectedly, topics which in themselves were closely connected and needed the mutual illustration they could give each other'. The law of shipping and of marine insurance, for example, 'could not be learned fully and accurately excepting in their connection', even though 'these topics had been heretofore regarded as in so great a degree isolated and independent'.[37] Parsons' second assertion proves the lie of his first. Clearly shipping and marine insurance *could* be understood in isolation, because they had been. Parsons' 'connection' was not a clarification but an invention. Similarly, early nineteenth-century projects of manuscript statutory recovery and publication (for example William Waller Hening in Virginia, Thomas Cooper in South Carolina) *created* an authoritative corpus of provincial law at a scale that could supersede locality.[38]

'Crystallisation', therefore, is an induced process, the product of intellectual labour, 'the fabrication of order'.[39] How much so is demonstrated by Hoyos' specific example, Jameson's *Constitutional Conventions* (1867). Jameson did not react to an accumulation of material, observe incipient crystallisation under way, and record it. He invented the law of constitutional conventions.

The significance of Jameson's move to bring the constitutional convention 'within' law is clear, given the history of the convention. From ratification through the controversy over the Alien and Sedition Acts,[40] attempts to redress the Yazoo land fraud,[41] serial acts of state formation, the Nullification crisis,[42] the Dorr War,[43] Bleeding Kansas,[44] and secession, the constitutional convention had been

[36] G Webb, *The Office and Authority of a Justice of Peace* (Williamsburg, VA, William Parks, 1736); Zephaniah Swift, *A System of the Laws of the State of Connecticut: In Six Books* (Windham, CT, printed by John Byrne 1795–96).

[37] Theophilus Parsons, *A Treatise on Maritime Law, Including the Law of Shipping; the Law of Marine Insurance; and the Law and Practice of Admiralty* (Boston, MA, Little, Brown & Company, 1859) v, vi.

[38] See W Waller Hening, *The Statutes at Large*, 13 vols (Richmond, VA, 1809-); T Cooper and DJ McCord (eds), *The Statutes at Large of South Carolina, Edited Under Authority of the Legislature*, 10 vols (Columbia, SC, AS Johnson, 1836–41); Edwards (n 34) 36–40.

[39] M Neocleous, 'Theoretical Foundations of the 'New Police Science'' in MD Dubber and M Valverde (eds), *The New Police Science: the Police Power in Domestic and International Governance* (Stanford, CA, Stanford University Press, 2006) 27, 25–29.

[40] On which see C Tomlins, 'Republican Law' in E Gray and J Kamensky (eds), *Oxford Handbook of the American Revolution* (Oxford, Oxford University Press, 2013).

[41] Ibid.

[42] Ibid.

[43] On which see S Wilentz, *The Rise of American Democracy: Jefferson to Lincoln* (New York, NY, WW Norton & Company, 2005) 539–45.

[44] Ibid 715–19.

the embodiment of the sovereign people, 'beyond law's horizon'.[45] Conventions, being extra-legal, were by their very appearance disorderly, ill-defined. But, in addition, much of their active history had been one of popular disorder. Jameson fabricated that disorder into something more purposeful, a taxonomy of conventions that loosened their claim on sovereignty by confining sovereign action to a single and rare species of institution, the revolutionary convention, that was, by (his) definition, an extra-legal expression of sovereign violence. All other conventions became subaltern institutions, merely one functional department of constitutional government among many.

In nineteenth-century US terms, the underlying metaphysics of Jameson's project appear as a continuation of those of the earlier Federalist project of reducing all to law, relocating law in the hands of juridical elites, and resituating it at a remove from the locality. (This was not, Edwards demonstrates, exclusively a Federalist project by any means.) [46] Jameson's particular motivation in 'de-institutionalising and disembodying the people',[47] Hoyos suggests, lay in the use of the convention as the means to engineer Southern secession. It is worth noting, however, that his doctrine of limitations was pressed into service to discipline Reconstruction-era conventions.[48] Just as I have argued that Cooley's and, later, Hammond's turn away from the material retrofitting of Blackstone's substance emphasised an interest in a supervening legal continuity, in sameness over change, so Jameson supplied the means to establish additional modes of disciplining the people and their agents.

There are important resonances, it seems to me, between Roman Hoyos's chapter and that of Angela Fernandez. Fernandez discusses another first treatise – Reeve's *Law of Baron and Femme* (1816) – and asks essentially the same question of it: what are the underlying metaphysics of law as refracted through the legal consciousness of Tapping Reeve?[49]

Fernandez's curiosity is aroused for quite specific reasons. Why did Reeve countermand Blackstonian wisdom, itself grounded in *Coke Upon Littleton*, on the matter of coverture and married women's right to will property? A large part of her answer is supplied by an analysis of the social specifics of Tapping Reeve's life in early republic Connecticut (his kinship connections and religion), and from that analysis emerges a highly contextualised socio-metaphysical answer. In effect, Reeve was a feminist. As interesting, however, are those legal metaphysics: how was it that Reeve could offer the legal answer he did?

One possibility, the least interesting, is suggested by Nathan Dane's comment on the question in his *Abridgement*, in which he relied upon Reeve. 'The notion that a wife has no will, is a mere fiction without foundation in fact'.[50] One might

[45] Hoyos (n 30) p 118.
[46] Edwards (n 34) 3–25.
[47] Hoyos (n 30) p 125.
[48] Ibid p 126.
[49] A Fernandez, chapter 3 of this volume.
[50] N Dane, *A General Abridgement and Digest of American Law, with Occasional Notes and Comments*, vol 1 (Boston, MA, Cummings, Hilliard & Co, 1823) 371.

read this to indicate that Reeve had done no more than identify the principle underlying coverture as a legal fiction, which of course it was (no one thought a woman's will was physically absorbed into that of her husband).[51] A more interesting possibility is suggested by the coincidence of interests between the 'fading' New England Federalist, Reeve, in 1816, and the isolated anti-New Deal progressive-turned-reactionary, Roscoe Pound, a century later, whose interest in Reeve Fernandez remarks: both were motivated by a Federalist metaphysic. That is, at widely separated moments of headlong legal change (the early republic; the 1930s) both were tucking law away in a safe place, the taught tradition celebrated by Pound in his *Formative Era*, of which Reeve and his Litchfield law school was the first identifiable American incarnation.[52] The metaphysics of the taught tradition celebrated the authoritative juridical intellect, ascribing to it the sole capacity to declare what the law really was. And Reeve, dancing a fascinating two-step with the Democrat Zephaniah Swift, used *Baron and Femme* to declare it.

The character of what Reeve declared is becoming familiar to us: first translocality; second the mobilisation of favoured fictions against a fiction disfavoured. On the question that most interests Fernandez, the question of marital unity, Reeve announces he will approach the issue:

> independent of any authorities; as if it were a question wholly novel, respecting which there had been no adjudications, and was now to be decided upon principle. In such case, unshackled with precedents, nothing can govern us, in deciding the question, but what is reasonable and right.[53]

The result is a kind of transcendental reconstruction of English law that floats free of authoritative moorings beyond Reeve's own persona as lawyer, teacher, judge and author. Again, rather than crystallisation, we have here an act of invention – of seeding – around which crystallisation might occur. At least until *Fitch v Brainerd* (1805), Reeve the teacher (and judge) is vindicated in substance by the circumstances of Connecticut case law, but more important is his lifelong enactment of the claim that the authoritative legal intellectual's statement of the law cannot be controverted by merely empirical evidence to the contrary.

Like other authors in this collection, Fernandez touches on the matter of personal motivation in regard to Reeve's decision to produce *Baron and Femme*, notably his need for income after his retirement as Chief Justice of the Connecticut Supreme Court. This is of interest as a point of comparison with the personal motivations of other treatise writers. One issue not addressed is the extent to which *Baron and Femme* was written throughout in the same vein as the passages on which Fernandez concentrates in her essay. Was the rebellion on husband and wife typical for Reeve or exceptional? Interestingly, in the case of

[51] Hartog (n 19) 43–44, 93–135.

[52] Pound (n 2) 161; C Tomlins, 'History in the American Juridical Field: Narrative, Justification, and Explanation' (2004) 16 *Yale Journal of Law & the Humanities* 323, 372–75.

[53] T Reeve, *The Law of Baron and Femme; of Parent and Child; of Guardian and Ward; of Master and Servant; and of the Powers of Courts of Chancery. With an Essay on the Terms, Heir, Heirs, and Heirs of the Body* (New Haven, CT, printed by Oliver Steele, 1816) 137.

master and servant, Reeve is at one with Blackstone. In his 1795 *System of the Laws of Connecticut*, Swift again argues differently, citing local Connecticut practice. In his 1822 *Digest*, however, Swift reluctantly falls into line. Reeve's translocality trumps Swift's locality on this question too.[54]

The theme I have chosen to stress here – legal literature doing the work of strategic intervention in the formulation/reformulation of the scale of law – is reinforced by Jim Phillips' chapter on John George Marshall's Nova Scotian JP manual.

Marshall's manual is another first, and it is clearly animated by its own metaphysic. It is neither a reproduction nor an abridgement of pre-existing manuals, although organisationally it is influenced by them. It is a normative commentary on law, or perhaps better on Nova Scotian legal culture, not as it is but as it as it should be (or as Marshall would like it to be).

Personally, I have long been fascinated by JP manuals for what they tell one, both through abridgement and substance, of the application of English law in early America. As Phillips indicates, homegrown eighteenth-century manuals circulated both as abridgements and as expositions of local law. The *Conductor Generalis; or The Office, Duty and Authority of Justices of the Peace* (title varies) was published in numerous editions between 1711 and 1794 in New York, Philadelphia, Woodbridge, New Jersey, and Albany, New York. The various editions of the *Conductor* were abridgements of English manuals: Dalton's *Countrey Justice*, Burn's *Justice of the Peace*, and most commonly Nelson's *Office and Authority of a Justice of Peace*. Without exception, the abridgements were extensive, indicating the limited applicability of English law. The *Conductor* was used widely throughout the middle colonies (Pennsylvania, New Jersey, New York, Delaware). Virginia manuals were more closely attuned to local statute law. Charles Warren's *History of the Harvard Law School* identifies George Webb's *Office and Authority of a Justice of Peace . . . Collected from the Common and Statute Laws of England, and Acts of Assembly, now in Force; and adapted to the Constitution and Practice of Virginia* (Williamsburg, 1736), as the first law book written by an American precisely because it was not simply an abridgement.[55]

Marshall's manual is as fascinating as these eighteenth-century manuals, I think, but for a different reason. While the eighteenth-century manuals give one access to the locality and plurality of law in the British American colonies – their lack of uniformity, whether with each other or with English law and practice – Marshall's manual expresses impatience with locality and seeks uniformity. It offers a pointed critique of localised administration and application of law. The substance of local law is readily observable in the manual, but just as important are the limits that Marshall desired to set on its administration, the sharply negative appraisal of local officers' competence, the emphasis on their jurisdictional confinement and the restraint of local discretion within their sphere, and, overall, the didactic and

[54] C Tomlins, *Law, Labor, and Ideology in the Early American Republic* (Cambridge and New York, Cambridge University Press, 1993) 263.

[55] C Tomlins, *Freedom Bound: Law, Labor, and Civic Identity in Colonizing English America, 1580–1865* (Cambridge and New York, Cambridge University Press, 2010) 353–54 (n 67).

peremptory tone of legal authority spoken from a level far above local administrators. The de-localising thrust of the manual is obvious. Its legal consciousness identifies translocal uniformity both in administration and the locus of authority as the desired objective. The manual 'is a strategic production, with the explicit purpose of disciplining and educating the relatively unlettered in one part of the colony while bringing them the rule of law in the form of central statutory authority and direction'.[56]

Phillips' essay introduces us explicitly to the legal treatise as communicative device. Marshall is addressing a clearly identified audience and his objectives are quite instrumental. One wonders whether the manual was used in the manner he intended, particularly in light of Lyndsay Campbell's chapter on 'Libel Treatises and the Transmission of Legal Norms', which addresses the transit of information itself, the communicative arc connecting writer to reader and what lies at the reader's end of the arc. Treatises are books, books have authors but also readers; reader response theory suggests that the latter are more important in determining the eventual destiny of the artifact than the former, active agents whose own work of interpretation imparts independent meaning to a text often distinct – sometimes wholly at odds – with authorial intent. As Campbell says, multiple local factors could impinge upon how readers might respond to a text, 'the material conditions under which it made its appearance, the political situation in which it was interpreted, and the legal traditions already in operation'.[57] Perhaps the didactic character of the legal treatise is dictated precisely by authorial determination that reader response should not hold sway. There are very good reasons why the rule-expositions and 'frameworks' characteristic of the treatise/abridgement/manual end of the legal literature spectrum take on the structural qualities of a cage: they are attempts to evacuate discretion. In short, we encounter strategy at both ends of law's spectrum, strategic readings as well as writings, each an attempt to contain or prevent undue agency on the part of the reader/writer's counterpart at the other end of the communicative arc.

Campbell tells us quite a lot about the substance of libel law in the early nineteenth-century Anglo-American world, but this is by way of necessary build-up to the real pay-off here, the demonstration of strategic reading in the trial of newspaper editor Joseph Howe in 1835 Halifax for libelling the city's magistrates. Howe, defending himself, successfully mobilised Thomas Starkie's *Treatise on the Law of Slander and Libel* (2nd edn, 1830) to claim its doctrine of broad qualified privilege, introducing the defence to Nova Scotian courts for the first time. Starkie's was not the first or, it seems, the leading treatise on libel at the time. Precedence and, initially, greater influence belonged to Francis Ludlow Holt's *The Law of Libel*.[58] But certain structural and substantive characteristics of

[56] J Phillips, chapter 10 of this volume, p 219.

[57] L Campbell, chapter 8 of this volume, p 166.

[58] F Ludlow Holt, *The Law of Libel: In Which Is Contained a General History of This Law in the Ancient Codes, and of Its Introduction, and Successive Alterations, in the Law of England. Comprehending a Digest of All the Leading Cases upon Libels, from the Earliest to the Present Time* (London and Dublin,

Starkie's treatise favoured Howe as reader. As Campbell puts it, Holt organised his text 'according to Blackstone's logic: offences against God first and ordinary people last'. His view of the liberty of the press – that it meant freedom from prior restraint but not from liability – 'echoed Blackstone's'. Starkie, on the other hand, took Blackstone on by distinguishing a substantively free press from the merely open press that immunity from prior restraint meant. Organisationally, too, Starkie's treatise advantaged the self-defendant Howe, notably in the clarity of its description of trial procedure and possible defences. Whereas Holt 'scattered' the situations 'in which liability had not been found . . . among the instances in which it had', Starkie 'carefully articulated not only the elements of the case for the plaintiff or the public but also . . . the grounds for attributing – or not – the injury to the defendant', and in his second edition set out the broad 'qualified privilege' doctrine on which Howe would rely.[59]

As a practical matter, then, Starkie was a far more usable text in the hands of a non-professional. At least as important to the success of Howe's strategic reading, however, was the character of the receptor region. In population and development, Nova Scotia was a low density colony with a limited legal establishment, whose quality, we know from George Marshall's dyspeptic writings and feuds (and Howe's offending newspaper article), was suspect. Howe's jury ignored the advice, on the law, of the attorney general and Chief Justice. One wonders how frequently Nova Scotian juries acted in derogation of judicial advice, and indeed whether they risked 'English' penalties in so doing. In Howe's case, the authority of the transatlantic treatise, skillfully invoked, trumps provincial knowledge and in so doing creates a local anomaly. What a contrast with the dense legal culture of Massachusetts where the legal establishment clearly had the initiative and could police reception, which is to say police reader response, with much greater authority. There the legal establishment could not only quarantine the law of libel from alien germs, like Starkie's qualified privilege, it could also severely limit the home-grown defences that *were* available. 'In Massachusetts . . . goodness of motive and justifiability of ends were in the eye of the judicial beholder'. Successfully exercising discretion, the judiciary used it to police the transit of ideas, but also to mould textual trajectories to the demands of social order. 'A treatise's place', concludes Campbell, 'depended on the stakes it raised and the power of the tradition it purported to affect'.[60]

Slowly, but successively, we are building up an account, a history, of the Anglo-American legal treatise; or perhaps simply a set of possible characters for this form of literature – as erasable palimpsest but simultaneously uncancellable expression

1812); T Starkie, *A Treatise on the Law of Slander, Libel, Scandalum Magnatum, and False Rumors; Including the Rules Which Regulate Intellectual Communications Affecting the Characters of Individuals and the Interests of the Public, with a Description of the Practice and Pleadings in Personal Actions, Informations, Indictments, Attachments for Contempts, &c. Connected with the Subject* (London, W Clarke & Sons, Law Booksellers, 1813).

[59] Campbell (n 57) p 170.

[60] Ibid p 180.

of the ever-same (Parker); as strategic intervention in ongoing legal debates but also as blank-slate seed crystal (Hoyos, Fernandez); as professional uniformalising agent (Phillips) but also as unpredictable reader resource (Campbell). What Barry Wright adds to this mélange of characteristics in his chapter on 'Treatises, Digests and Criminal Law Codification' is further and trenchant consideration of the treatise's intertextual qualities. As Wright underlines, the treatise is a text in a text-rich environment, a text that interacts with other texts, in this particular case with codes. This is in part a case of resemblance in ends: the treatise interacts with digests, special commission reports and legislative enactments in that all have as their objective the production of organisation and synthesis, what I have been describing as a constant pushing and pulling to engineer shifts in scale. But it is also, Wright shows, a matter of textual resemblance, of mixed genre. In its array of definitions, examples and notes, Thomas Macaulay's Indian Penal Code (1837) structurally resembles a treatise as well as strategically seeking similar ends. Blaine Baker offers the same intimations of resemblance in the opposite direction. 'In structure, [Joseph Story's] treatises are near-codes, written around general principles presented as rules'.[61] One wonders what other texts we might nominate as intertextual companions, or antagonists, of treatises in the process of scalar intervention, organisation and synthesis: case reports of course, but thinking more broadly than that, and back to the essays discussed so far or to be discussed the list might also include newspapers, pamphlets and broadsides, accounts of famous and notorious trials, expressions of local custom and knowledge, theatrical and religious materials, reform literature, and so forth.[62]

Horwitz and Simpson offer contrasting commentary on the relationship between the treatise and codification. Horwitz, we have seen, describes the treatise as the common lawyers' retort to codifiers:

> If the strongest suit which those who favoured legislative codes could play was the accusation that the common law was inconsistent, the trump card available to the defenders of elite judicial law-making was their demonstration that the common law was in fact reasonable.

In the US case, '[t]he treatise tradition arises in direct response to the codification movement of the 1820s and 1830s'.[63] Simpson disagrees. 'A number of treatises were written in the form of codes, *the code being the next logical* step in the process of systematization beyond the discursive treatise'. Citing several post-1870 English treatises (including Fitzjames Stephen's 1876 *Digest of the Law of Evidence* and 1877 *Digest of the Criminal Law*) Simpson argues that '[t]hese works were all consciously conceived of as steps toward codification, and were modeled on the form of the Indian codes'.[64] The question whether indeed there *was* a 'codification movement' in

[61] Baker (n 26) p 88.

[62] For a stimulating discussion of the general question of legal intertextuality, see S Wilf, *Law's Imagined Republic: Popular Politics and Criminal Justice in Revolutionary America* (Cambridge and New York, Cambridge University Press, 2010) 3 9–13, 193–94.

[63] Horwitz(n 1) 460.

[64] Simpson (n 3) 666 (emphasis added), 666–67.

the 1820s and 1830s US is germane to assessing Horwitz's contention.[65] Were there no codification movement as such, the early 'formative era' treatises of Story *et al* might be better seen as expressions of a broad systematising mentality quite coherent with a codifying impulse rather than strategically antagonistic to it. But Wright's chapter shows that Simpson too has overstated his case. Whereas Macaulay's IPC expressed Benthamite hostility to the common law, Stephen's later *General View* (1863) and *Digest* (1877), though intended as codes in the making, and prefatory to his Draft English Code (1878) were written in an attempt to compromise with the common law rather than replace it. In Wright's analysis, textual structure and strategic intent clearly intermingle both in Macaulay's case and in Stephen's, but with different effects. Macaulay's *Examples* and *Notes* both exhibit qualities analogous to the treatise form – synthetic restatement and critique – but with the goal of vacating the common law and judicial discretion. In Stephen's case, in contrast, code and treatise are united in one intertextual form seeking compromise with another intertextual form, the common law itself. Unavailingly, it turns out. Rather than an expression of the hostility of defenders of elite judicial law-making to codification, as Horwitz would have it, Stephen's treatise project is itself done in by that hostility. And rather than demonstrate the lack of any need for codification by writing their own systematising treatises, the judicial establishment (personified in Lord Chief Justice Cockburn) instead simply invokes its own claims to supreme juridical authority. In effect this is a strategic move downscale, or perhaps better, to a different scale altogether – an invocation of an aesthetic of complexity to defeat the disenabling expression of an organisational synthesis considered appropriate enough for barbarian colonies, but not for 'the internal lands of the island' (as Mike Brogden put it long ago and in a different – though definitely related – context).[66]

Thus Wright's chapter shows us how the treatise becomes a weapon in wars of manoeuvre between common law juridical elites and utilitarian professionals, but in a fashion rather different from one would predict from reading *either* Horwitz or Simpson. In adding an account of Canadian criminal law codification, Wright argues that the conditions of settler colonies lent themselves to the more successful realisation of treatise/code intertextuality, as the example of George Burbidge's Canadian code (1892) demonstrates. Burbidge moves seamlessly, it would seem, from the Canadian edition of Stephen's *Digest* (1890) to 1892 code precisely along the arc of intertextual compromise between code and common law unsuccessfully attempted by Stephen in England. This was possible, Wright concludes, because '[c]ommon law culture was weaker in the colonies and codification had more constitutional momentum'. Codification 'enhanced the effectiveness and legitimacy of British rule in India' while in Canada it helped shore up the new Dominion amid 'the challenges of post-colonial nation-building'.[67]

[65] On this, see RW Gordon, 'Review: The American Codification Movement' (1983) 36 *Vanderbilt Law Review* 451.

[66] M Brogden, 'An Act to Colonise the Internal Lands of the Island: Empire and the Origins of the Professional Police' (1987) 15 *International Journal of the Sociology of Law* 179.

[67] B Wright, chapter 9 of this volume, p 200.

If codification projects at the grand level (an imaginary English equivalent of the IPC) elicited juridical hostility, and even the more cautious approach of Stephen resulted in failure, the intertextual mode of analysis that I have attributed to Barry Wright and that I will now attribute also to Lindsay Farmer reveals that an important level of doctrinal formalisation and professional consolidation in English criminal law did nevertheless come about during the nineteenth century. And once again, the effect of formalisation and consolidation is alteration in the scale of law – an assertion that can be refined in light of juridical defences of common law complexity to 'enhanced ability to slide up and down scale, or to vary scale'.

Significantly, Farmer eschews a narrow definition of treatise in order to write instead about the 'literature' of the law, and in particular the law's 'practical literature'.[68] Practical literature covers a wide variety of forms, most of which we have by now encountered: JP and parish officer handbooks, dictionaries, institutional texts, formal treatises, and reform-oriented literature aimed both at reformers and the general public. The question is, how do these texts interact? Do they all pull in the same direction, as it were? What are the tensions among them? Farmer's account is of a movement with which we have become very familiar, a movement in the direction of jurisdictional translocality – up and away from the local lay courts and lay officers of early-modern Britain (and its American mainland colonies), and the literary forms that serviced them, and toward widening translocal hierarchies and a professionalised national criminal bar. The means of movement are distinct from codification, whether of the Benthamite or the Stephensian variety, but the direction is the same.

Particularly interesting here is the emergence of the treatise as a particular form of text that services translocality, a text written by practising lawyers *for* practising lawyers, providing essential legal information and highly practice-oriented modes of organisation and reference. By emerging from the diverse literature of the criminal law as 'the dominant form during the nineteenth century',[69] the treatise substitutes – in a fashion similar to that described in Wright's chapter – for other 'official' legal texts to which professionals needed access if they were to professionalise the criminal law successfully: case reports, legislative syntheses and so forth. As Farmer says, in the absence or extreme disorganisation of such other sources, these practice-oriented treatises (manuals, guidebooks) became the fullest available statements of the law. Effectively, they became the law.[70]

[68] L Farmer, chapter 7 of this volume, p 145.

[69] Ibid p 146.

[70] Mitra Sharafi has explored the significance of this phenomenon in explicitly colonial settings. Legal treatises were especially important in the British Empire, she says, for two related reasons. First, their summaries of different areas of law compensated for difficulties in stocking law libraries. In the absence of settled case law or clear legislation or volumes of case reports, 'judges relied upon them in their decisions.' Second, precisely because they could 'become' the law in this way, treatise writing offered self-interested groups (her example is the Parsi community in British India) a means to shape the law to communal advantage). See Mitra Sharafi, *Parsi Legal Culture in British India* (book manuscript in progress), chapter one.

Given the authoritative status thrust upon them, it is fascinating to learn that the treatises in question were often written by young and, one supposes, relatively inexperienced lawyers. In light of Campbell's chapter, one must also wonder whether their structure and organisation rendered them usable by lay people or instead hindered that use. We are looking here at the formation of a specific expertise – a professionalised criminal law in place of localised lay courts and local knowledge. Usually an expertise creates barriers to entry, intellectual as well as credential. Is that the case here?

Farmer's account also raises interesting questions about the distinctions, or lack of them, between texts such as WO Russell's *Treatise on Crimes and Misdemeanors* and David Hume's *Commentaries on the Law of Scotland Respecting Crimes*, and George Marshall's JP manual. Both Russell and Hume, of course, are much more substantial works than Marshall, and devoted to exposition of a body of law rather than the ambit of an office. Still, it is striking that Hume brusquely dismisses elegance.

> I have no intention of bringing forward a Philosophical Treatise of Criminal Jurisprudence, in which the history of the human species, with respect to this branch of the science of law, is to be traced; and an attempt made to ascertain, on abstract and universal principles, the nature of the several offences, and the application and proportion of punishments.[71]

What counts is practicality and efficiency – and authorial authority. 'Crimes were treated in order of their practical importance', rather than according to more traditional schema. Hume had himself 'gone through the Books of Adjournal' which began in 1524, 'to develop an authoritative statement of the practice of the law' – and 'to save others the labour of the like research'.[72] Equally important is Farmer's demonstration of the emergence of principle *from* practice, followed by the isolation of principle as a guide to practise. Practice reveals principle; principles structure practice. Both are intertextual and scalar moves, moves from one genre and scale of text to another and back. One has the impression, however, that intertextuality is increasingly limited – that as criminal law's professionalisation continues, the treatise becomes ever more hermetic, more abstracted. Treatise and profession becomes the significant interaction, formulating law as expertise plus the means to its efficient application, very much at a remove from the intertextual concatenation that serviced 'wide public interest' in crime and criminal law at the outset of professionalisation (local lay knowledge, instruction manuals, reform literature, etc).[73] We end the nineteenth century with a criminal law structured by treatise-driven forms of practical codification and by supralocal sameness. The next phase of creating ever greater distance between law as expertise and its social effects – academicisation – sees the twentieth century's textbook.

Barry Wright and Lindsay Farmer having dealt with the criminal law treatise in its nineteenth-century heyday, Stephen Waddams recounts the history of the

[71] D Hume, *Commentaries on the Law of Scotland Respecting Crimes*, 4th edn (Edinburgh, Bell & Bradfute, 1844) I, 14.

[72] Farmer (n 68) 157, n 67, Hume (n 71) 3, 18.

[73] Ibid 153.

treatise in its 'highest' private law incarnation of contract, at the moment of modern contract law's emergence and maturation. Waddams' chapter allows us to assess the interaction of treatise with doctrinal innovation, in what seems to me the most favourable and sympathetic environment for Horwitz's crystallisation argument, the high mandarin genre of contract doctrine. Interestingly, once again, as in the original case of Blackstone, what appears to be the initial point of departure is a civilian consciousness – in this case Pothier's 1761 *Traité des Obligations*, and more particularly its translation in 1806. Like Waddams, Patrick Atiyah identifies Pothier and his will theory of contract as, in effect, the seed that first caused doctrinal crystallisation in English law. 'The subsequent English authors were all more or less influenced by Pothier's approach', Atiyah writes, 'as well, of course, as by the growing signs of its acceptance in the English Courts'.[74] We should note that high in the order of praise visited upon Pothier was an aesthetic judgment. Waddams quotes Best J in 1822 – 'luminous method, apposite examples, and a clear manly style' – and Addison in 1847 – 'elaborate and elegant'.[75] As in Blackstone's case, the civilian legal consciousness had imparted an initiating aesthetic and synthetic capacity that simply evaded the common lawyers (with the notable and lonely exception of the incomparable Littleton to prove the rule). Civilians could, we have seen, fly high above the clutter and chaos of locality and unsystematic adumbration that was the early-modern common law. Interesting then is the case of Henry Colebrooke who attempts to write the first English contracts treatise in the civilian manner – and fails dismally. By the early nineteenth century, in the wake of Lord Mansfield, the function of the first common law contracts treatise has been superseded: it is no longer to tell an elegant and neat (and crystallising) story of legal origins and conceptual development, it is to mediate the output of juridical authority for the guidance of the profession; it is not, as in Blackstone's case, to declare its own authority by a stylish demonstration of command, but instead to distill, modestly, principle from authoritative precedent and guide professional practice by that derived authoritative principle. (Hence the fervid retrofitting of the elegant Blackstone.) Here it seems is the same professional demand for guidance as in the criminal law arena, but with the addition (unlike the noxious trade of criminal law) of plenty of authoritative centralised juridical disquisition to (modestly) synthesise. Colebrooke's first was a failure primarily because, by the time he wrote, professional demand had narrowed style to what was useful. Subject area limits authorial license. Waddams comments that the civil law ideal 'order, science, elegance, logic, and principle' continued to influence English writers, but also notes how the demands of the subject and of the reader forced authors to distance themselves from the ideal.[76]

Particularly interesting in Waddams' account, I think, is the shift away from Pothier in the later nineteenth century as the imprint of the German historical

[74] PS Atiyah, *The Rise and Fall of Freedom of Contract* (Oxford, Oxford University Press, 1979) 400.
[75] S Waddams, chapter 6 of this volume, p 130.
[76] Ibid p 135.

school on English legal writing becomes marked. Thus Pollock credits Savigny rather than Pothier as inspiration. However, Savigny proves no lasting substitute. I was fascinated to see, in Waddams' analysis of Pollock, that as Pollock finds himself distanced from *both* Pothier and Savigny, he 'loses' his thread: his own style becomes impossibly awkward, trapped in passive construction and convoluted sentences. The cause appears to be the problem English writers faced in crafting assertions of their own authorial authority, required if their interpretations of English legal materials – adjudged cases – were to be credited, without appearing explicitly to do so. In the English treatise tradition, Waddams reminds us, the author had little interpretive authority per se, reliant instead upon an interaction between writer and authoritative judicial opinion. Even the vain, pompous Pollock is reduced to incoherence by this bind. Mastering his interaction with the judge was in an important sense the key to creating a distinctive style for the English common law treatise writer, a lesson that both Pollock and Anson seem to learn through a deft combination of fawning deference and manipulation – each seeking judicial approval, each creating authority for their own work by procuring recognition of it in judicial opinions.

Two other matters are worth some attention. First, the culmination of the course of nineteenth-century treatise writing in the area of contracts is the re-expression of the law of *contracts* as the law of *contract*: a conceptually unified and coherent region of doctrine. Waddams says this is the re-expression of plurality as a singularity, and this seems entirely justified, but what kind of singularity? 'Contract' per se is ambiguous. Is it a noun or a verb? Might we not as readily think of 'contract' as a quasi-gerund – ie a move from the law of *contracts* to the law of *contracting*, from plural and distinct *events* to a way of understanding a form of *behaviour*. Here again arises the question of scale: have we made a move along a scale, from plurality to singularity, or have we jumped from one scale to another, from plural and distinguishable acts to a mode of action?

Second, what can we learn from the authorial war between Pollock and Anson, notable for the manoeuvres on both sides, won it would appear by Pollock in the short term, but not in the long. One wonders why, and how, a treatise 'survives'? In this case Anson starts out behind, but as Waddams attests, Anson's treatise, praised (condescendingly) by Pollock as 'elementary', became 'the standard student textbook'.[77] In a paper presented at a University of London conference in honour of William Twining (2010), Wes Pue offered an acute analysis of the relativities of change in the substance and structure of Anson's treatise over the course of the twentieth century that demonstrated Anson's success was due in no small part to successor editors, who undertook much more than the retrofit of new cases and new law that Parker describes as the fate of Blackstone during the nineteenth century. Yet they did so while remaining conceptually tethered by Anson's traces, elaborately and explicitly articulating the necessity that the treatise express at the same time sameness and difference within its own intellectual

[77] Ibid p 143.

structure – each a condition of its continued existence, neither adequate to grant it lasting epistemological integrity, the result a stumbling corpse that Pue likened to the undead who populate contemporary popular culture. Word by word, line by-line, the entire content of Anson's treatise has been overhauled incrementally to accommodate successive innovations in contract law. Yet the editors must claim sameness even as their own efforts undermine the claim, and even as the claim in turn undermines their own efforts.[78]

Is the quasi-death of *Anson*'s *Law of Contract* the product of actions or reactions? That is, does the leading treatise in its perpetual reappearances lead, or does it follow, always desperately trying to catch up? Do the editors' moves indicate an alteration in the deferential relationship between writers and juridical authorities that characterised Pollock and Anson's original texts? And how much are their structural and substantive alterations attempts to systematise the 'complex devices' invented by courts so as 'to avoid results perceived to be unjust'?[79] Waddams argues that the very systematisation that the educative treatise attempts may induce legal rigidities that courts must then manoeuvre around. Here is a distinct form of strategic intertextuality, an interaction between judiciary and text that becomes a recurrent feedback loop of simplifying systematisation and complexifying exceptionalism, simultaneously a competition between distinct forms of authorship and authority. That this competition existed even at the deferential outset is suggested in Anson's letter to Lord Justice Thesiger, likening himself to an explorer who, Waddams acutely observes, is also an 'improver' – not simply a surveyor of terrain but a coloniser planning its use.[80]

CONCLUSIONS

When Morton Horwitz wrote about the legal treatise 35 years ago, his attention was focused on the treatise as an instrument, one that would help the legal historian 'grasp the structure of growth and decline in various areas of . . . law'.[81] Five years later, and at much greater length, Brian Simpson paid greater attention to form: 'I shall suggest that certain literary forms are closely tied to theories about the nature of law itself, and that this is particularly true of the treatise'.[82] But though they differed in focus and emphasis, Horwitz and Simpson were in agreement that the treatise could be tied to a particular phase of growth and decline, the phase of reasoned doctrinal hermeneutics that fashioned the systematised substance corroded by Realism's acid.

[78] WW Pue, 'Anson's Law of Contract' unpublished paper, presented at 'Legal Education And Scholarship – Past, Present And Future: A Workshop in Honour of William Twining' (Institute of Advanced Legal Studies, University of London, 20 October 2010). And see AWB Simpson, 'Contract: The Twitching Corpse' (1981) 1 *Oxford Journal of Legal Studies* 265, 266–67.

[79] Waddams (n 75) 144.

[80] Ibid 141–142.

[81] Horwitz (n 1) 461.

[82] Simpson (n 3) 633.

Here I think one sees a different approach under development, one that addresses the treatise not just as the means to instantiate a particular legal culture or legal ideology and a record of its alteration over time (although plainly it is that) but also as a means to achieve certain strategic ends, a means that must be read in conjunction with other legal texts and their authors if the end is to be identified. I have argued that shifts in scale are one strategic end that can be abstracted from treatises as a literary form, and that shifts in the locale of authority are another.

Yet we should not be satisfied with the conventional historian's move of adumbrating the appropriate contexts for our texts. The texts stand as objects for our aesthetic as well as our analytic contemplation. Parker reminds us that Blackstone was trained as a classical scholar, authored critical notes on Shakespeare, and had won a prize for a poem on Milton. It is also worth noting that Blackstone (1723–80) was a contemporary of William Hogarth (1697–1764), whom we know as an occasional satirist of law,[83] but whose fame as observer and critic lay elsewhere, in his *Analysis of Beauty* (1753), itself a systematic treatise on artistic representation that stressed (through a mnemonic system) that the parts of a form must always be understood in relation to that form's living whole, and simultaneously sought to represent organic form not at rest but in total movement. 'Structure, organism, movement were felt to be all inseparable aspects of a single reality, which could further be grasped in terms of variety, intricacy, and simplification'. Beauty resided in 'living process, in the forms realised in their vital tensions, movements, oppositions, and harmonies, with sensual fullness'.[84] Hogarth's drawings, necessarily still-standing, are movement frozen – in their cessation they are pregnant with motion, dialectical images.[85] In Hogarth, as in Leibniz, 'the line of beauty' (a key concept) was the curve, or fold, which expressed living tension, not the straight line, which was merely mechanical extension.[86] Hogarth 'protest[ed] against post-Galilean mechanism in terms of the living nexus of forces that involve a ceaseless conflict and fusion of symmetries and asymmetries'.[87] What might we make of Blackstone's *Commentaries*, famous for their style, their beauty, in terms of this aesthetic? Does Blackstone manage to express living tension? What might we make of the treatises of the nineteenth century and of their innumerable progeny of updates in terms of an overarching aesthetic of mechanical extension, of 'mechanism'?[88] What aesthetics do we yearn to recover to imbue law with meaning?

I will end with a famous, very short, story. In Franz Kafka's 'A New Advocate', the bar is waiting to admit Bucephalus, once the warhorse of Alexander the Great.

[83] See, for example, Hogarth's 1724 engraving 'Some of the Principal Inhabitants of ye Moon, as they Were Perfectly Discover'd by a Telescope brought to ye Greatest Perfection' also known, as 'Royalty, Episcopacy and Law' at exhibits.library.northwestern.edu/spec/hogarth/politics3.html (accessed 21 April 2011). See also 'The Bench' (1758), at ://en.wikipedia.org/wiki/The_Bench_%28Hogarth%29 (accessed 7 May 2011).

[84] J Lindsay, *Hogarth: His Art and His World* (London, Hart-Davis, MacGibbon Ltd, 1977) ix, 185.

[85] W Benjamin, *The Arcades Project* (Cambridge, MA, Harvard University Press, 1999) 462 [N2a,3].

[86] Lindsay (n 84) 173–75.

[87] Ibid 185.

[88] On which see T Carlyle, 'Signs of the Times' in T Carlyle, *Critical and Miscellaneous Essays*, vol 2 (Boston, MA, James Munroe and Company, 1838).

Alexander is long dead, his age is over; no one knows any more where to find the gates of India. Dr Bucephalus has immersed himself in law books. 'Free', writes Kafka, 'his flanks unconstrained by the grip of his rider, in the still light of the lamp, far from the din of the battle of Issus, he reads and turns the pages of our ancient books'.[89] In Kafka's world, law books are secret, but Dr Bucephalus reads them. The story has been called a critique of myth written from the standpoint of justice. But how was it, asked Walter Benjamin, that law 'could be invoked against myth in the name of justice?' Perhaps what was new was that Dr Bucephalus did not practice law, he read it. 'The law which is studied *but no longer practiced*', Benjamin mused, was Kafka's opening to justice.[90] Justice resides in cancelled law.[91]

In Kafka's world, law is materialised in two media, books and files. The split differentiated the authority instantiated in secretive legal form from that inherent in law's incessant substantive replication as record. The late Cornelia Vismann's recent *Files: Law and Media Technology* brilliantly presents a history of the material world of files and records and their jurisdictional locales that is on the one hand a history of the file as the signifier of the state, of the authorisation of law in techniques of administrative recurrence and the media in which they are materialised; and simultaneously a history of law as *detritus*, old originals and discarded files left in the wake of the state's movement through time.[92]

Vismann's *Files* shows us how to write a history of how law is embodied as a technology – a history of the generation of documents, the establishment of registers, the keeping of records, the invention of files, and their locations; a history of law's recording media and of the distinct modes of manipulating what is recorded that they afford. In its various 'readings' of the treatise, this collection offers a clear opening to a similar history of the treatise, the most capacious of the file's formalised equivalents. The chapters gathered here have shown that the treatise has as many historical and material incarnations as the file, and can only be understood as a medium in light of its broad dispersal – of place and time, of function and form, of objective and aesthetic, of strategy and scale. They have shown that the legal treatise is indeed a book 'in action' – that its meaning lies not only in its exposition of law as a particular form of knowledge, but also in its purposeful advocacy of structures, both epistemological and jurisdictional, that animate the way that particular knowledge is expressed. Simultaneously they have searched for the meaning of the treatise as residue, as *detritus* – law at rest, useless old editions discarded in remote library stacks, full of the law before the law. What *is* the meaning of cancelled law? This collection creates openings to a history of the treatise as a second instance of law and media technology.

[89] F Kafka, 'The New Advocate' in M Pasley (trans), *The Transformation and Other Stories: Works Published During Kafka's Lifetime* (London, Penguin, 1992) 154–55.

[90] MW Jennings, H Eiland and G Smith (eds), *Walter Benjamin, Selected Writings, 1931–1934* (Cambridge, MA, Harvard University Press, 1999) 815 (emphasis added).

[91] For a distinctive variation on this idea, see Marianne Constable, *Just Silences: the Limits and Possibilities of Modern Law* (Princeton, NJ, Princeton University Press, 2005).

[92] C Vismann, *Files: Law and Media Technology* (Stanford, CA, Stanford University Press, 2008).

INDEX

Index

Index

www.ingramcontent.com/pod-product-compliance
Ingram Content Group UK Ltd.
Pitfield, Milton Keynes, MK11 3LW, UK
UKHW020803290926
15470UKWH00003B/928

9 781849 461412